HOME TODAY GONE TOMORROW

SNAPSHOTS from 40 YEARS on the ROAD - AUSTIN and BACK

by MUSIC VETERAN and MANAGER

MARK PROCT

with NETTIE REYNOLDS

Photos & Book Design by Mark Proct
Page 6 photo not credited photographer unknown
Page 140 CD cover courtesy of Atlantic Records
Text by Mark Proct & Nettie Reynolds
Project Direction: Nettie Reynolds
Cover art: Billy Perkins
Mark I Books
Austin, TX

Visit our website at www.facebook.com/HomeTodayGoneTomorrowTheBook
Email markproct@gmail.com

ISBN: 978-0-9905486-9-0

Printed by McCarthy Print
Print Production: Tim Koderl
Prepress Tech: Deaun Rosas
First Mark I Books Printing
Printed in Austin, TX USA

Special thanks to my wife Junhui, my parents Marlene & Jerry, sisters Jody & Gail, brother Brian, Nettie for helping me get this book completed, friends Tony Elfrez, Chris Kelly, Charlie Boswell, Vicky Moerbe, Joe Priesnitz, John McDermott & Esbit my dog of 14 loyal years.

Contents

Austin is hot these days and it's become the "little music town that could" with the good and bad that comes with that including more folks moving to the city and some folks bemoaning "those days gone by." But the constant in Austin that no behemoth condos or new downtown developments blocking the city skyline can take away from is our being the incubator and home for some of the most formative music in blues, country, and alternative rock then any city has ever known.

We were there when it wasn't cool and we'll be there way beyond the hype cycle of Austin coolness again, and I had the great fortune of seeing this amazing music over the last forty years and being part of some of those movements and bands in a myriad of jobs. I started out on the road as a young man coming down from NY and planting myself in Austin and in the time span of 40 years ended up working with some of the most talented musicians, everyone from Willie Nelson to The Fabulous Thunderbirds to Stevie Ray Vaughan, The Arc Angels and others.

This book offers photos from behind and beyond the stage, shots that I took over the time I spent with some of the best musical talent Austin has ever produced.

Austin's music history is constantly being rewritten and people are losing touch with the events and the memories and so it's time to share these. Austin is still the music capital of the world and there is no other town that attracts and fosters the musicians in the world from Willie to Stevie Ray to beyond, we'll never be rivaled in what we brought to the world.

The pictures I share in this book are mine, and they were shot with different cameras (way before digital and selfies) and I hope that you'll enjoy the history revealed in the pictures too. It's rare to be able to capture so much that has not been seen before. I'm glad I have that piece of history and that you can take this ride with me.

My story starts with the question, "How did a teenager from New York, end up in cowboy boots, cowboy hat and land in the center of Texas?" I can blame that on some of my early childhood friends. First Shelly Shulman for turning me onto the Rolling Stones, The Beatles and the Grateful Dead along with countless other great music (POCO, The Flying Burrito Brothers, NRPS and Commander Cody).

I found myself gravitating and listening to more and more country music and I took up playing the pedal steel guitar. Both being outside a typical New Yorkers understanding, my friends were all thinking I was crazy as country music was well outside the norm for New York City.

There are a couple more people I need to thank for those early music influences, Jon Sunshine for all those concerts we attended together especially Watkins Glen and of course for introducing me to Stu Schulman who ultimately got me to Texas. Stu was my pedal steel guitar teacher and a good friend who was living in New Paultz, NY. It wasn't long before Stu headed to Texas for his musical career though we continued to stay in touch.

In 1974 I was an electrical engineering student at Southeastern MA University and an aspiring pedal steel guitar player. At winter break of that year I boarded a Braniff Airlines flight to Austin, TX to visit Stu and his roommates Poodie Locke and Michael Schroeder all who were working for BW Stevenson. I didn't know it at the time, but this trip was going to change my life forever.

And so this book is not just a trip down memory lane but it also represents one of the most seminal times in Texas music and my great luck to be a part of all of it.

Austin today is not quite the same sleepy town that it was some forty years ago. My best recollection is just students, musicians and politicians. I spent three weeks during that winter break absorbing everything the town had to offer. Generous friends and an abundance of the music that I loved.

After three weeks I knew Austin was where I ultimately wanted to be. Those weeks passed so quickly and before long I was on my way back to New York. I finished my second semester of college, and then told my parents I was packing up and moving to Austin, Texas. To this day I know that saddened them, but I also know they were my biggest supporters and I can never thank them enough. In September 1975 with one suitcase, my steel guitar and Fender twin reverb I jumped into my 67 Pontiac and headed to Austin and as they say, "the rest is history."

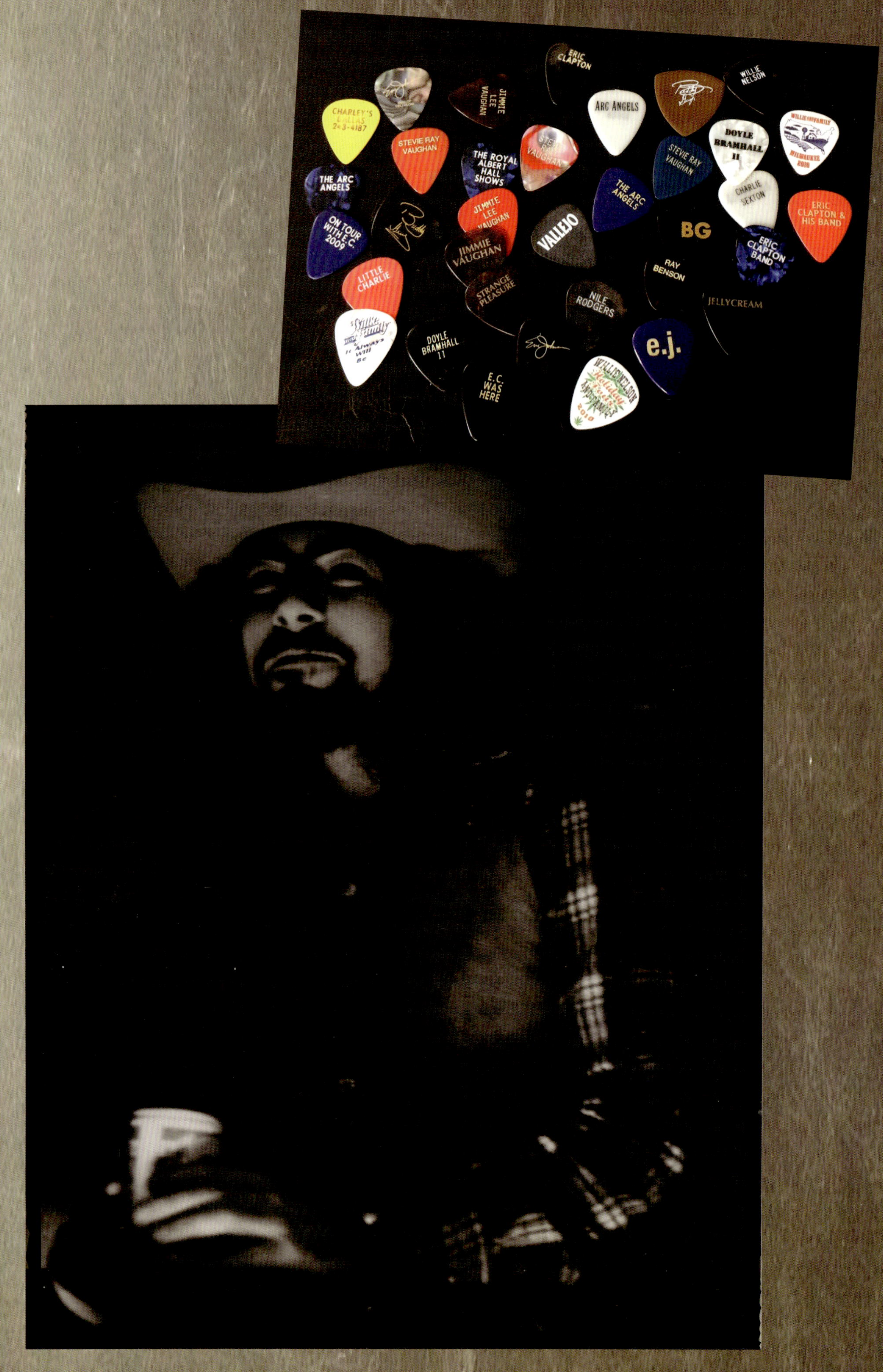
ERIC CLAPTON
JIMMIE LEE VAUGHAN
ARC ANGELS
WILLIE NELSON
STEVIE RAY VAUGHAN
THE ROYAL ALBERT HALL SHOWS
STEVIE RAY VAUGHAN
DOYLE BRAMHALL II
THE ARC ANGELS
JIMMIE LEE VAUGHAN
THE ARC ANGELS
CHARLIE SEXTON
ERIC CLAPTON & HIS BAND
ON TOUR WITH E.C. 2009
VALLEJO
BG
JIMMIE VAUGHAN
ERIC CLAPTON BAND
RAY BENSON
LITTLE CHARLIE
STRANGE PLEASURE
NILE RODGERS
JELLYCREAM
DOYLE BRAMHALL II
e.j.
E.C. WAS HERE

CHAPTER 1: ON THE ROAD AGAIN WITH WILLIE NELSON & FAMILY 1975-1976

After a three week visit, I returned to NY but I was determined to get back to Austin and make it a permanent home. I arrived back in Austin in 1975, and I reconnected with an old friend Stu Schulman and new friends Poodie Locke and Michael Schroeder.
At the time, Stu was still playing steel guitar in the B.W. Stevenson band though Poodie and Michael Schroeder had both gone to work for Willie Nelson. I knew I loved the music and I quickly realized I was never going to be a great steel player, but I knew I was going to stay in Austin. After a Willie Nelson concert, Poodie introduced me to Jerry Potter, the owner of Lone Star Sound who was providing Willie with a sound system for all of his concerts. I think with a little twisting of the arm Poodie convinced Jerry Potter to give me a job. I thanked Jerry for the work and let him know I would make the most of the opportunity. Truly this was the school of hard knocks and I never shied away from getting my hands dirty.

I was now working for Lone Star Sound. In early 1976 the Willie Nelson Tour left Austin for Lubbock and this was the start of a future of many honky-tonks, theaters and arenas.

July 1976 Willie planned for a huge 4th of July picnic in Gonzales, Texas. A stage was built in the middle of a field, Lone Star Sound along with Black Star Sound set up massive sound system to accommodate the expected crowd of over 100,000 fans.

After working the entire day of July 3rd, setting up the sound system, the sun rose with Leon Russell walking out on stage, sitting down at the piano and playing the opening notes to start the picnic. The crowds awoke to Leon followed by George Jones, Jerry Jeff and the Lost Gonzo band, Kris Kristofferson and Rita Coolidge along with a stellar lineup of other musicians. Willie Nelson's final set came to an end as a Texas thunderstorm was approaching. The show's finale was an incredible downpour that filled the roof of the stage with water and the weight of it threatening to collapse the roof. Willie's drummer Paul English saved the day by shooting five holes into the roof of the stage and the water dripped like a spigot over all the instruments and we called it a day.

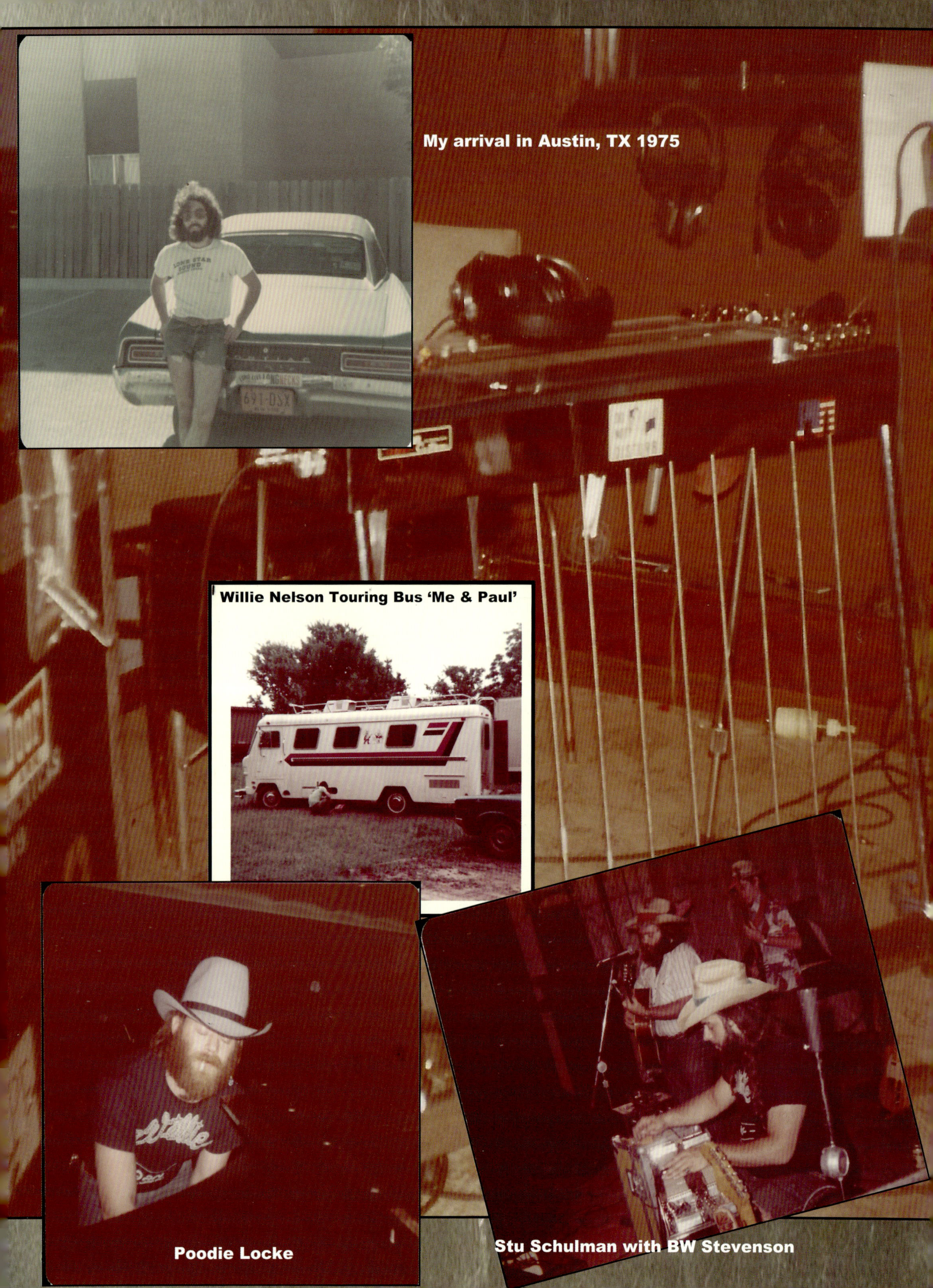

My arrival in Austin, TX 1975

Willie Nelson Touring Bus 'Me & Paul'

Poodie Locke

Stu Schulman with BW Stevenson

WILLIE NELSON & FAMILY 1976

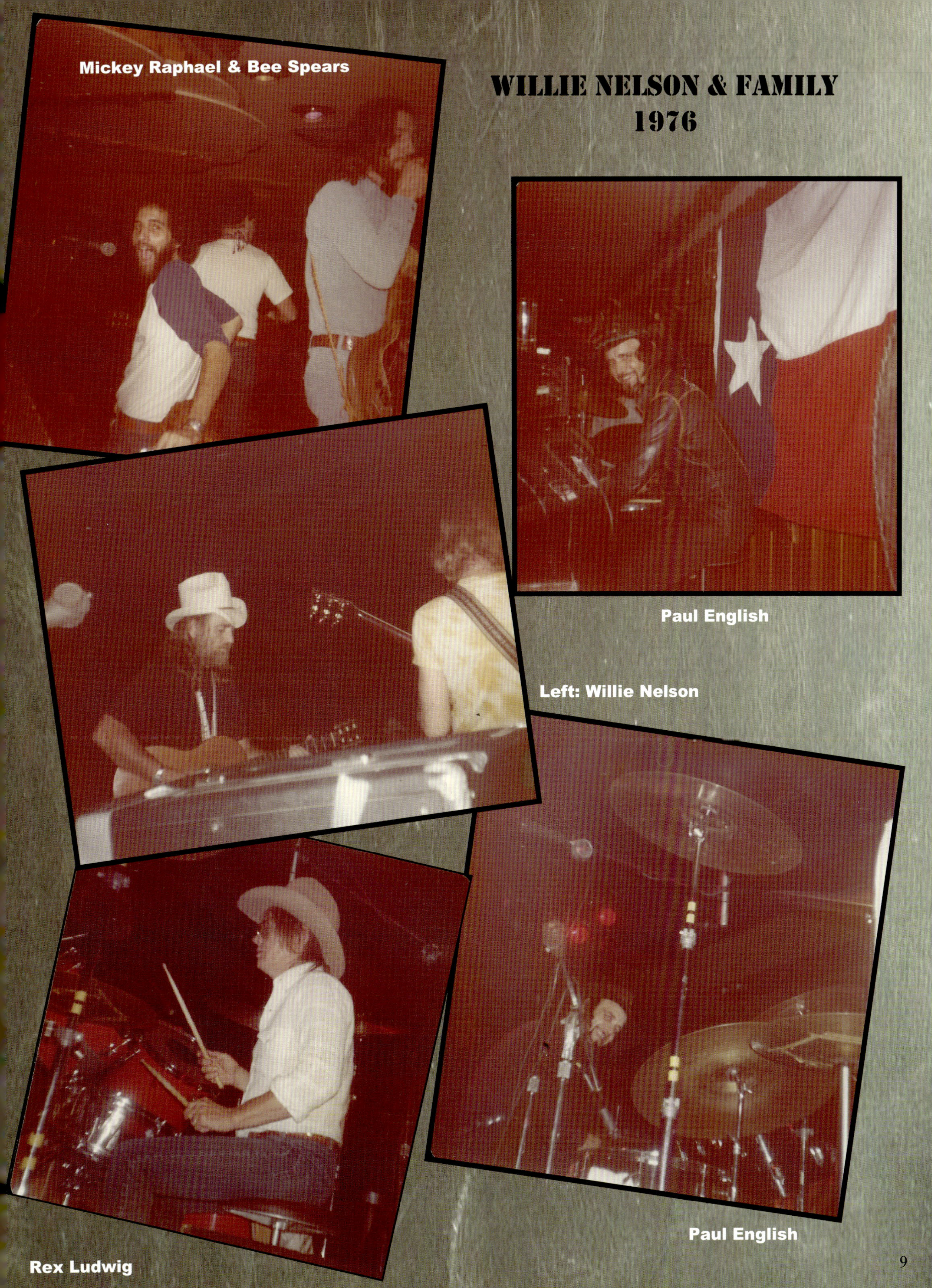

Mickey Raphael & Bee Spears

Paul English

Left: Willie Nelson

Paul English

Rex Ludwig

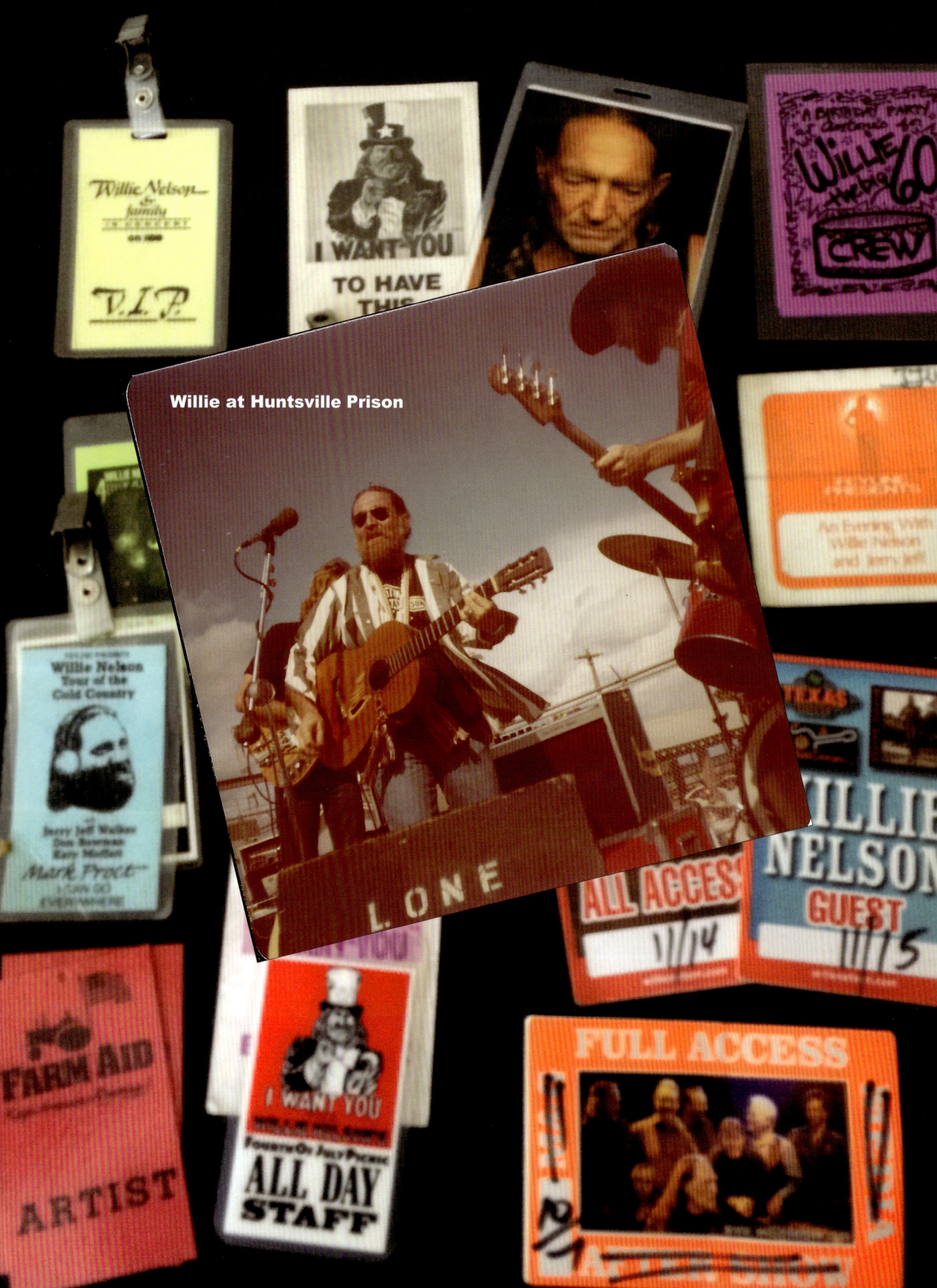

Willie at Huntsville Prison

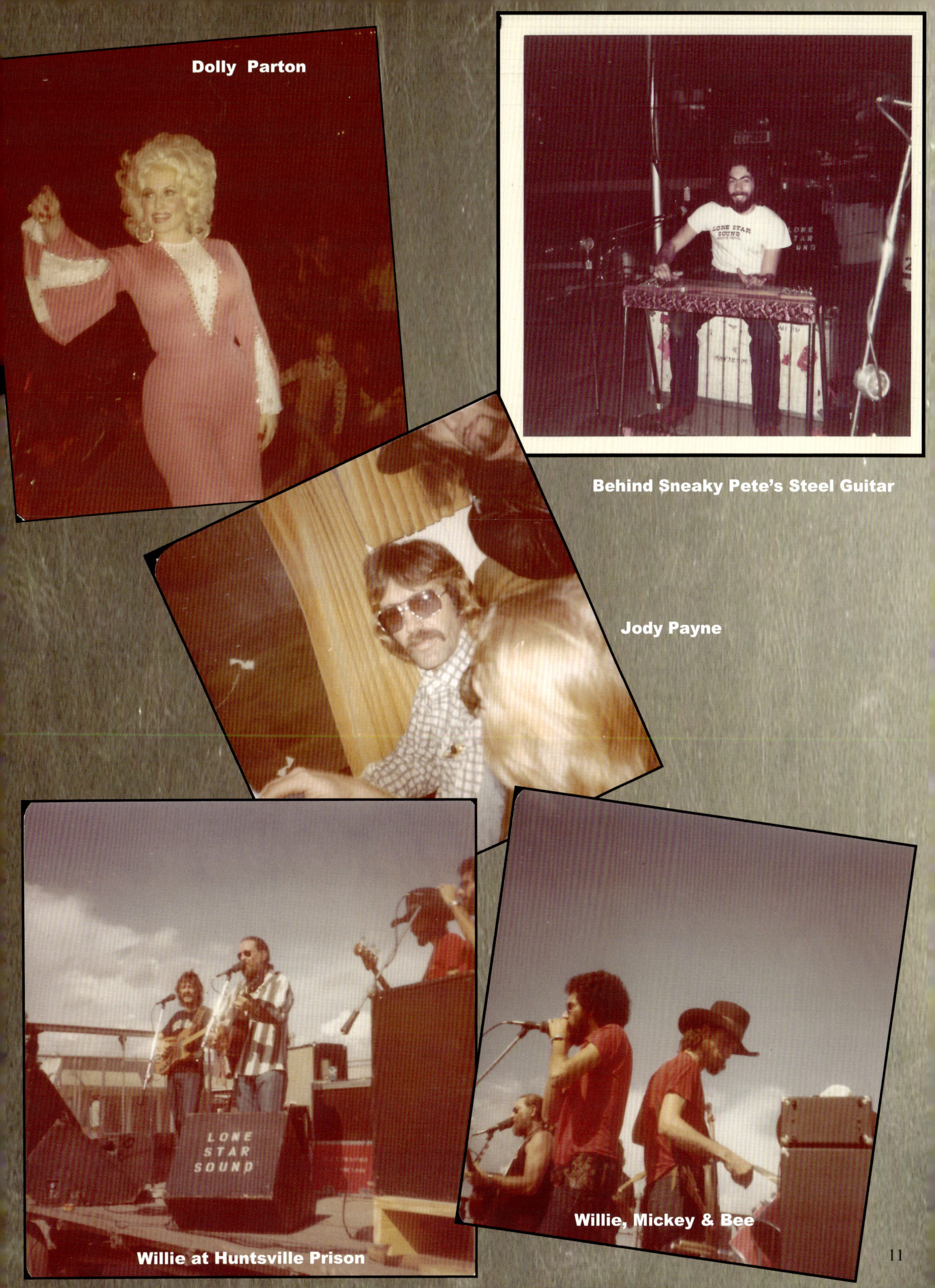

Dolly Parton

Behind Sneaky Pete's Steel Guitar

Jody Payne

Willie at Huntsville Prison

Willie, Mickey & Bee

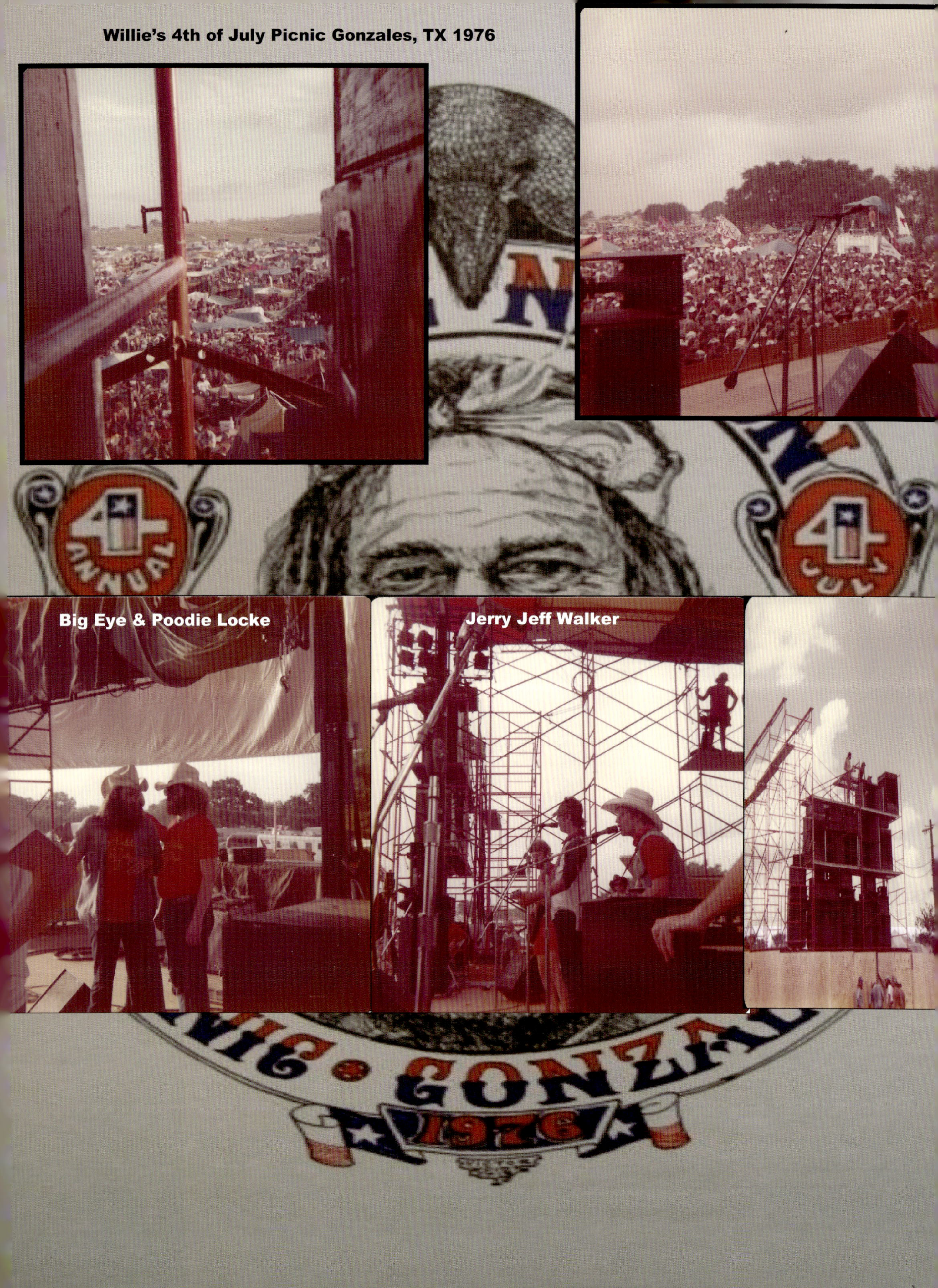

Willie's 4th of July Picnic Gonzales, TX 1976

Big Eye & Poodie Locke

Jerry Jeff Walker

WILLIE NELSON 4TH OF JULY PICNIC GONZALES, TX 1976

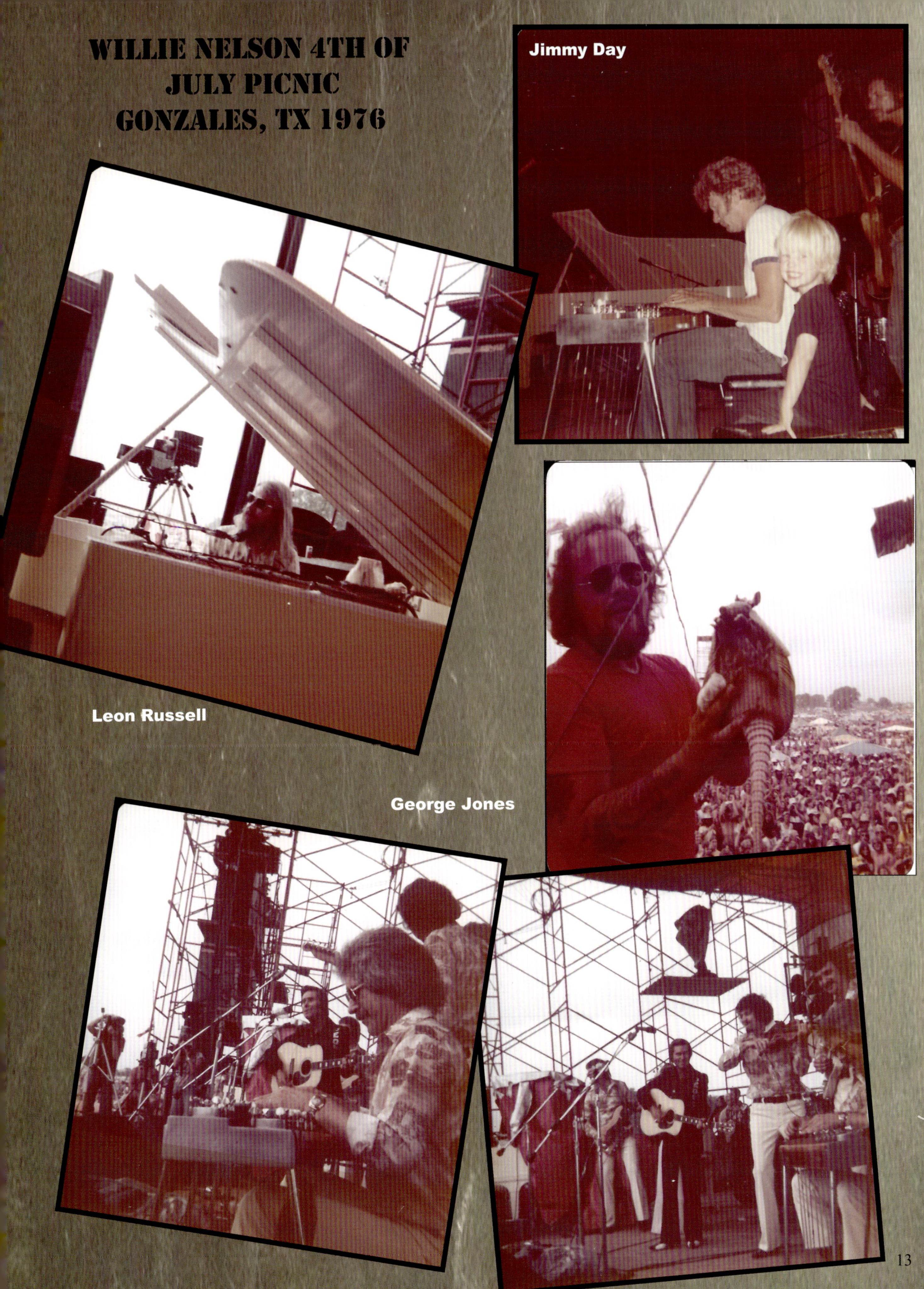

Jimmy Day

Leon Russell

George Jones

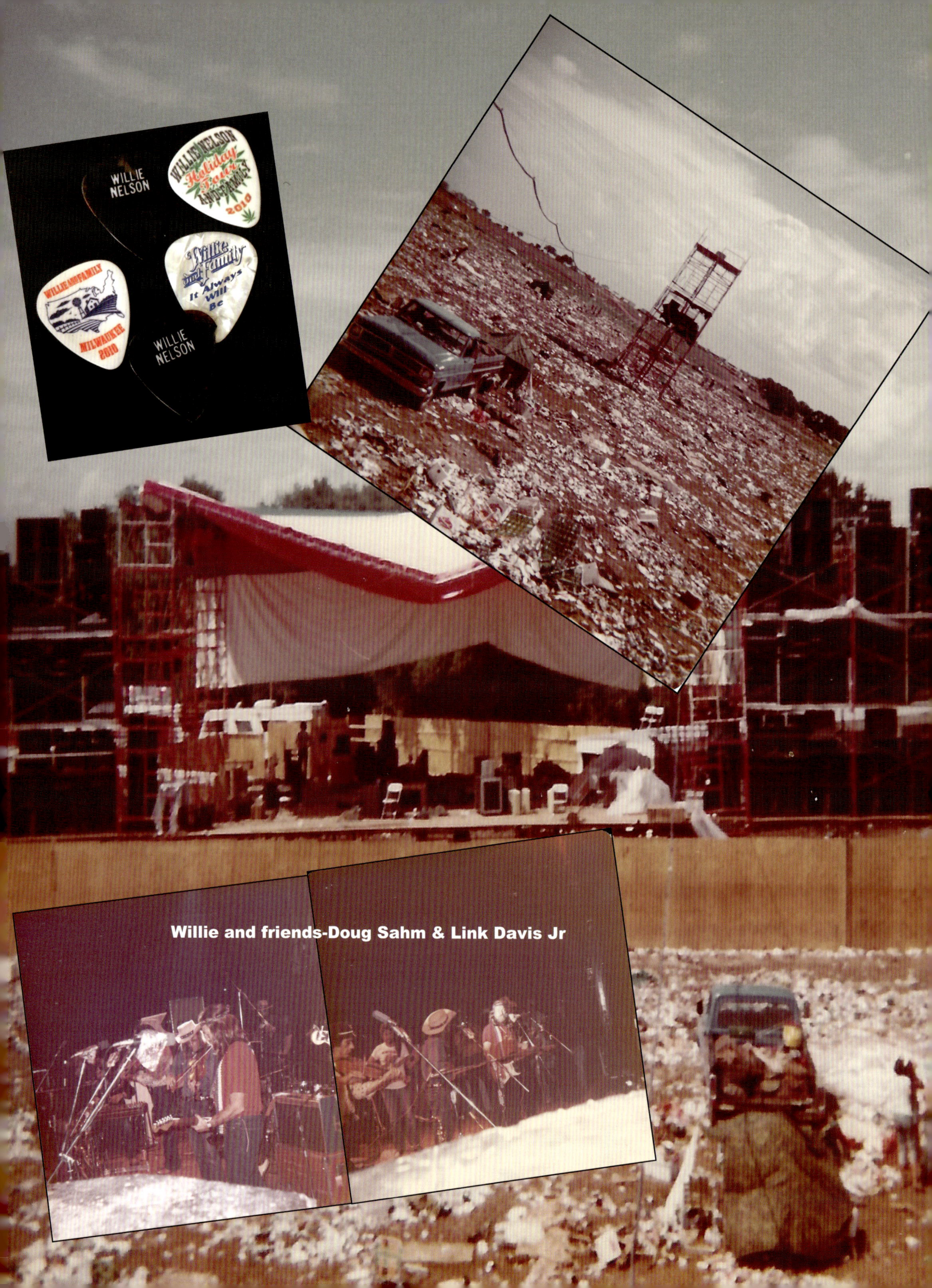

Willie and friends-Doug Sahm & Link Davis Jr

Chapter 2: Miles & Miles of Texas with Asleep at the Wheel 1977

With Lone Star Sound the work day was first in and last out at each venue. A day's pay could come after 16 plus hours of being on the job. This built up a work ethic that I would never lose. Having come off that 8 month tour with Willie, I knew I wanted to get back out on the road ASAP. That's when I got a call from Ray Benson and he offered me the position of house engineer for Asleep at the Wheel. I wanted to work for a band where even at a young age I would be offered a bit more job security so I hit the road with The Wheel. One of the hardest things I had to do was going to Jerry Potter and telling him I was leaving as Jerry was instrumental in giving me my start in the music business.

In 1977 I was out on tour with Asleep at the Wheel and we never stopped working – 200 plus gigs a year. During 77-78 we hardly ever came off the road. From the East Coast to the West Coast, North and South, Canada and then back again. At the time, Asleep at the Wheel had very little radio play but they were reinventing the sounds of Bob Wills and the musical style of Texas swing. The band was playing beer joints, some colleges, an occasional rodeo, and supporting many of the top country acts of that time.

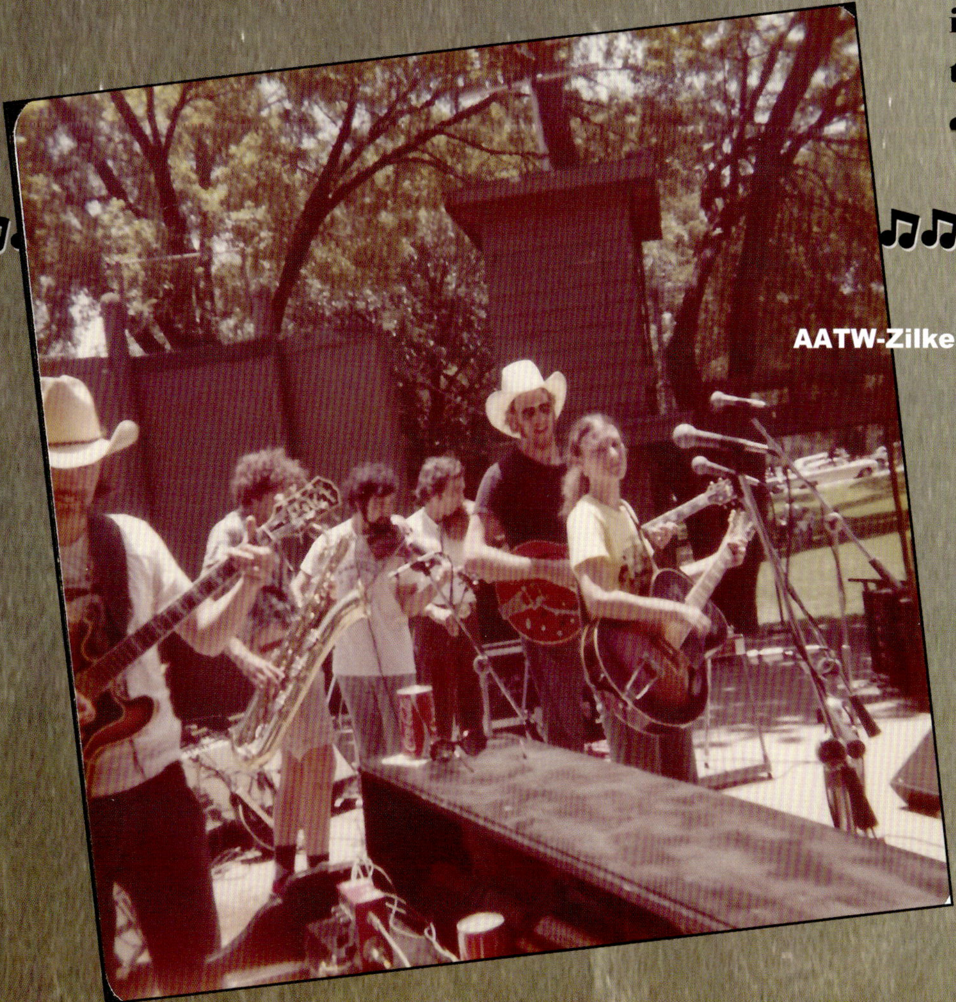

AATW-Zilker Playhouse Austin 1977

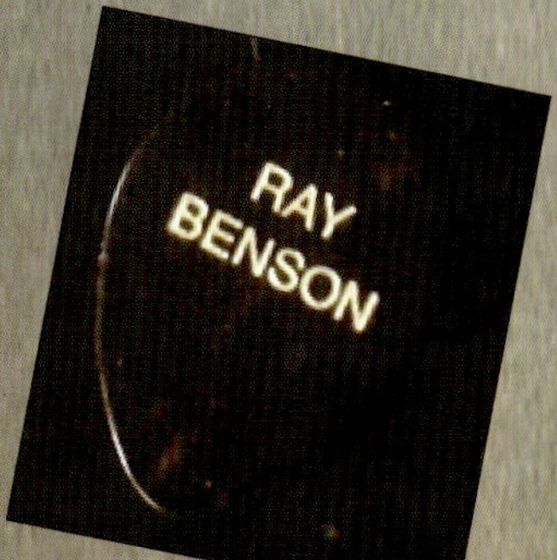

RAY BENSON

AATW-Ray Benson, Chris O'Connell & Leroy Preston

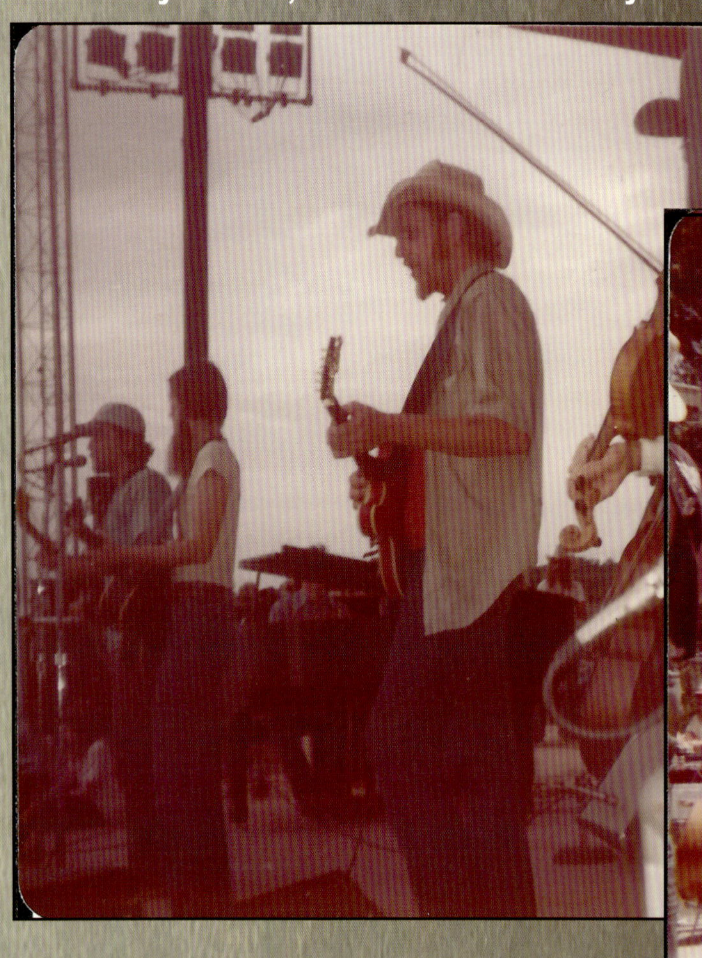

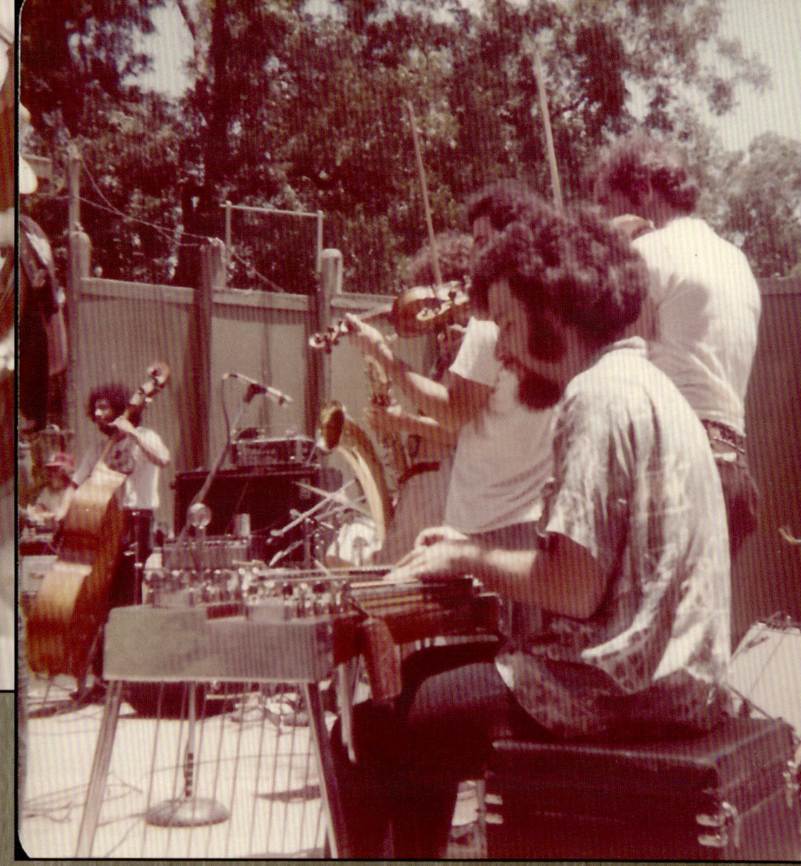

Tony Garnier

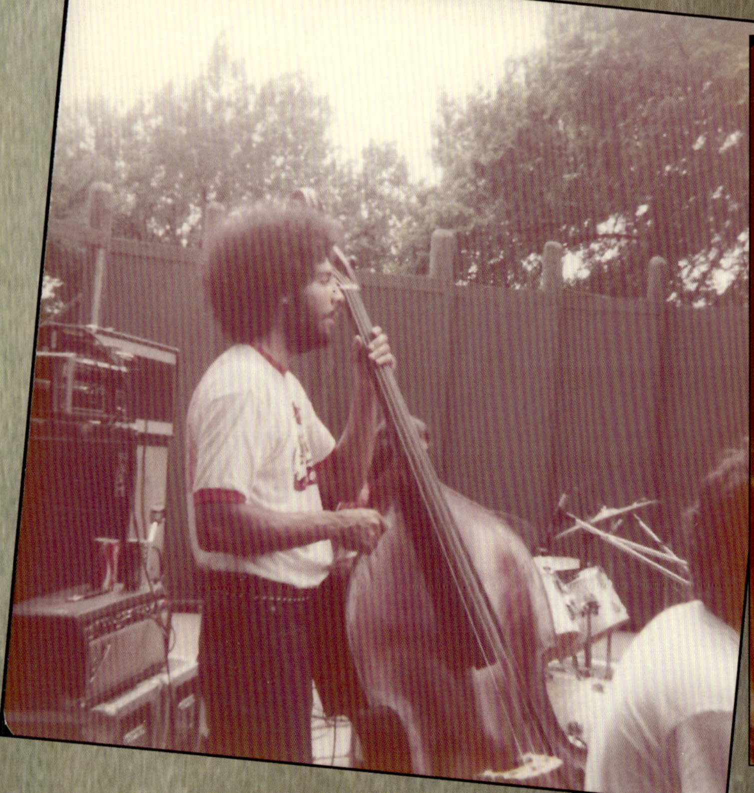

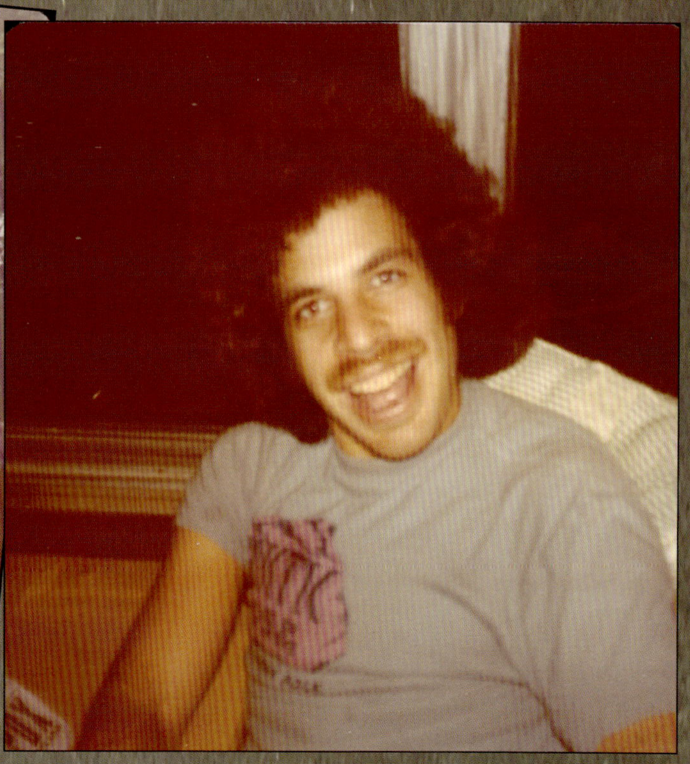

Lucky Oceans

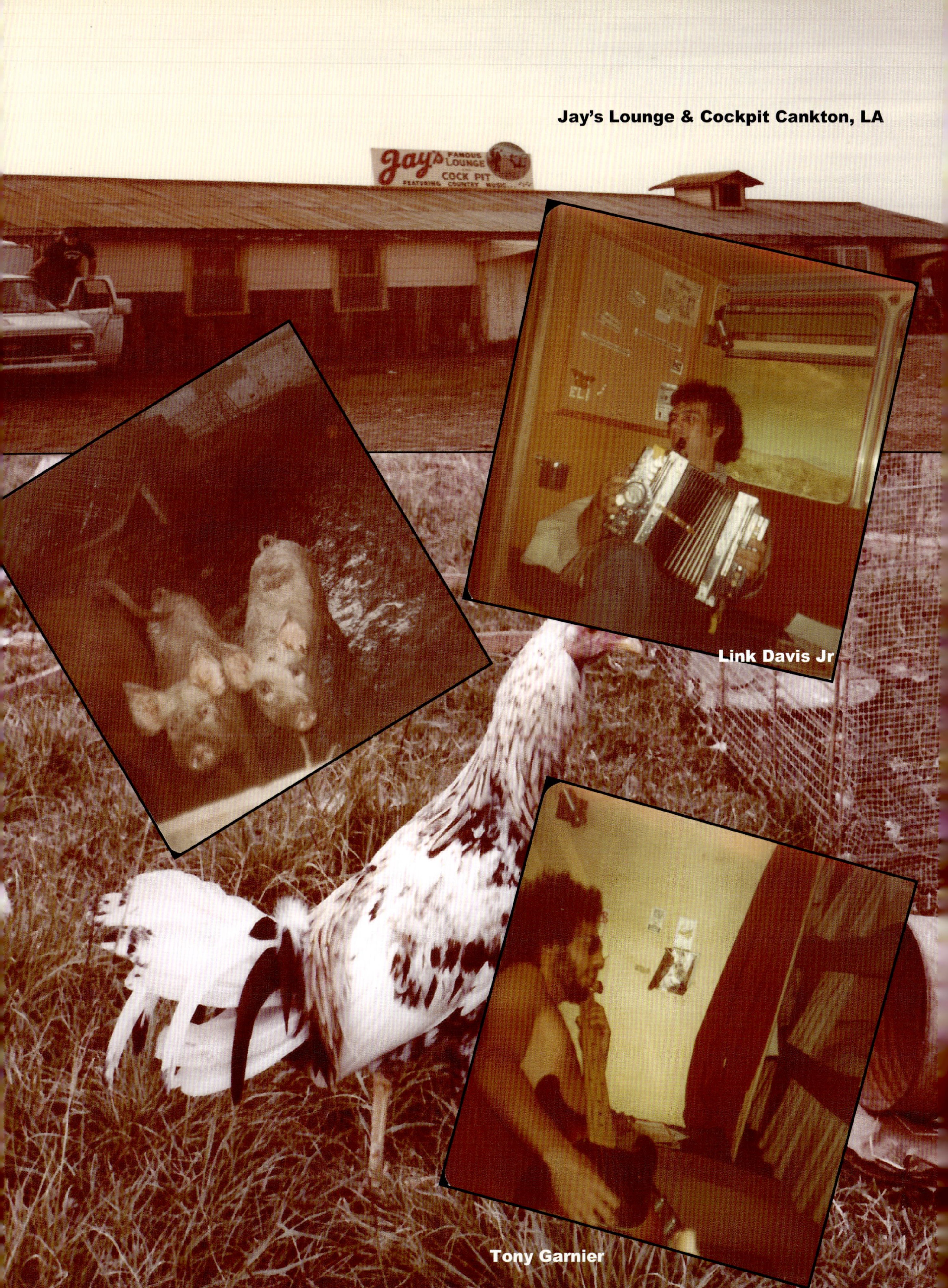

Jay's Lounge & Cockpit Cankton, LA

Link Davis Jr

Tony Garnier

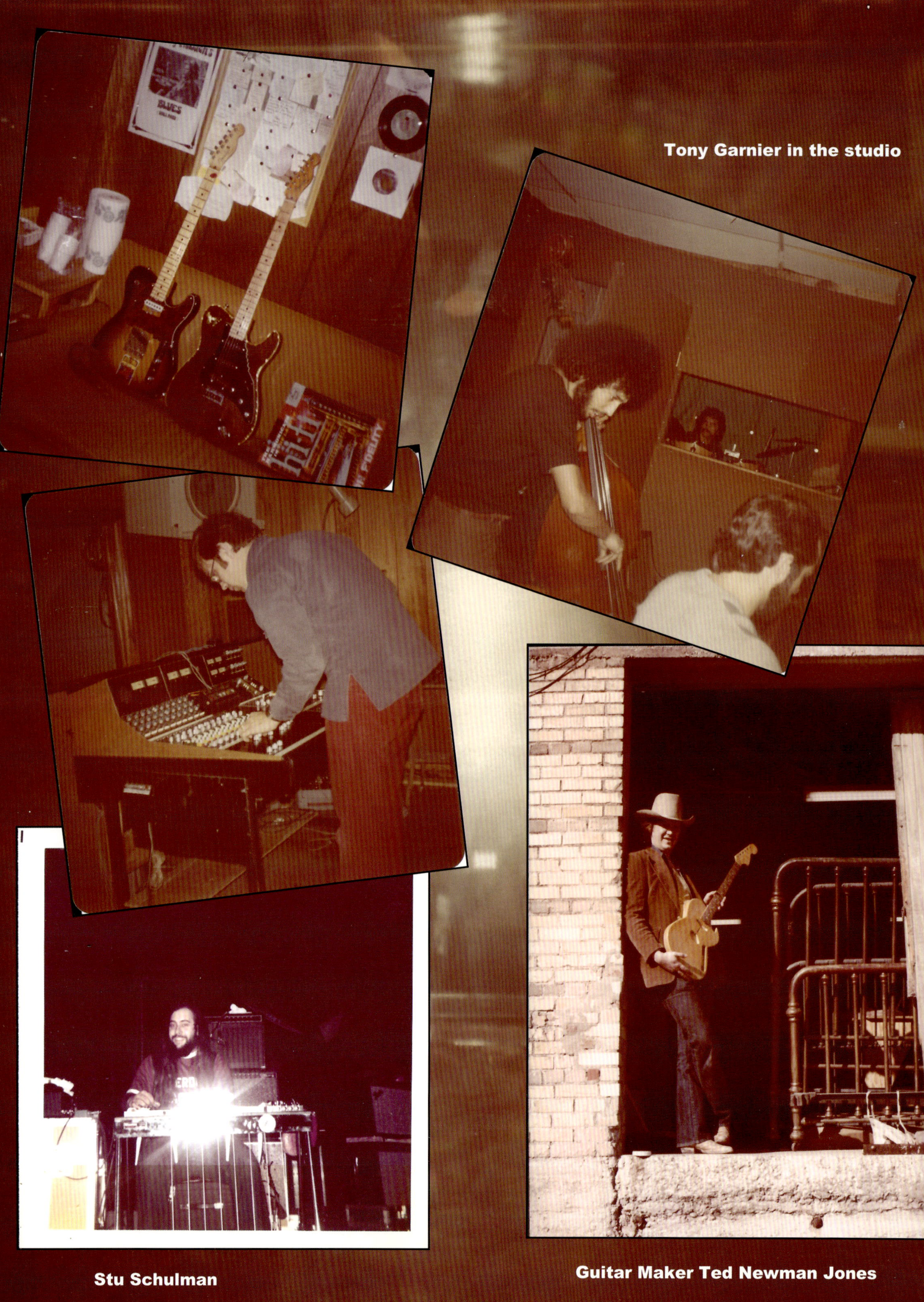

Tony Garnier in the studio

Stu Schulman

Guitar Maker Ted Newman Jones

Chapter 3: Leavin' Texas with Jerry Jeff Walker 1978

After a disagreement with Ray Benson, I left the Asleep at the Wheel tour and headed back to Austin. I was only home for a short period of time before I got a call from the Jerry Jeff Walker crew asking if I would be interested in driving their equipment truck. I accepted the temporary job, jumped into the truck and after a short stint as a truck driver I was offered a full-time position on Jerry Jeff's crew. At the height of his career in 1978, Jerry Jeff was selling out concert venues and touring with Willie Nelson.

One show in particular was very special for me: Arrowhead Stadium in Kansas City with Willie Nelson and The Grateful Dead.

The crew and band were all one big family. Everyone was treated as an equal and it was friends working for friends. Coming from NY there were so many lines drawn and in Austin it just wasn't that way. That's why I loved it.

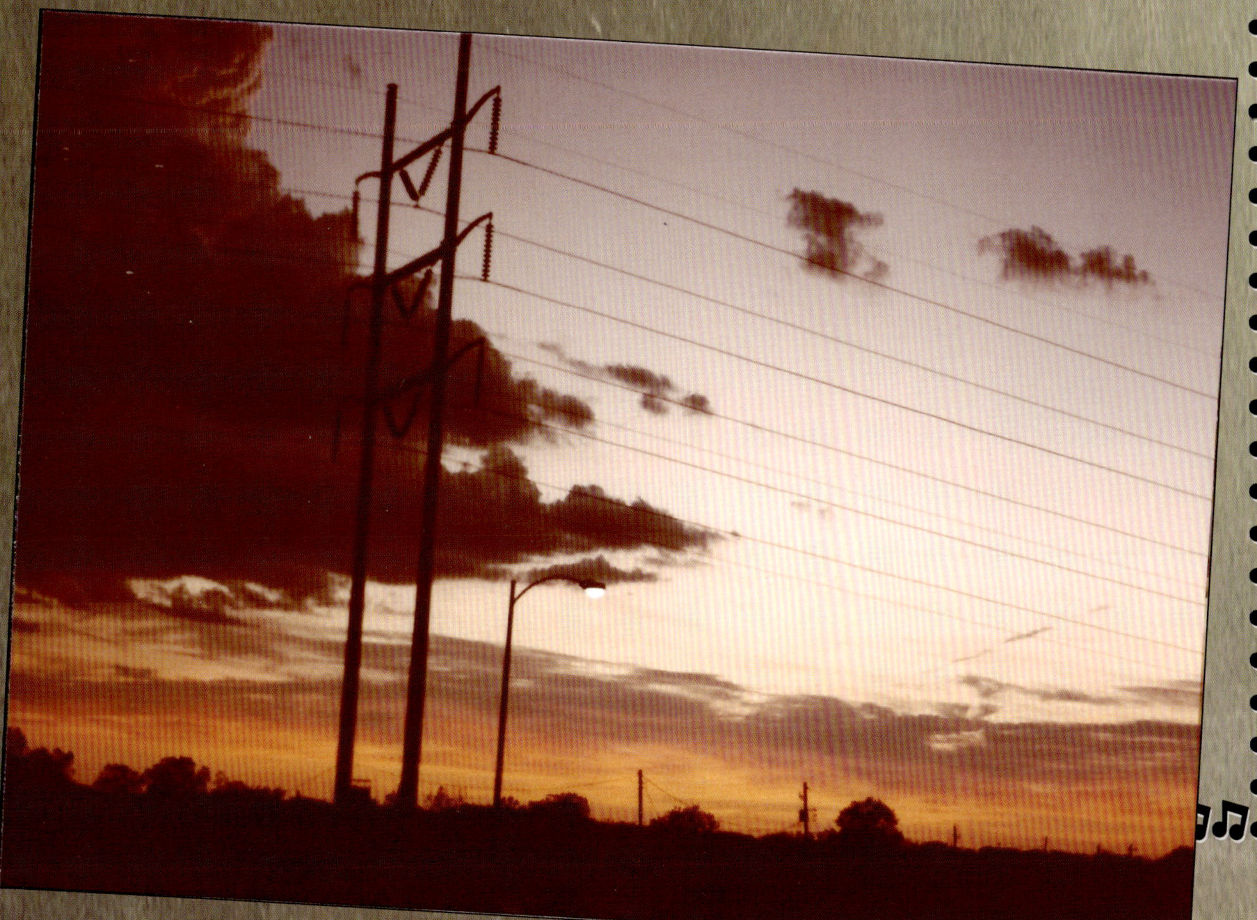

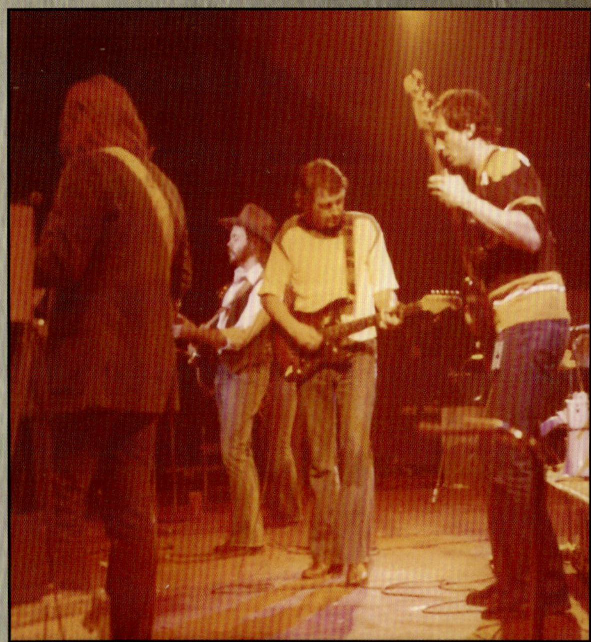

Jerry Jeff Walker Band

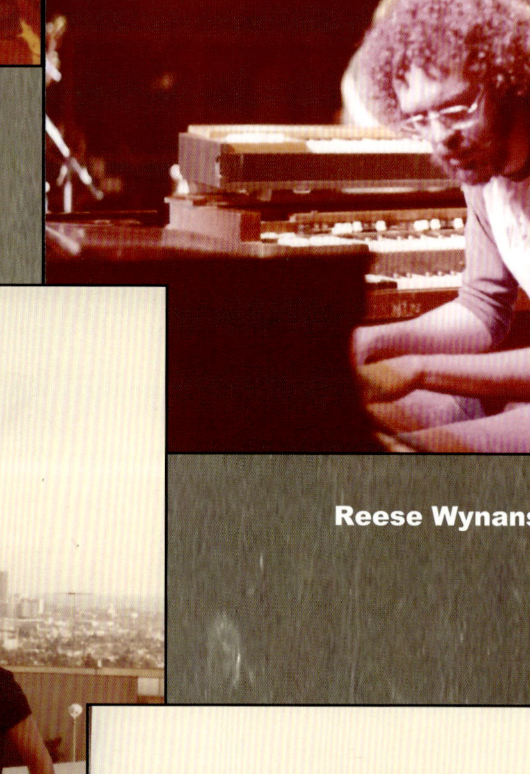

Reese Wynans

Bobby Bowles & Bobby Lemons

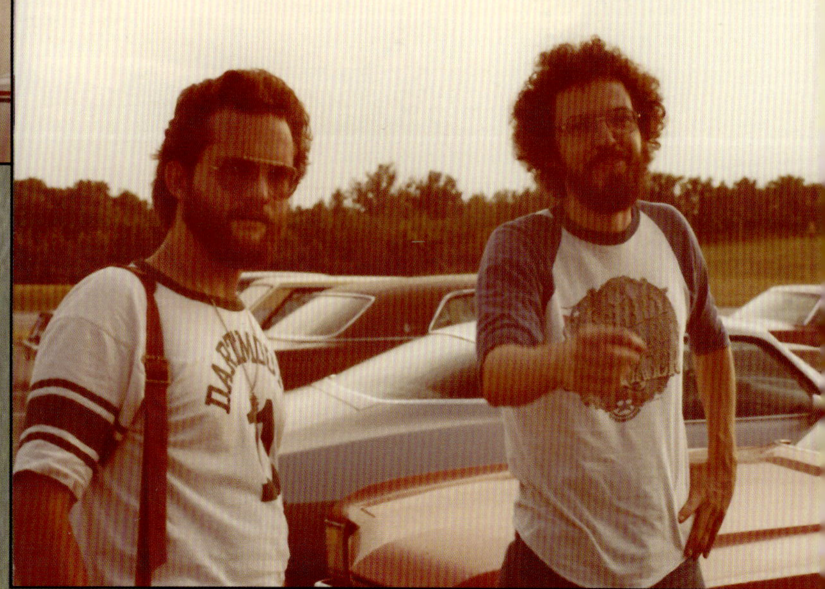

Freddy Krc & Reese Wynans

ARROWHEAD STADIUM
WILLIE, THE GRATEFUL DEAD & JERRY JEFF
1978

Joe "Beast" Aronson, Willie & Snake

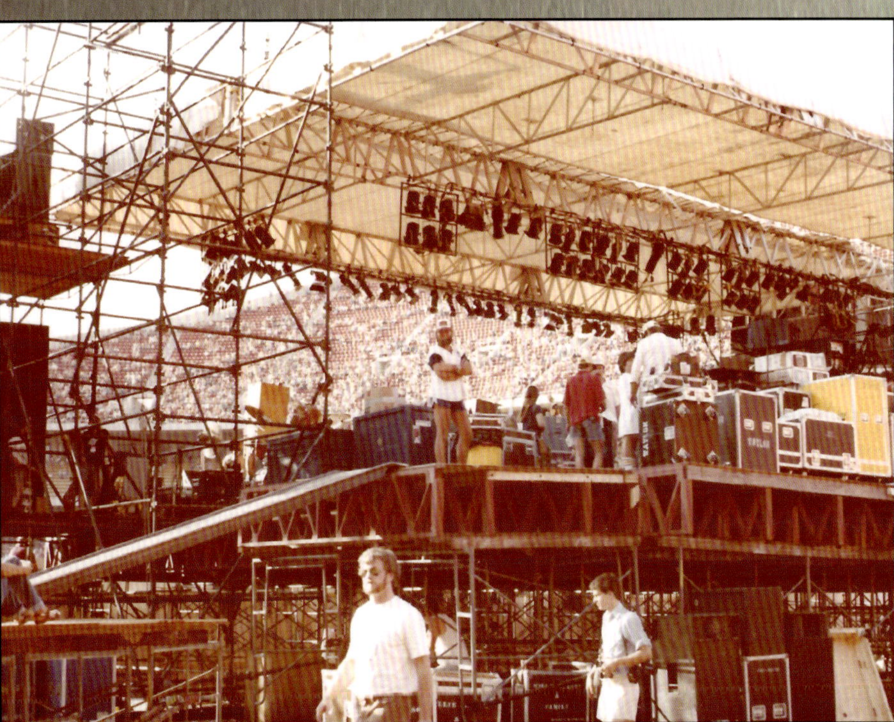

Poodie Locke "Up On Stage"

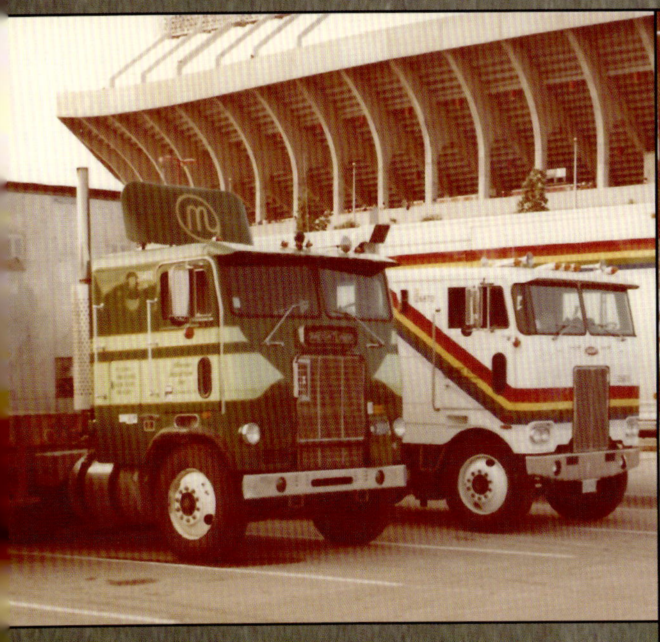

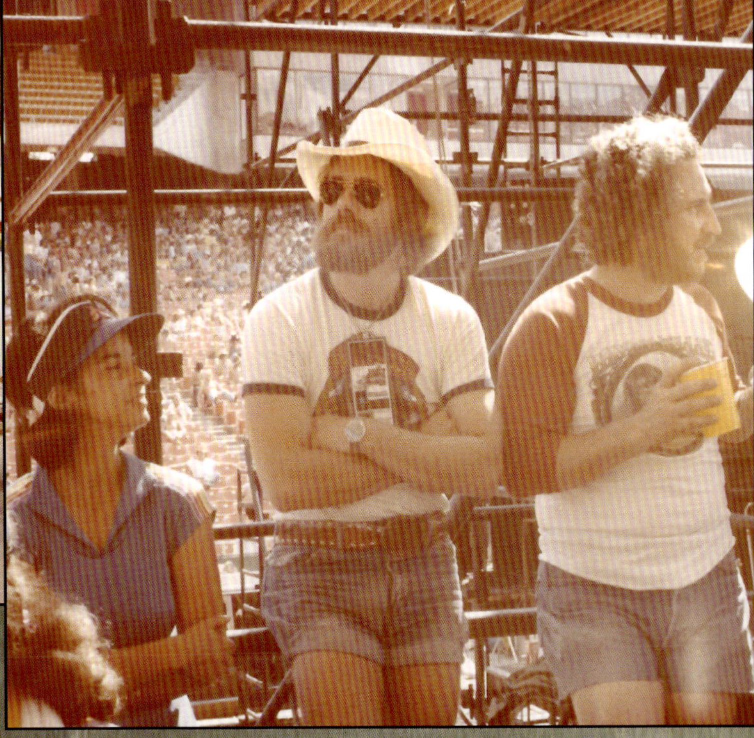

Buddy Pruitt

Bobby Lemons & Rut Rutledge

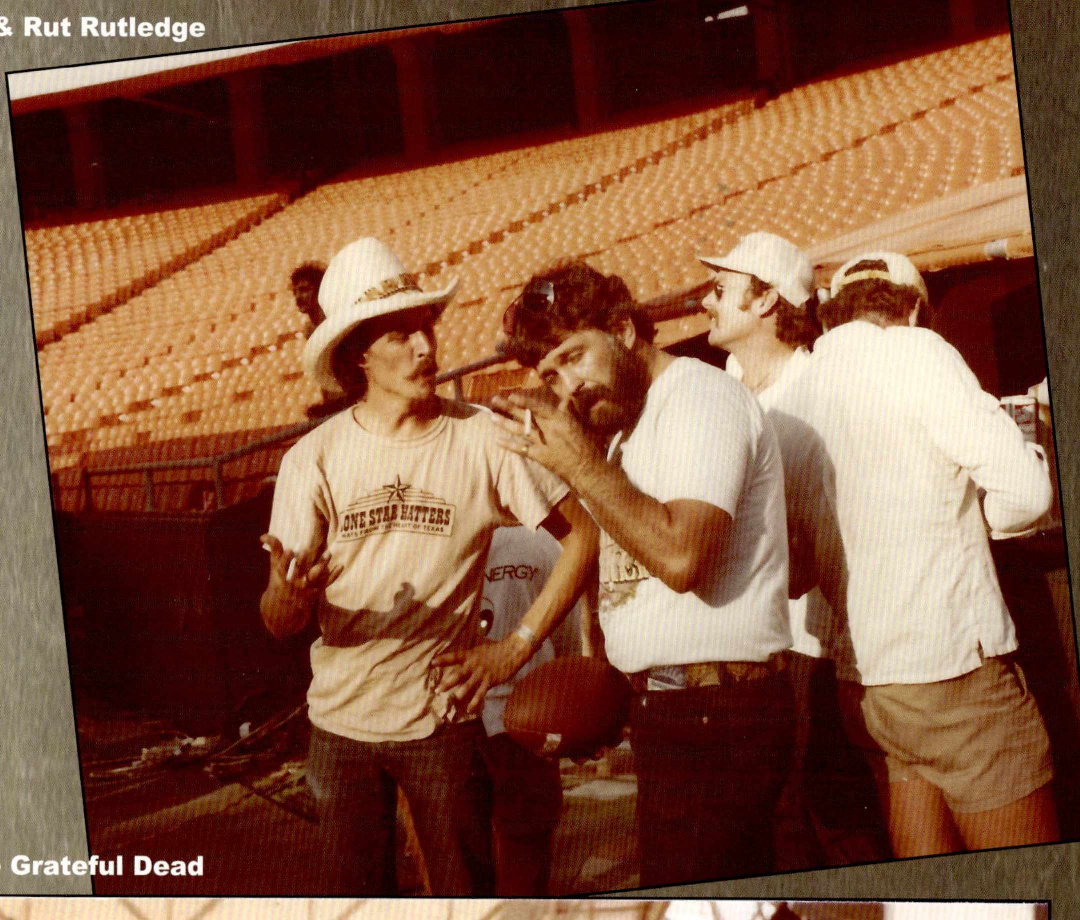

Phil Lesh of The Grateful Dead

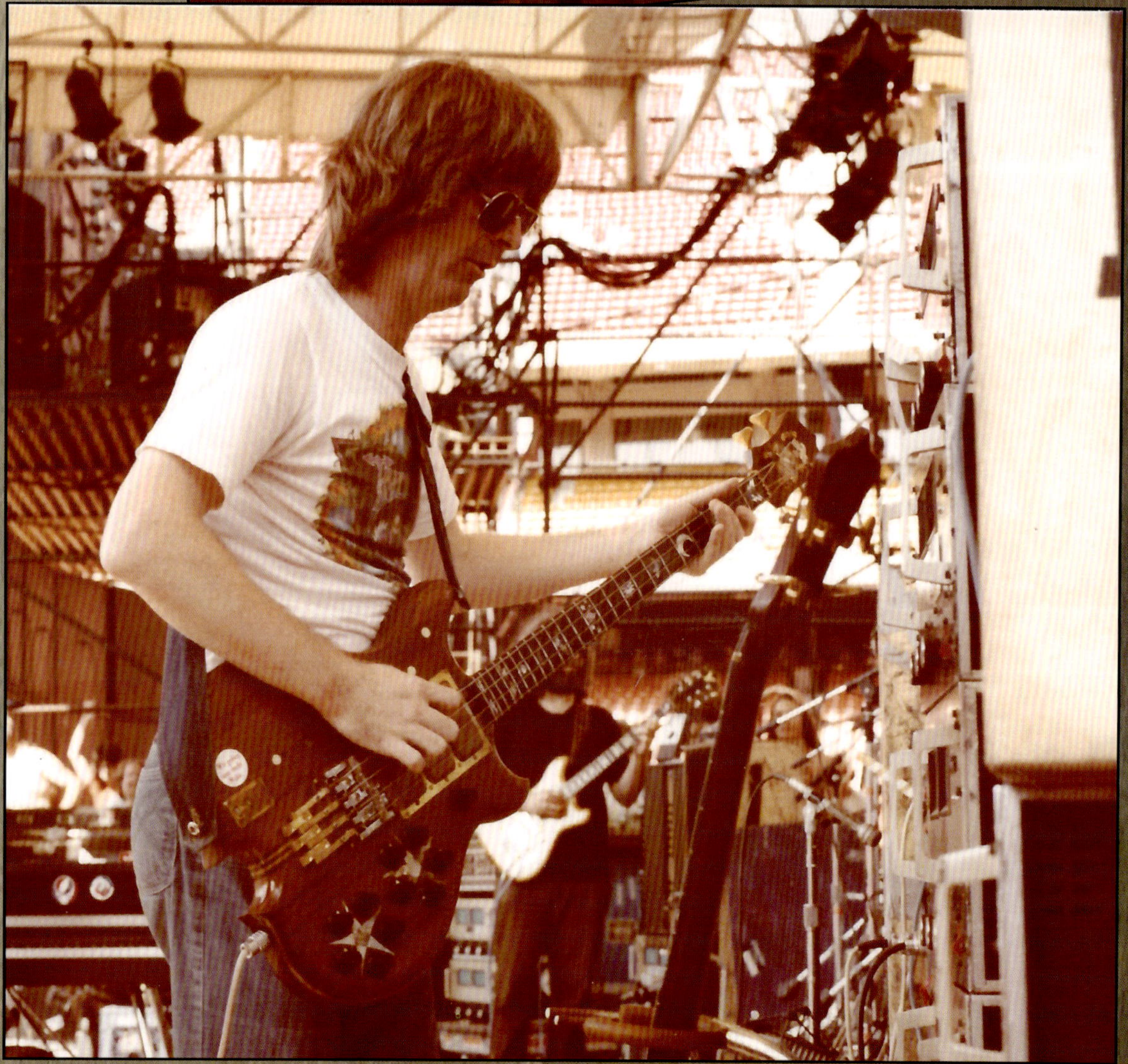

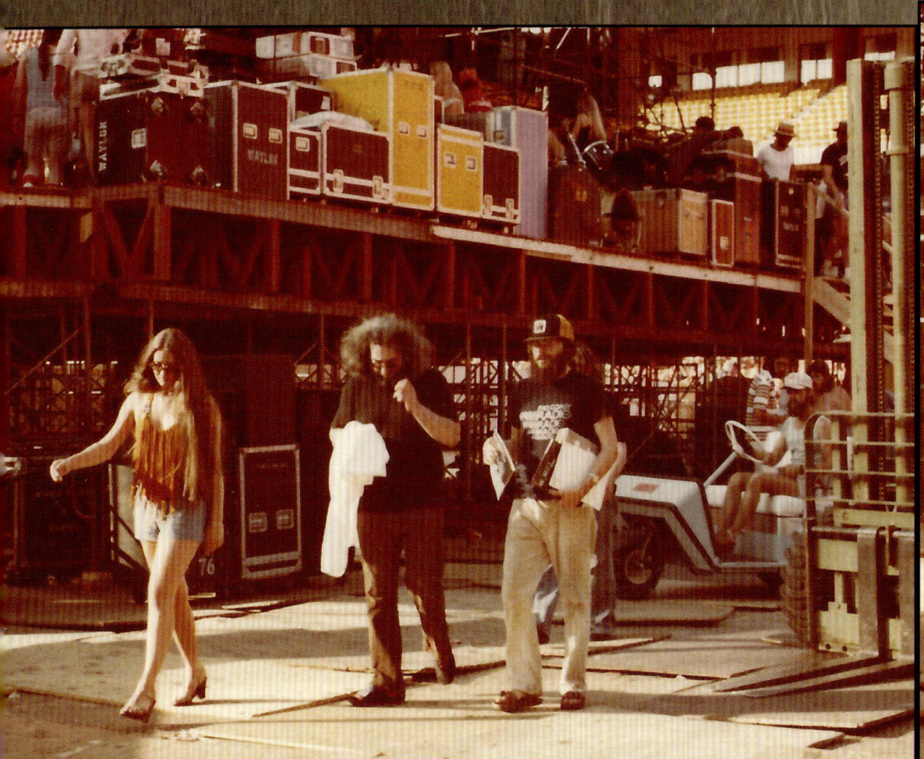

Jerry Garcia of the Grateful Dead

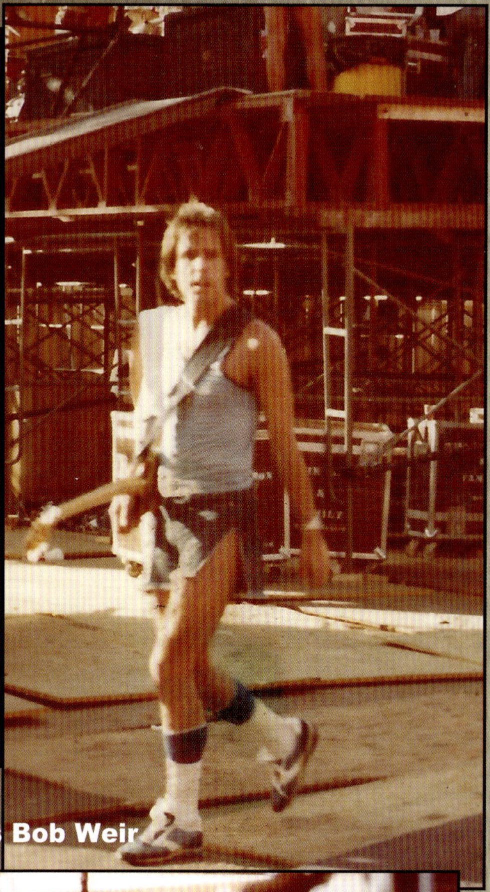

The Dead's Bob Weir

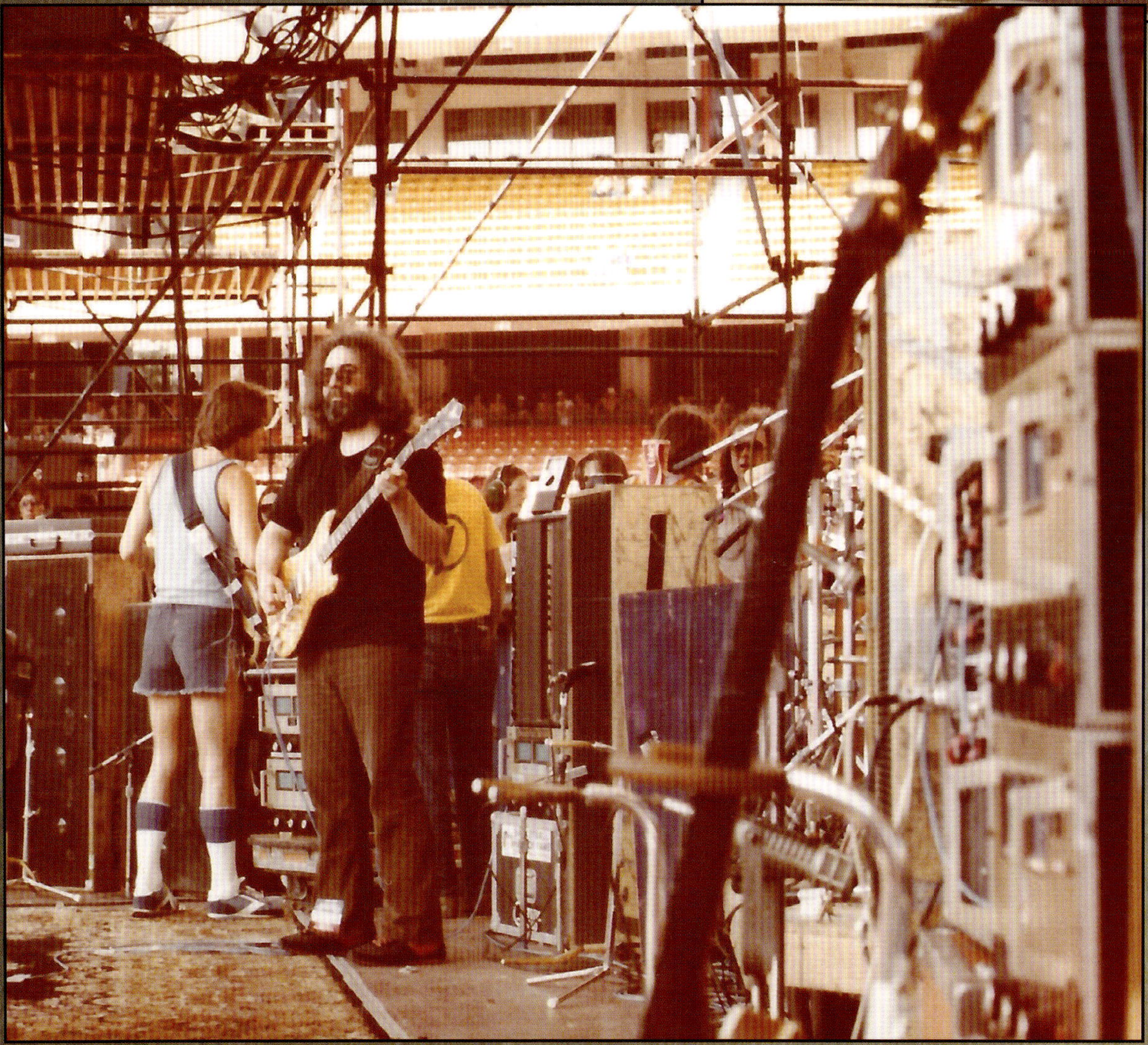

Jerry Garcia

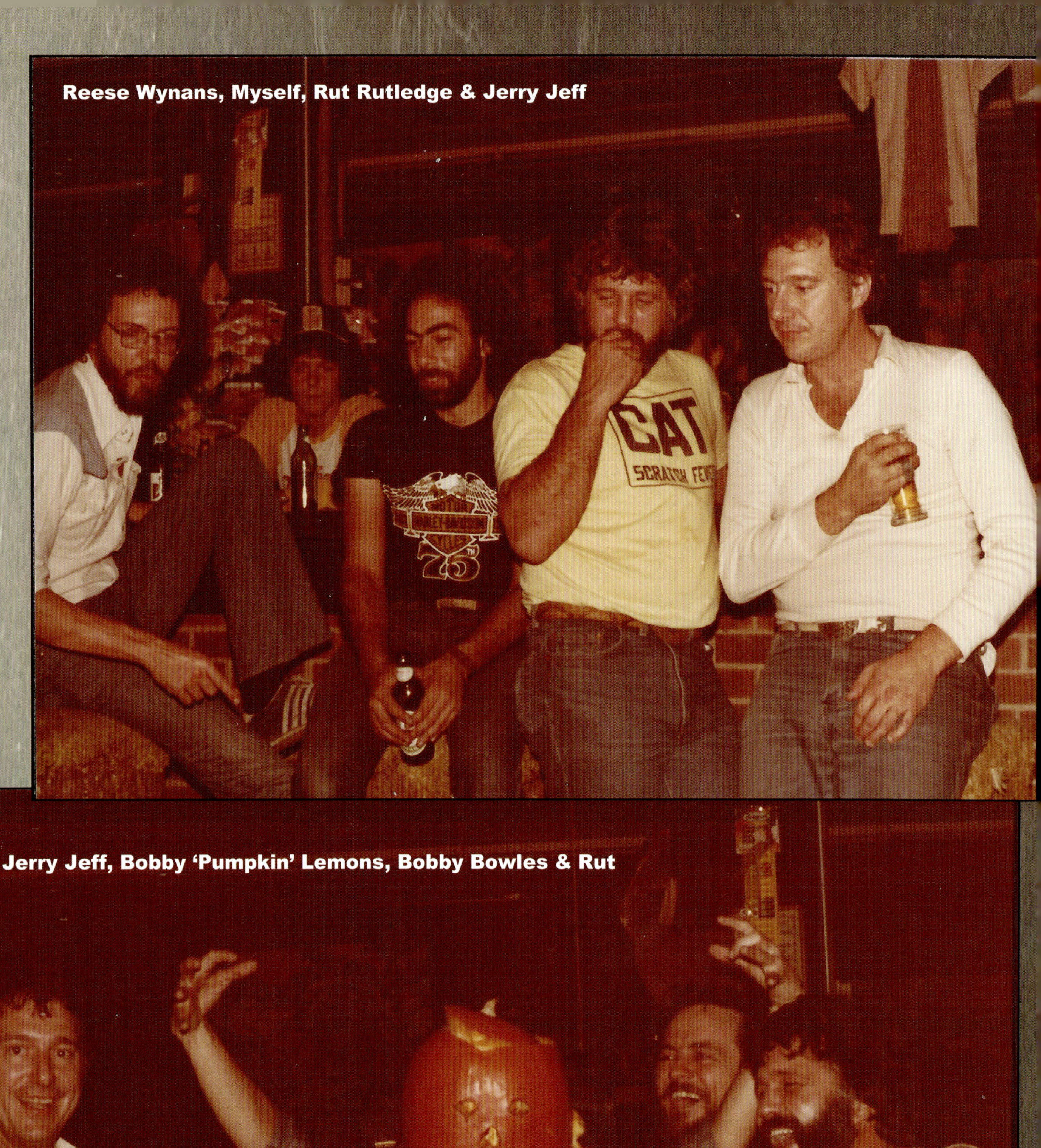

Reese Wynans, Myself, Rut Rutledge & Jerry Jeff

Jerry Jeff, Bobby 'Pumpkin' Lemons, Bobby Bowles & Rut

Chapter 4: Honky Tonkin' with Delbert McClinton 1979-1981

After Jerry Jeff's decision to quit touring, we headed back to Texas, and it was time to look for a new gig. As luck would have it, it didn't take long before I received a call from Jerry Jeff's ex tour manager asking if I was interested in working for Delbert McClinton as the house engineer. Delbert was one of my favorite artists, so this was an easy decision taking this job.

Starting in 1979, I hit the road with The Delbert McClinton band and it was a year of honky tonks, festivals and supporting everyone from Willie Nelson to James Brown to Charlie Daniels.

By 1980, Delbert was back in the studio recording what would be his biggest hit, "Giving It Up for Your Love," which led to an appearance on *Saturday Night Live*, and reuniting me with old friends on the Willie Nelson tour as Delbert spent much of that year opening shows for Willie.

After four continuous years on the road, Delbert made the decision to take some time off and I was left to find a new gig.

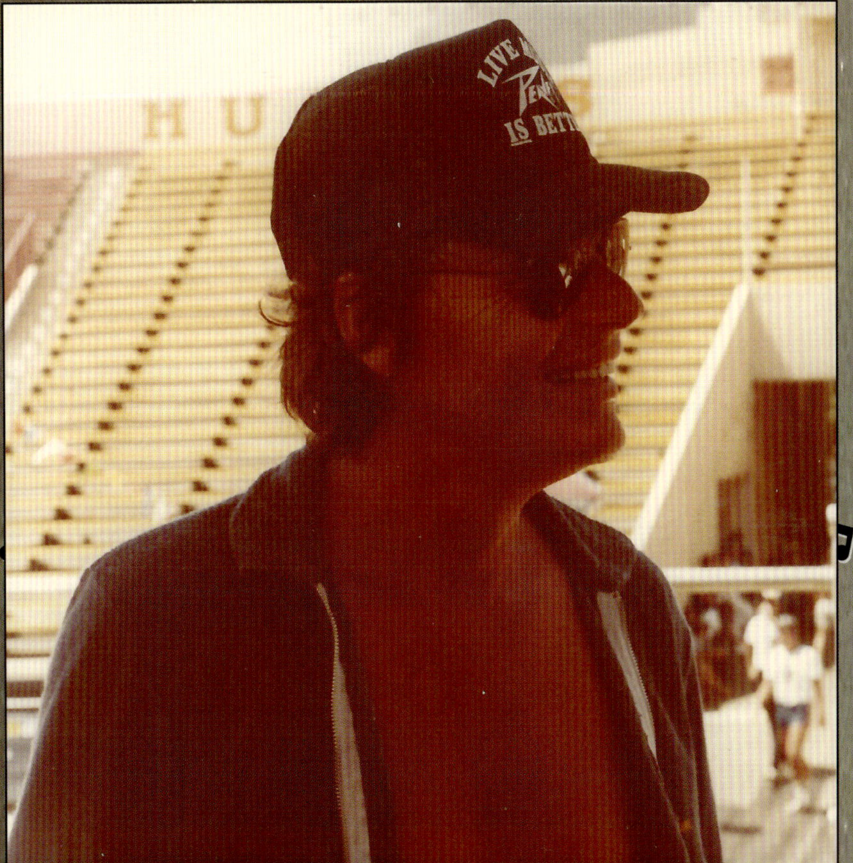

Delbert McClinton

Broke down Again!

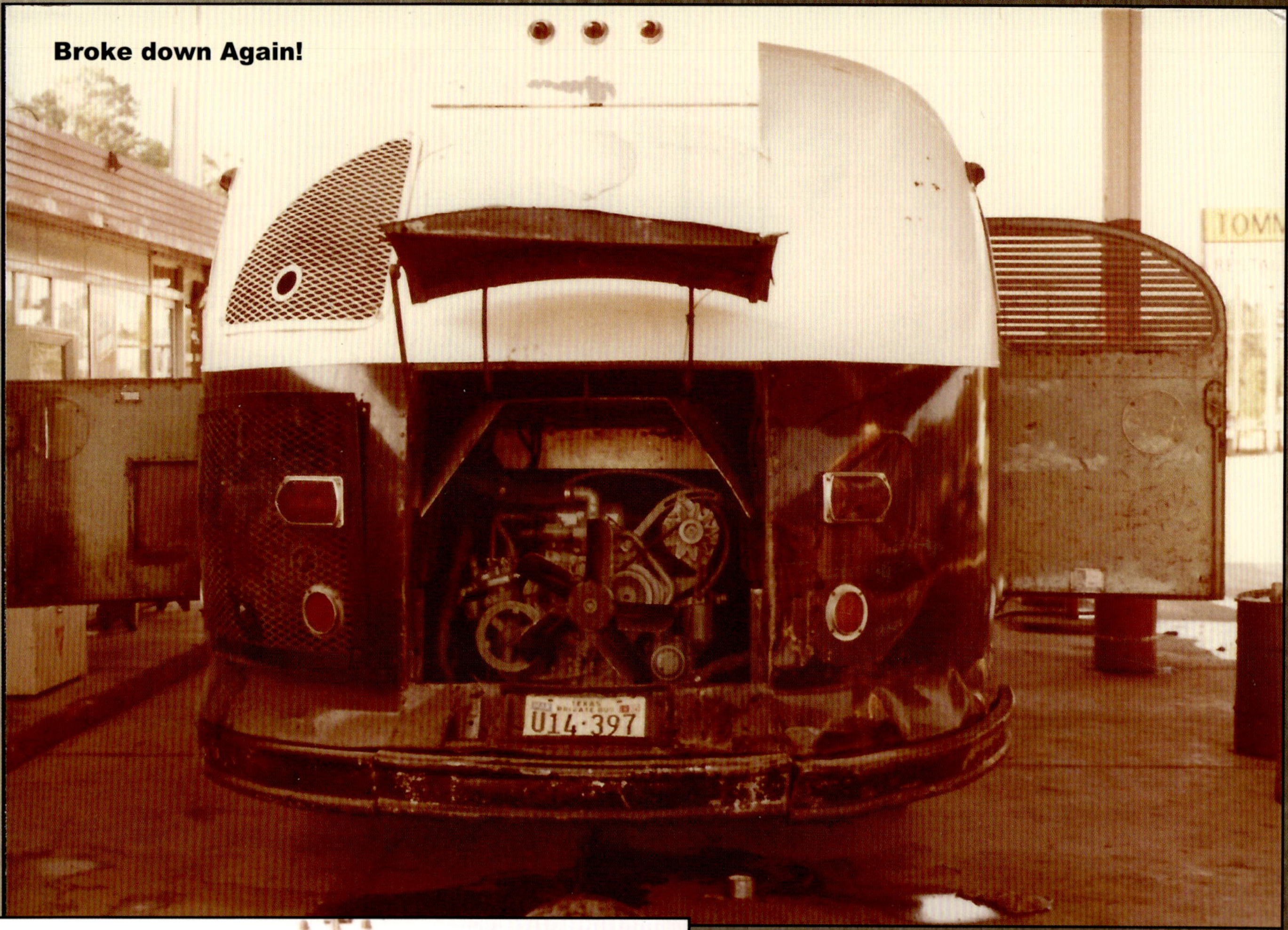

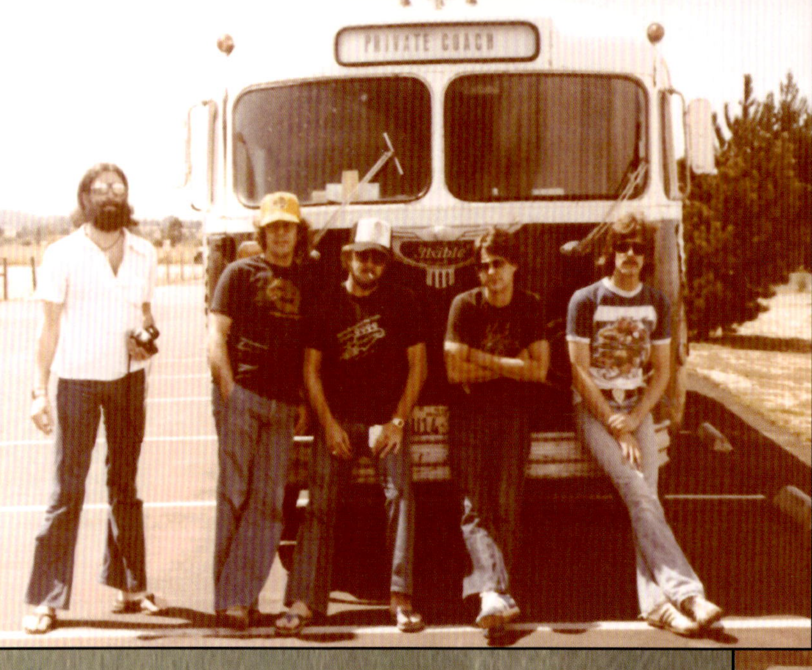

Billy Burke, Robert Harwell, Billy Sanders, James Pennybaker, Ron Cobb

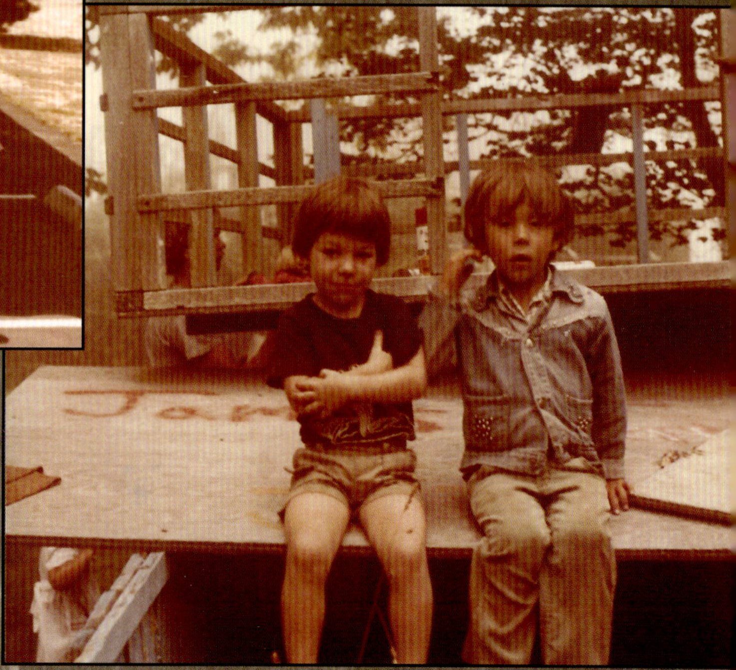

Clay McClinton & Friend on Martha's Vineyard

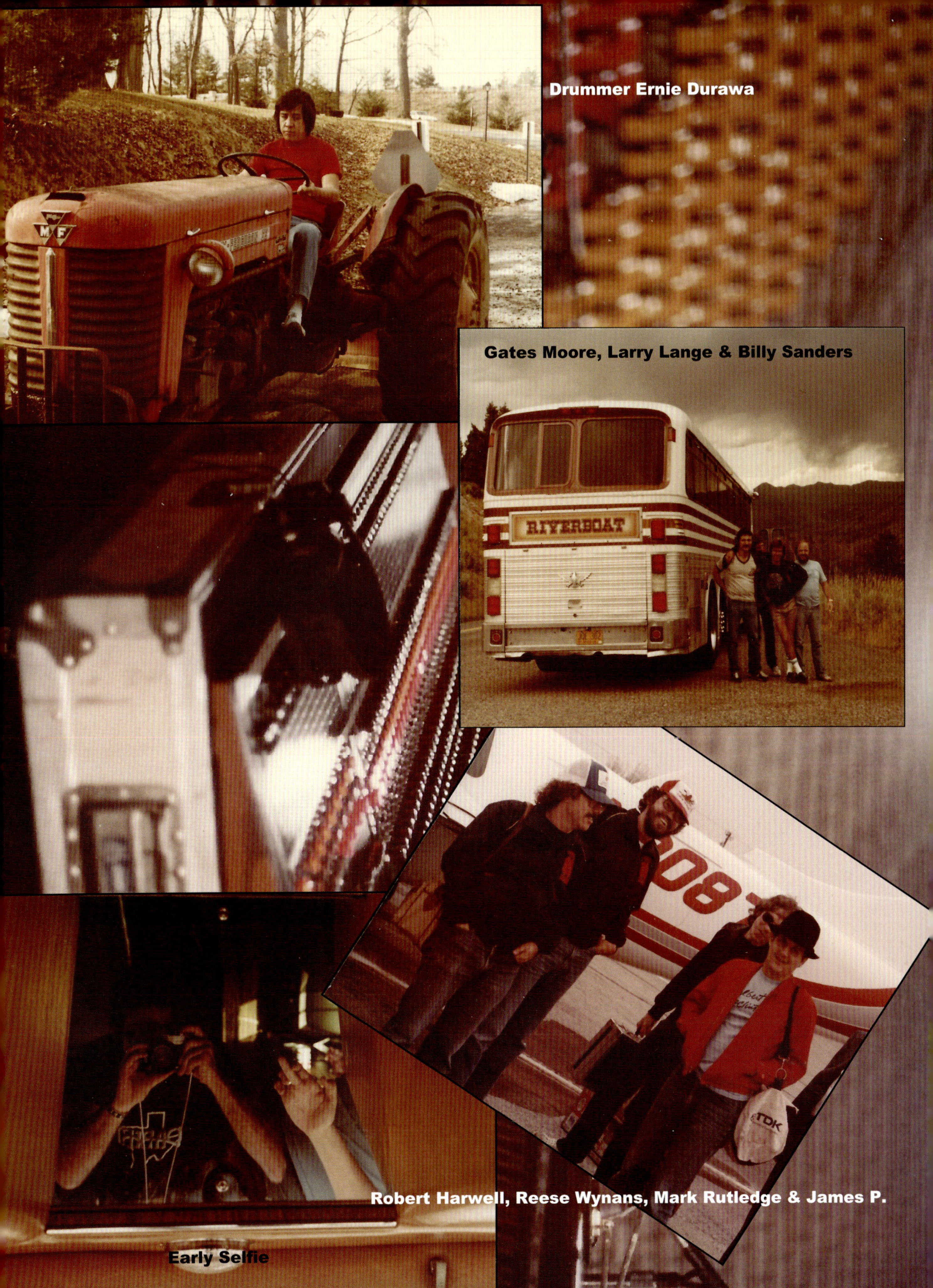

Drummer Ernie Durawa

Gates Moore, Larry Lange & Billy Sanders

Robert Harwell, Reese Wynans, Mark Rutledge & James P.

Early Selfie

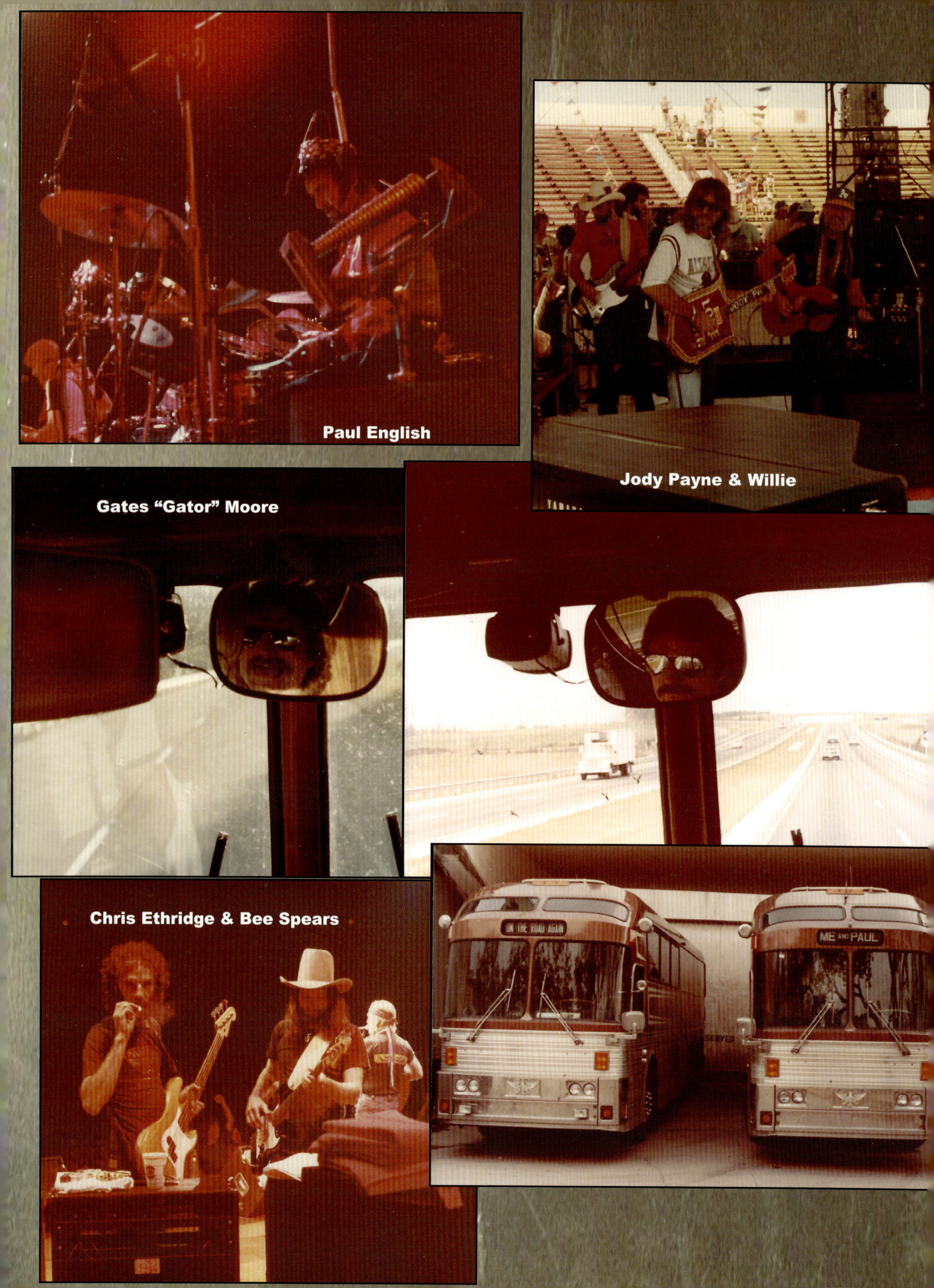

Paul English

Jody Payne & Willie

Gates "Gator" Moore

Chris Ethridge & Bee Spears

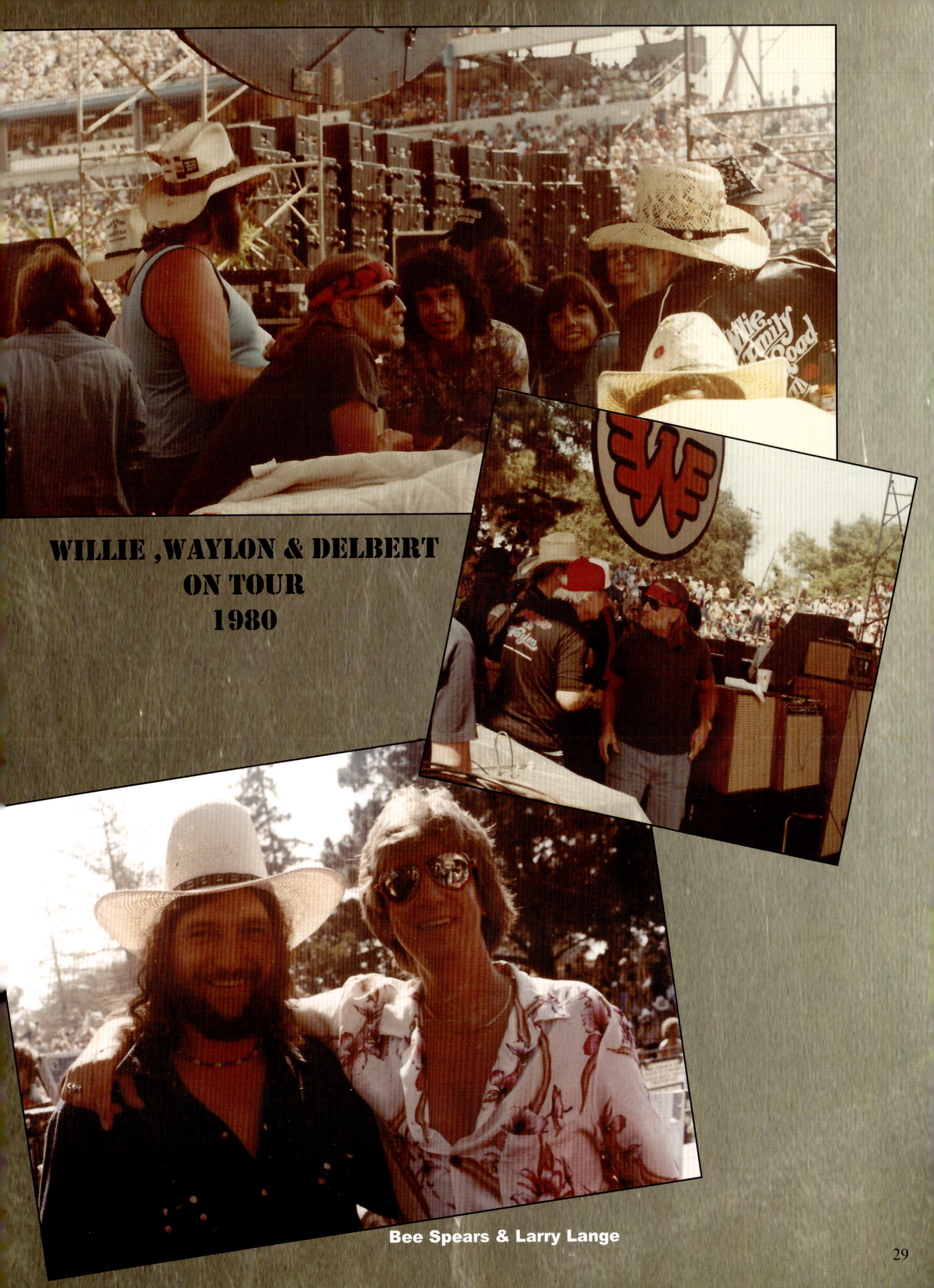

WILLIE ,WAYLON & DELBERT
ON TOUR
1980

Bee Spears & Larry Lange

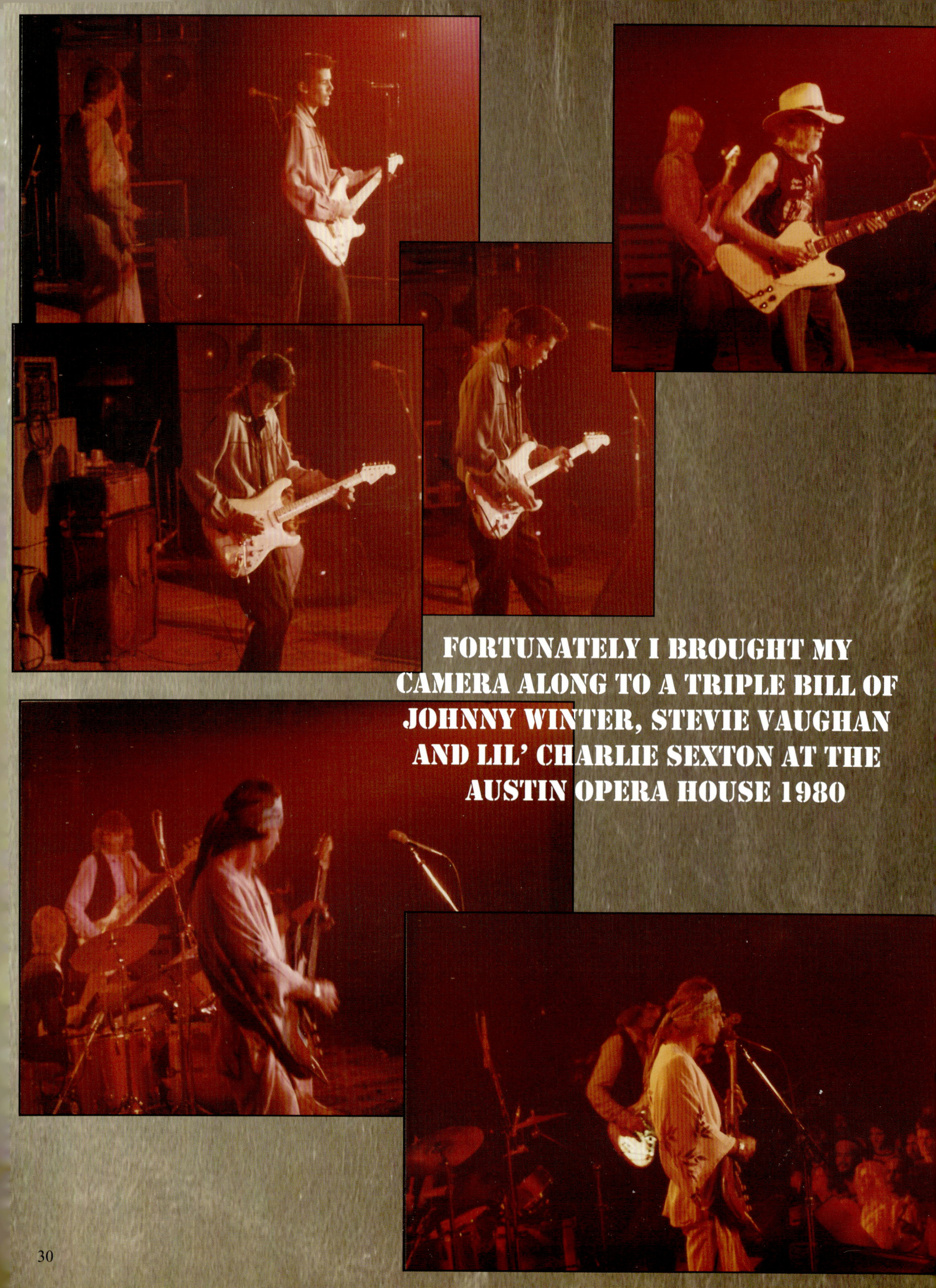

FORTUNATELY I BROUGHT MY CAMERA ALONG TO A TRIPLE BILL OF JOHNNY WINTER, STEVIE VAUGHAN AND LIL' CHARLIE SEXTON AT THE AUSTIN OPERA HOUSE 1980

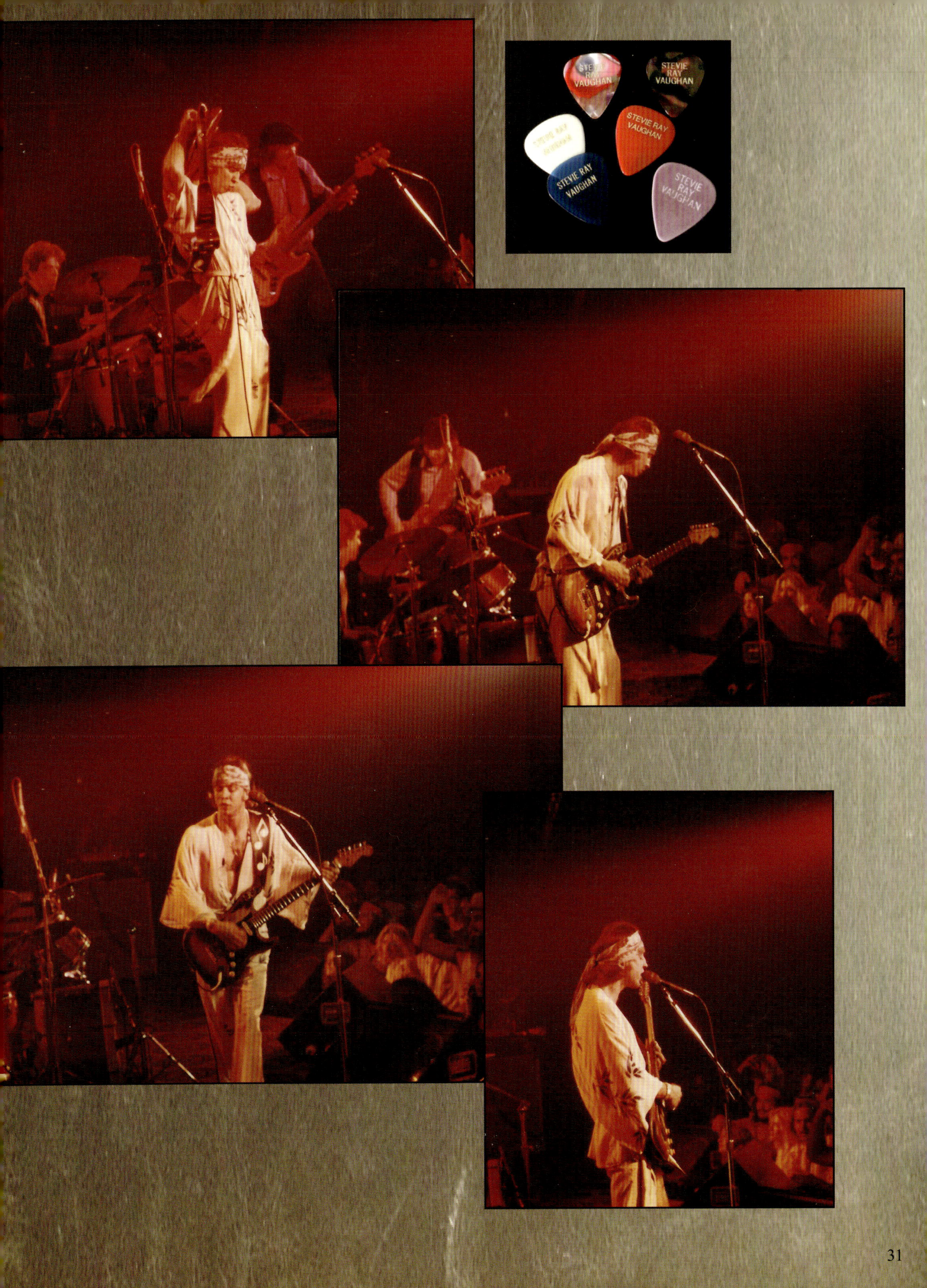
VAUGHAN
STEVIE
RAY
VAUGHAN
STEVIE RAY
VAUGHAN
STEVIE RAY
VAUGHAN
STEVIE
RAY
VAUGHAN

Chapter 5: Hot Dog & a Roadmap with The Fabulous Thunderbirds

Back in Austin, I got a call from an old friend, Dave Gardner who had worked for Blackstar Sound and was presently working for the T-birds as their audio engineer. Dave told me they needed a tour manager and offered me the job. In the past, Jimmie Vaughan had called me two or three times offering me a job, and previously each time I thanked him but passed on the offer.

When Dave called, the timing couldn't have been any better, as the T-birds had a new album coming out, a planned tour of Europe and I was looking for work. I had never tour managed before nor had I ever toured Europe but I felt I had the confidence to do both.

In the winter of 1983, I headed to London with the T-birds to start the tour. They played one show in London and after that show we boarded a ferry heading out to the North Sea and toward our destination of Norway. It was a 24 hour trip in sub-zero weather and if you stood on the deck too long your hands would freeze.

This tour took us through Scandinavia, Central Europe and back to England. The tour was a huge success as we found an incredibly enthusiastic and loyal fan base. At the shows the people just loved the music. Thirty days in Europe and we headed back home to resume a non-stop schedule of touring from East Coast to West Coast.

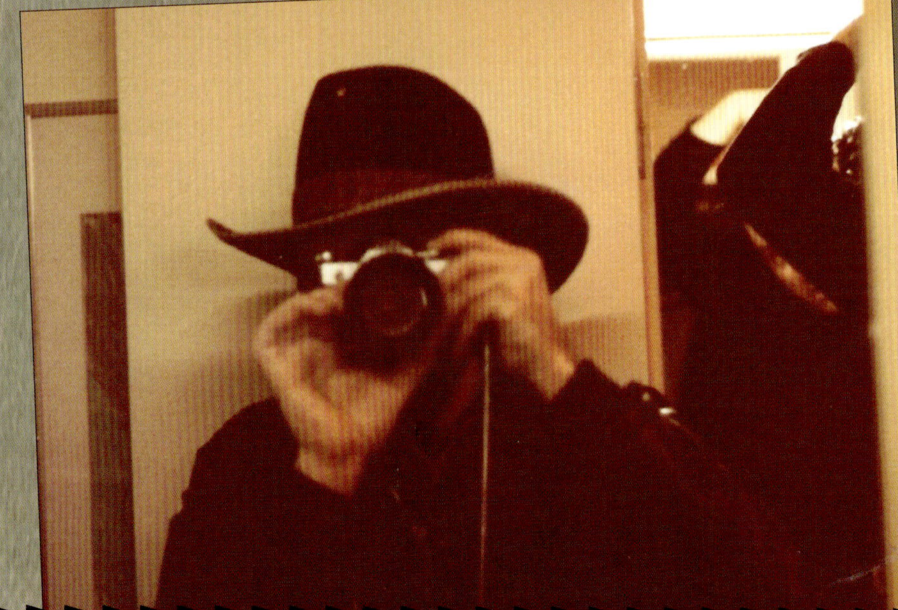

Opposite Page
Production Mgr. Mick Kluczynski, Kim & Jimmie

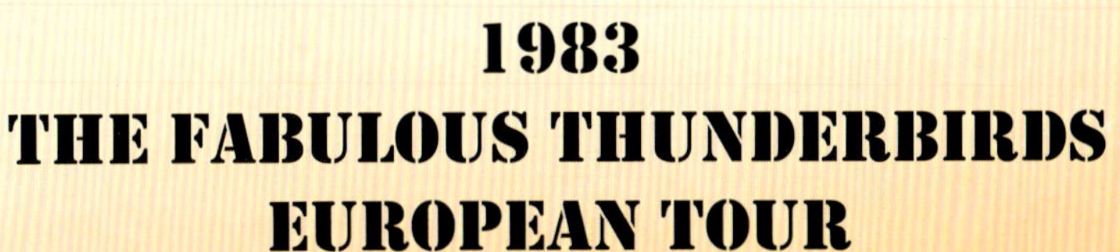

1983 THE FABULOUS THUNDERBIRDS EUROPEAN TOUR

Kim Wilson & Jimmie Vaughan

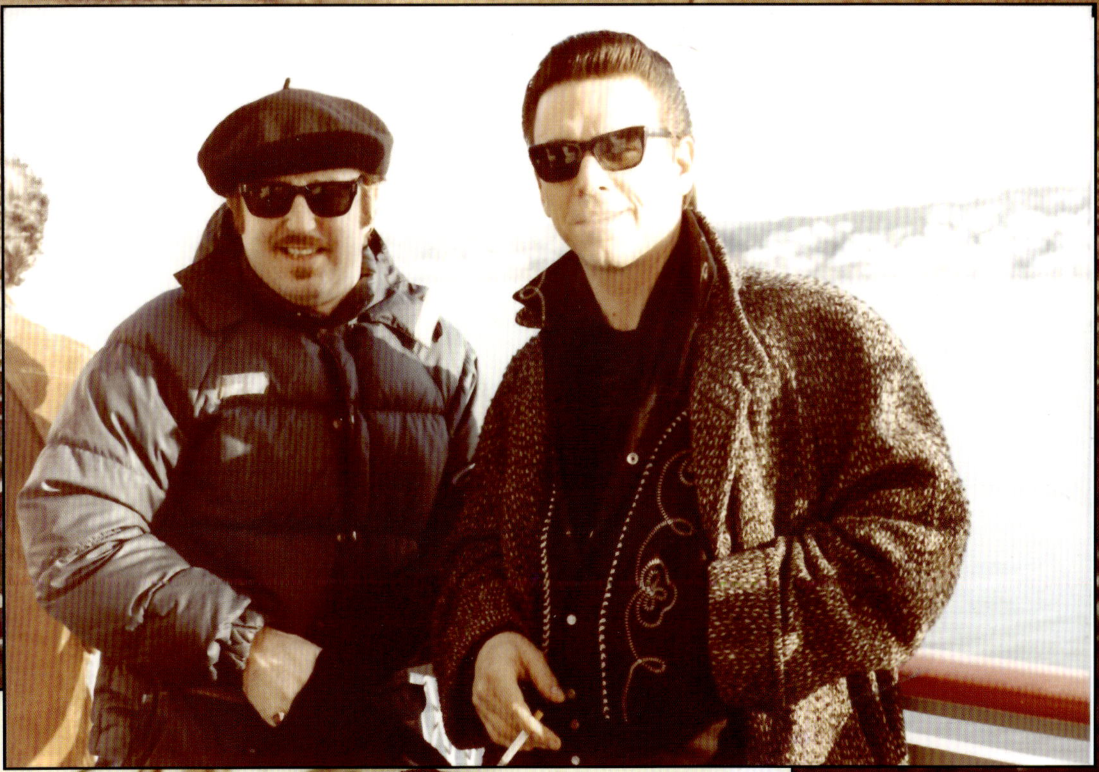

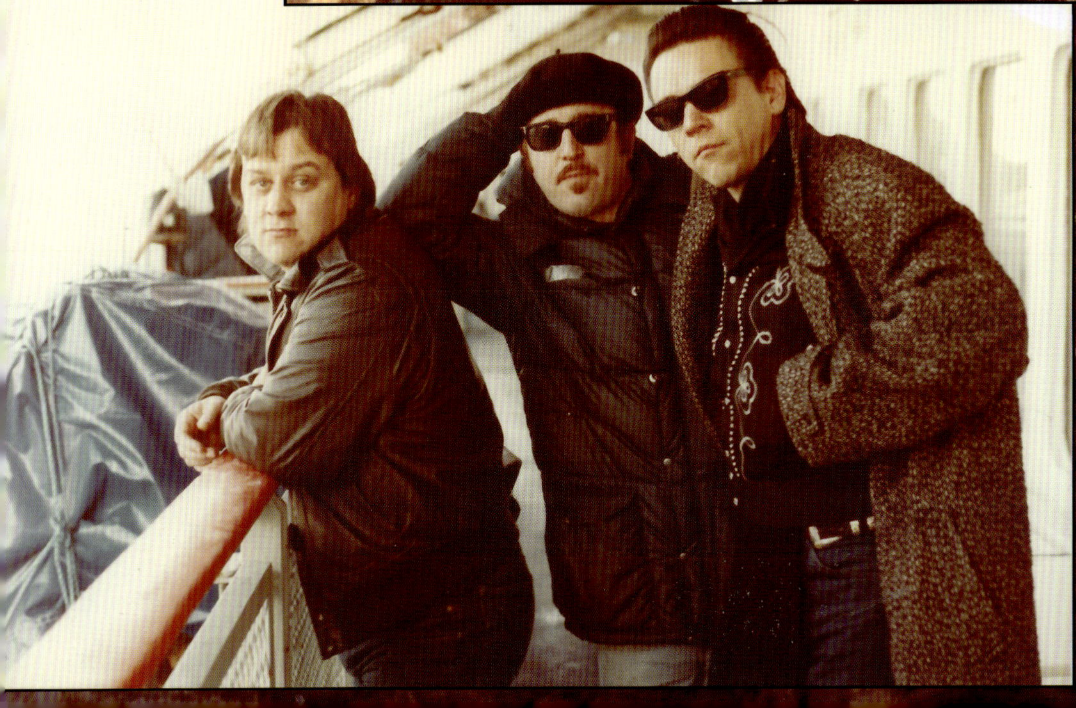

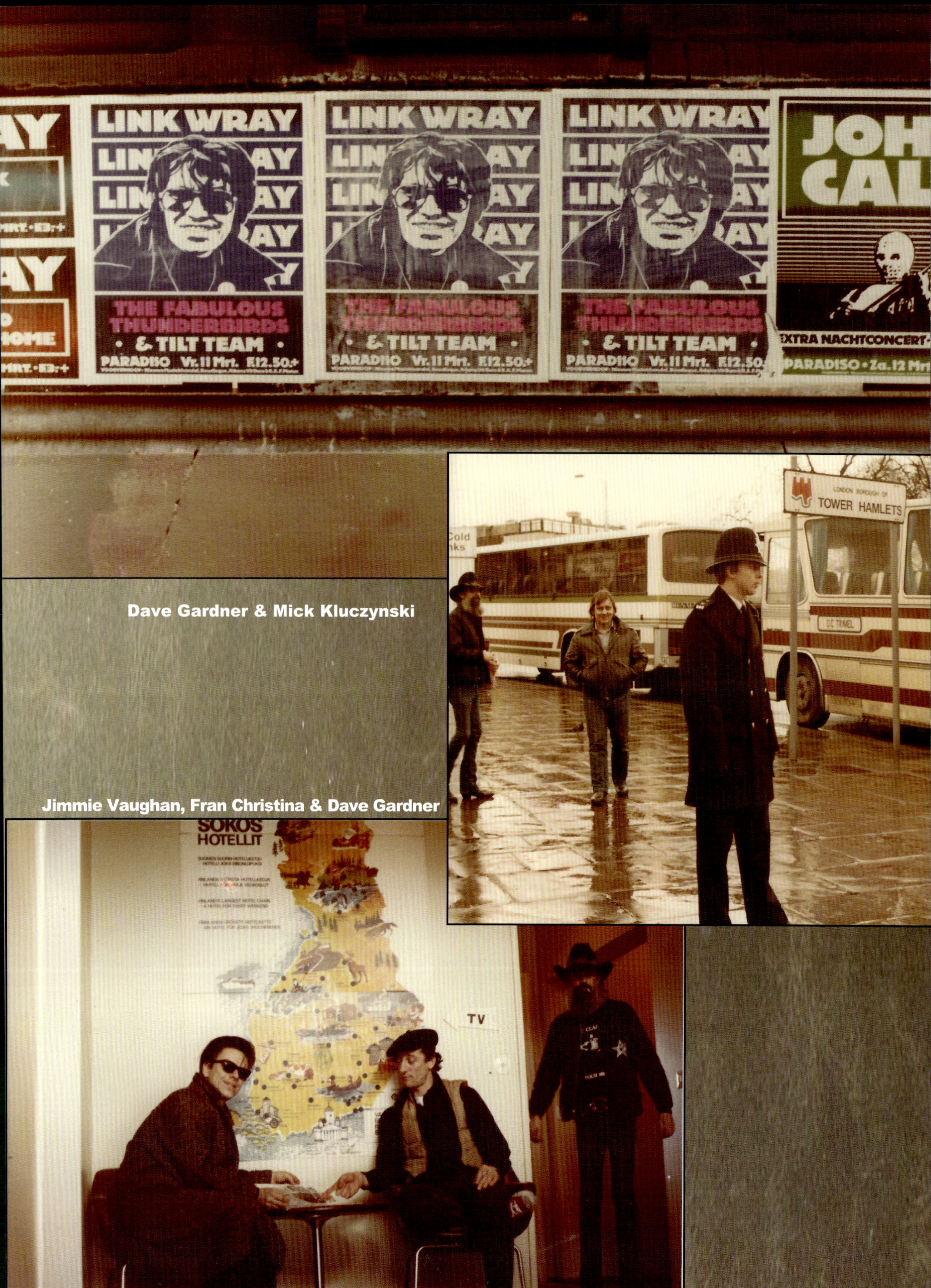

Dave Gardner & Mick Kluczynski

Jimmie Vaughan, Fran Christina & Dave Gardner

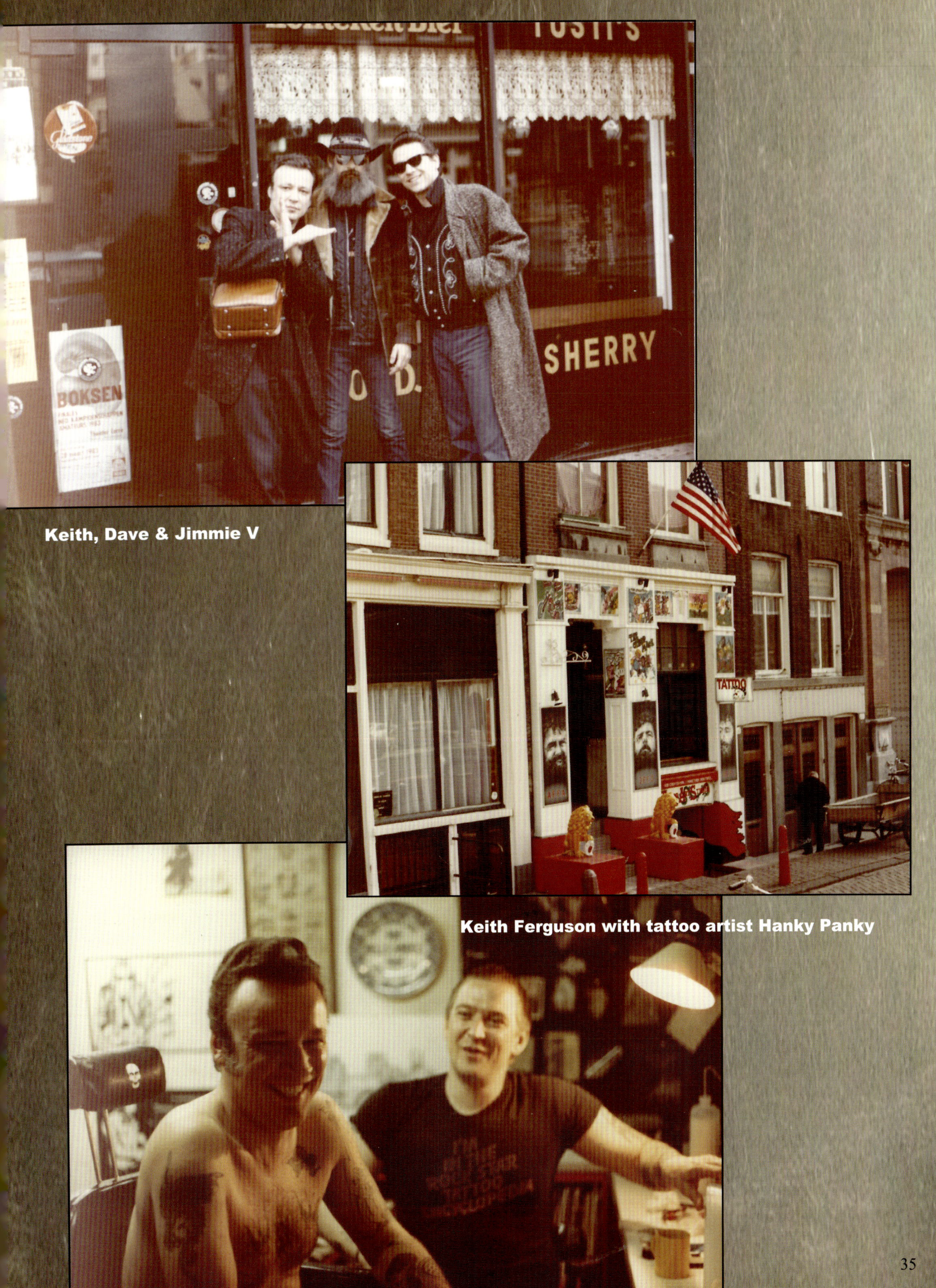

Keith, Dave & Jimmie V

Keith Ferguson with tattoo artist Hanky Panky

Chapter 6: Can't Tear It Up Enuff with the Fabulous T-Birds

Before heading to Europe Chrysalis Records gave us a small budget to produce an MTV-style video for the new release "T-Bird Rhythm" . With a tiny budget of $10,000, a director and a camera man on skates we produced two videos, "Can't Tear It Up Enough" and "How Do You Spell Love?".

Filmed at the Continental Club and Dan's Hamburgers on South Congress well before the street became 'SOCO'.

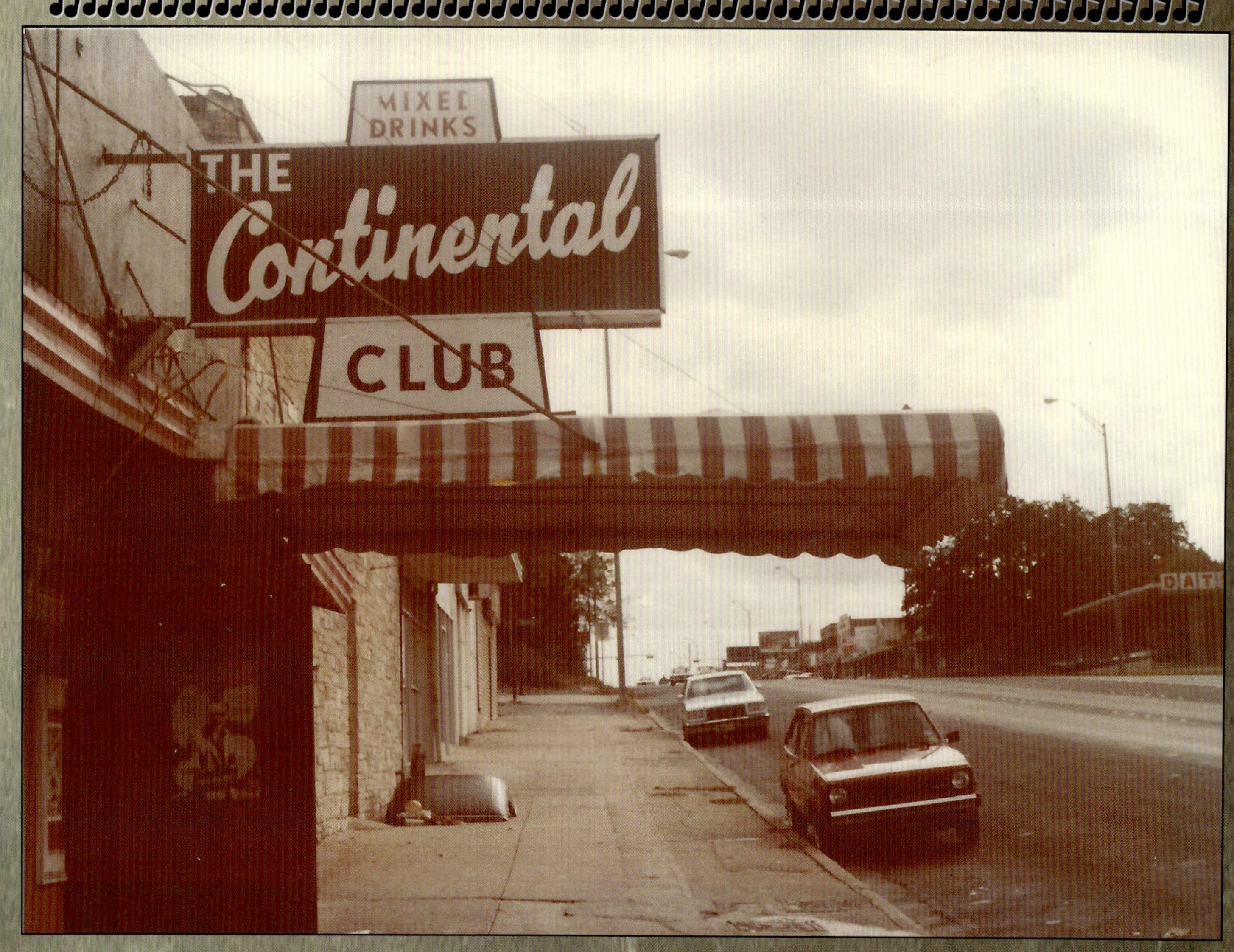

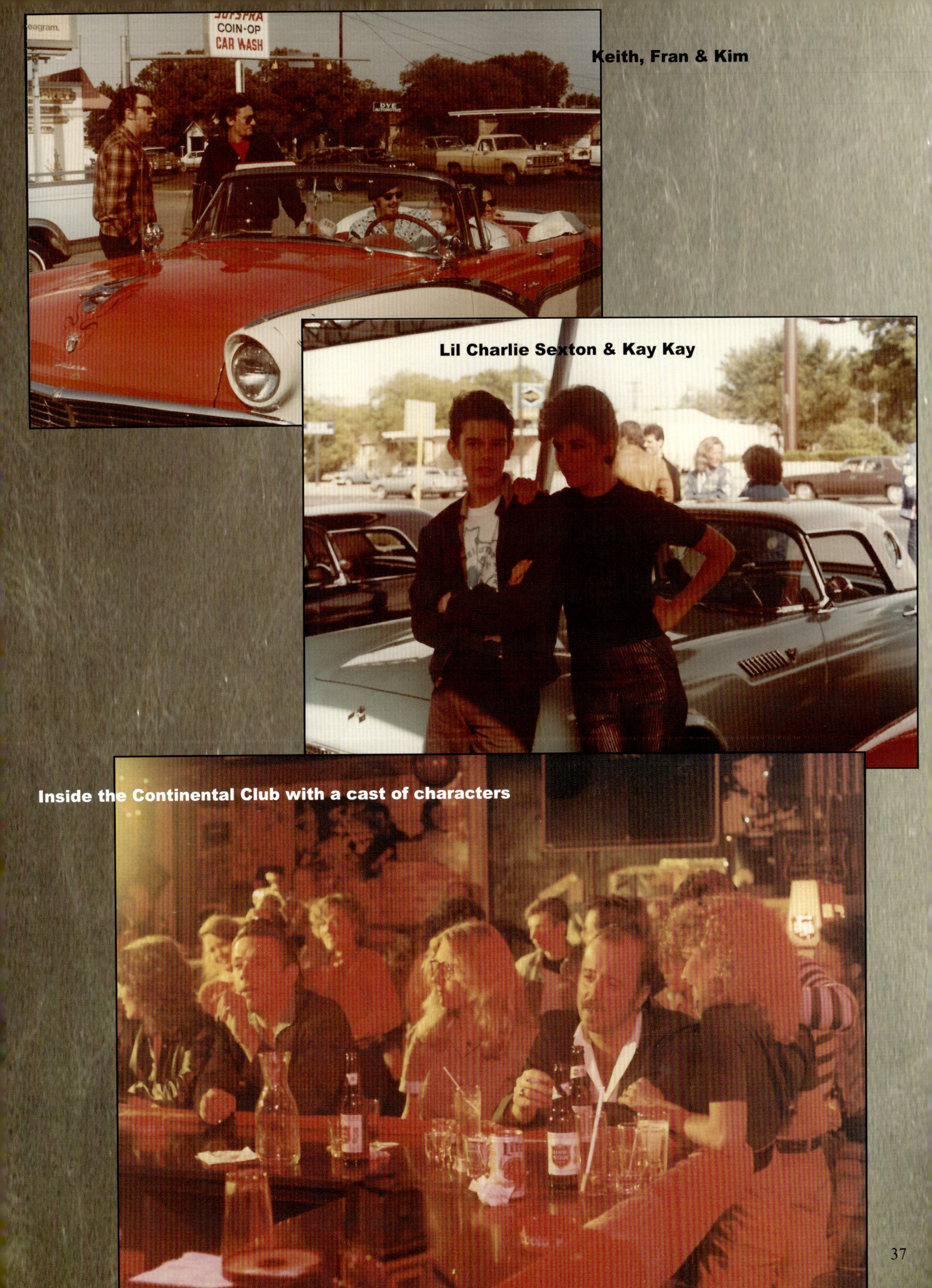

Keith, Fran & Kim

Lil Charlie Sexton & Kay Kay

Inside the Continental Club with a cast of characters

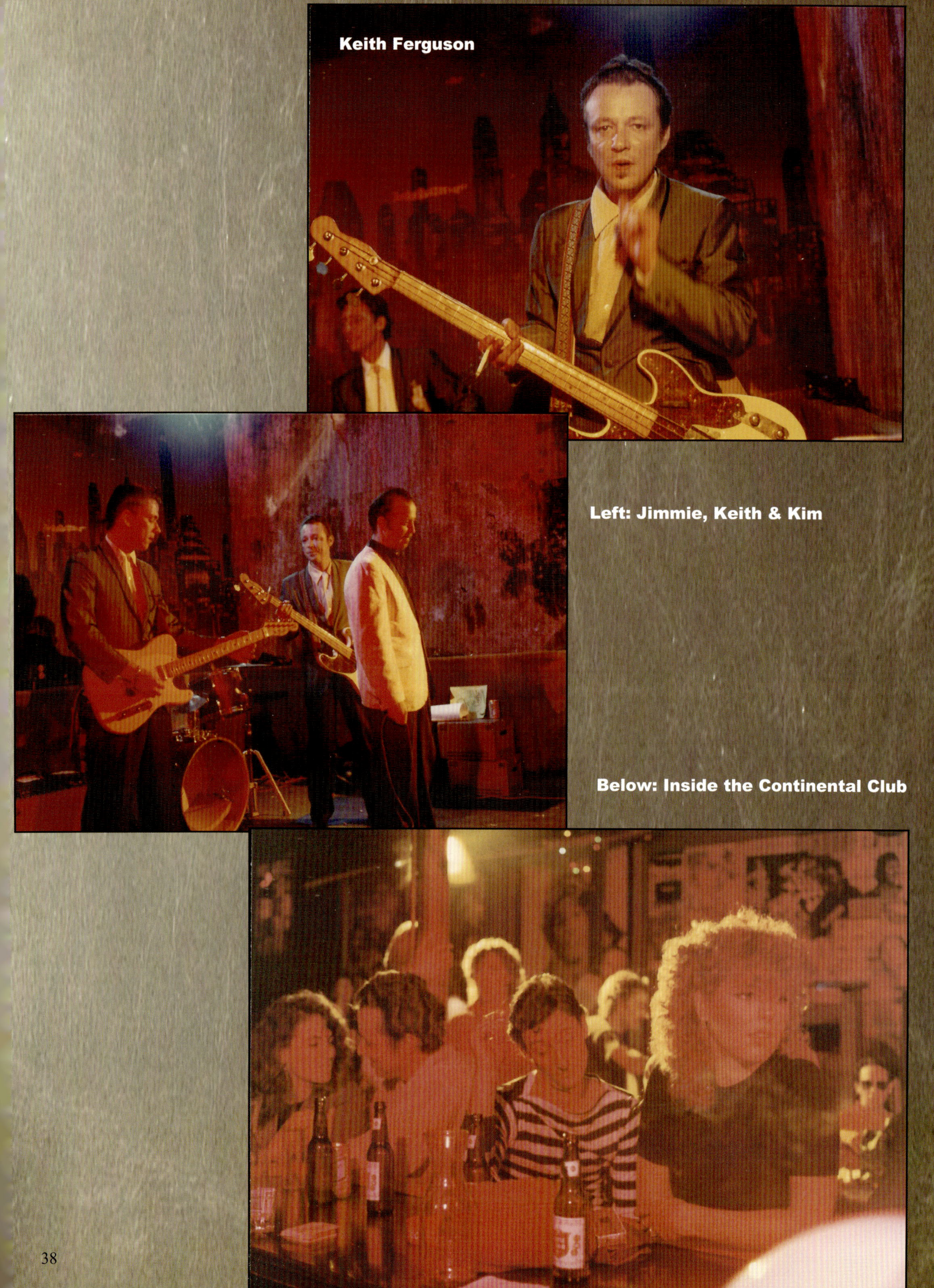

Keith Ferguson

Left: Jimmie, Keith & Kim

Below: Inside the Continental Club

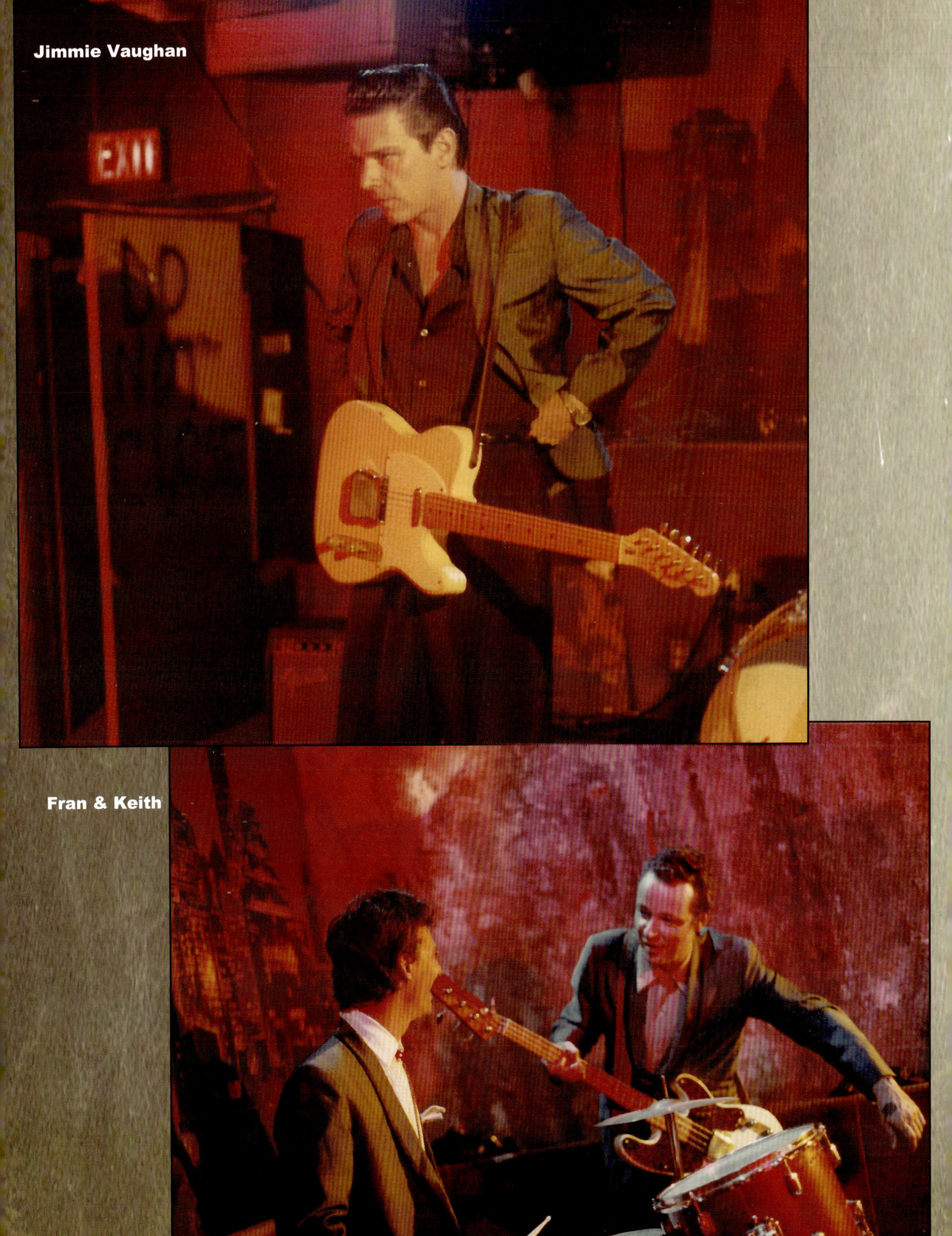

Jimmie Vaughan

Fran & Keith

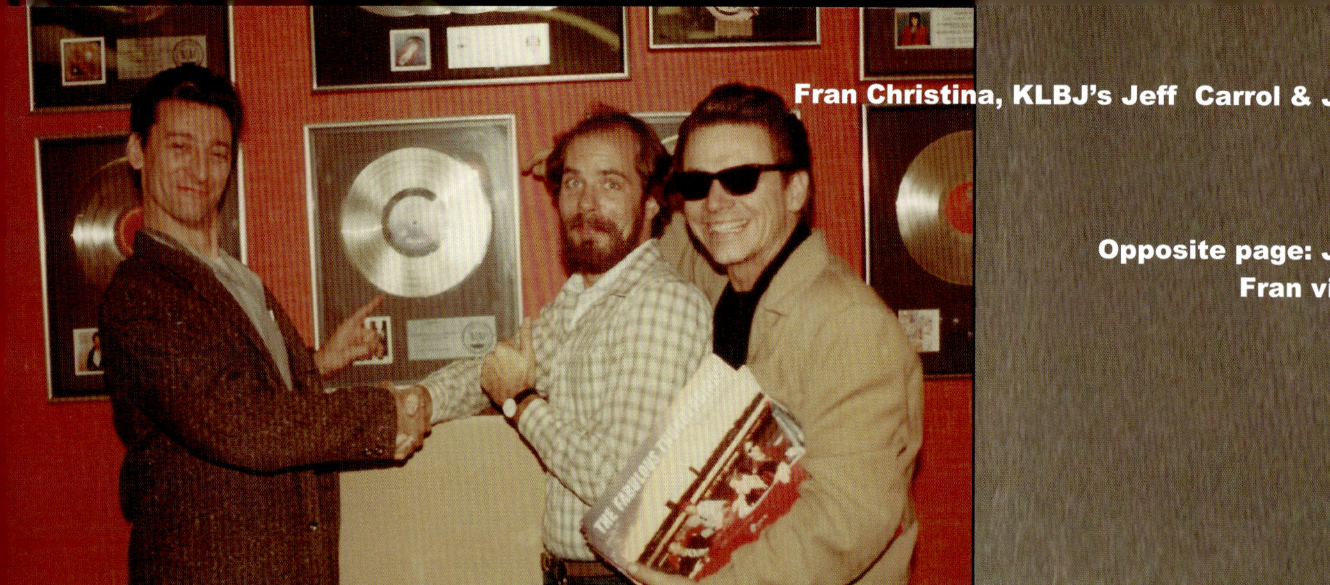

Fran Christina, KLBJ's Jeff Carrol & Jimmie V

Opposite page: Jimmie & Fran visit KLBJ

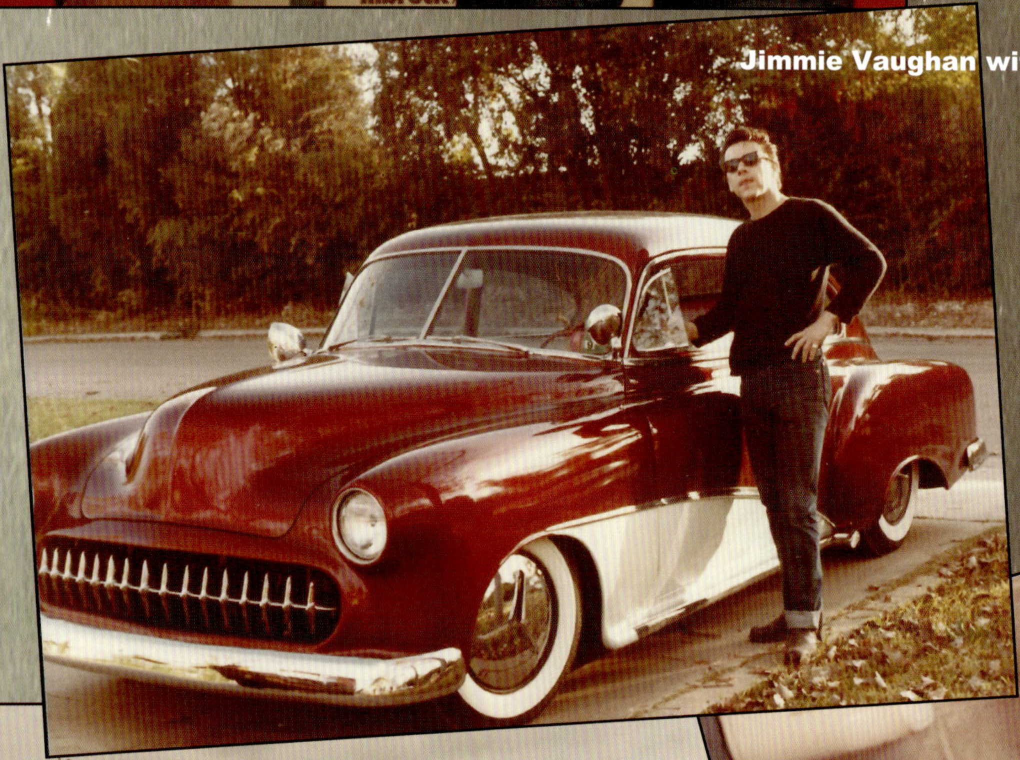

Jimmie Vaughan with his 1950 Chevy

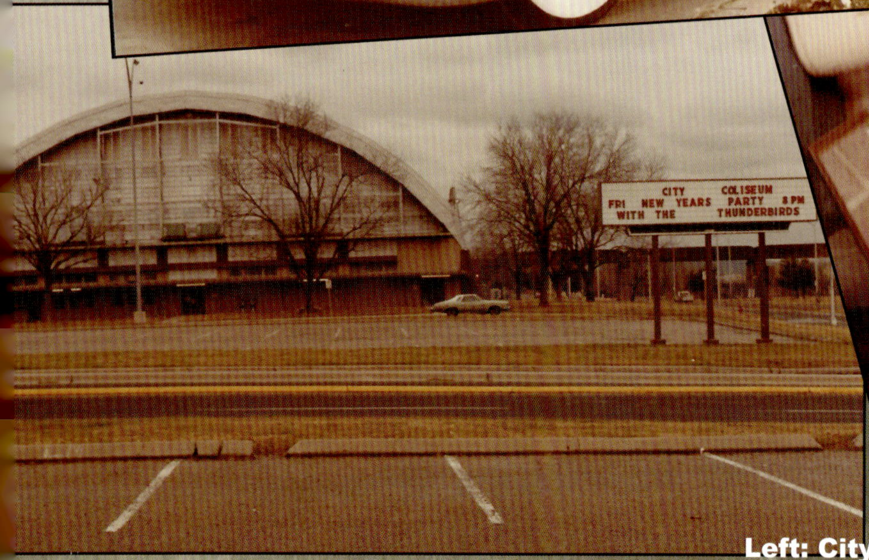

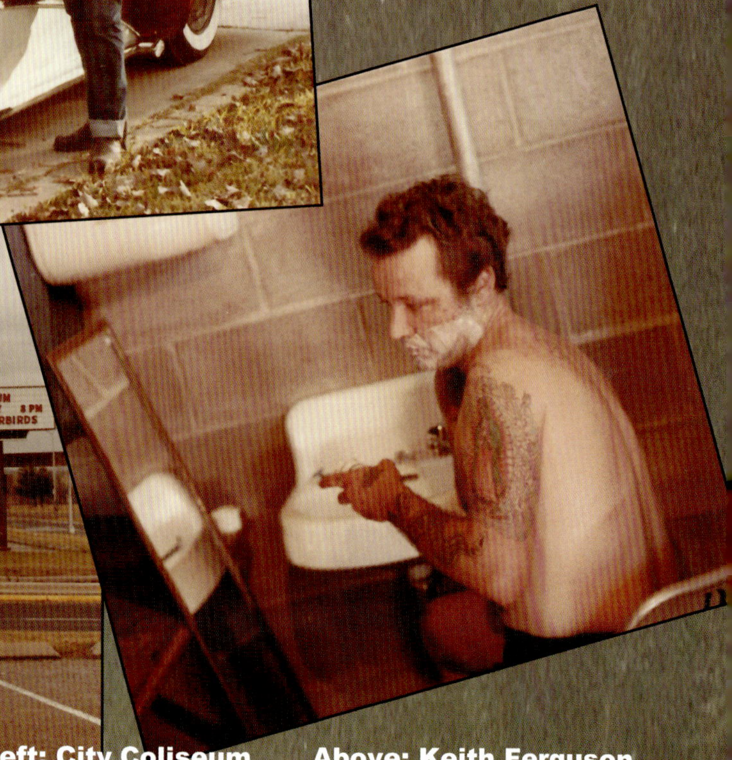

Left: City Coliseum

Above: Keith Ferguson

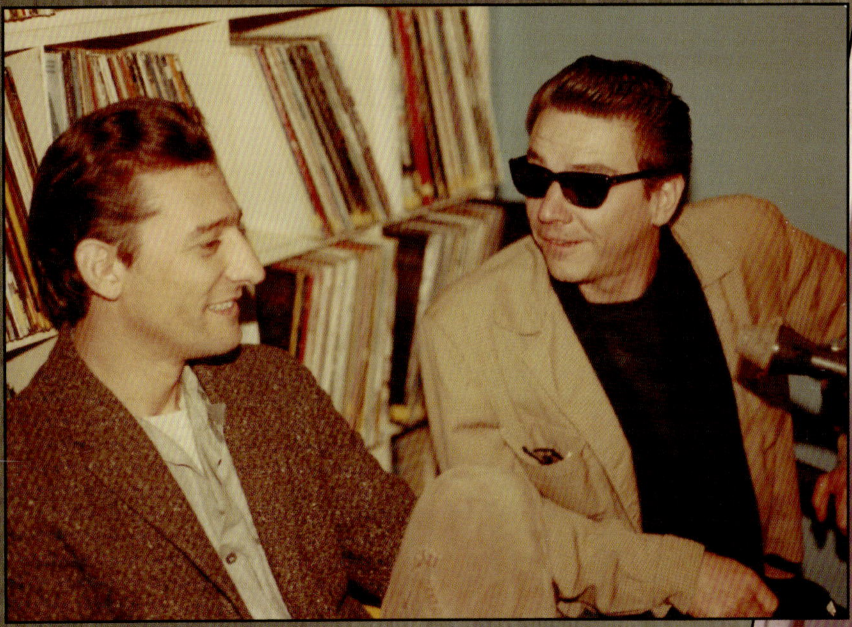

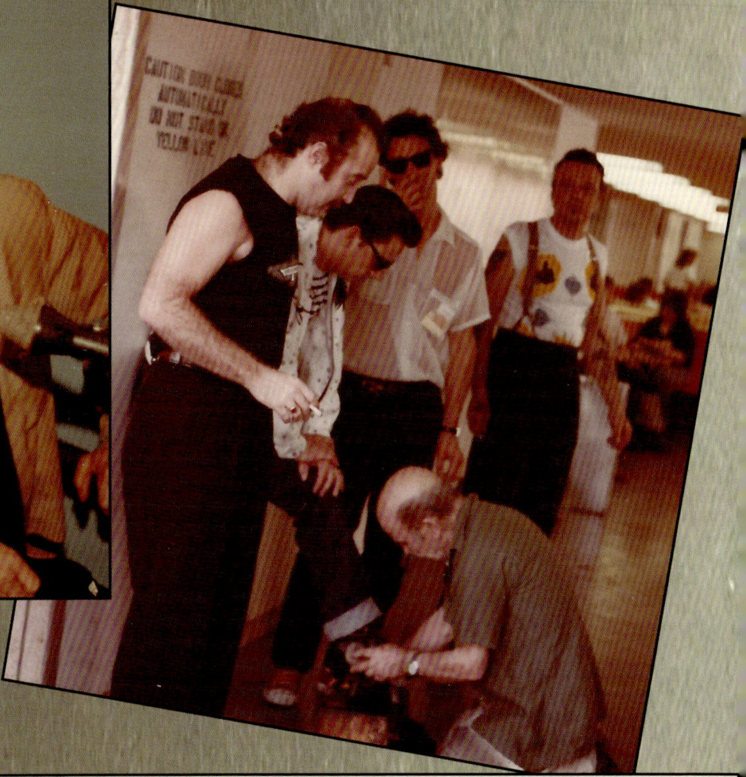

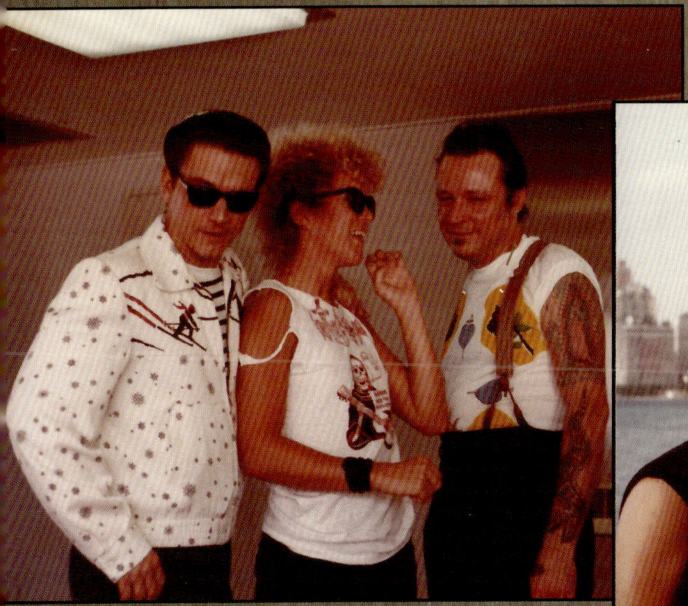

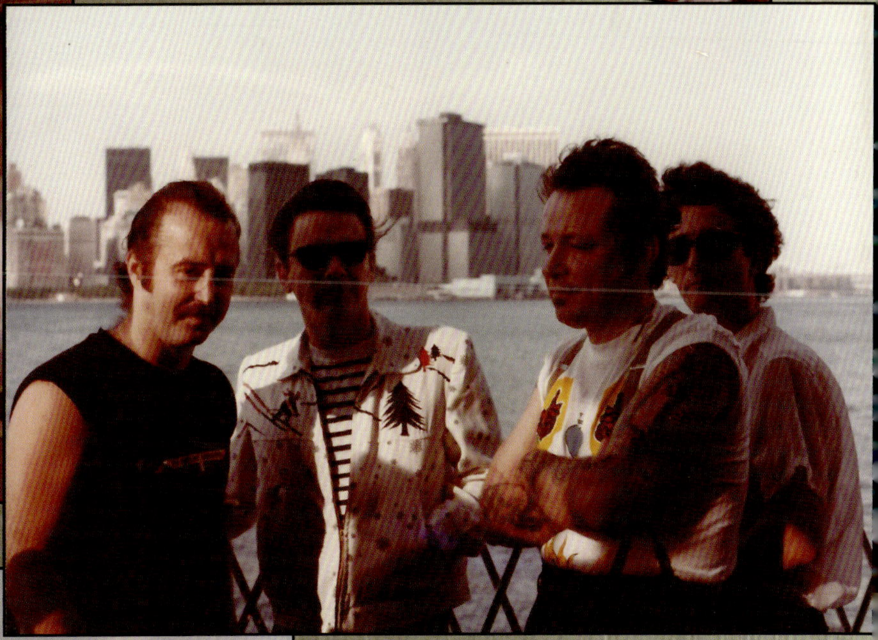

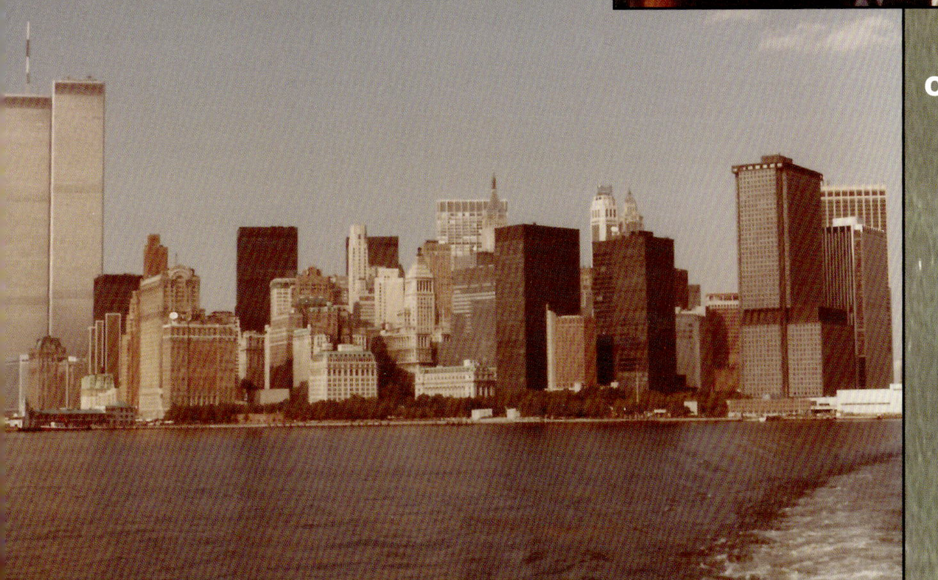

On the New York Circle Line Ferry

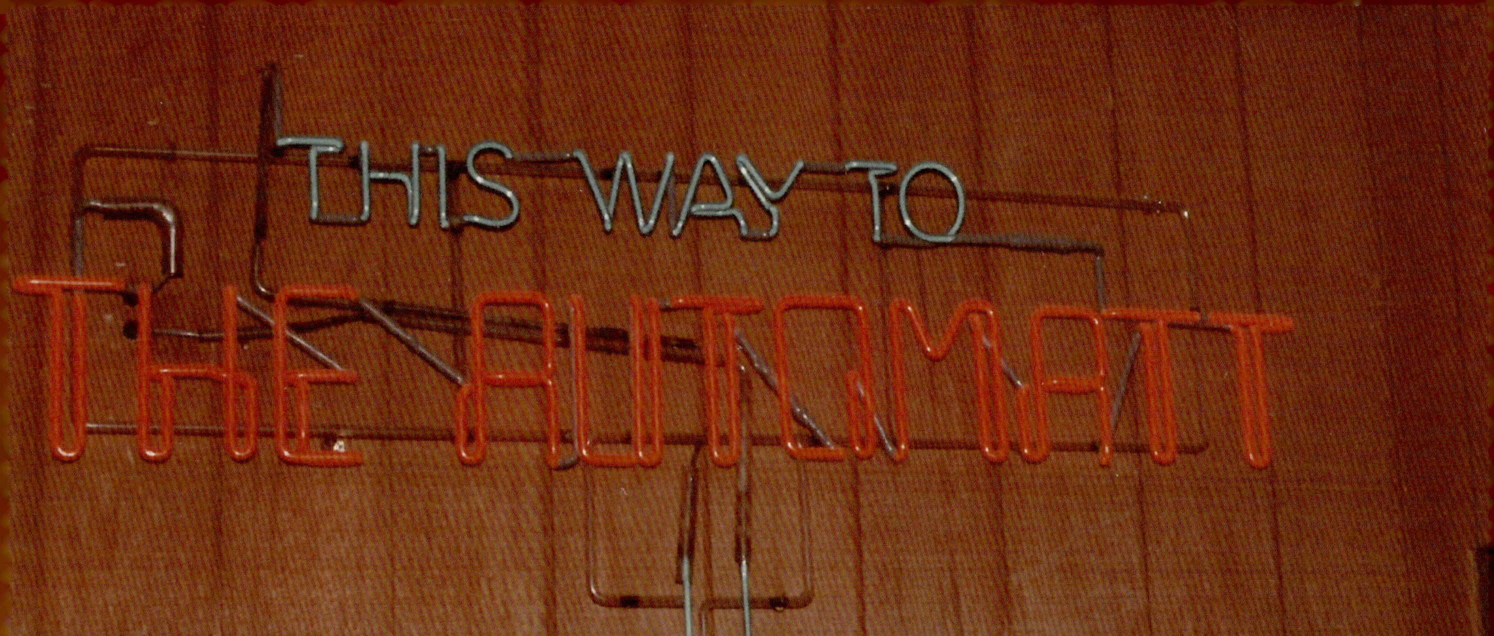

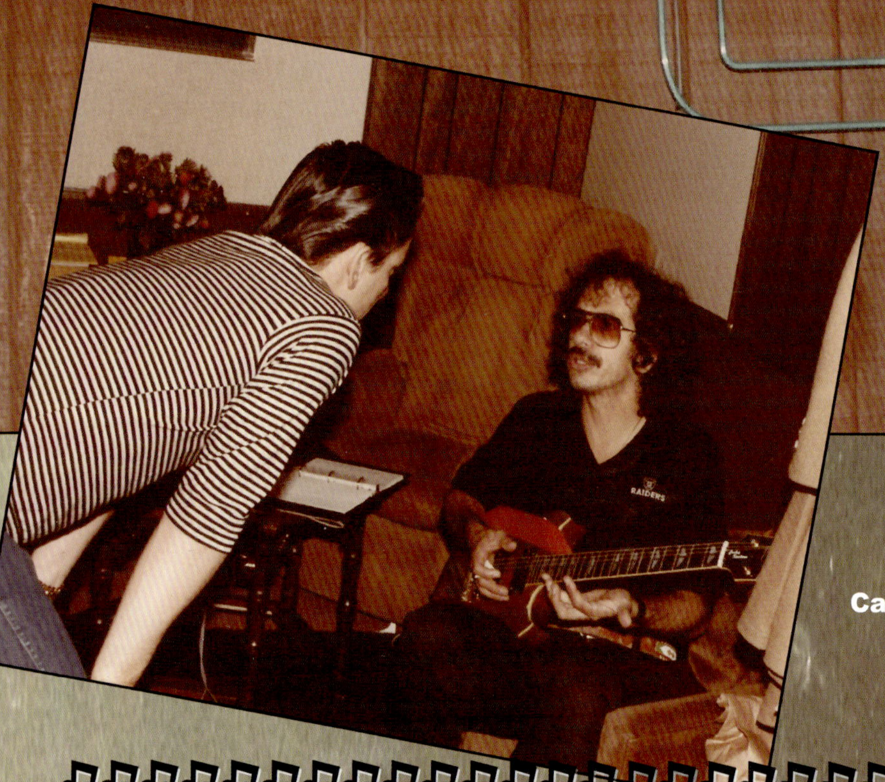

Carlos Santana & Jimmie Vaughan

Chapter 7: Havana Moon with Carlos Santana

At the time the T-birds were creating quite a following amongst other musicians. In April 1983 we traveled to San Francisco and recorded at the AUTOMATT with the legendary producer Jerry Wexler, along with Muscle Shoals alumni Barry Beckett. Carlos Santana was a big fan of the T-bird's sound and hoped to create an album infusing Carlos' Latin influences with the blues. I still think to this day that album was way ahead of its time and stands the test of time.

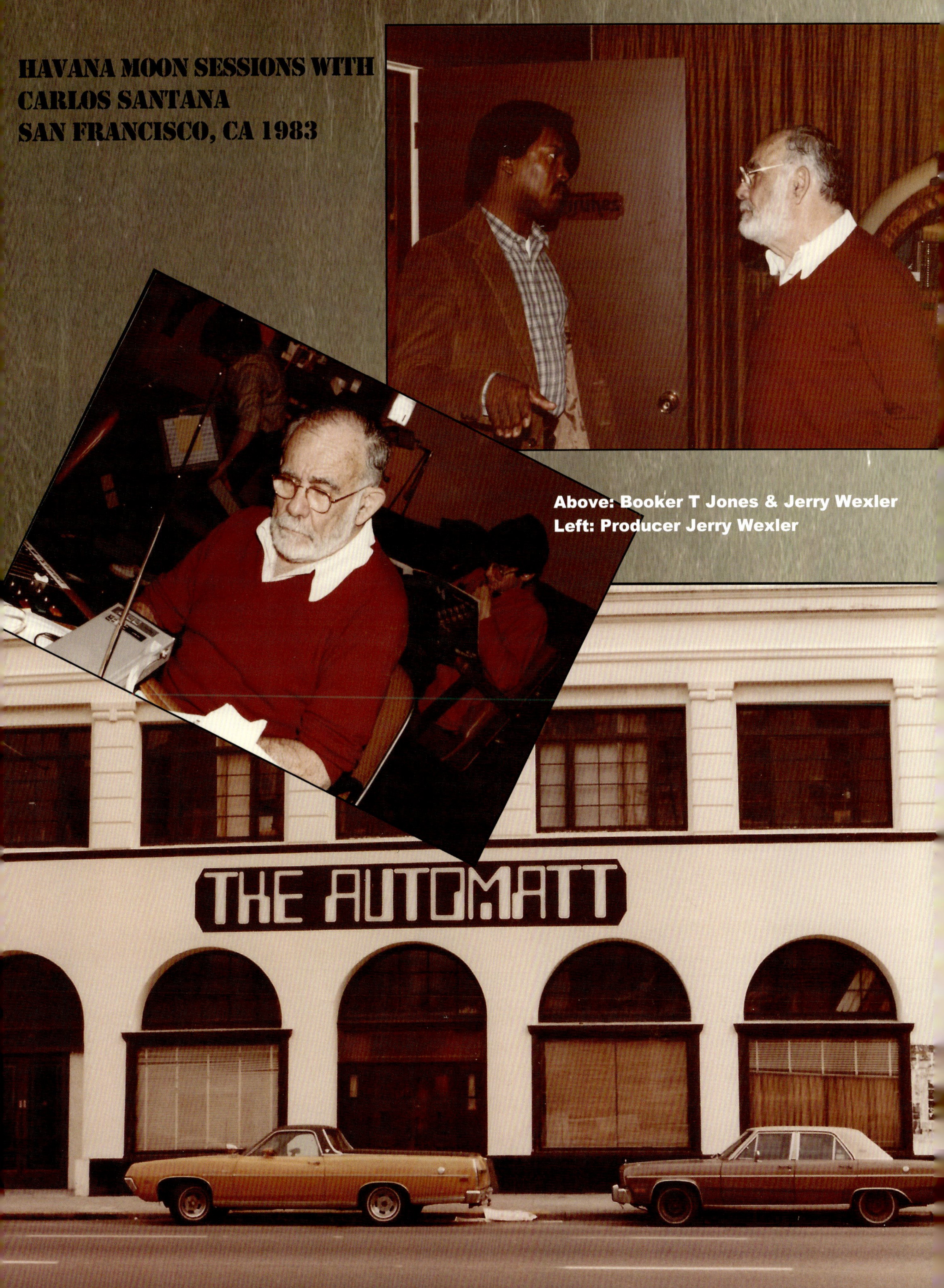

Above: Booker T Jones & Jerry Wexler
Left: Producer Jerry Wexler

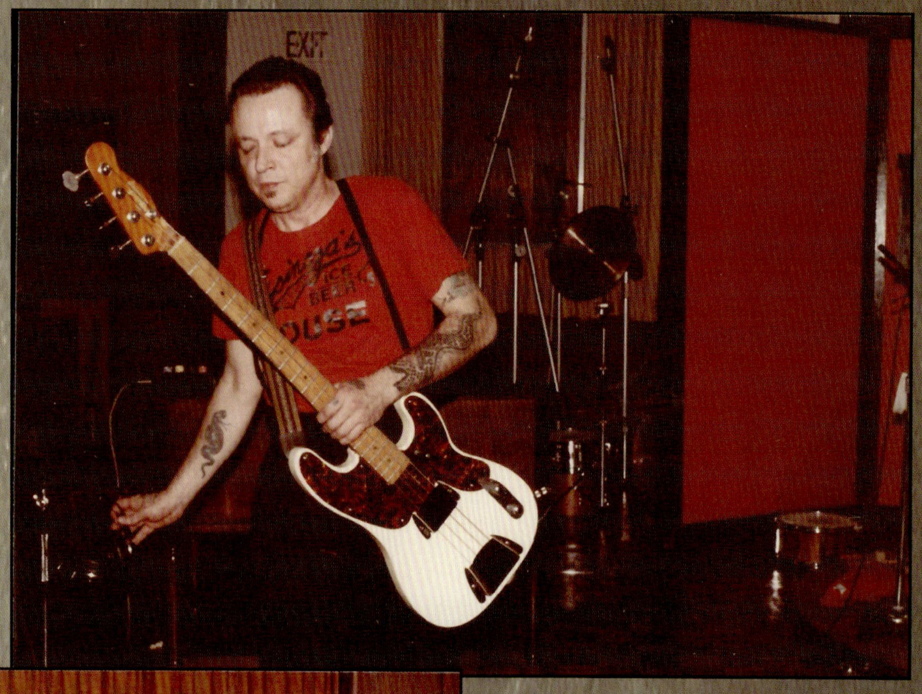

Keith Ferguson

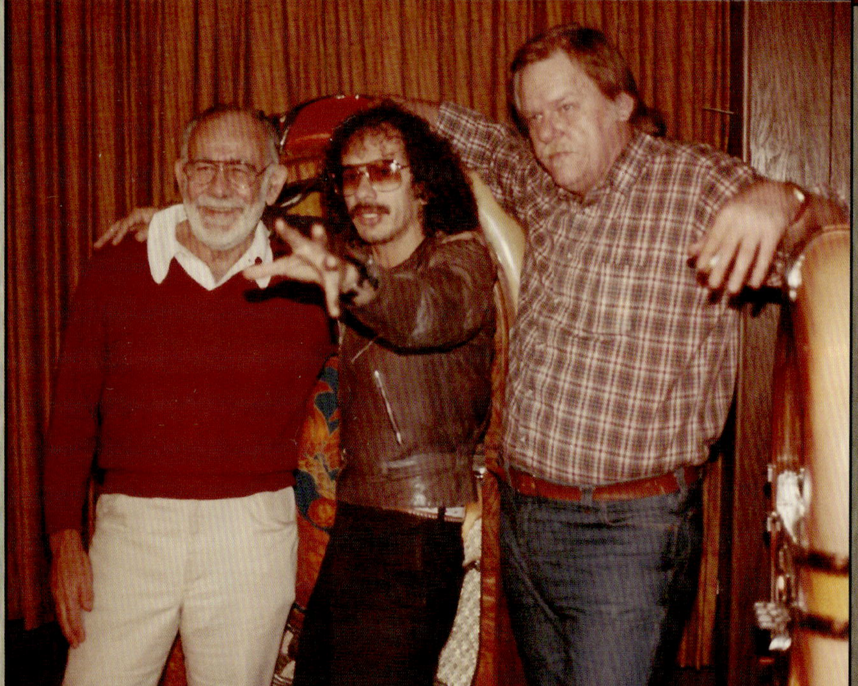

Jerry Wexler, Carlos Santana
& Barry Beckett

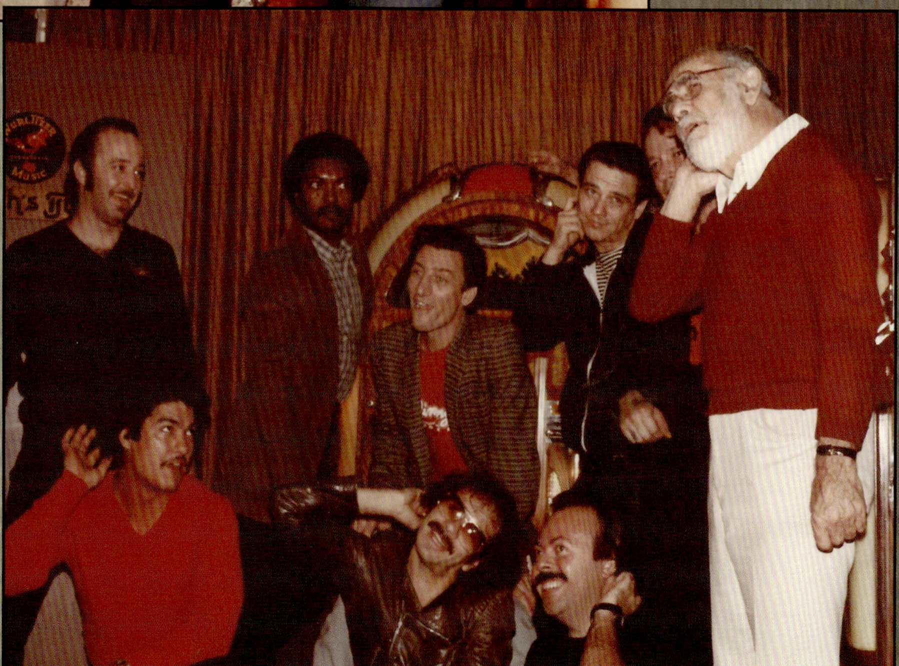

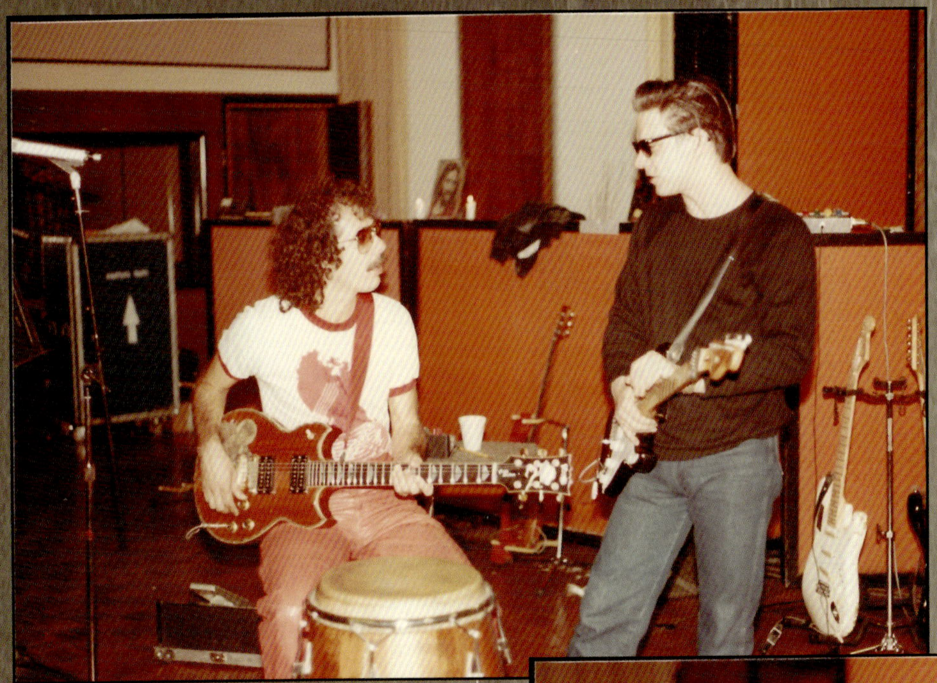

Carlos & Jimmie

Fran Christina

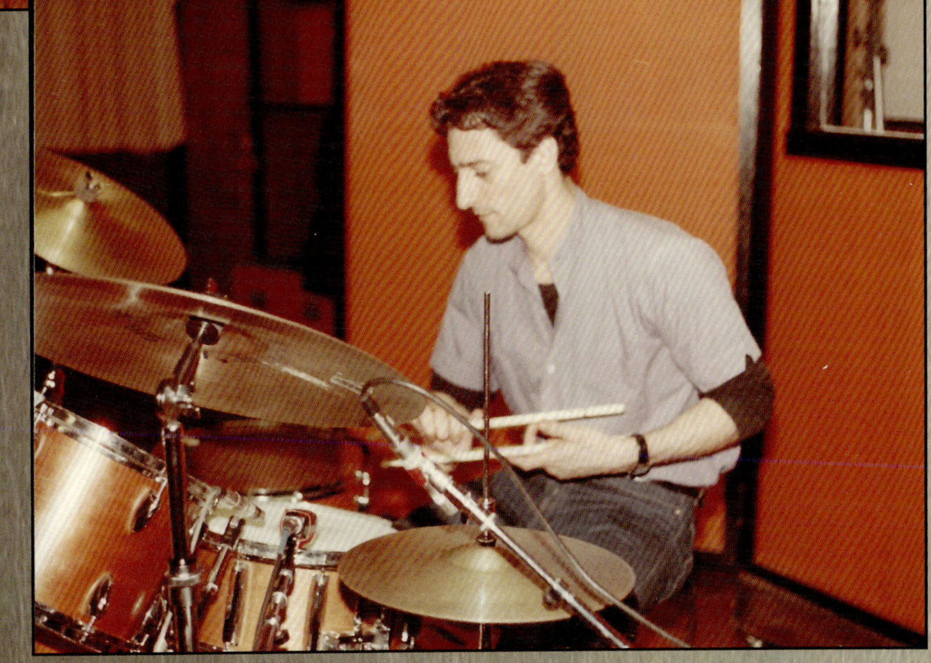

Keith, Carlos & Jimmie

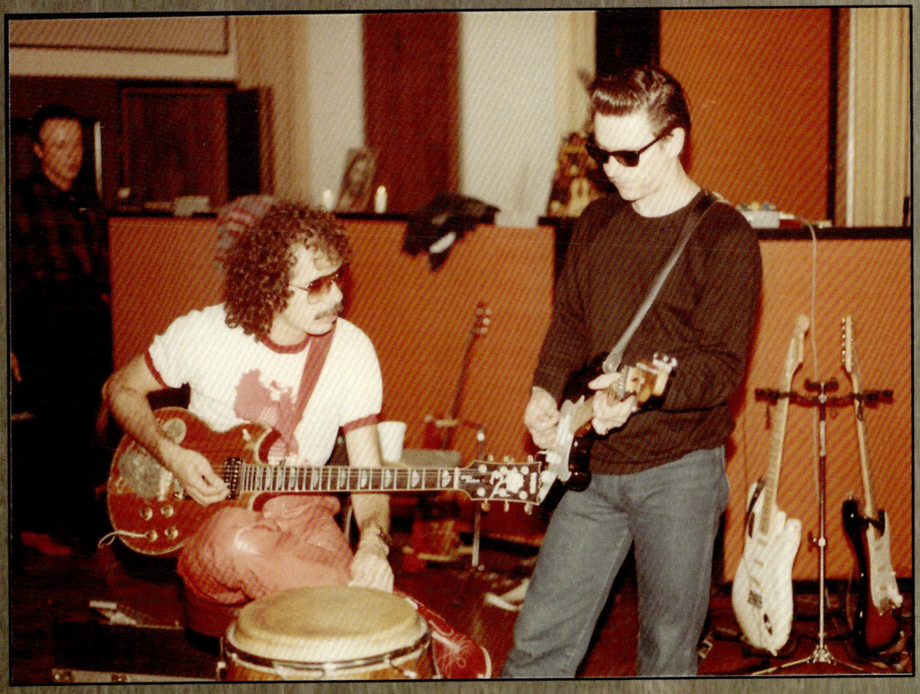

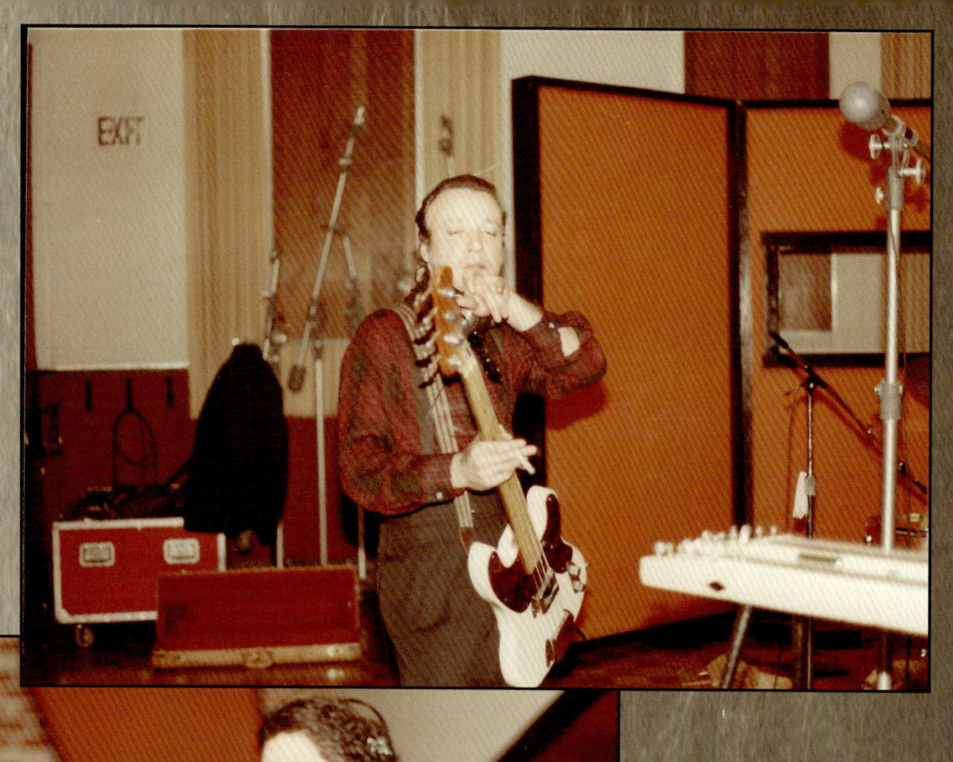

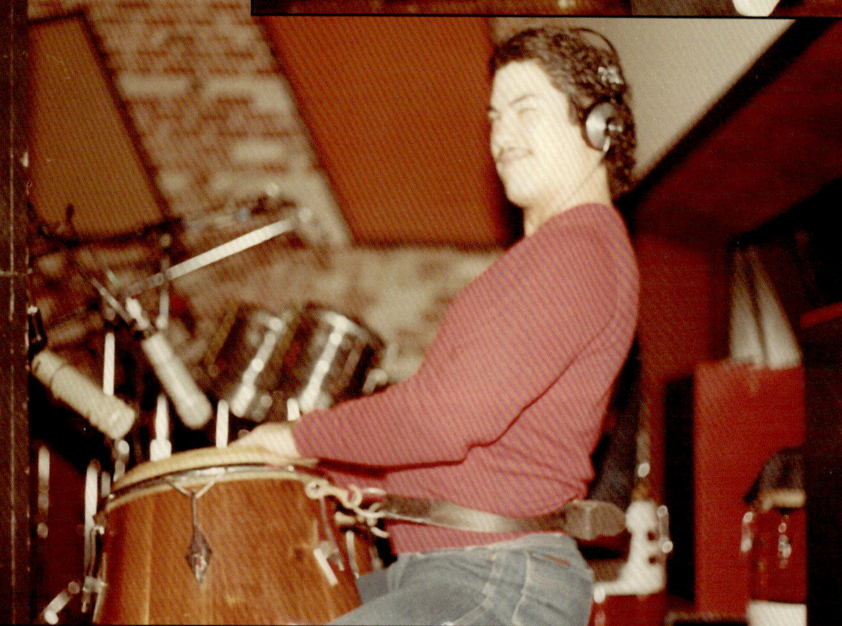

Above: Bassist Keith Ferguson
Left: Percussionist Raul Rekow
Below: Booker T Jones

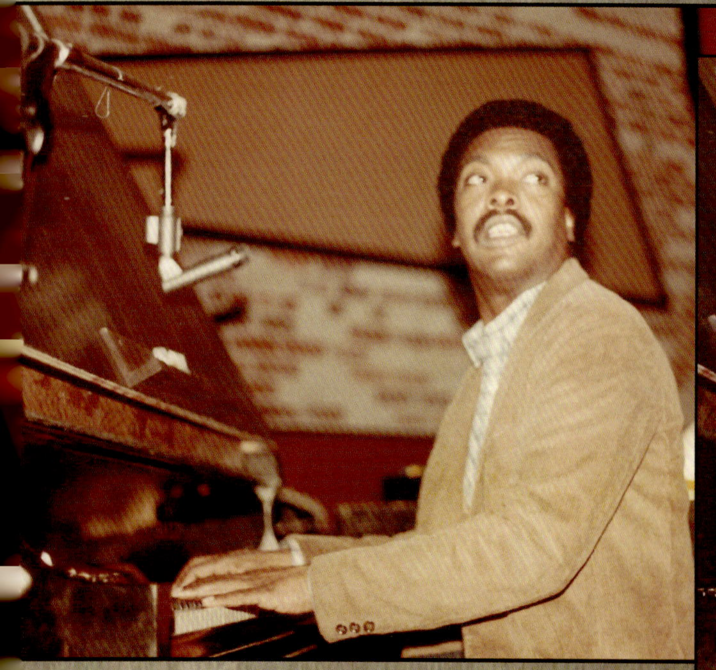

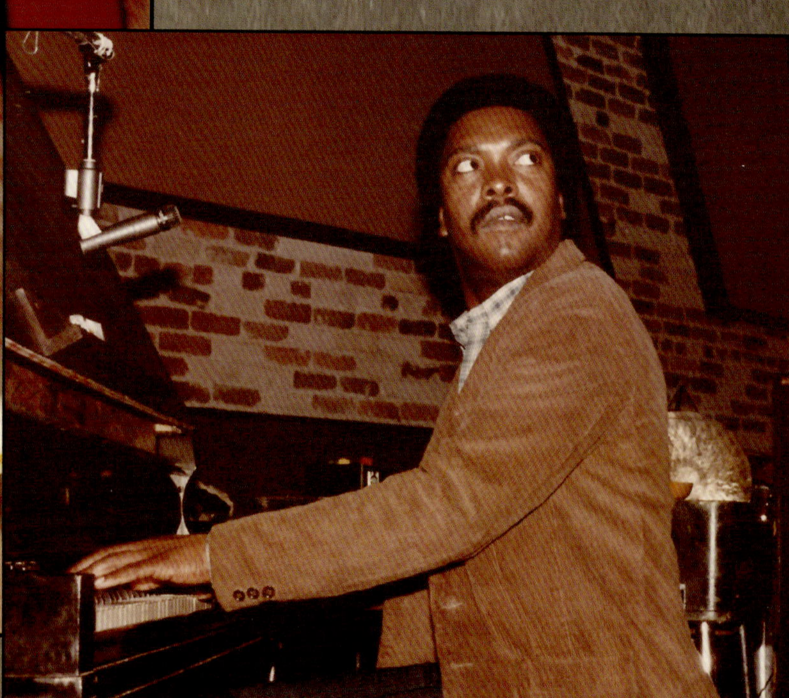

Fran Christina, Booker T &
engineer Jim Gaines

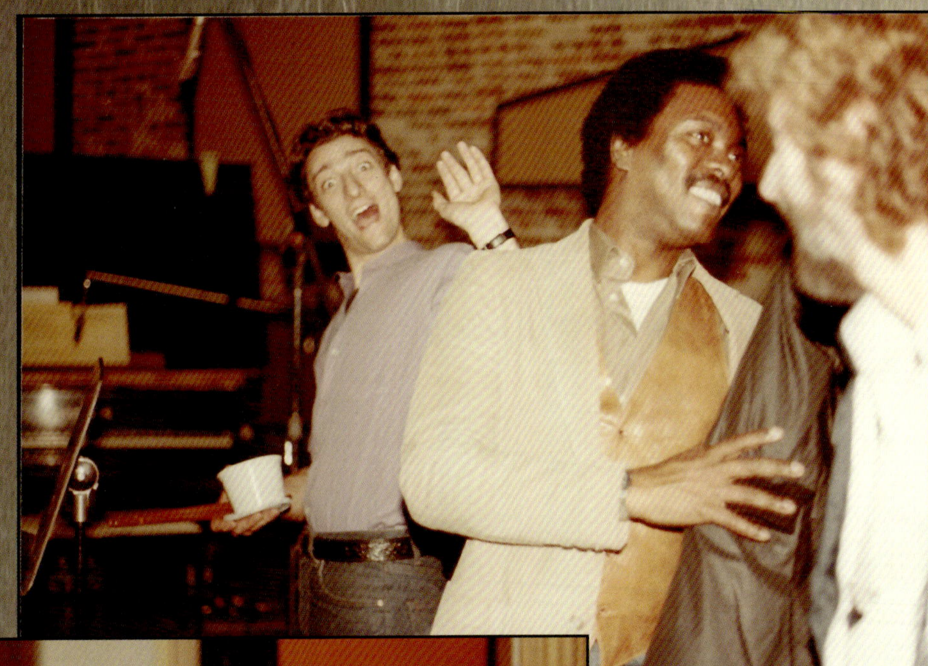

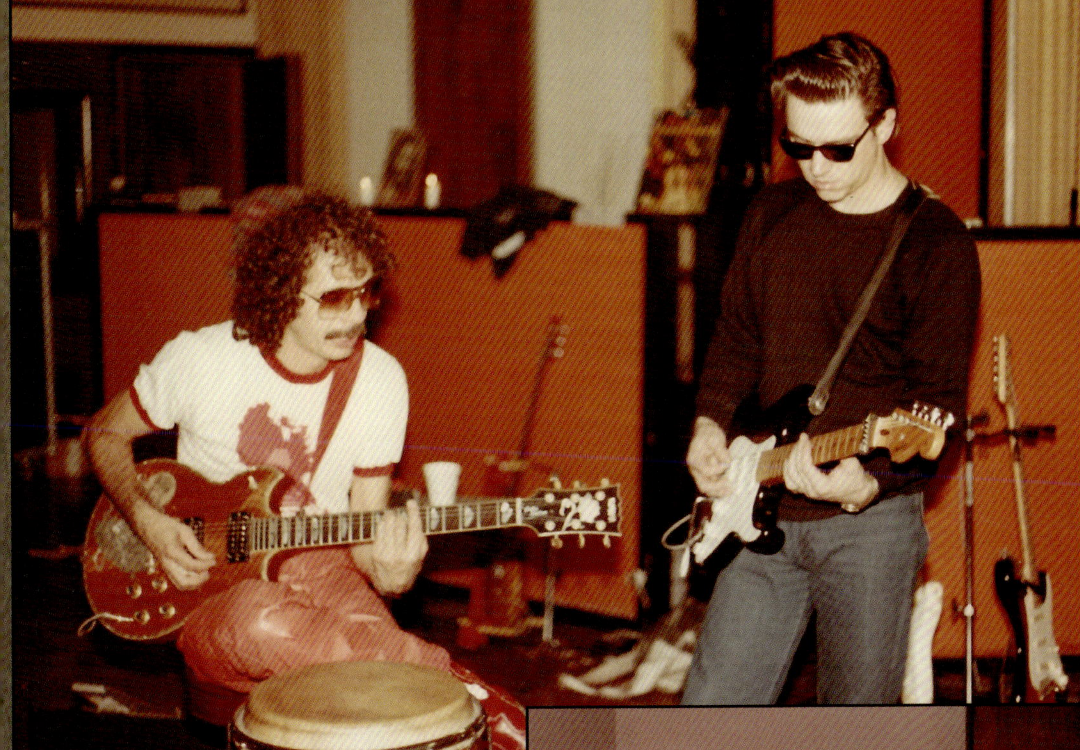

Carlos & Jimmie

Fran giving Carlos a guitar lesson

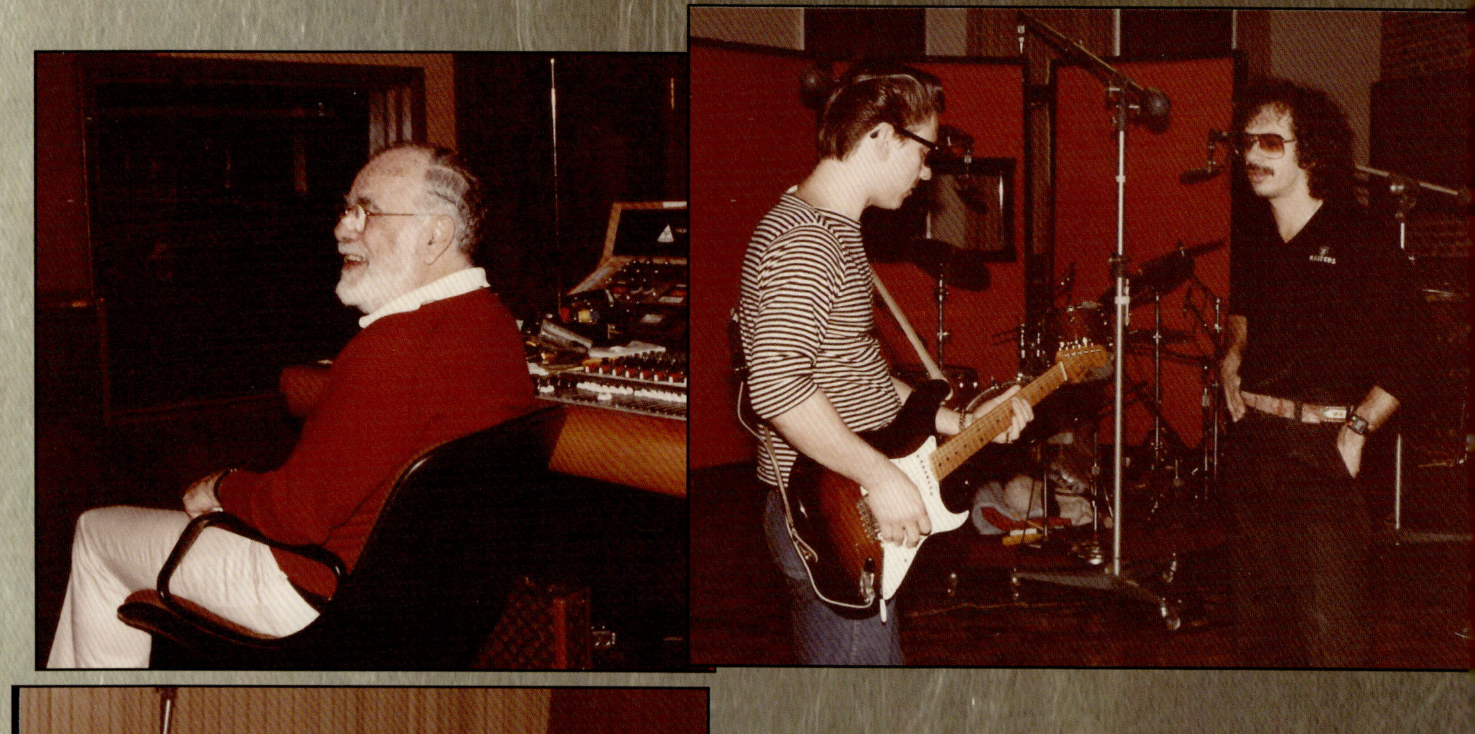

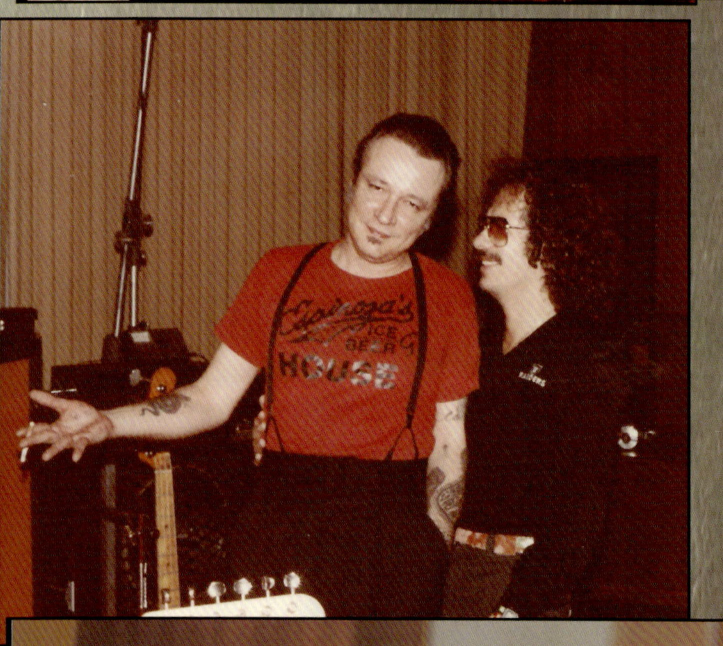

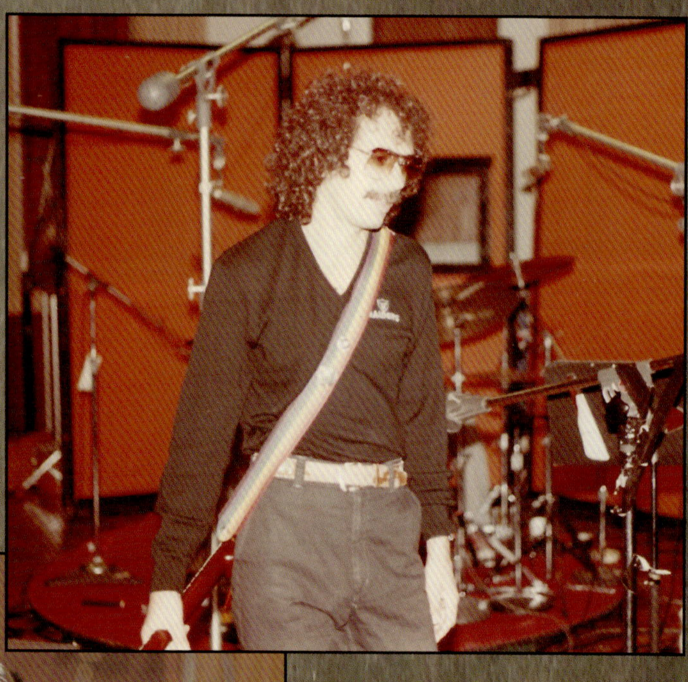

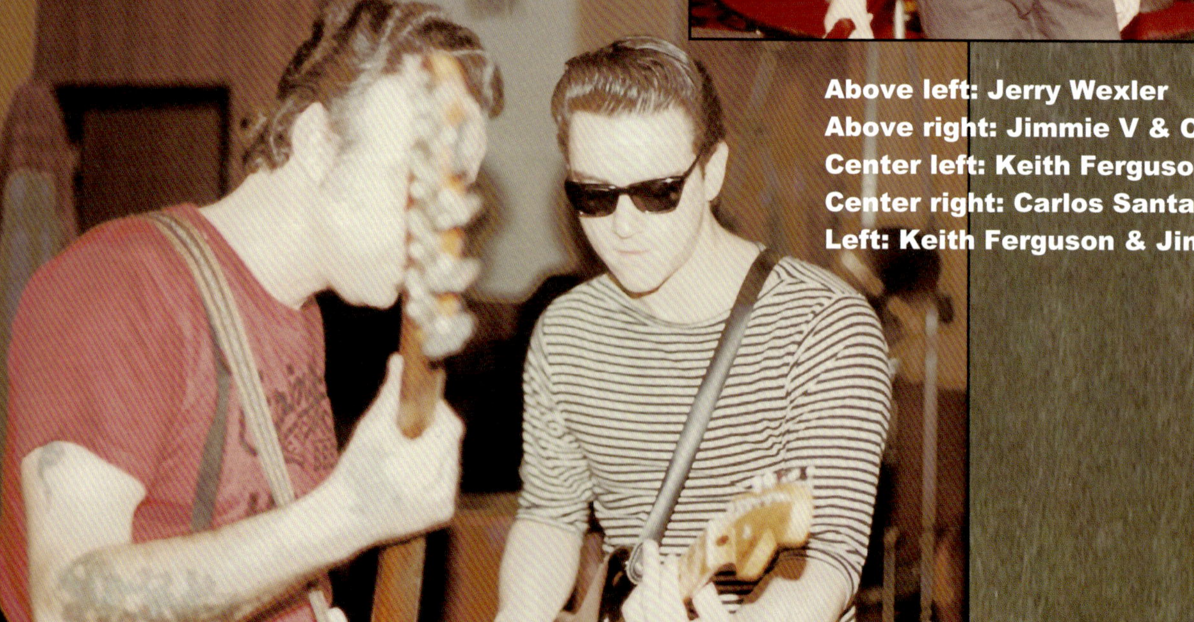

Above left: Jerry Wexler
Above right: Jimmie V & Carlos Santana
Center left: Keith Ferguson & Carlos
Center right: Carlos Santana
Left: Keith Ferguson & Jimmie Vaughan

Chapter 8: The T-Bird River Fest

In 1983, French Smith and I launched the first T-Bird River Fest, with a plan to offer great music at a low ticket price, by inviting friends of the band to come to Austin and perform. After the success of the first festival, we produced a decade of River Fests with line-ups including Stevie Ray, Carlos Santana, Bonnie Raitt, Nick Lowe, Greg Allman, Joe Ely, Delbert McClinton, Little Feat and even the Red Hot Chili Peppers (who played twice).

Keep an eye on the Austin skyline as it dramatically changes each year!

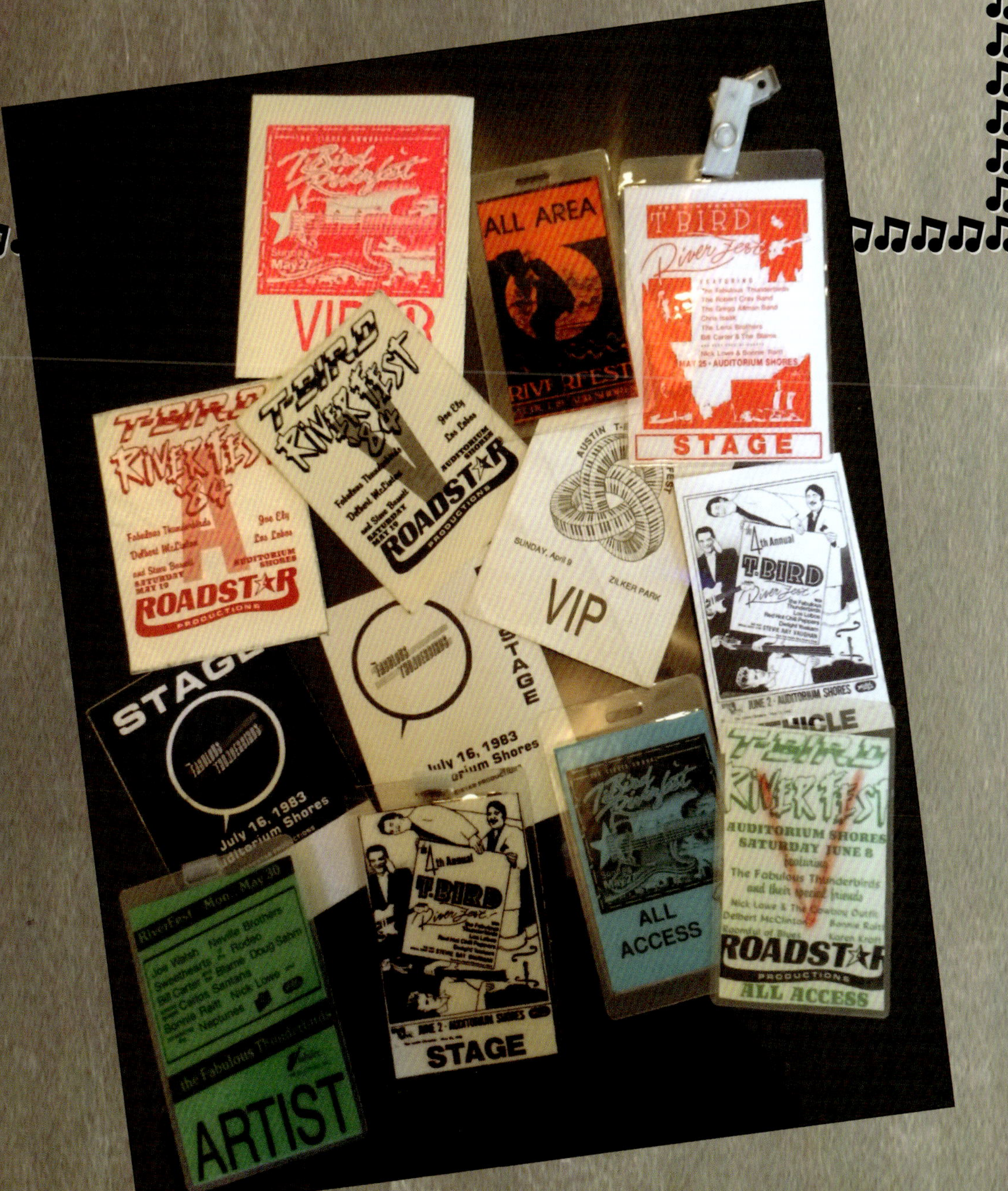

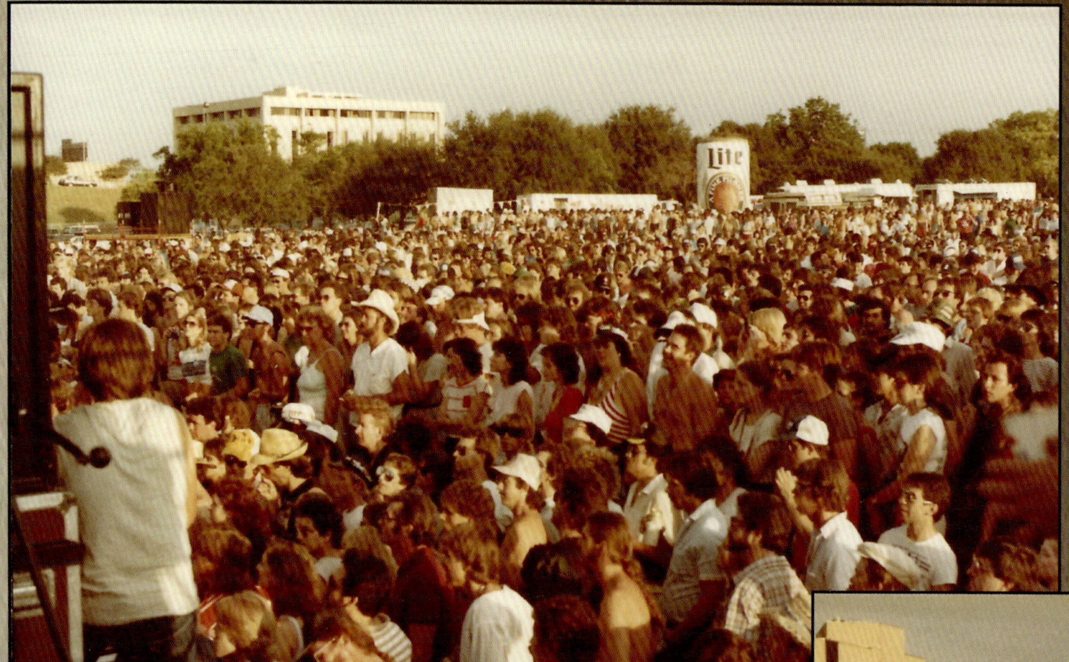

Above: Riverfest crowd
Right: Joe Ely
Below: Joe Ely

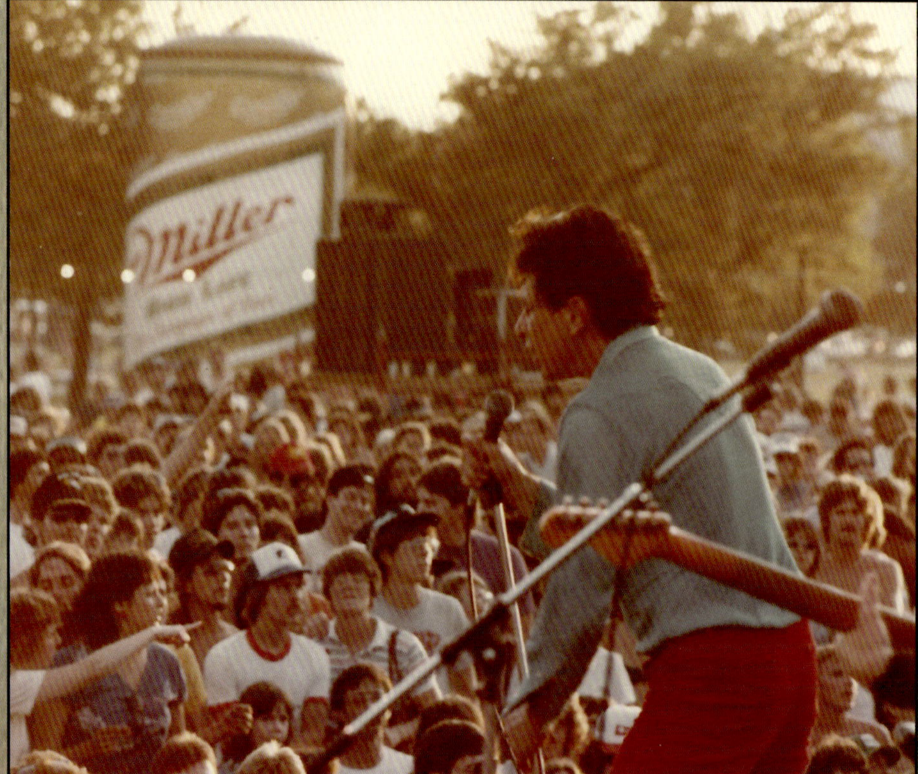

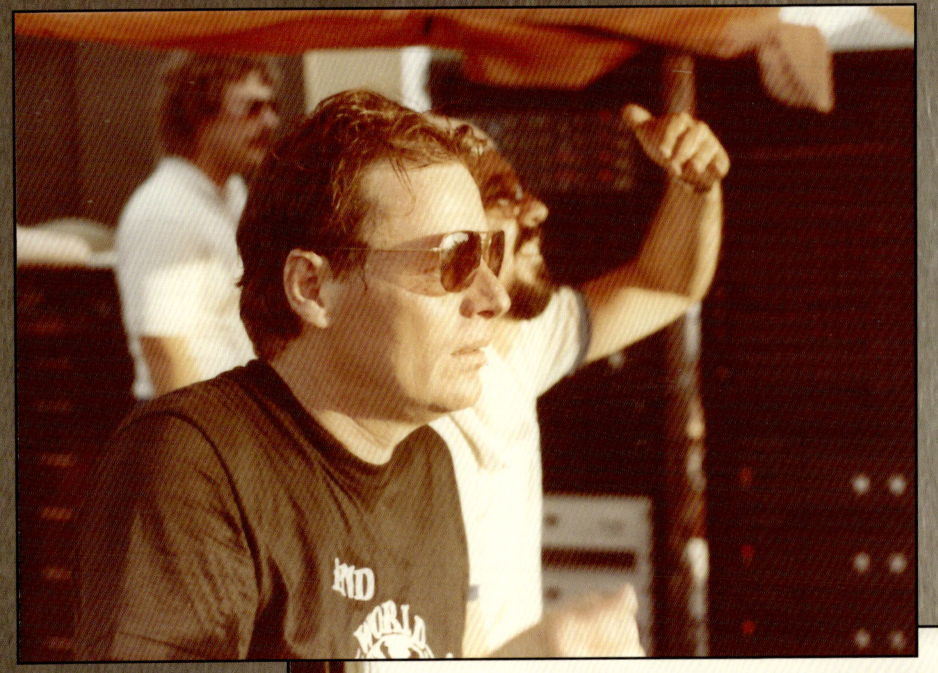

Delbert McClinton

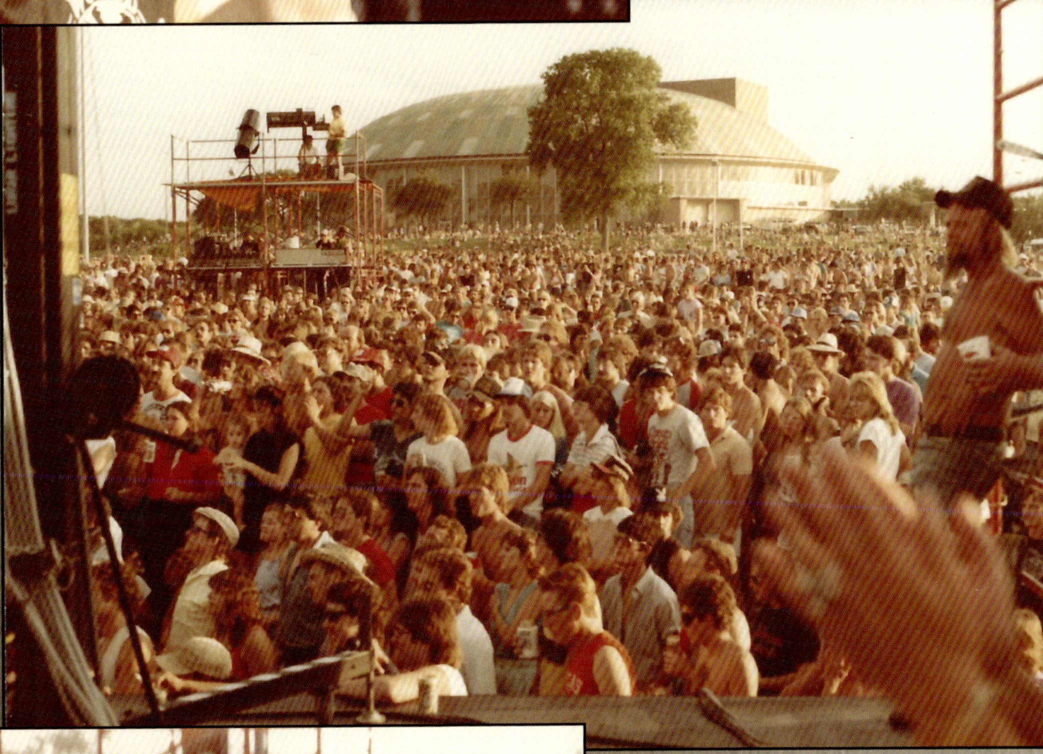

Crowd with Palmer Auditorium in background

Joe Ely with Lil Charlie looking on

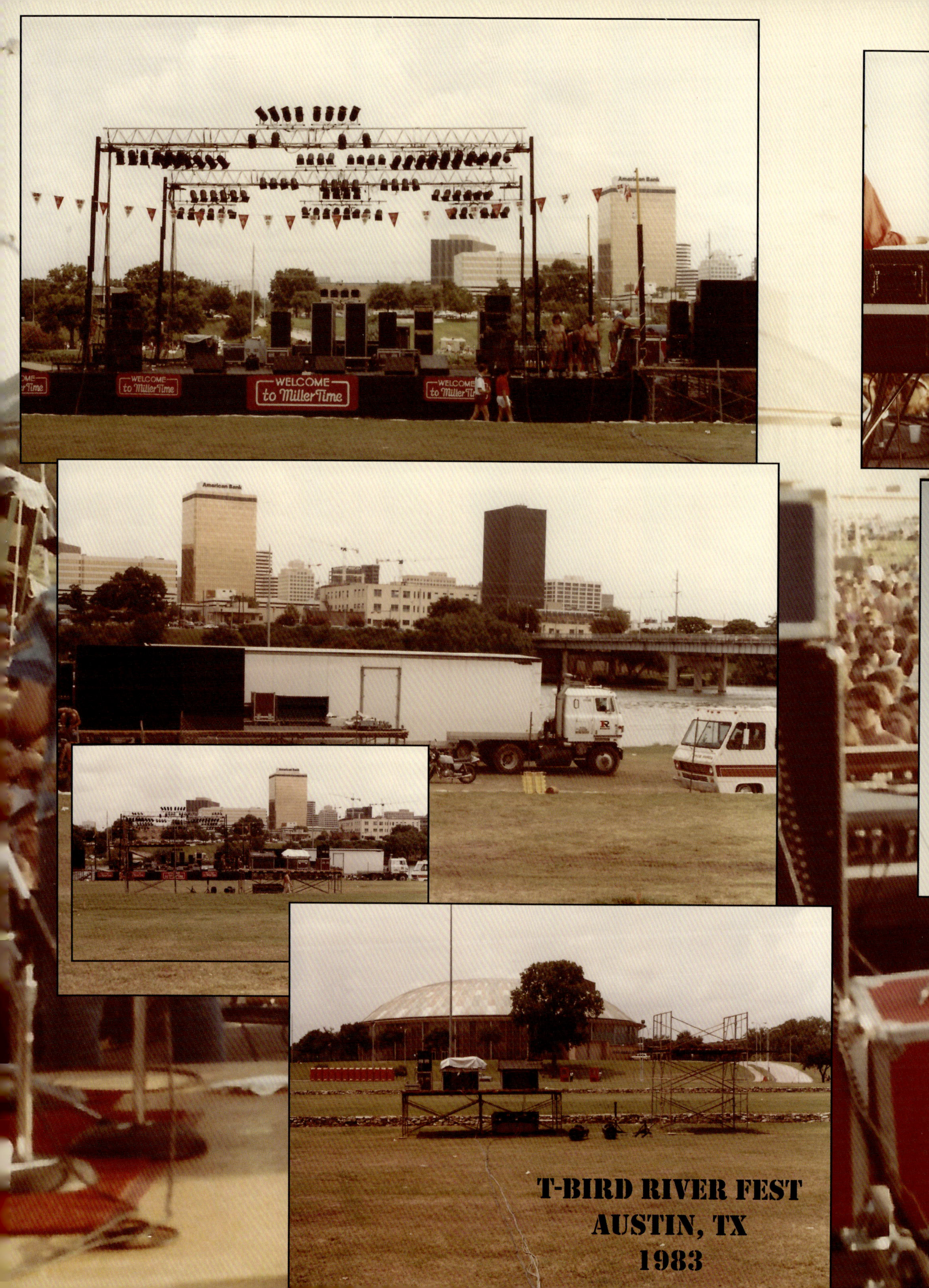

T-BIRD RIVER FEST
AUSTIN, TX
1983

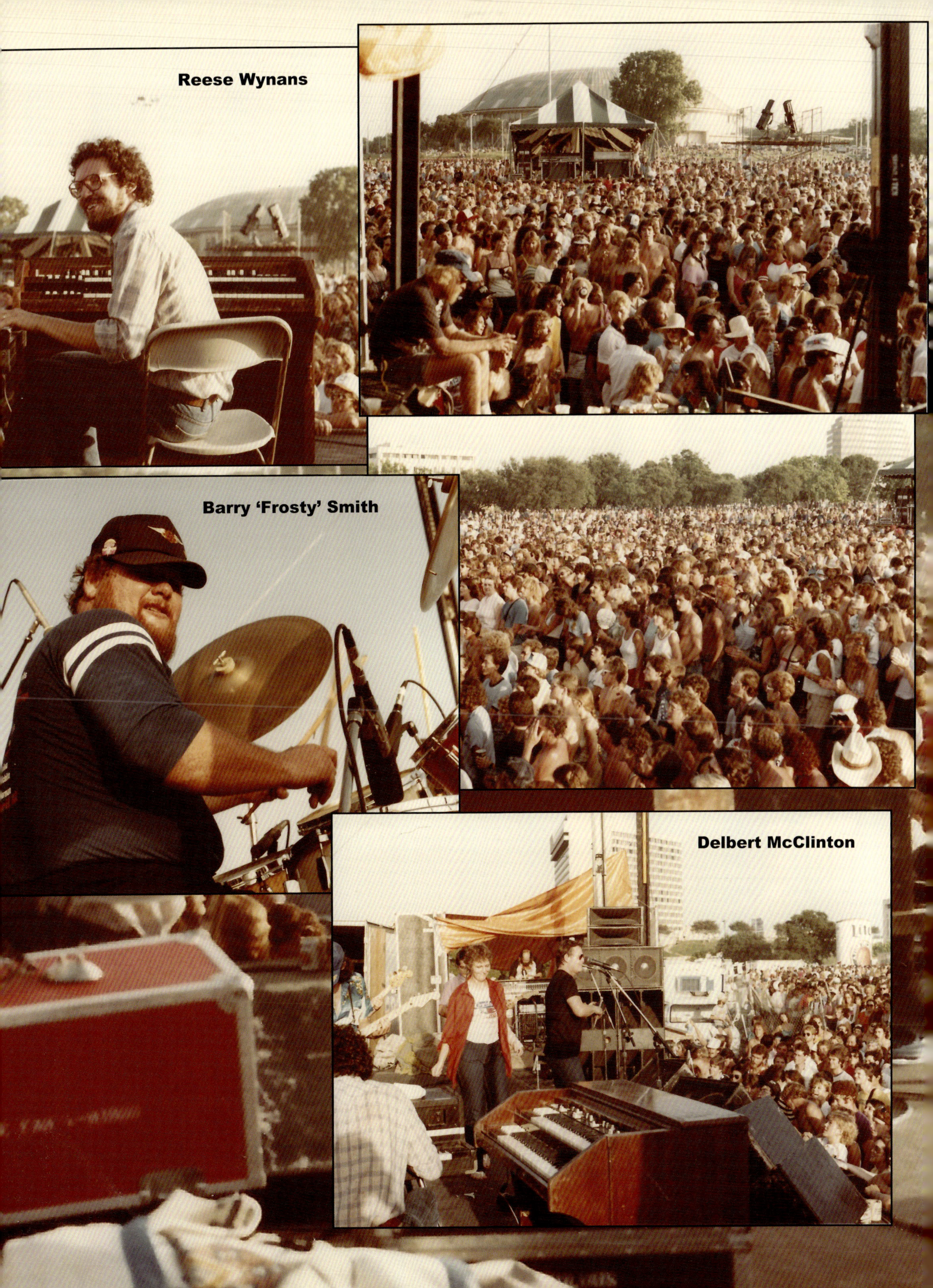
Reese Wynans
Barry 'Frosty' Smith
Delbert McClinton

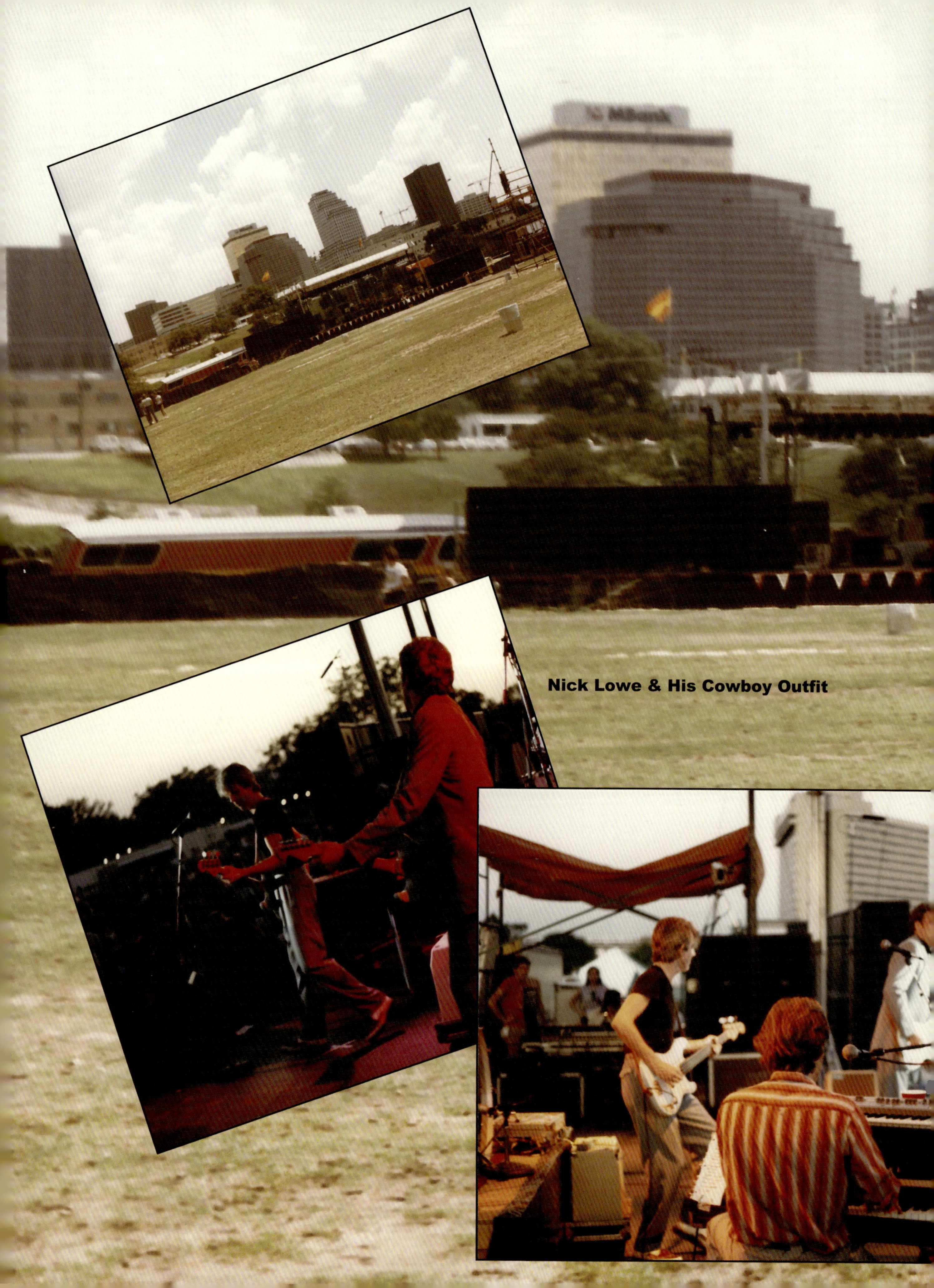

Nick Lowe & His Cowboy Outfit

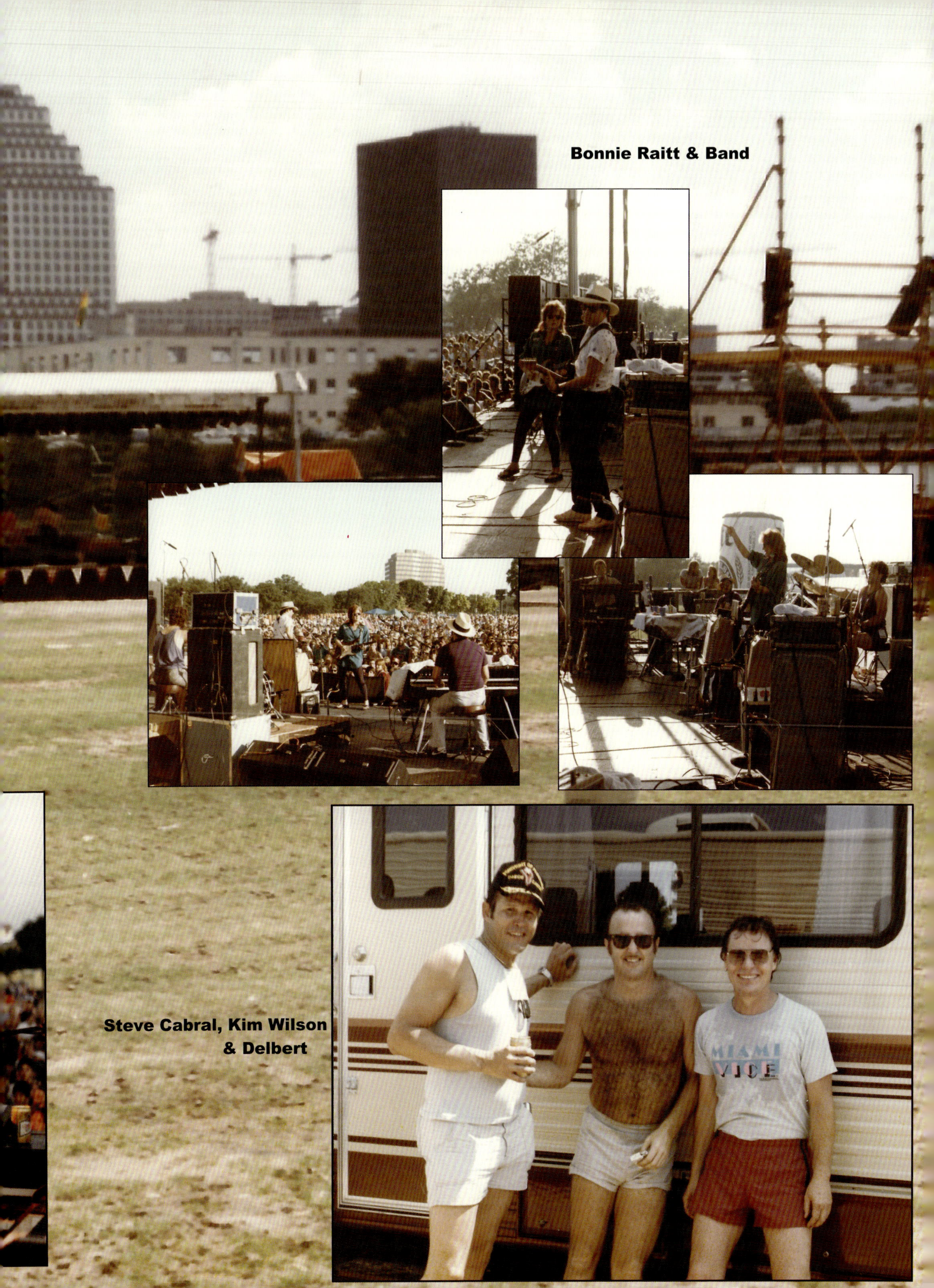

Bonnie Raitt & Band

Steve Cabral, Kim Wilson
& Delbert

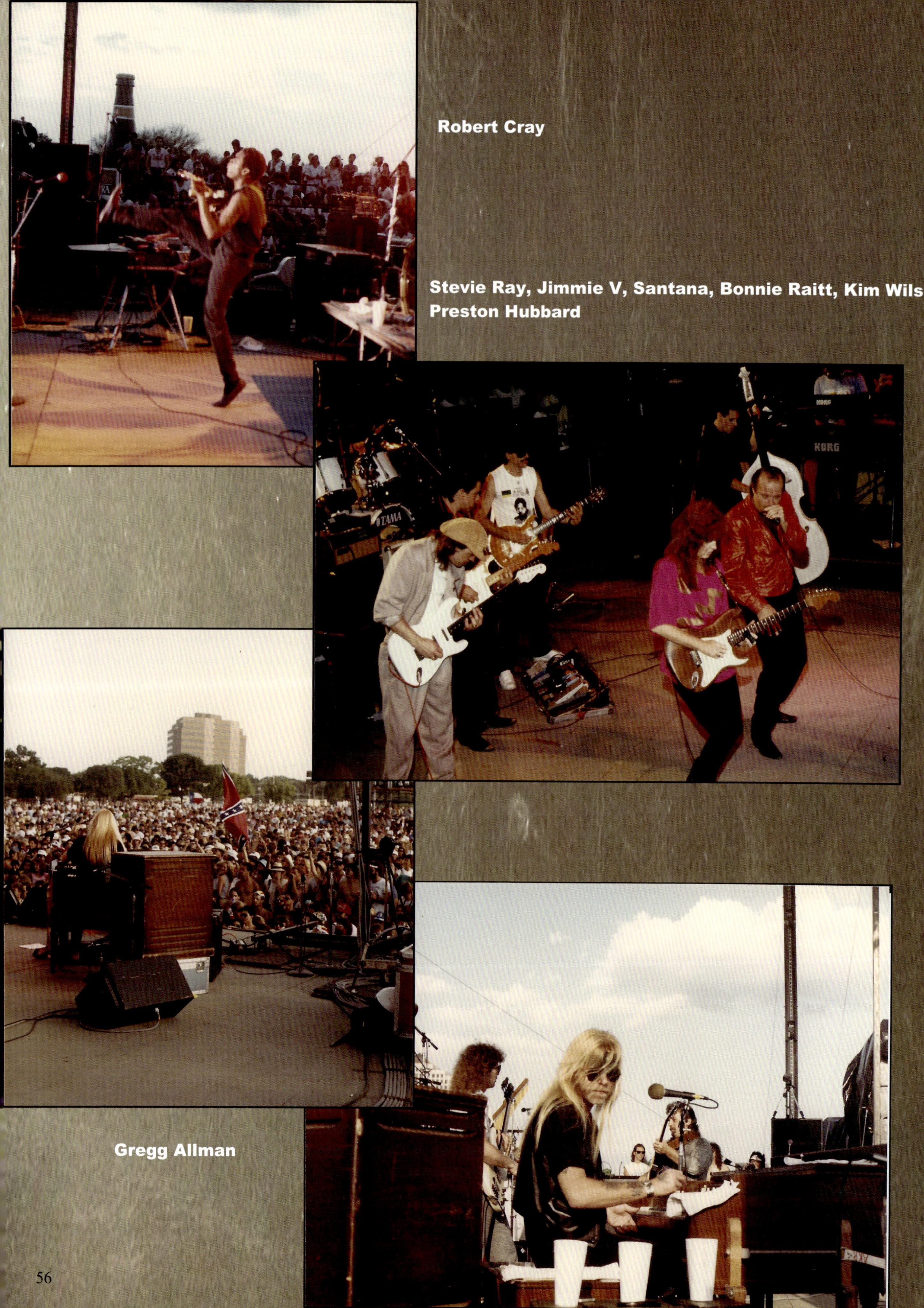

Robert Cray

Stevie Ray, Jimmie V, Santana, Bonnie Raitt, Kim Wilson
Preston Hubbard

Gregg Allman

Chapter 9: Roll, Roll, Roll with Stevie Ray & The Fab T-Birds

With a few weeks off from a busy Fabulous Thunderbirds schedule I was on my way to Honolulu along with Stevie Ray, Double Trouble and Jimmie Vaughan. It was 1984 and prior to the release of Stevie Ray's new CBS Record "Couldn't Stand the Weather," he had been invited to perform at the CBS Records Convention.

By this time I found myself very comfortable with the tour manager position. I was well organized, very respectful of the band and I started to push them in the right direction. Jimmie Vaughan and Kim Wilson were considered to be the leaders of the band while drummer Fran Christina was always the sensible one.

Then there was bassist Keith Ferguson. Keith was feared by many though underneath the tattoos was an incredibly smart individual with a very unique vision of the world. When I first started touring with the T-Birds we had to share hotel rooms and many a night I found myself rooming with Keith. Keith was one not to sleep much so I found myself up late and chatting till the early morning hours. Keith was finding the grueling touring schedule tedious and always preferred to be closer to home.

I knew our touring schedule was only getting tougher and with the success of the European Tour we would be spending a significant amount of time touring outside of the USA. Jimmie, Kim and Fran were all enthusiastic about the upcoming tours but not Keith. The band made a very difficult decision in 1984 to replace Keith Ferguson with Preston Hubbard. One of Preston's first gigs was getting on an airplane, flying to Germany and performing with the band at the Berlin Jazz Fest. We couldn't look back as London was looming around the corner.

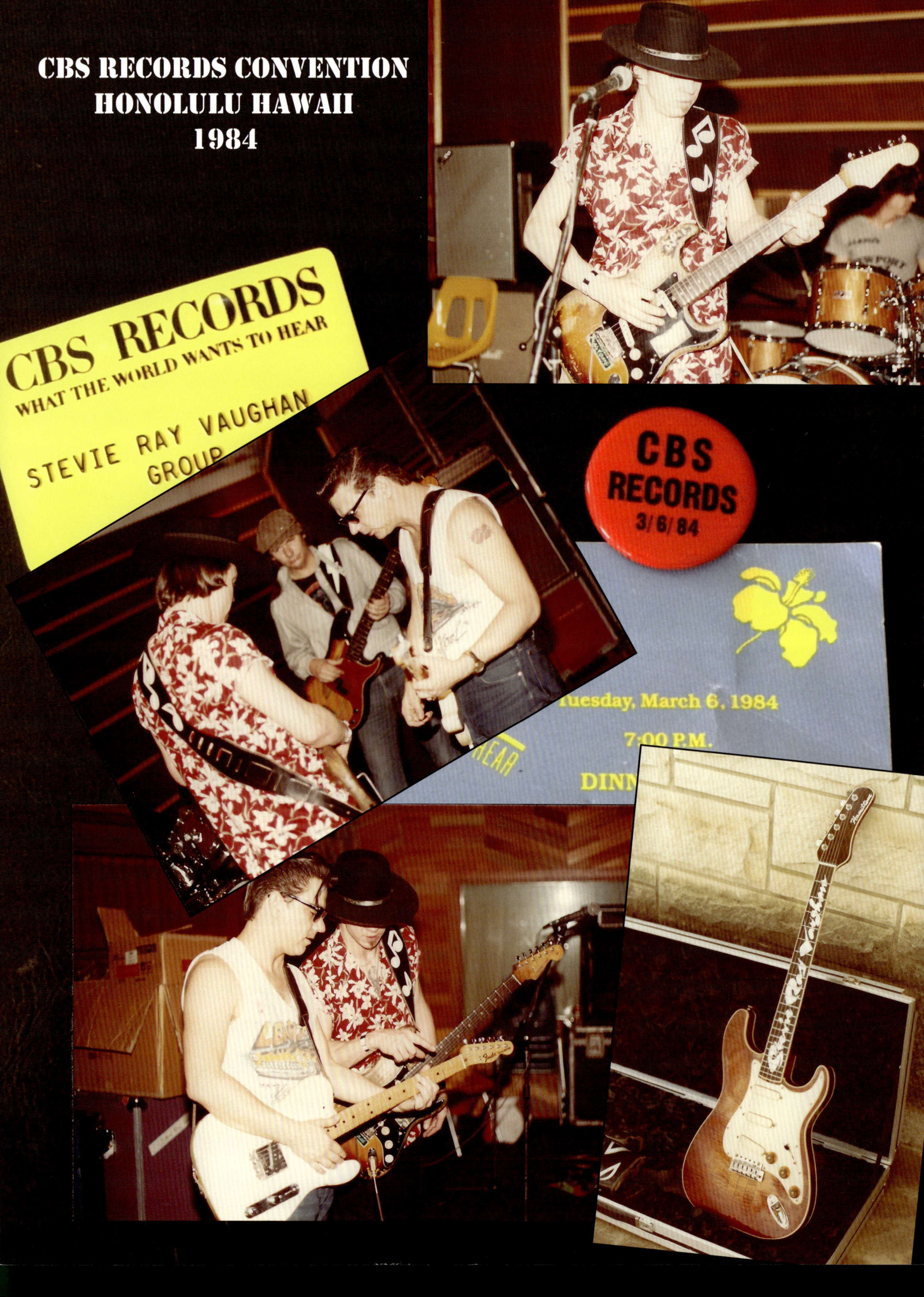
CBS RECORDS CONVENTION
HONOLULU HAWAII
1984
CBS RECORDS
WHAT THE WORLD WANTS TO HEAR
STEVIE RAY VAUGHAN
GROUP
CBS
RECORDS
3/6/84
Tuesday, March 6, 1984
7:00 P.M.
DINN

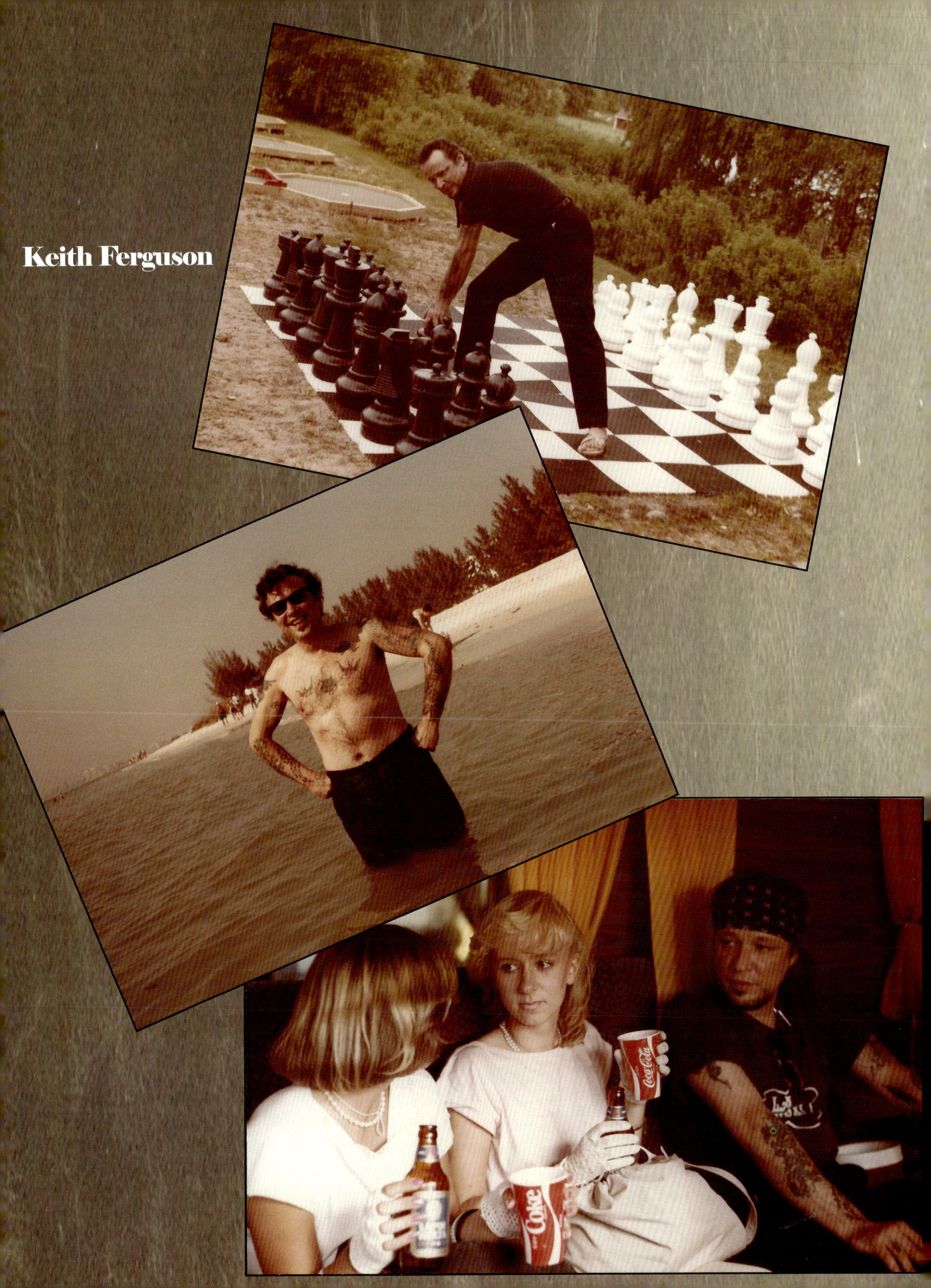

Keith Ferguson

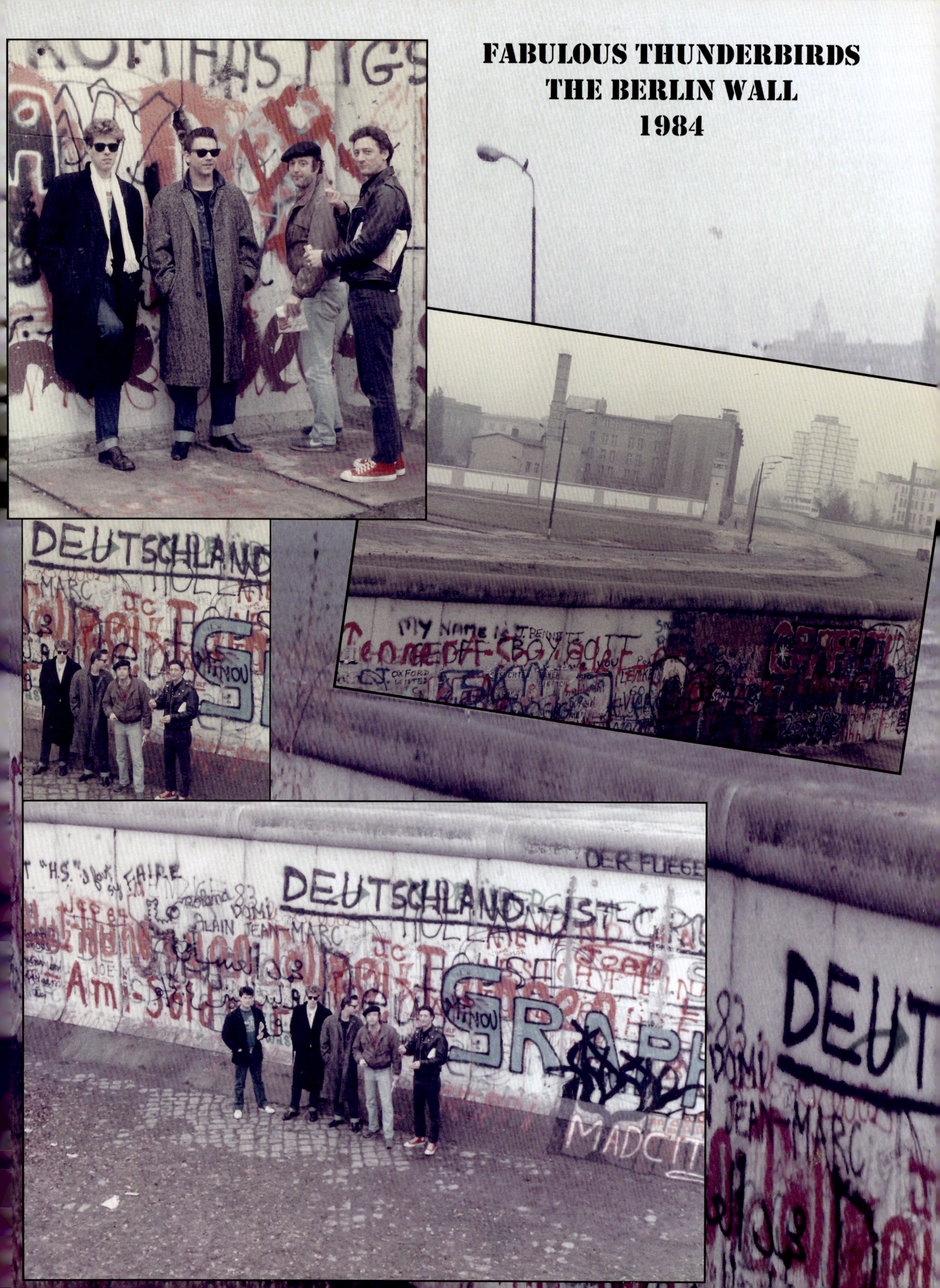

FABULOUS THUNDERBIRDS
THE BERLIN WALL
1984

FABULOUS THUNDERBIRDS
BRUGGE, BELGIUM
1985

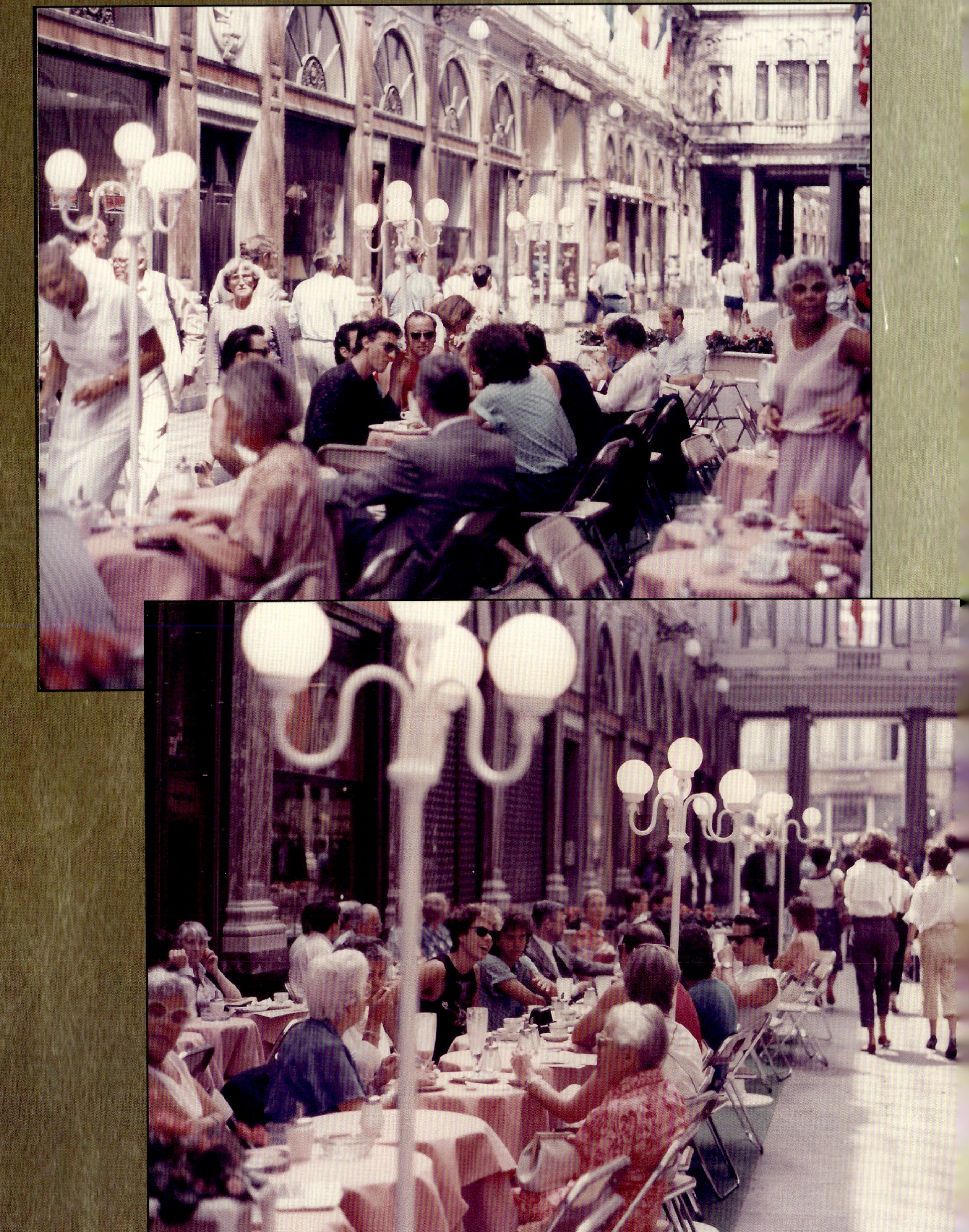

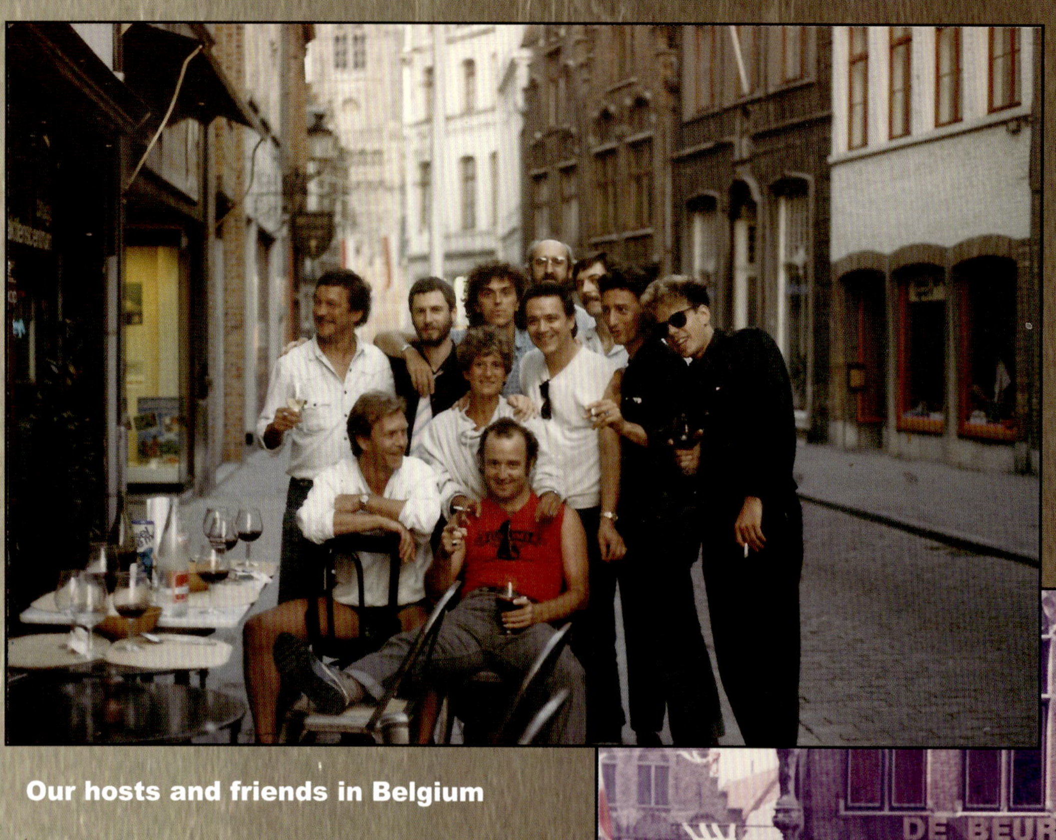

Our hosts and friends in Belgium

Jimmie & Kim on the streets of Brugge

Jimmie & Fran

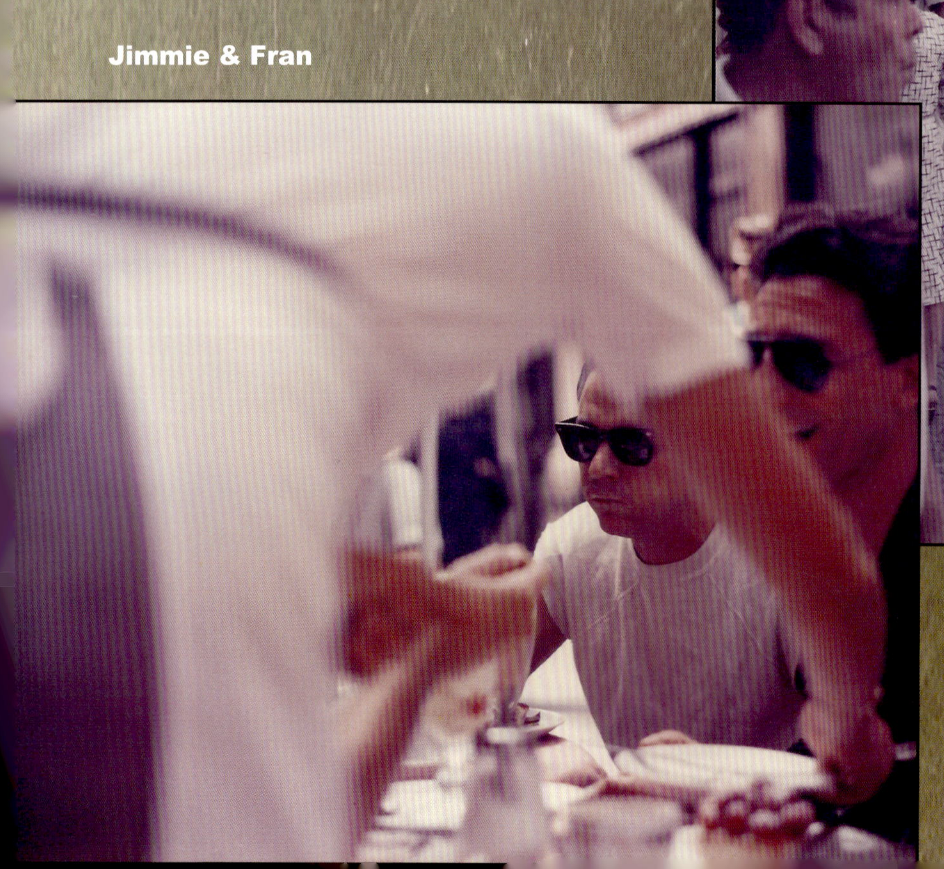

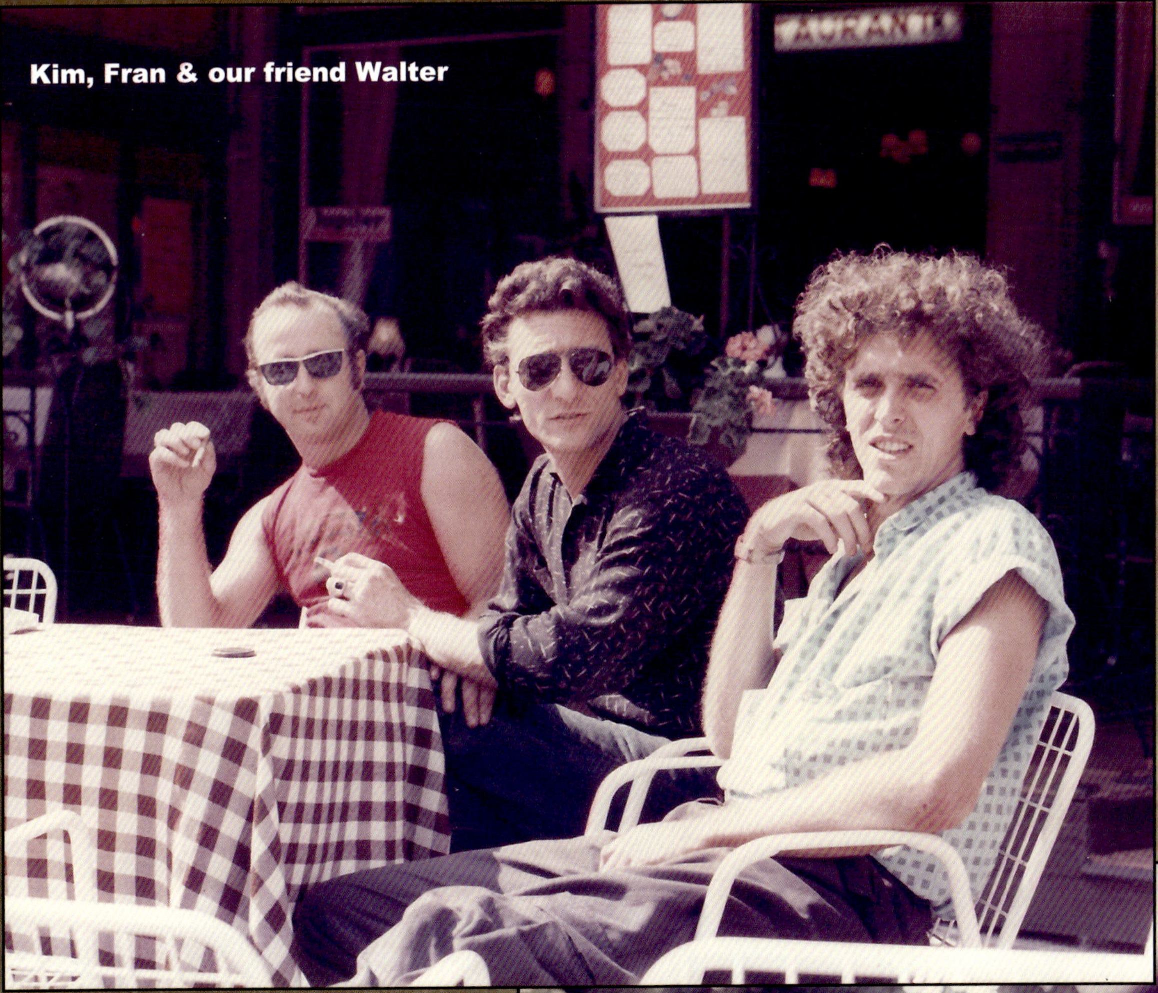

Kim, Fran & our friend Walter

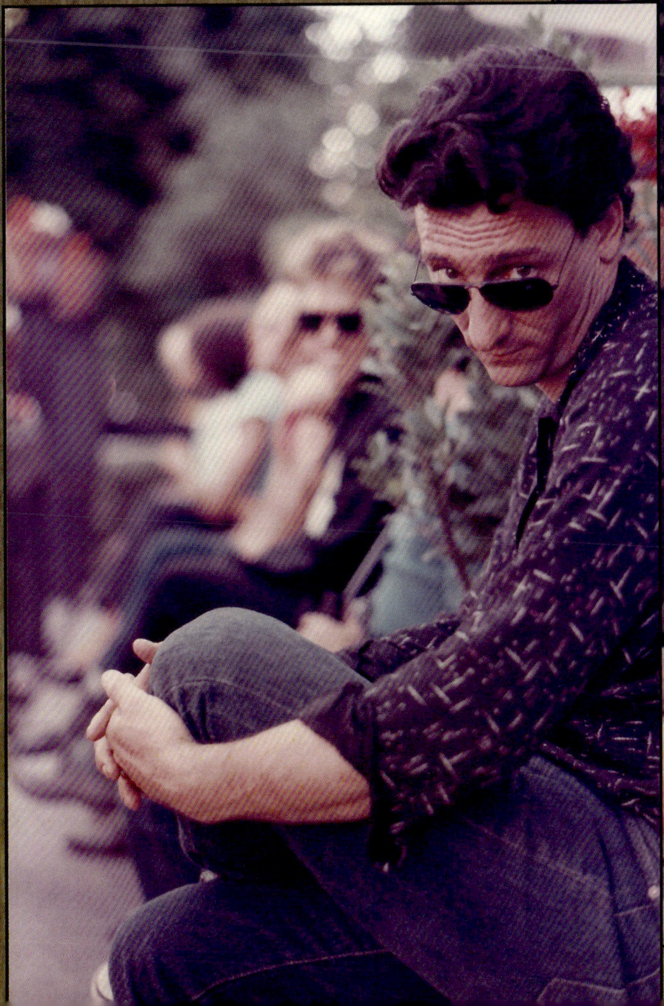

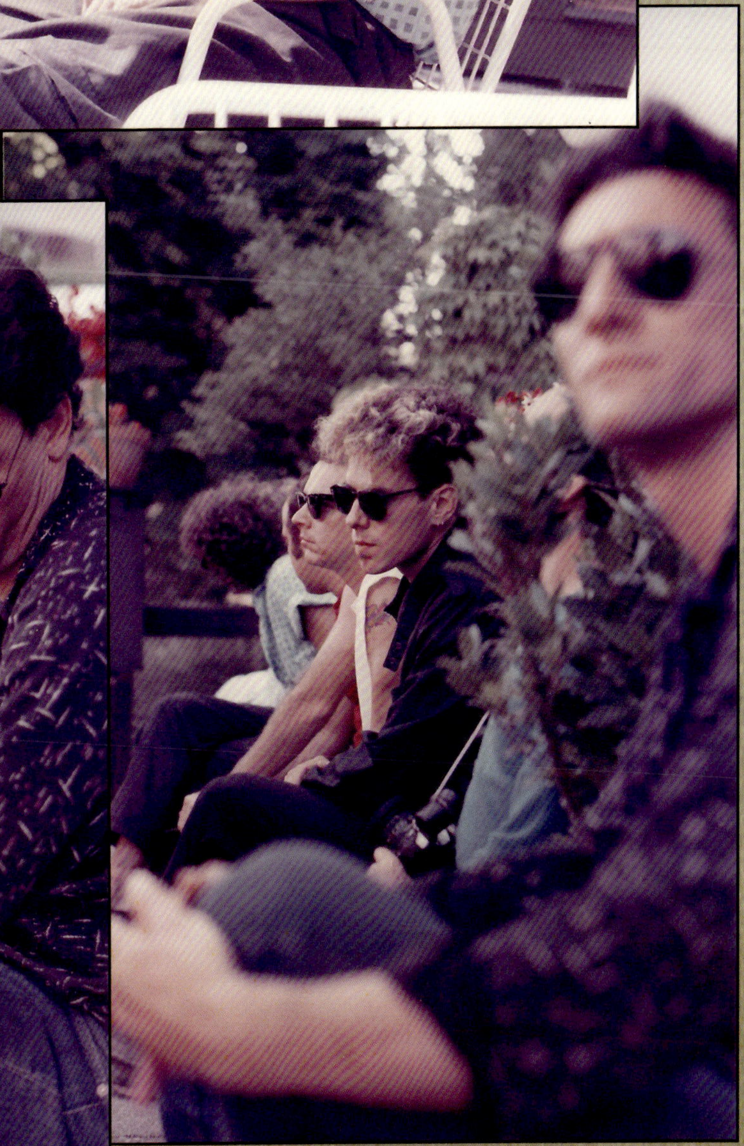

Fran Christina enjoying the sights

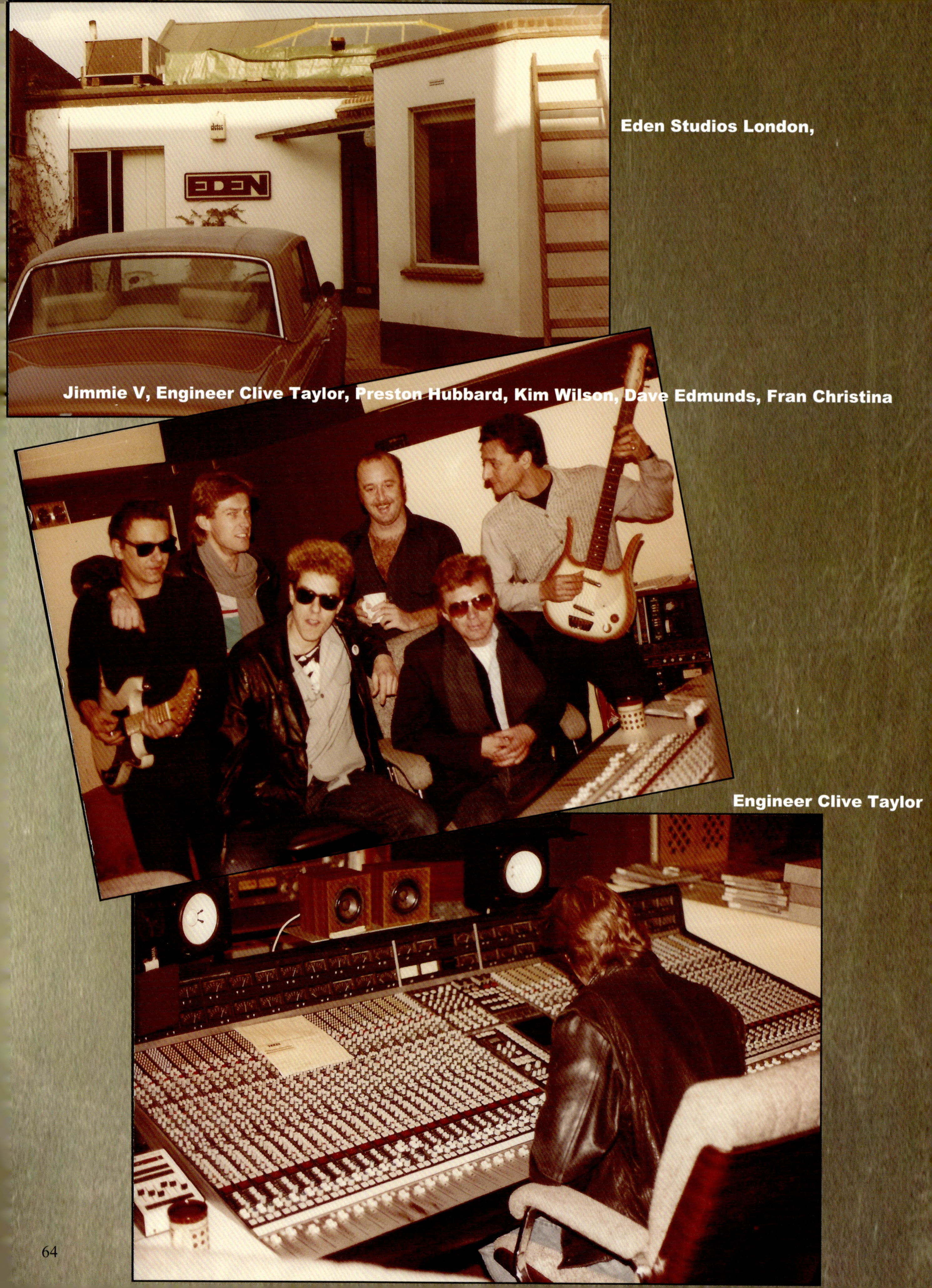

Eden Studios London,

Jimmie V, Engineer Clive Taylor, Preston Hubbard, Kim Wilson, Dave Edmunds, Fran Christina

Engineer Clive Taylor

Chapter 10: Tuff Enuff with the T-Birds

1985 saw the T-birds going to London and starting the recording of *Tuff Enuff* with Dave Edmunds at the helm. Dave had been coming out to see us in London and had been a big fan since the T-birds had previously toured with his band *Rockpile*. The basic tracks were cut in less than 2 weeks with two additional weeks of overdubbing and mixing. I returned to Austin hand carrying the reels of tape with the final mixes.

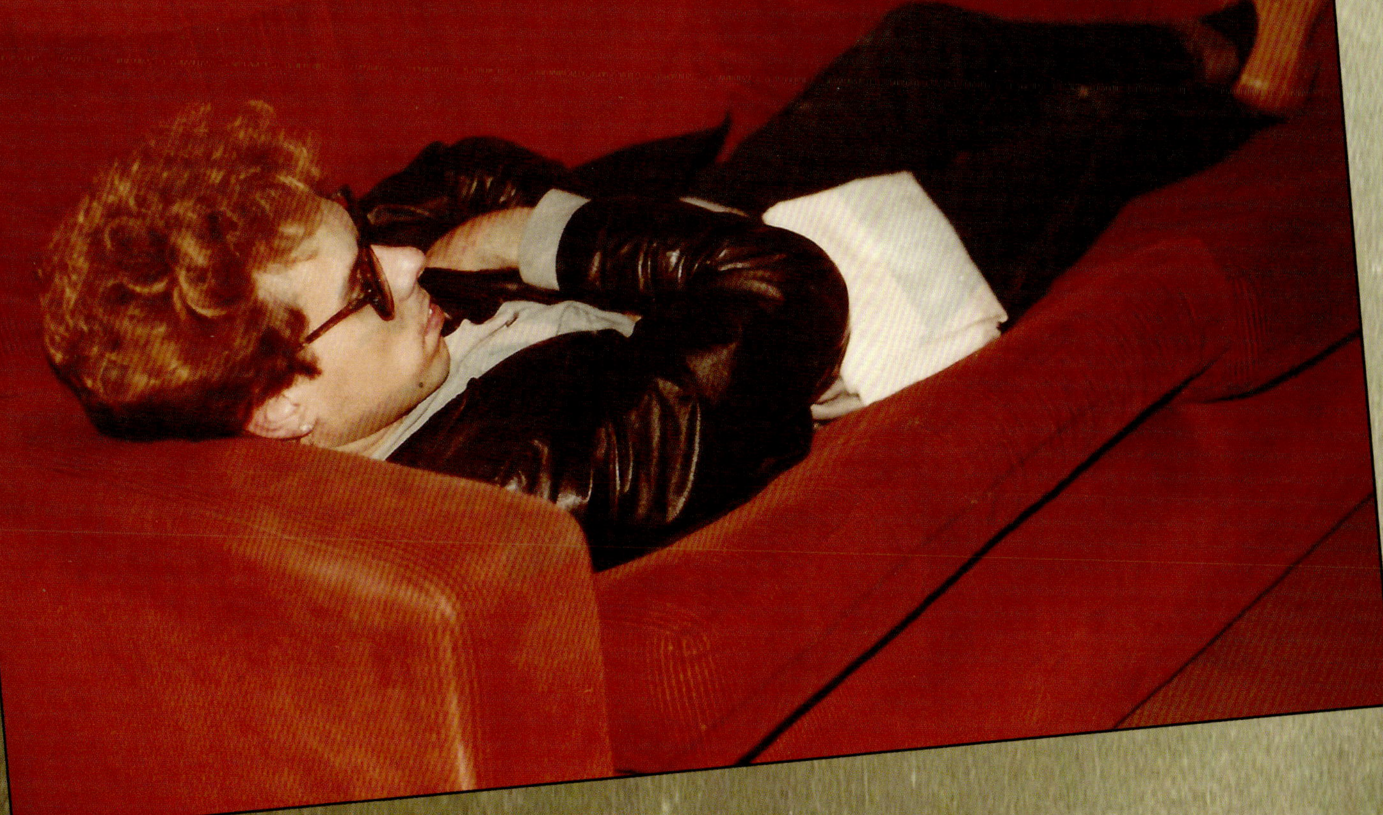

Preston Hubbard hard at work

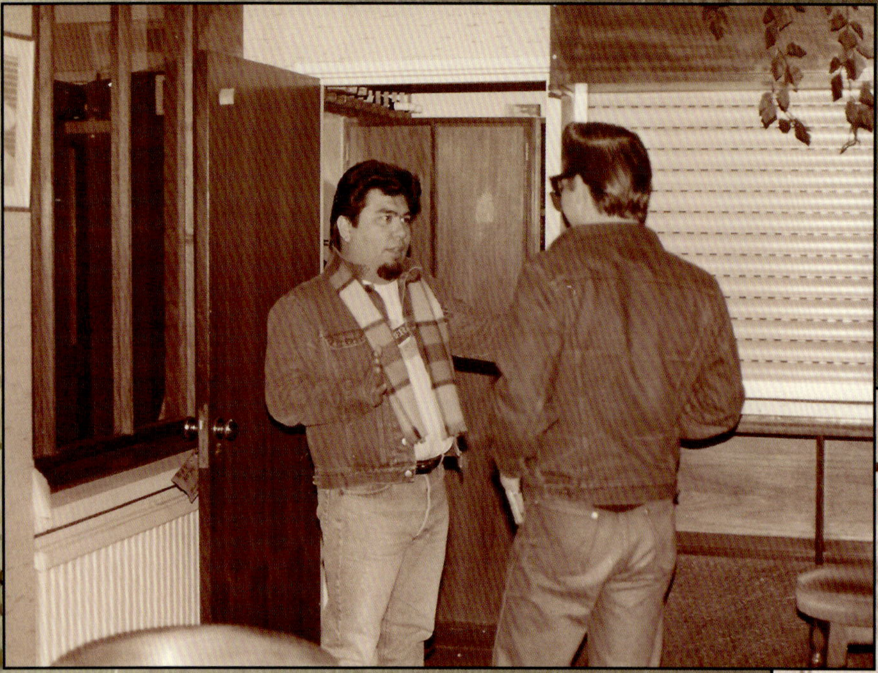

Cesar Rosas (Los Lobos) & Jimmie Vaughan

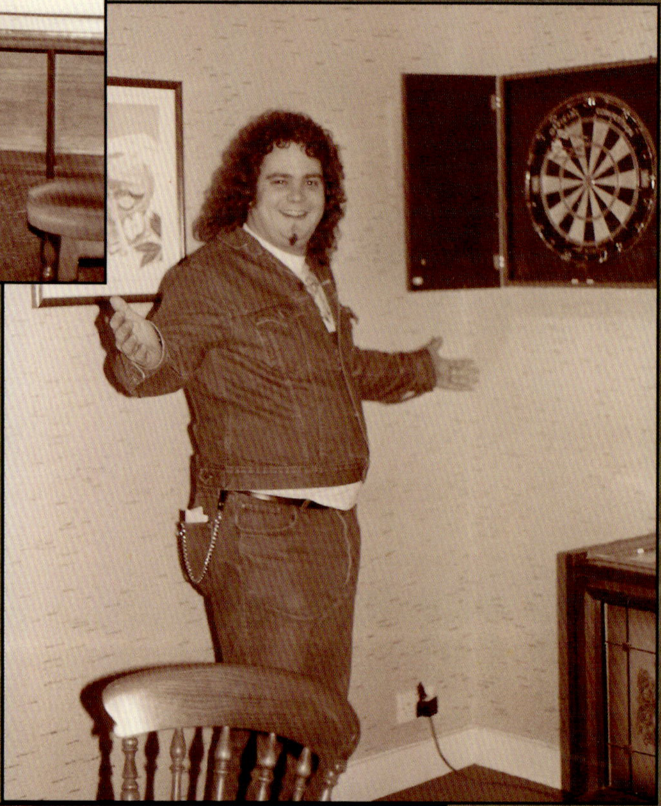

Los Lobos Tour Mgr. Bondo

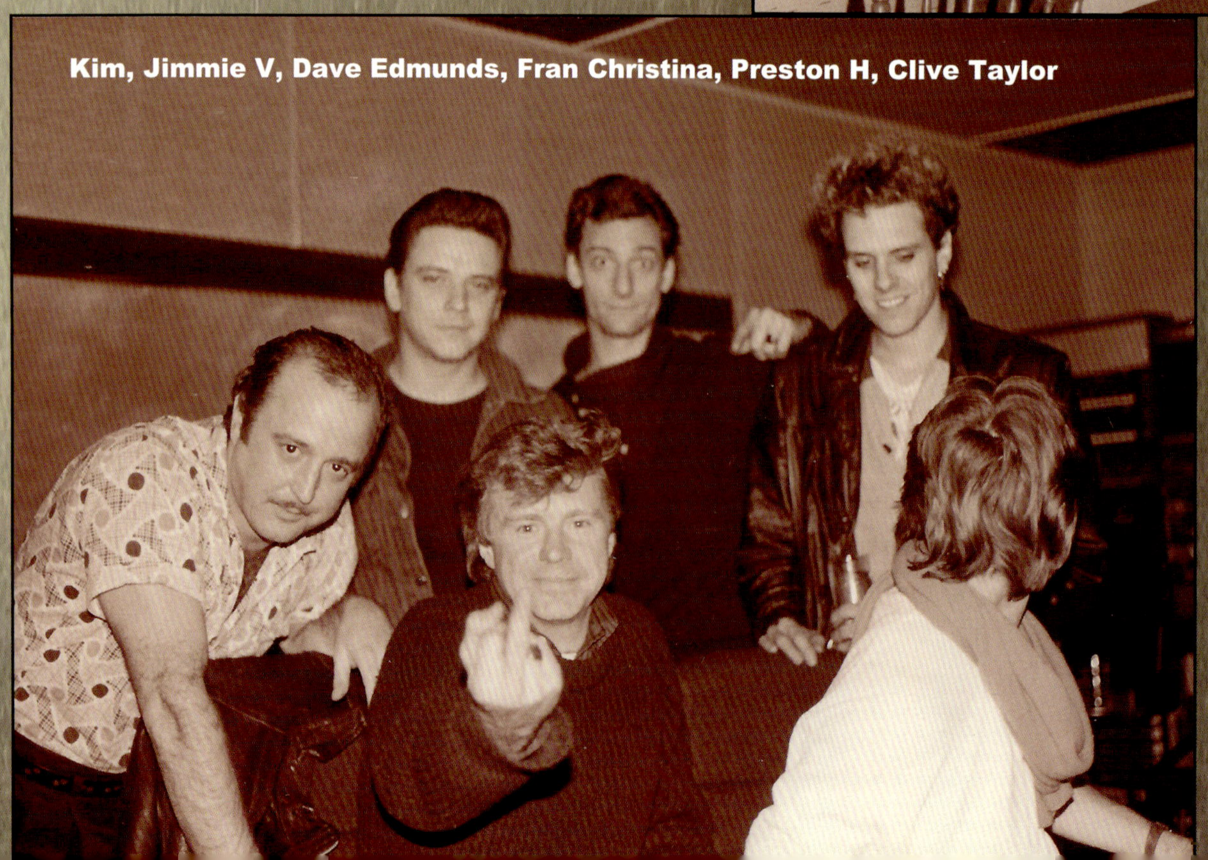

Kim, Jimmie V, Dave Edmunds, Fran Christina, Preston H, Clive Taylor

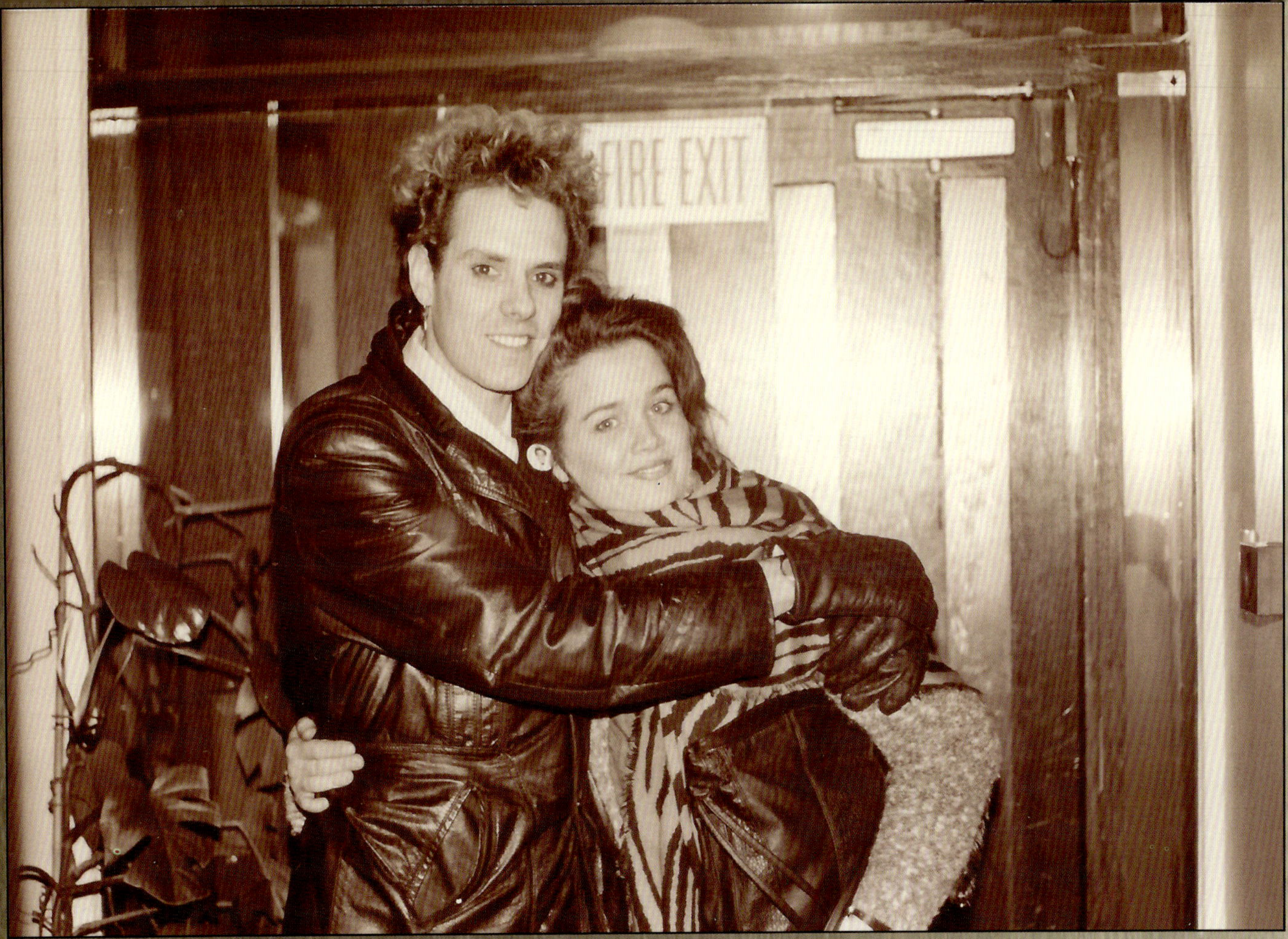

Above: Preston Hubbard & Julie Speed

Below: Kim Wilson, Columbia Hotel Night Manager & Cesar Rosas

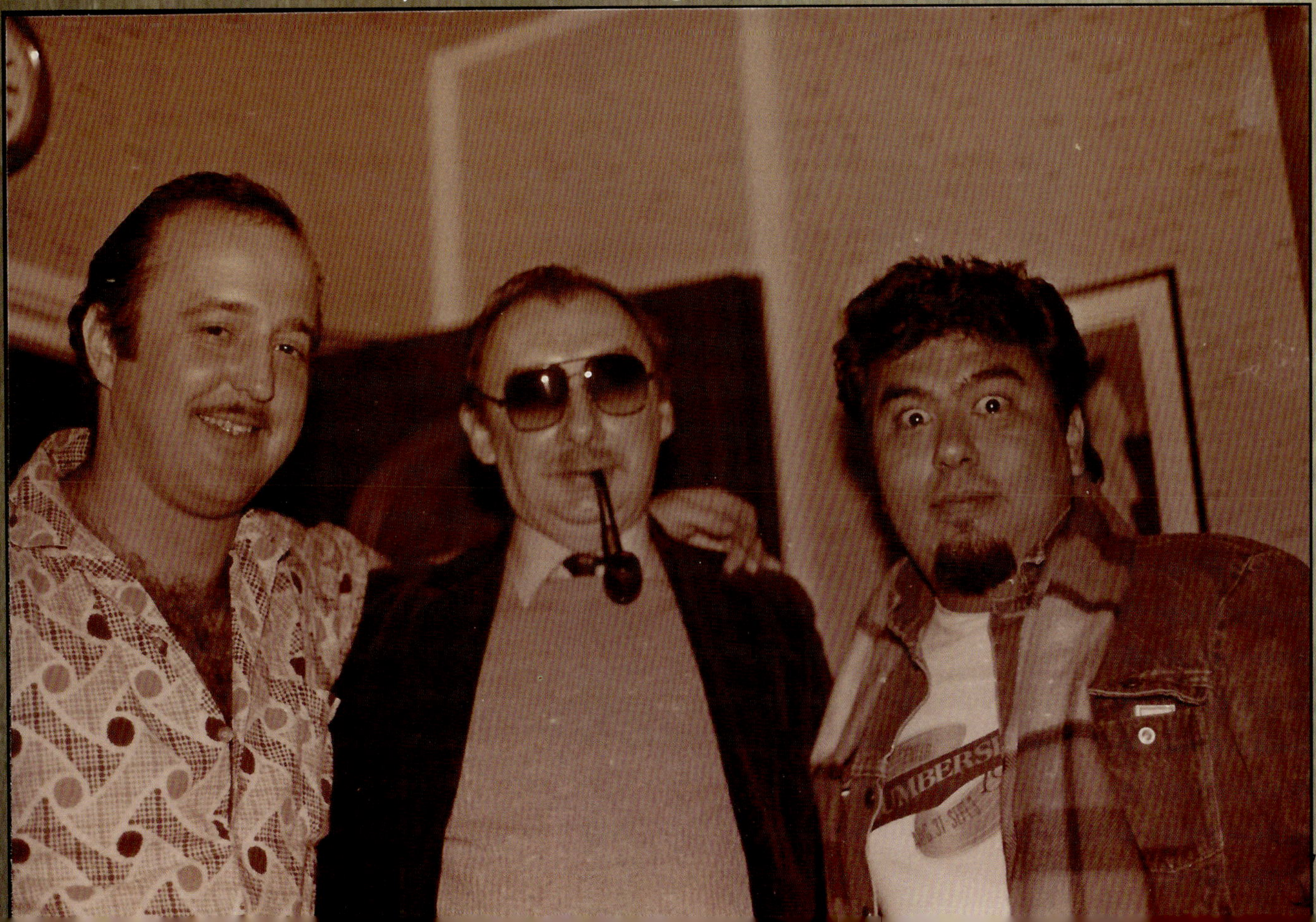

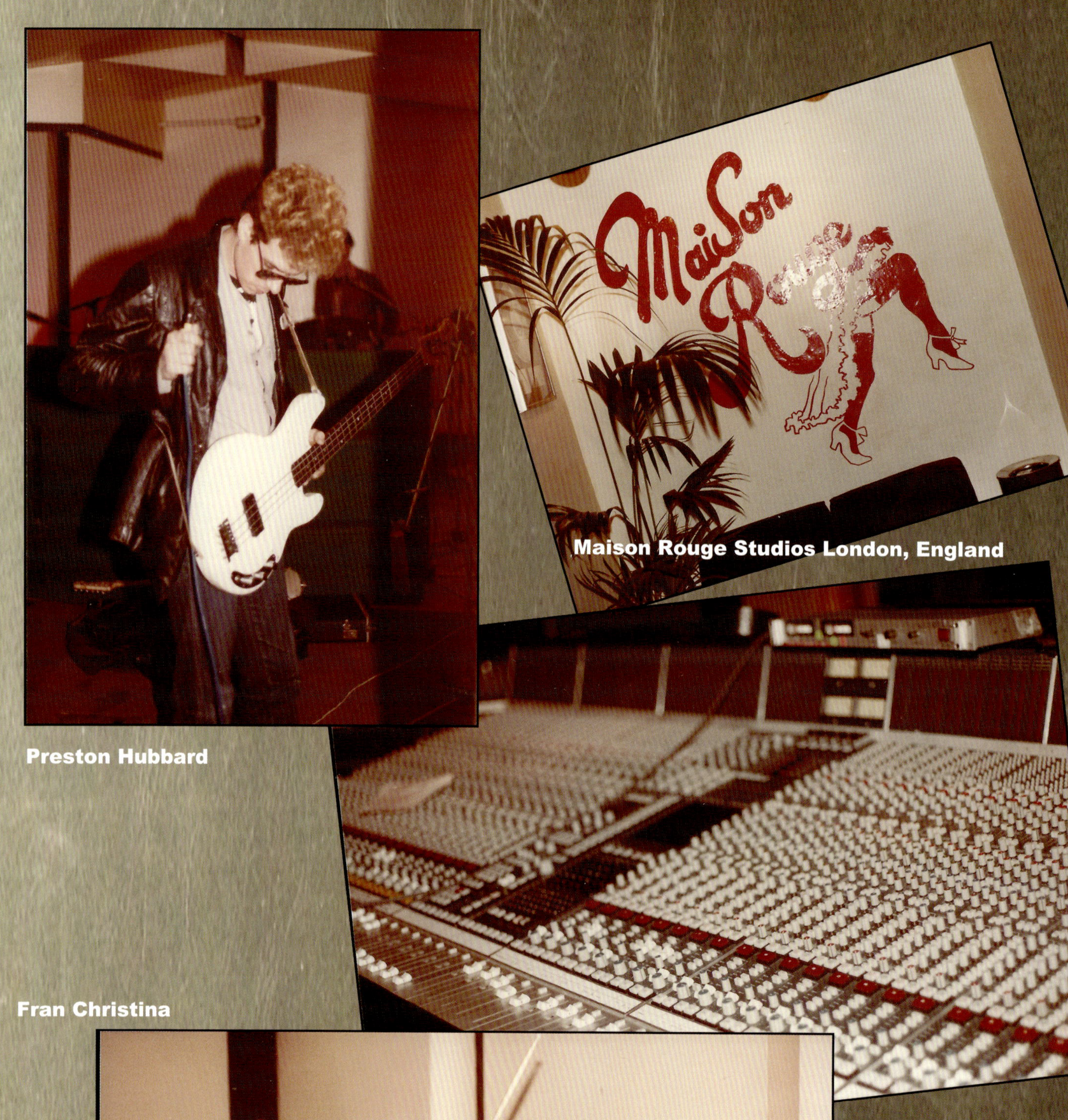

Maison Rouge Studios London, England

Preston Hubbard

Fran Christina

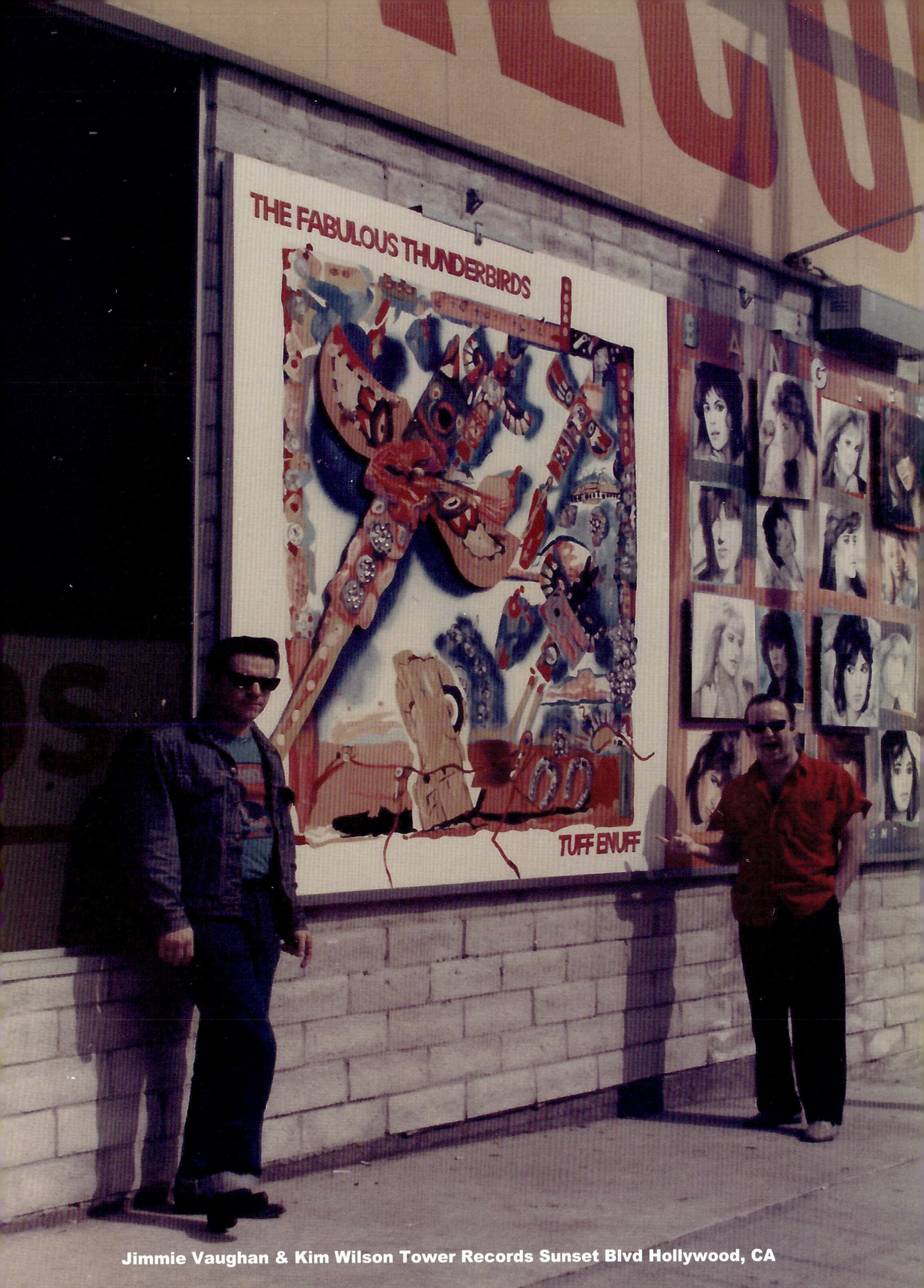

Jimmie Vaughan & Kim Wilson Tower Records Sunset Blvd Hollywood, CA

FABULOUS THUNDERBIRDS WRAP IT UP VIDEO HOLLYWOOD, CA 1987

Shot at Liberace's former Hollywood Hills home

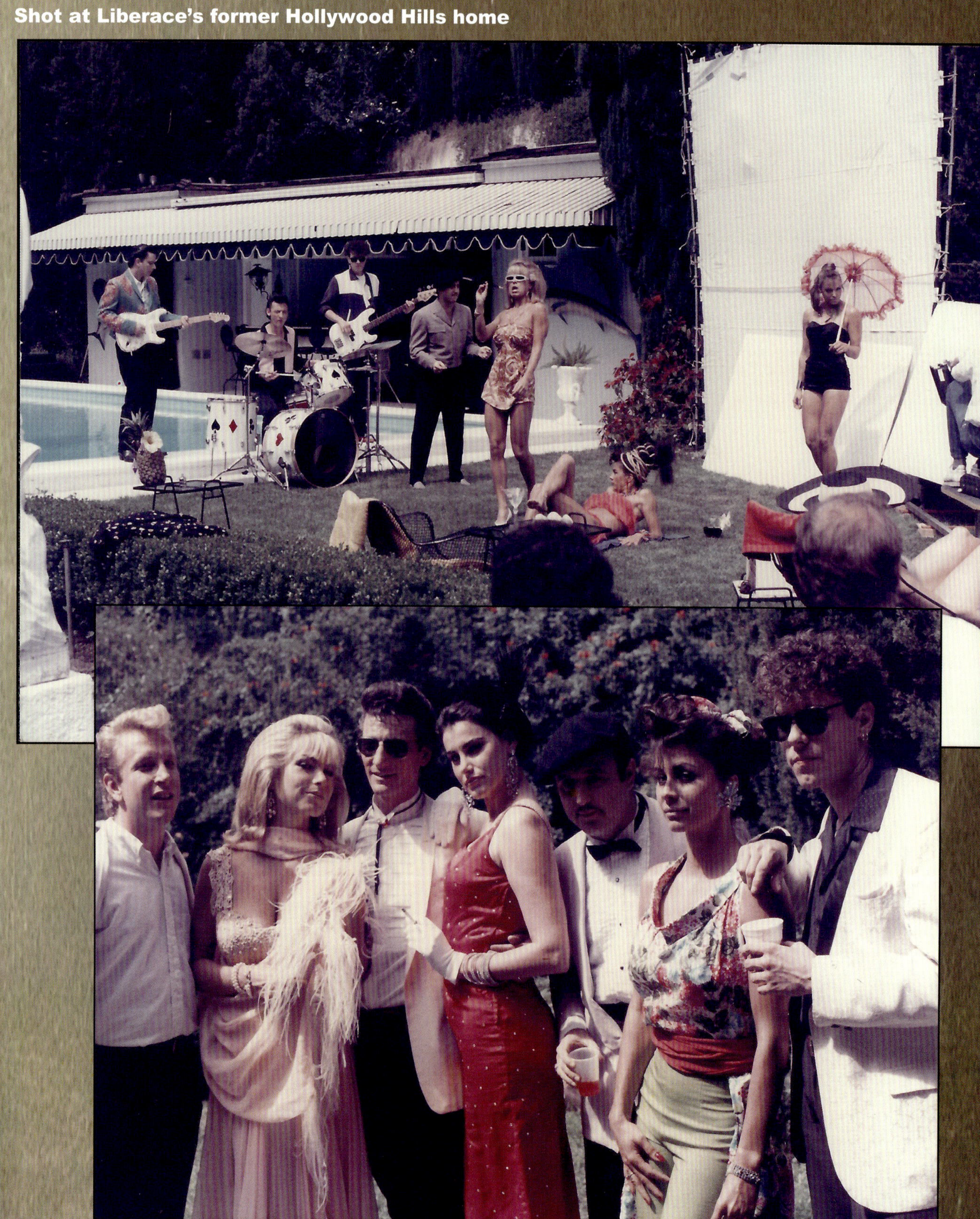

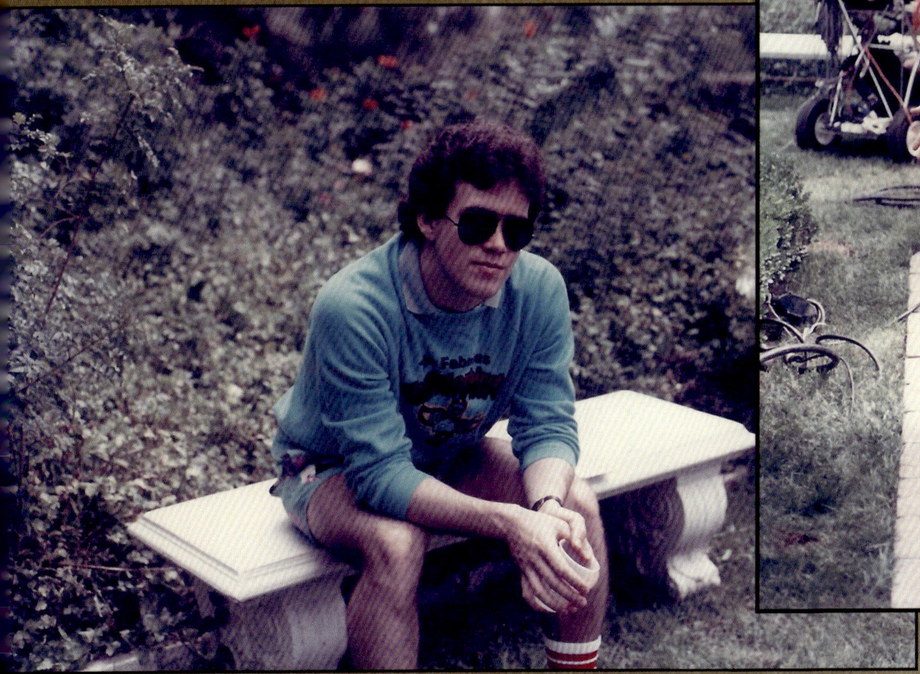

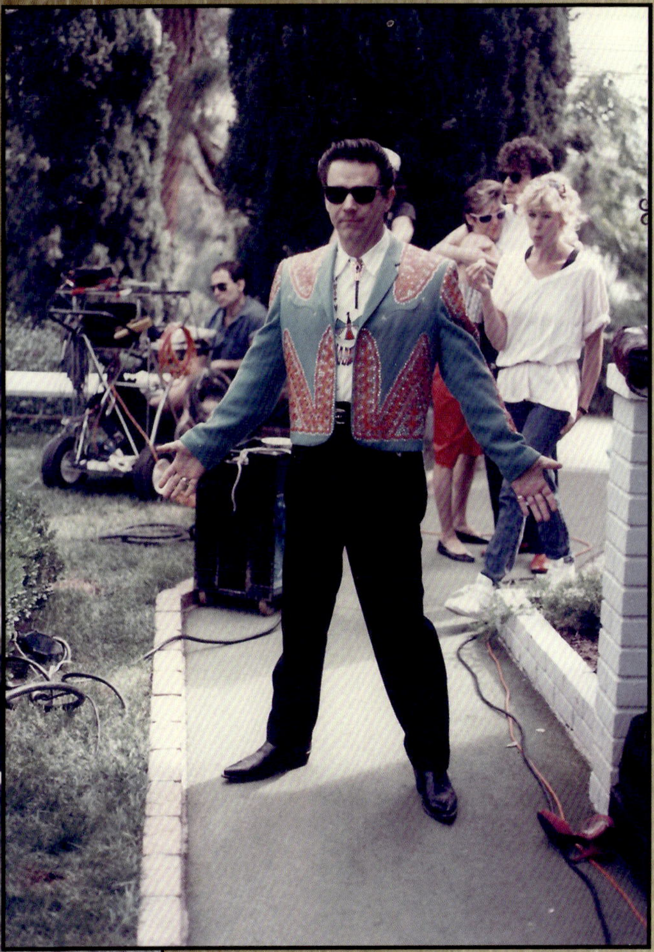

Jimmie Vaughan

Our first product mgr-Diarmuid Quinn CBS Records

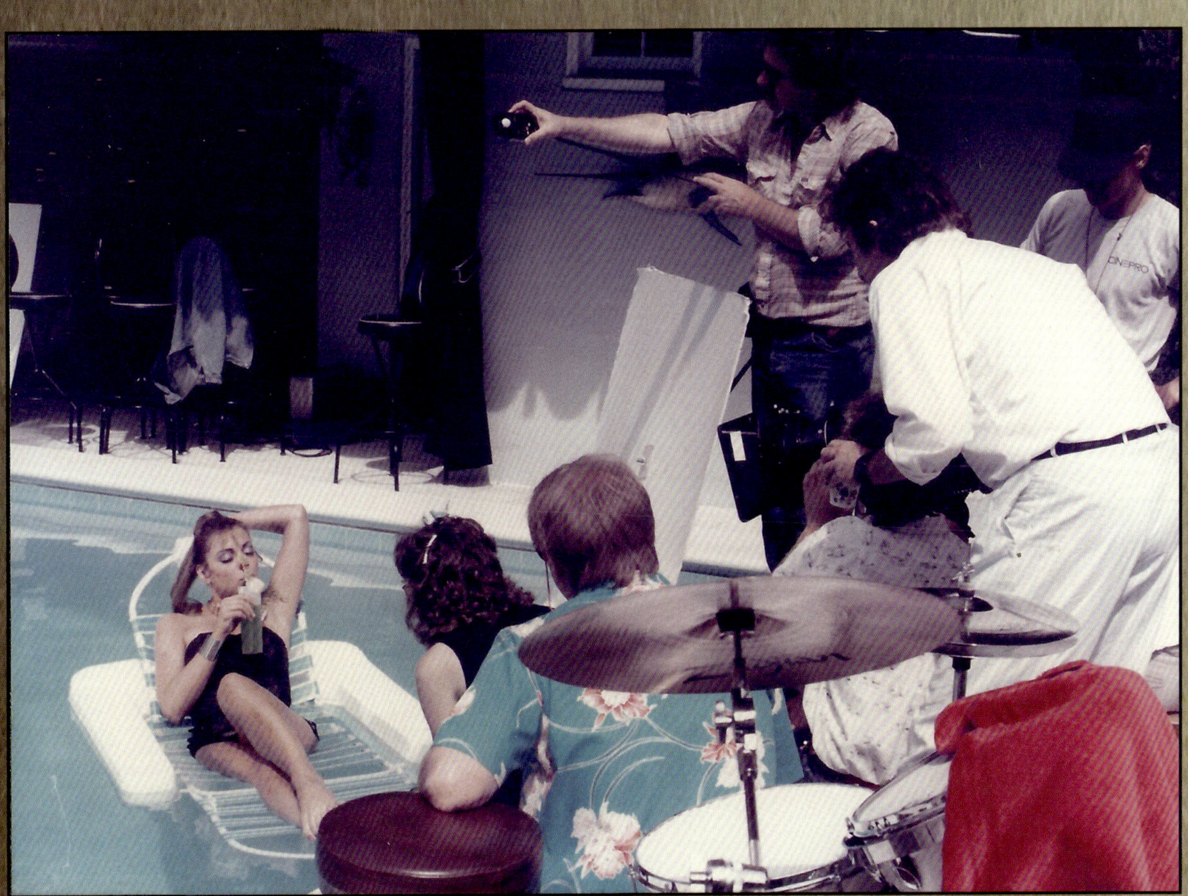

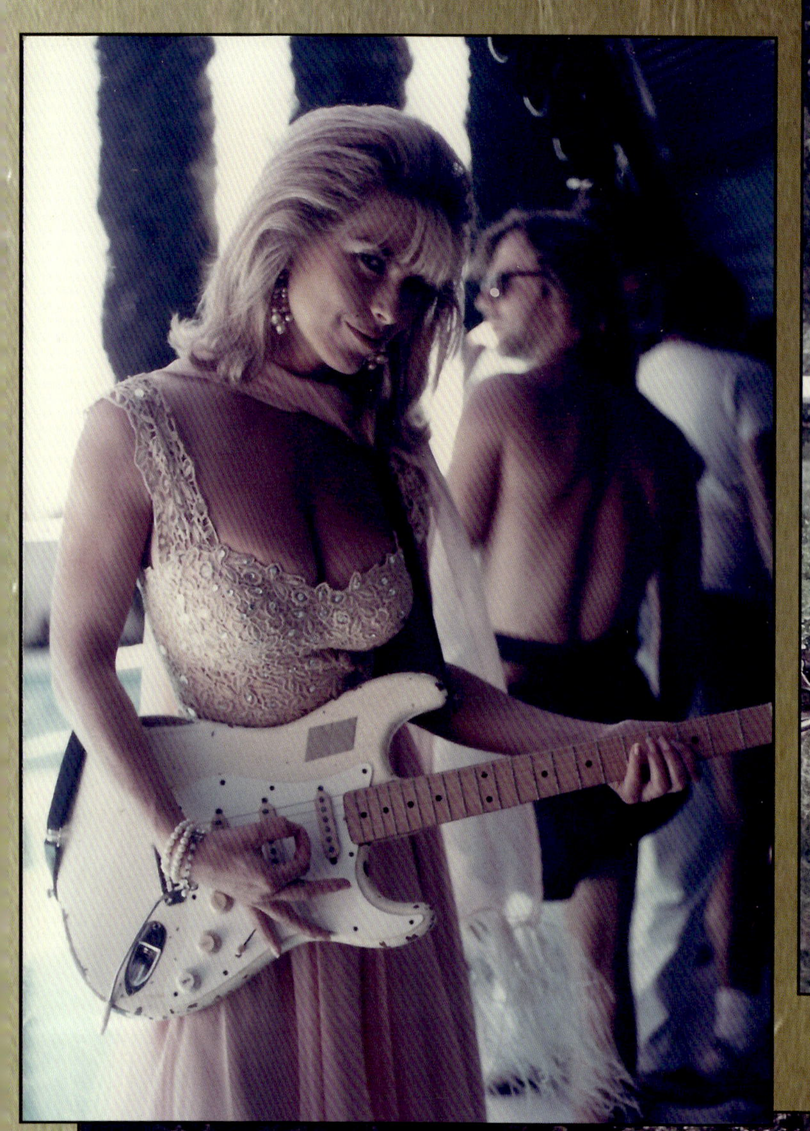

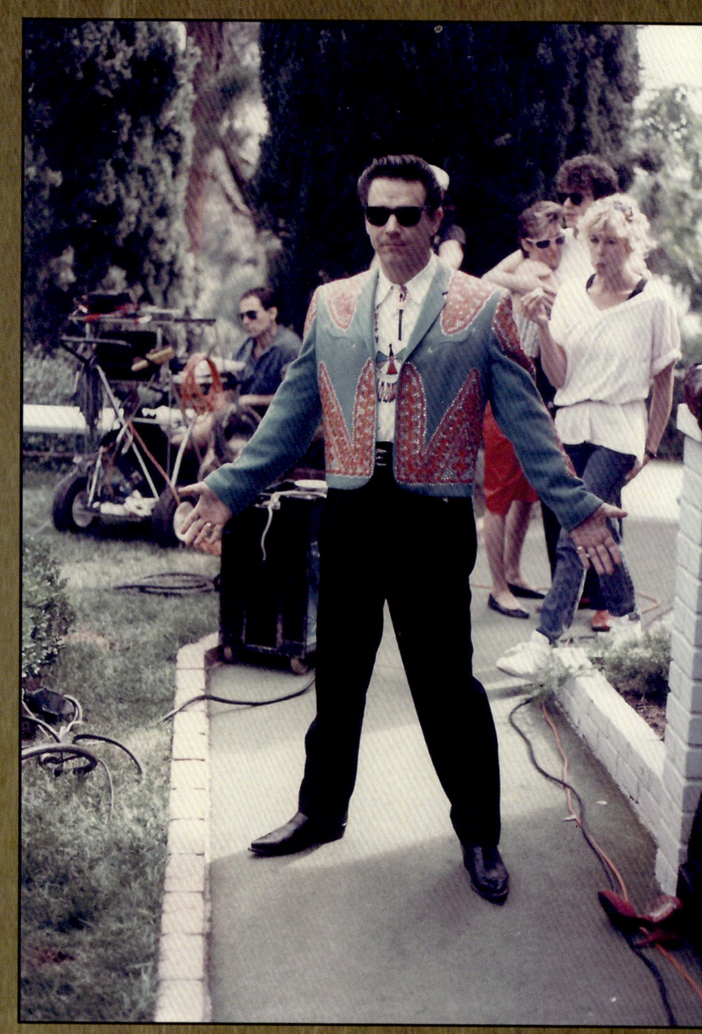

Jimmie Vaughan

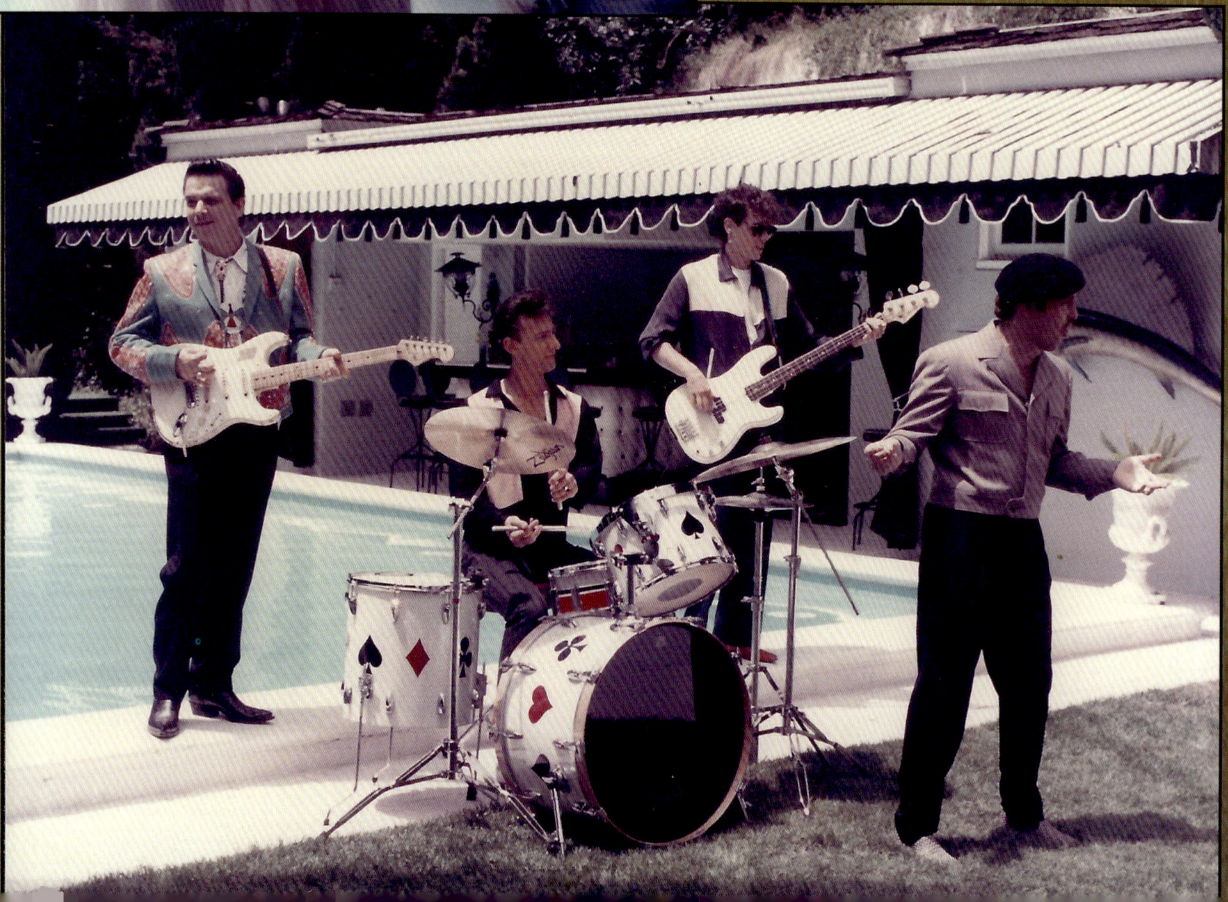

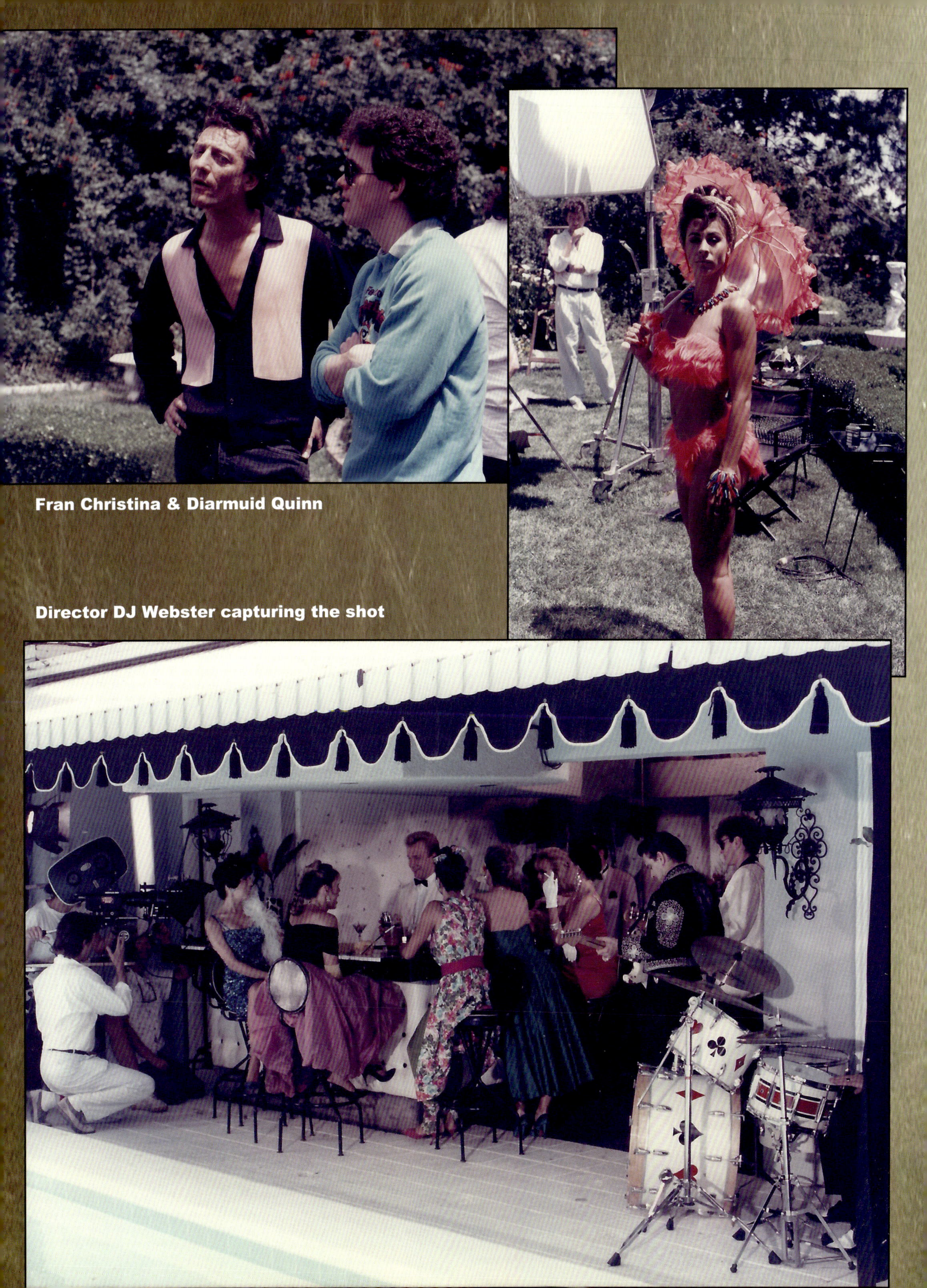

Fran Christina & Diarmuid Quinn

Director DJ Webster capturing the shot

Jimmie, Kim, Fran, Preston, Diarmuid Quinn, DJ Webster

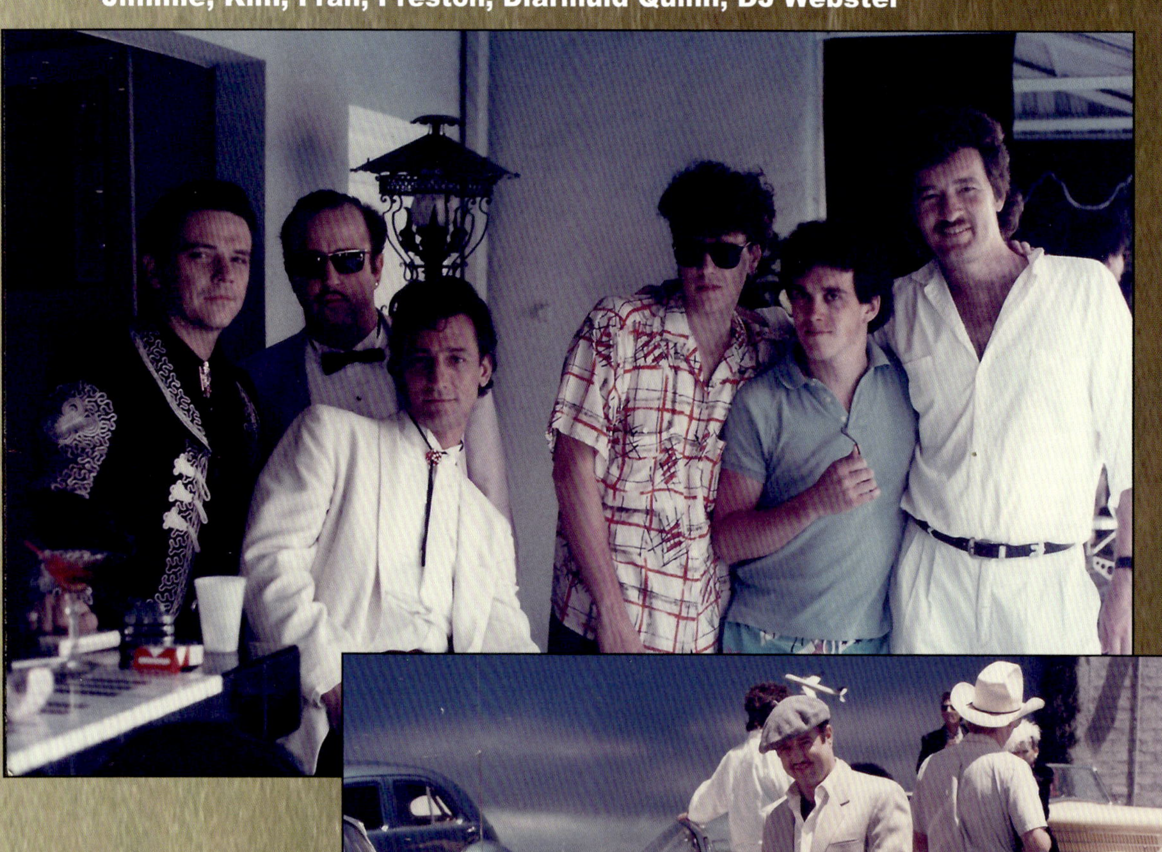

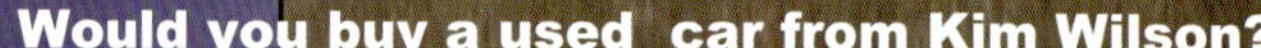

Would you buy a used car from Kim Wilson?

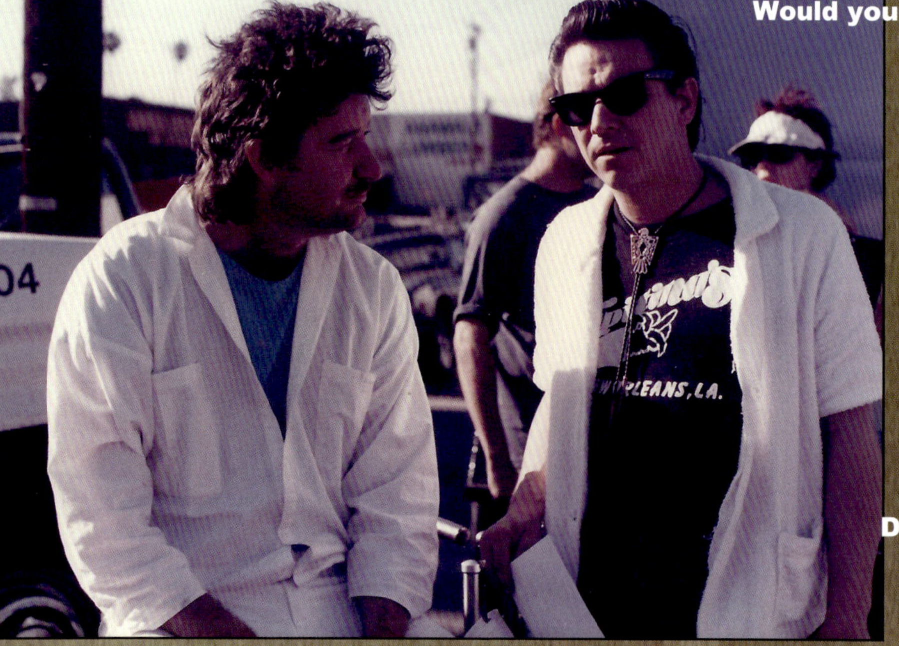

Director DJ Webster with Jimmie

Chapter 11: Powerful Stuff – On the Road with the Thunderbirds

The Tuff Enuff album was completed, we had a new home at CBS Records and we did what we knew best and headed back out on the road. As the album was just starting to make waves in the US market Stevie invited the T-birds to support his upcoming tour of Australia and New Zealand.

It was very much a family affair as both bands and crews headed to Australia for a month long tour. Stevie's star was shining in Australia as he was selling out large arenas throughout the tour. While in Sydney we were all invited to board a yacht and tour the Harbor as CBS Records presented Stevie and Double Trouble with gold plaques and also to celebrate Jimmie Vaughan's and Preston Hubbard's birthdays. It was 1986 and the future looked very bright.

TBirds Touring with Bob Seger

The success of Tuff Enuff took everyone by surprise as the album generated two top ten hits, two top ten MTV videos and sold well over a million copies. A year of non-stop touring, appearances with Johnny Carson, David Letterman and even Howard Stern all helped to fuel the fire. A good portion of the year was spent touring with Bob Seger on his sold out North American Tour.

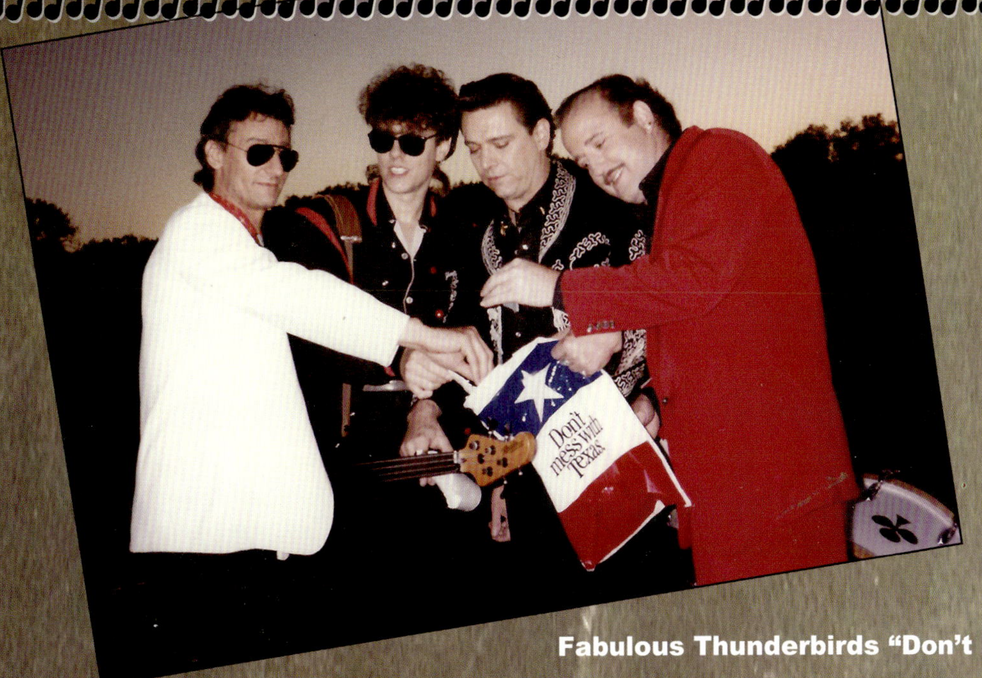

Fabulous Thunderbirds "Don't Mess With Texas"

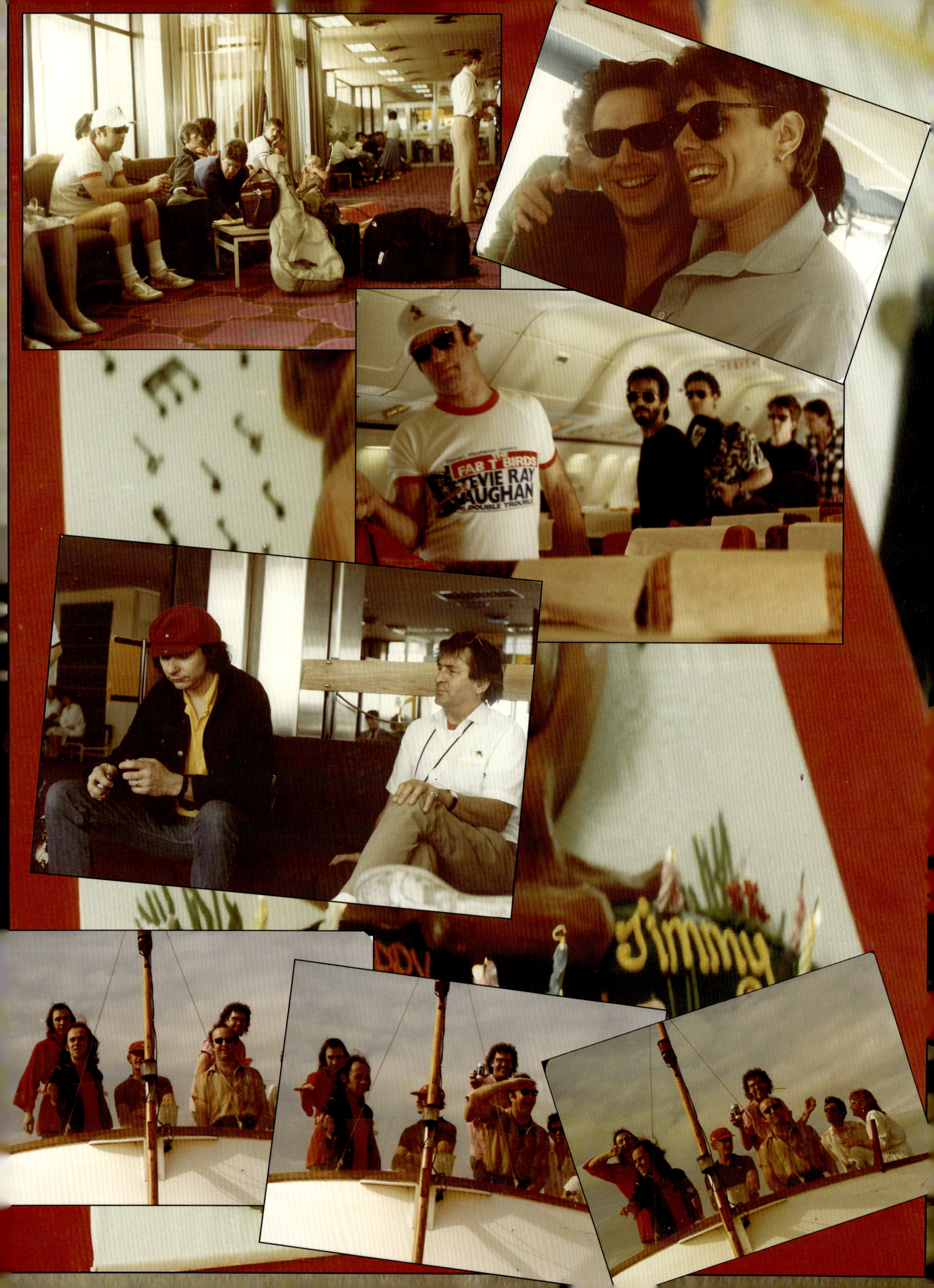

FAB T'BIRDS
TEVIE RAY
AUGHAN
Jimmy

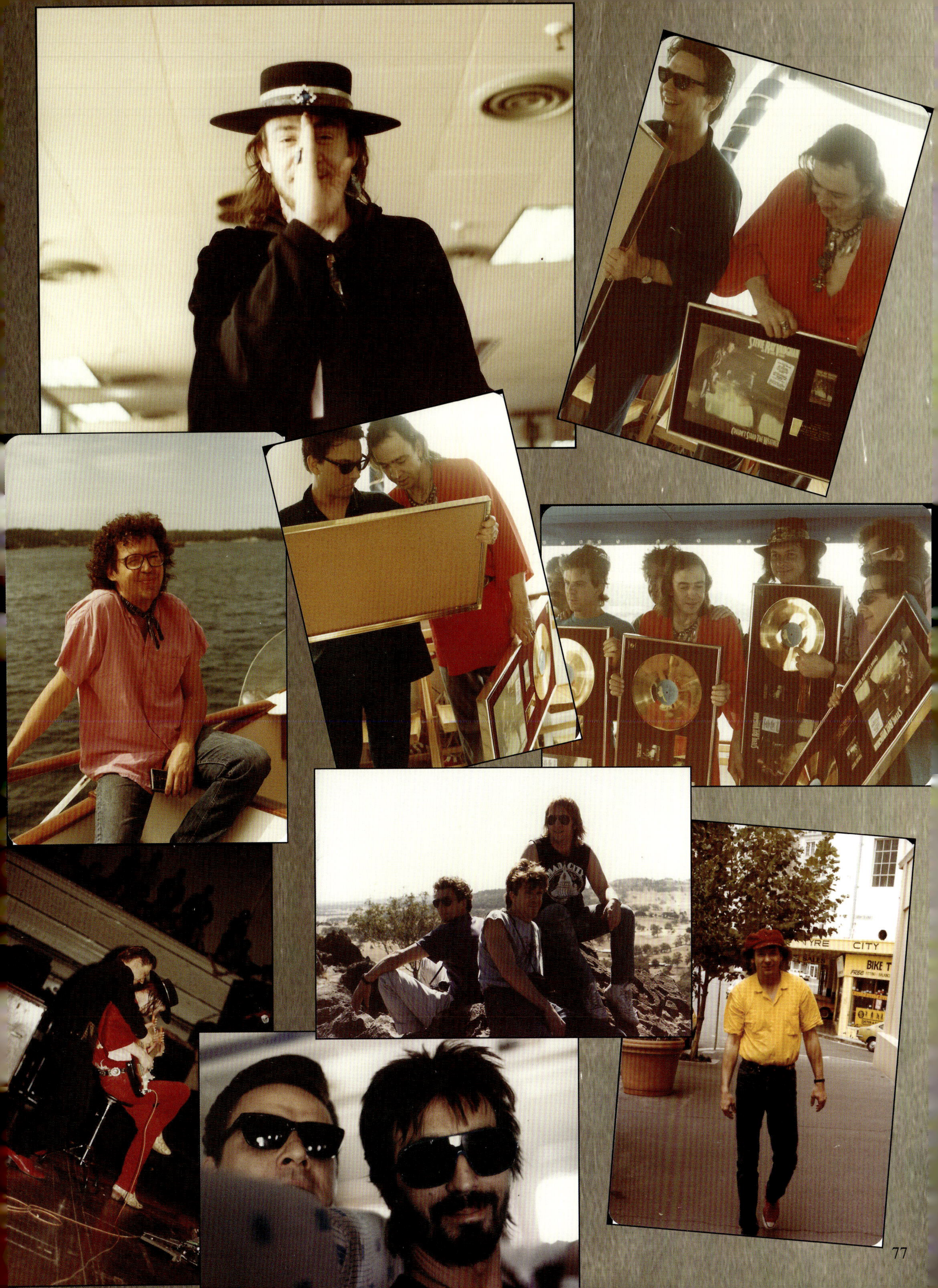
CITY

Al Priest, Chris Layton & Fran Christina SRV/T-Bird Australian Tour

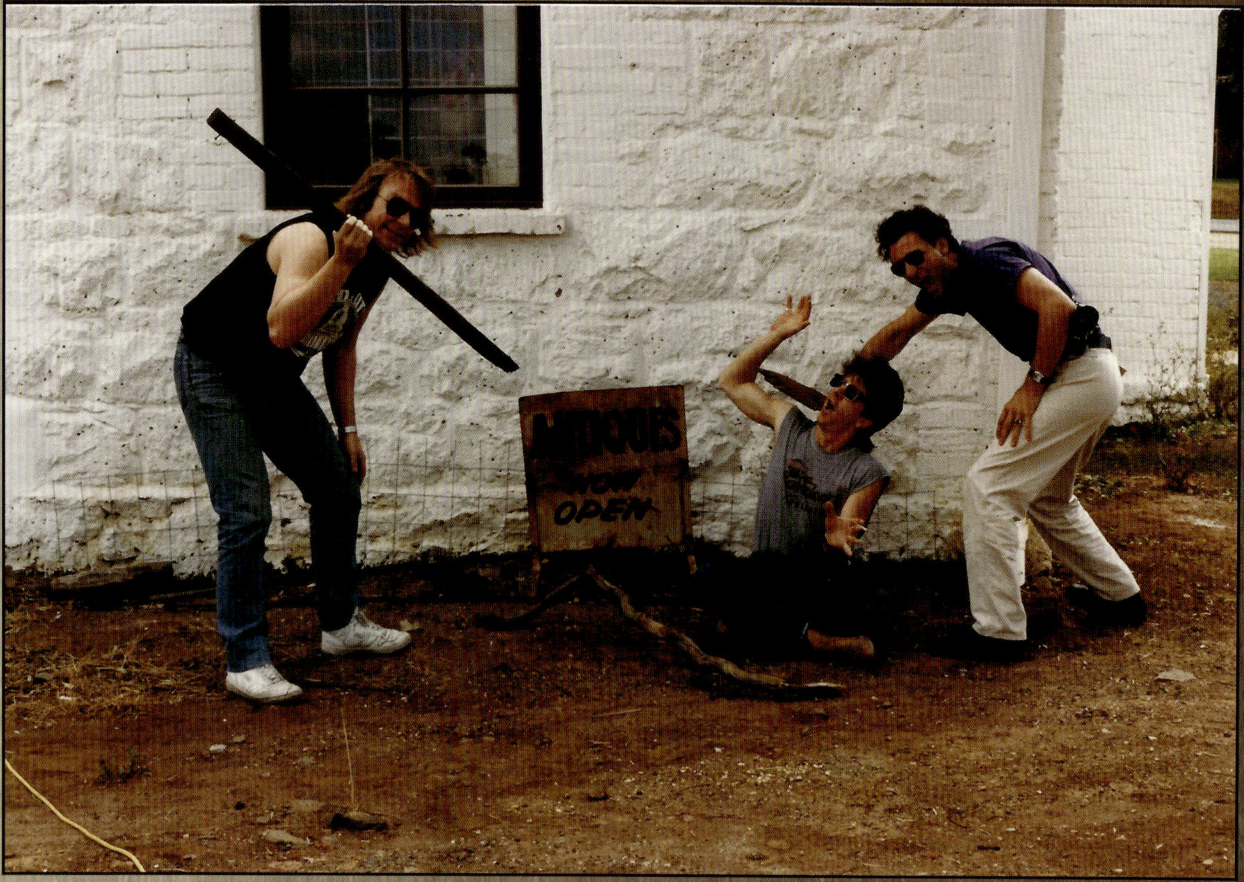

Jimmie V & Tony Garnier Madison Square Garden NY, NY

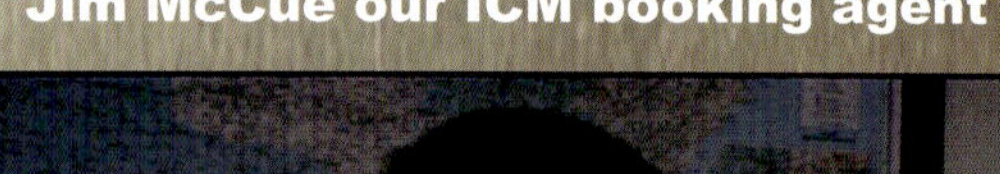

Jim McCue our ICM booking agent

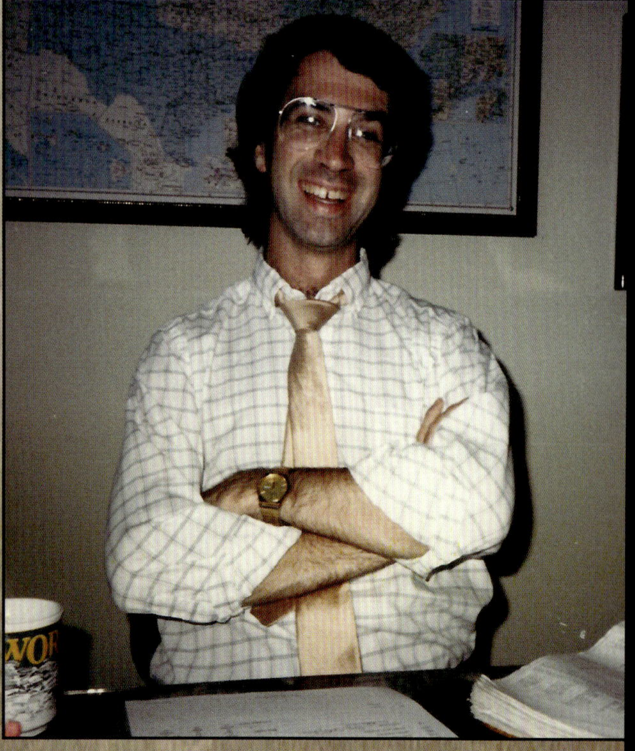

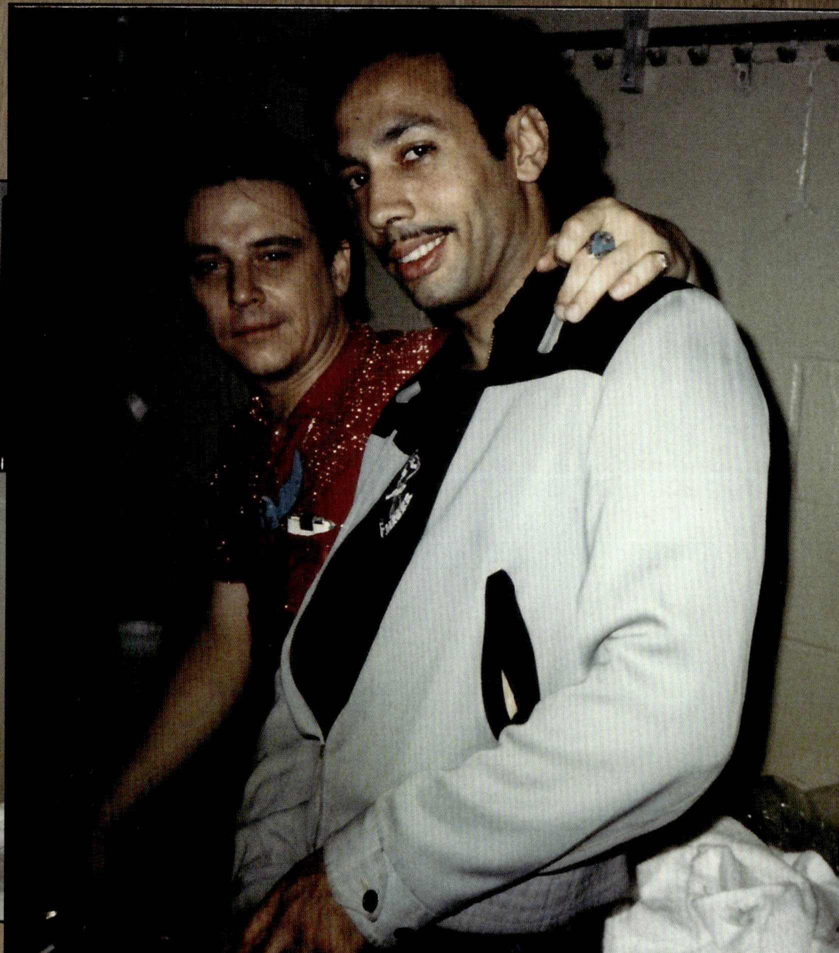

ON TOUR WITH THE T-BIRDS
1986-1987

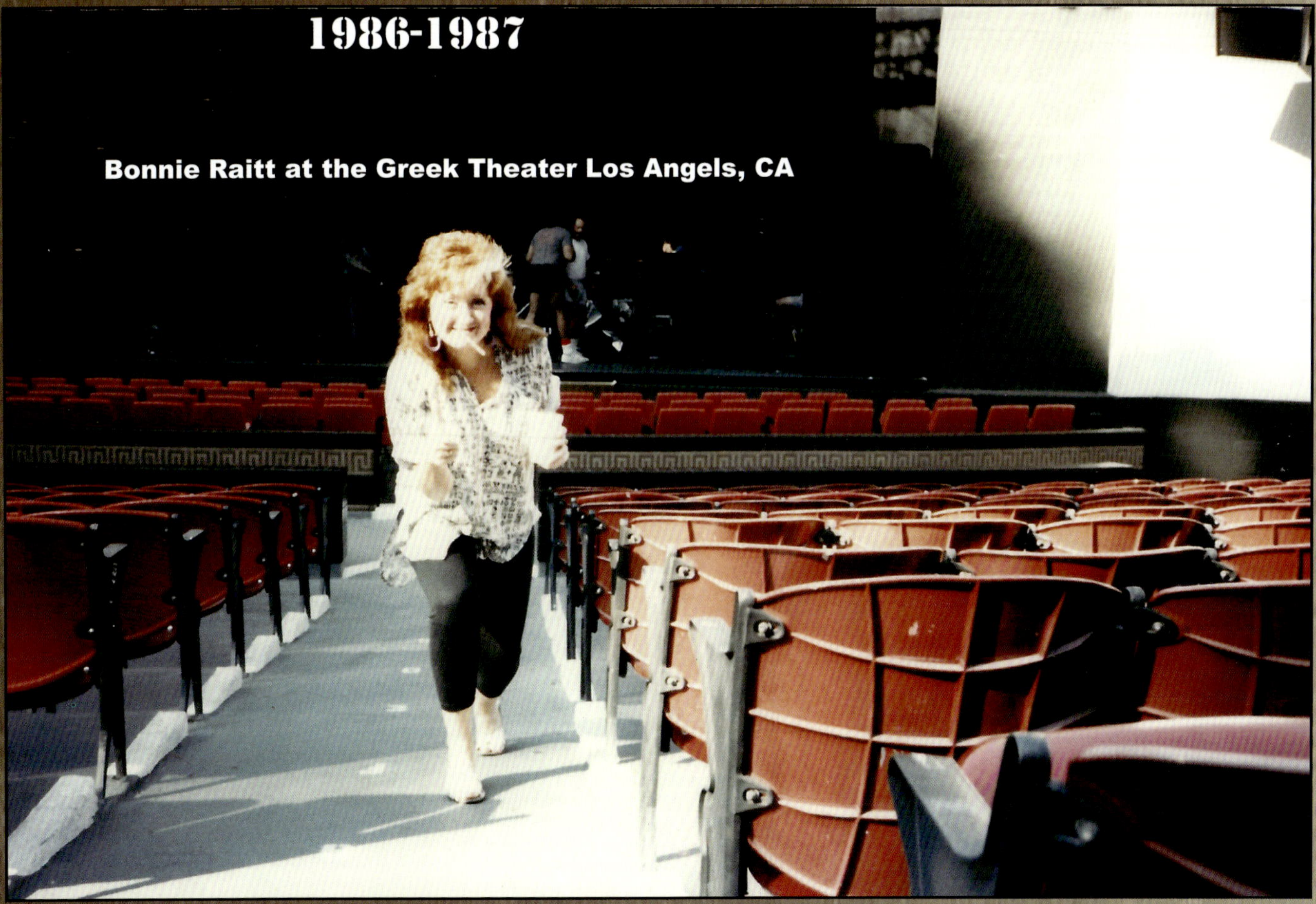

Bonnie Raitt at the Greek Theater Los Angels, CA

Jr Brantley, Fran Christina, Dave Edmunds, JLV, Bob Dylan, Kim Wilson, Preston Hubbard
Madison Square Garden NY, NY

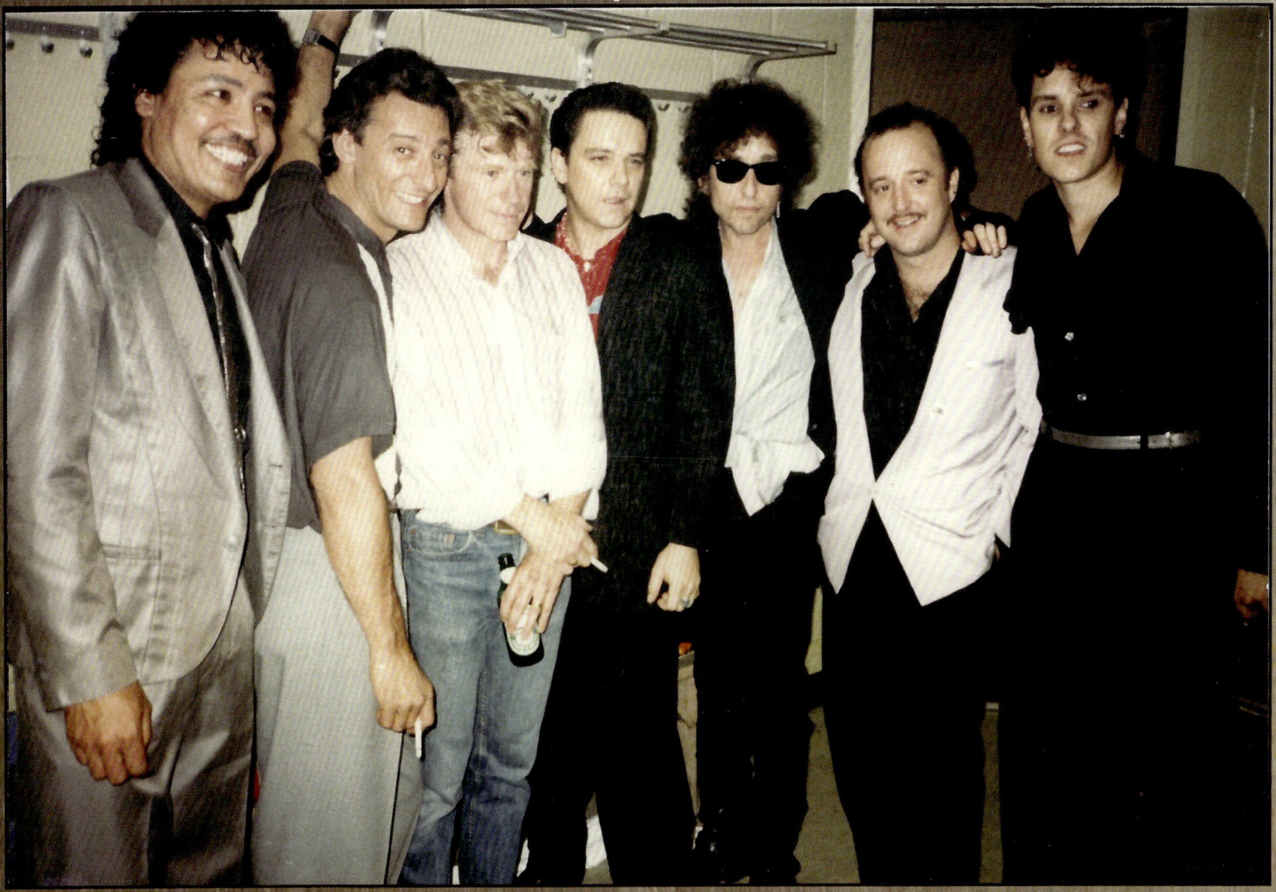

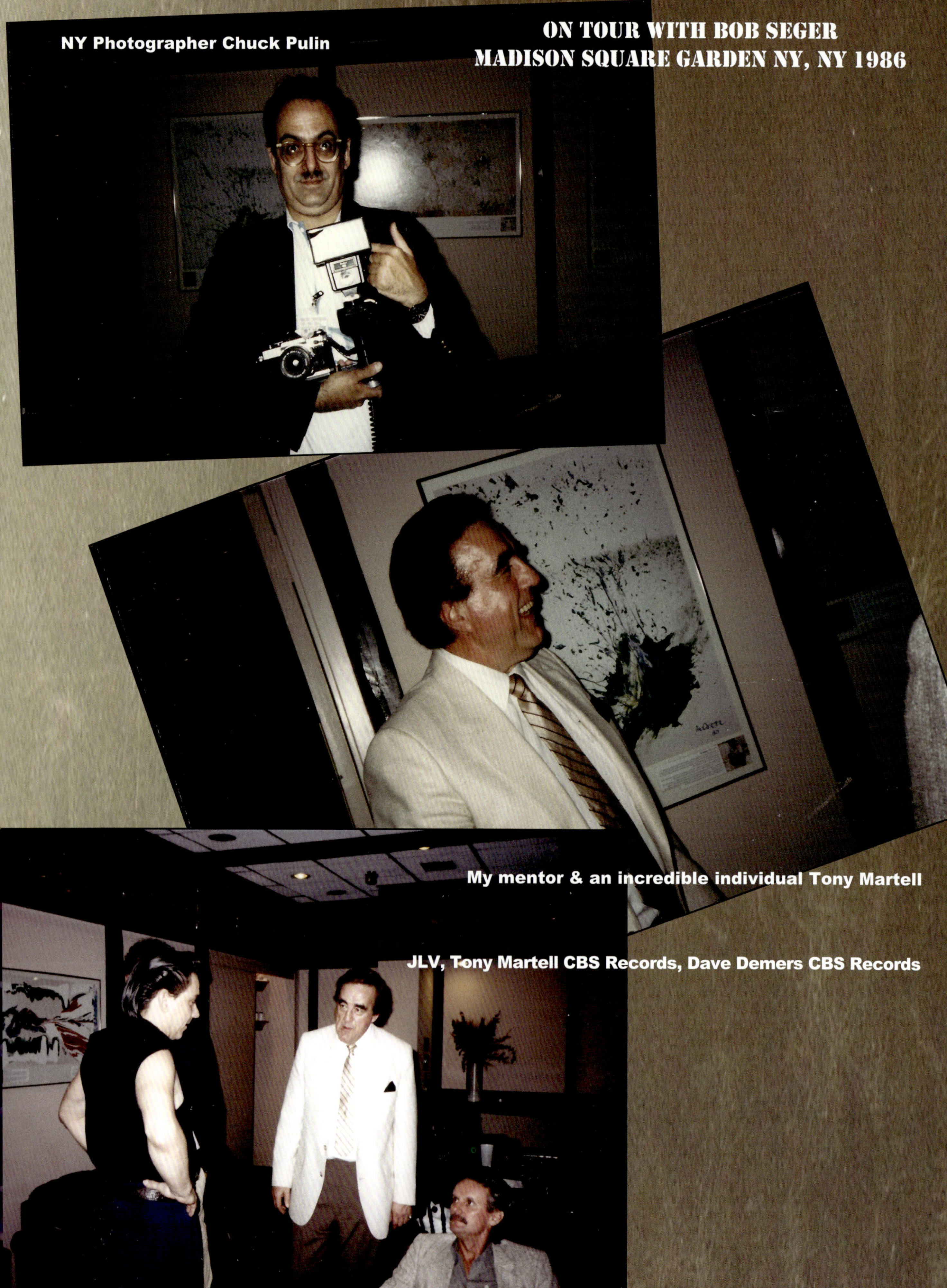

ON TOUR WITH BOB SEGER
MADISON SQUARE GARDEN NY, NY 1986

NY Photographer Chuck Pulin

My mentor & an incredible individual Tony Martell

JLV, Tony Martell CBS Records, Dave Demers CBS Records

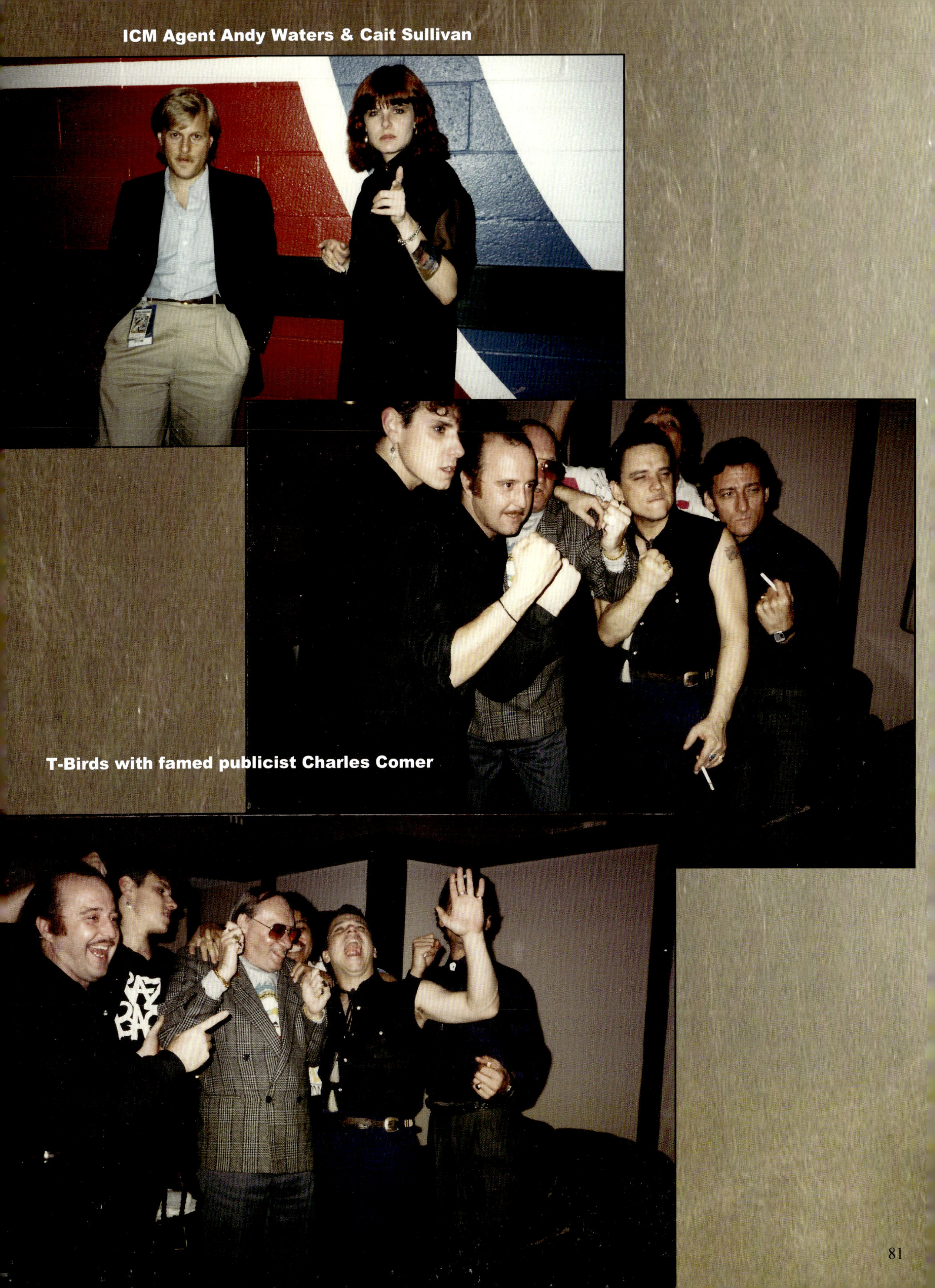

ICM Agent Andy Waters & Cait Sullivan

T-Birds with famed publicist Charles Comer

The Fabulous Thunderbirds Marching Band

Marlene & Jerry Proct on stage at Madison Square Garden

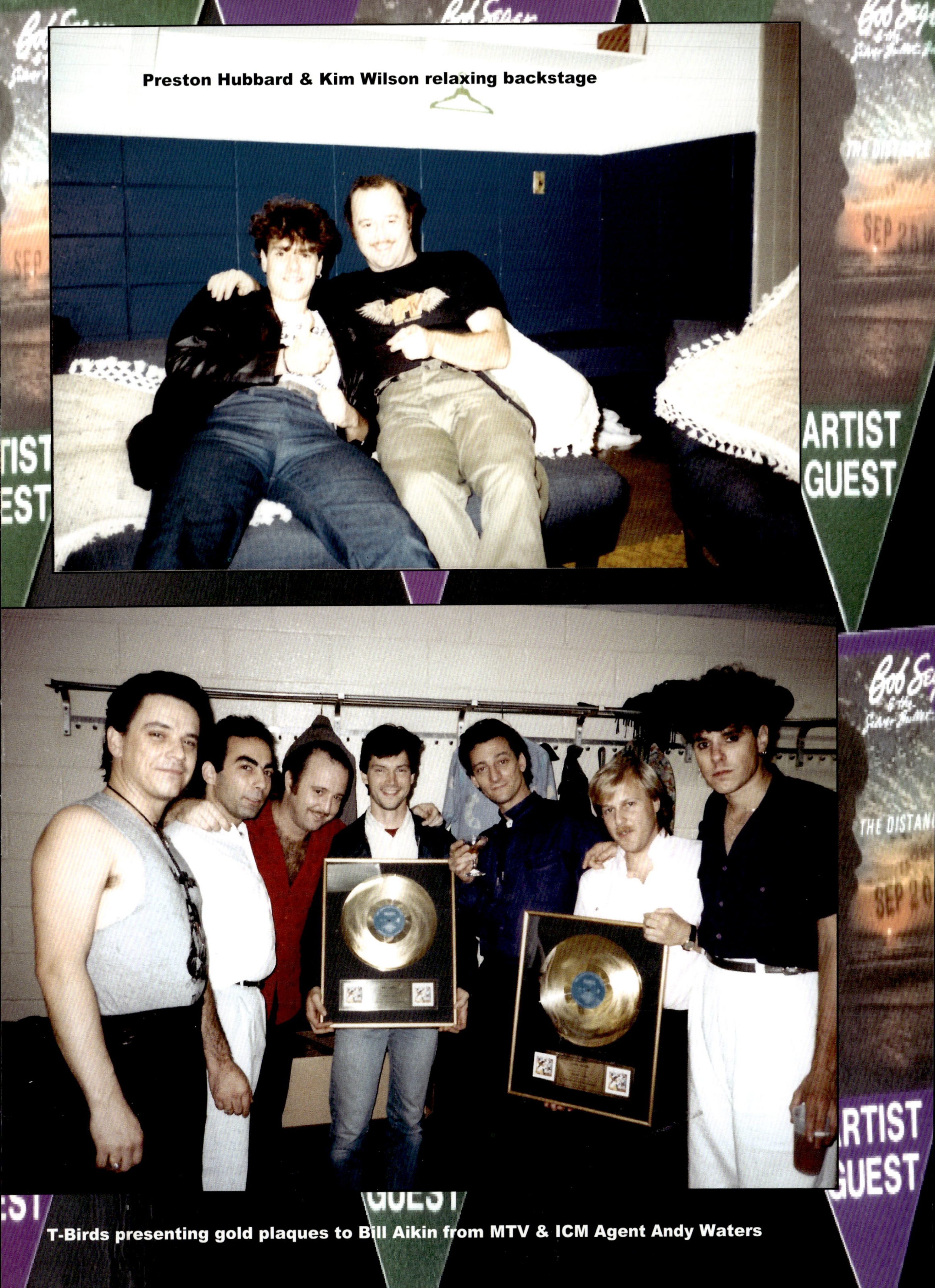

Preston Hubbard & Kim Wilson relaxing backstage

T-Birds presenting gold plaques to Bill Aikin from MTV & ICM Agent Andy Waters

My good friend Cait Sullivan's daughter Marissa backstage at Madison Square Garden

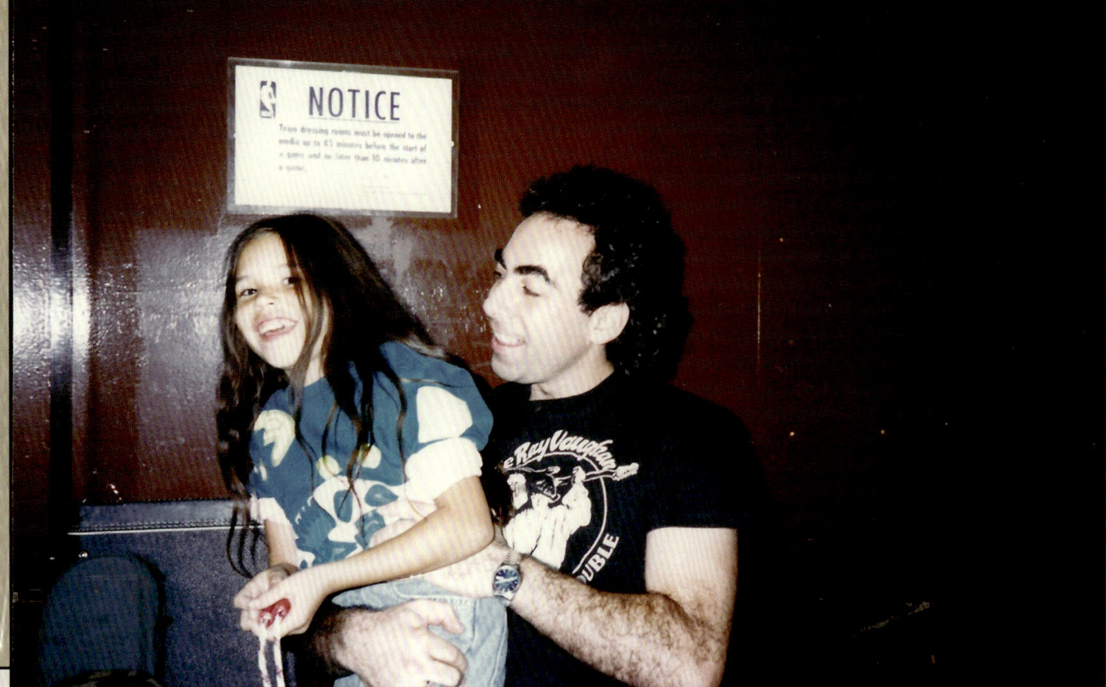

Our longtime business manager & friend Bill V

Our amazing CBS Records publicist Sue Sawyer

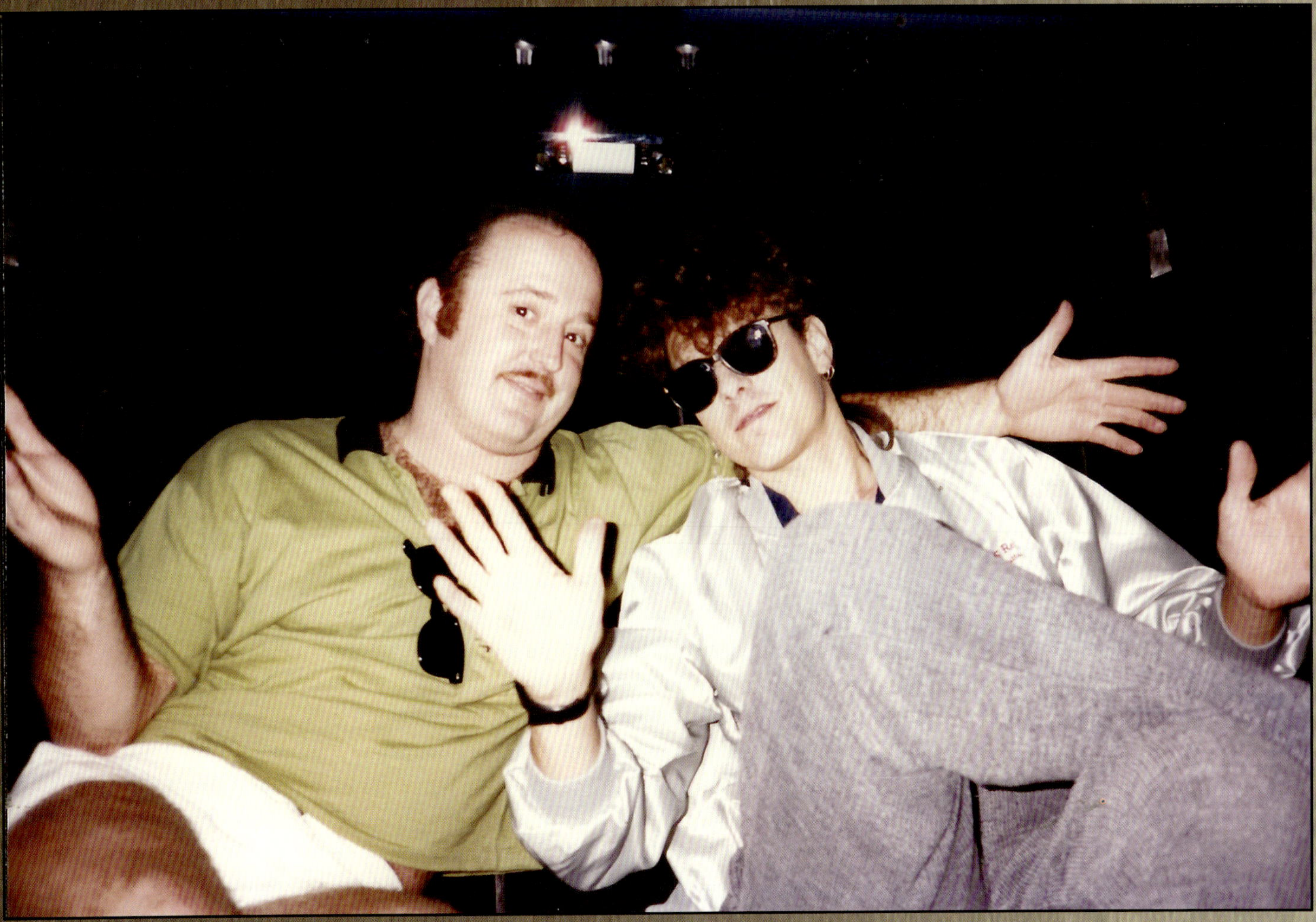

Above: Kim & Preston

Below: Fran with brother Richard Christina

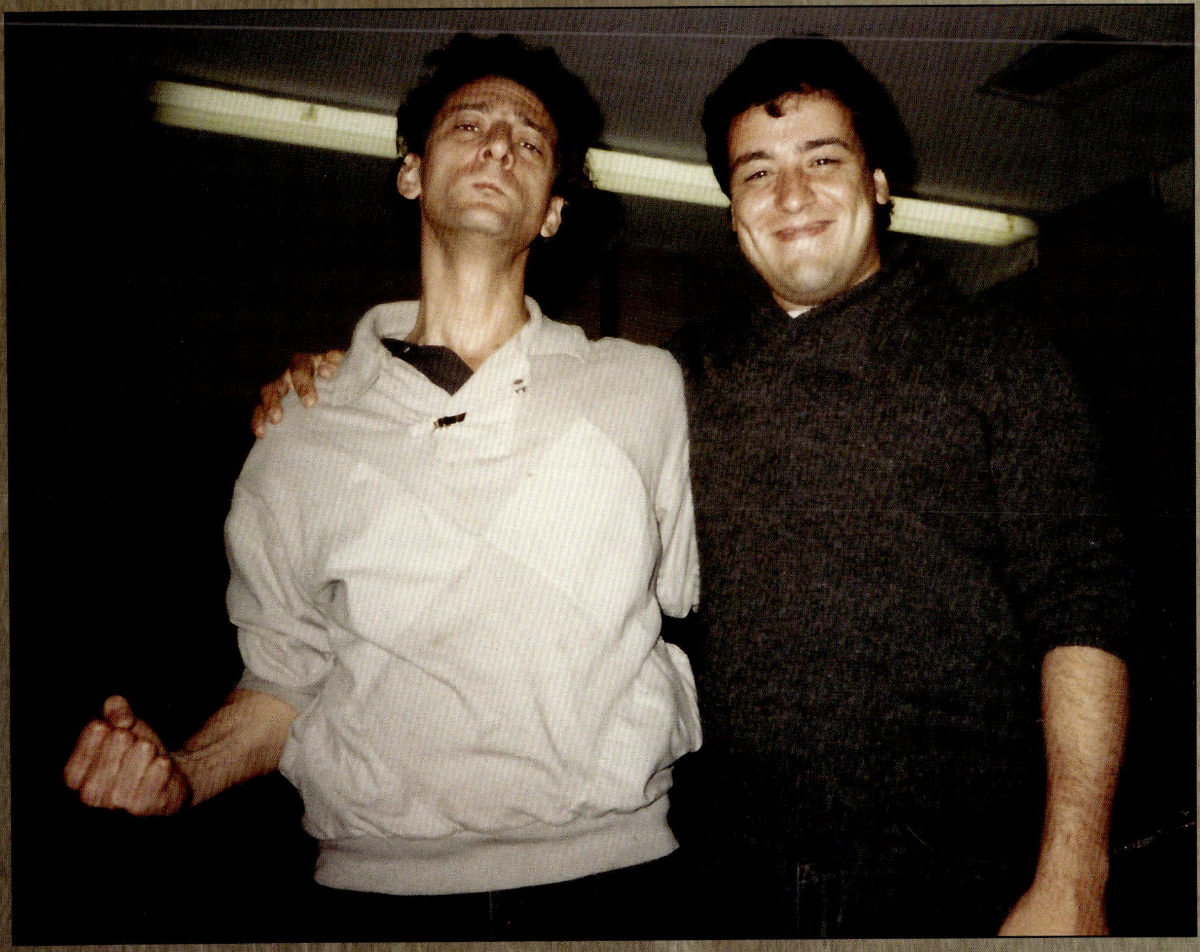

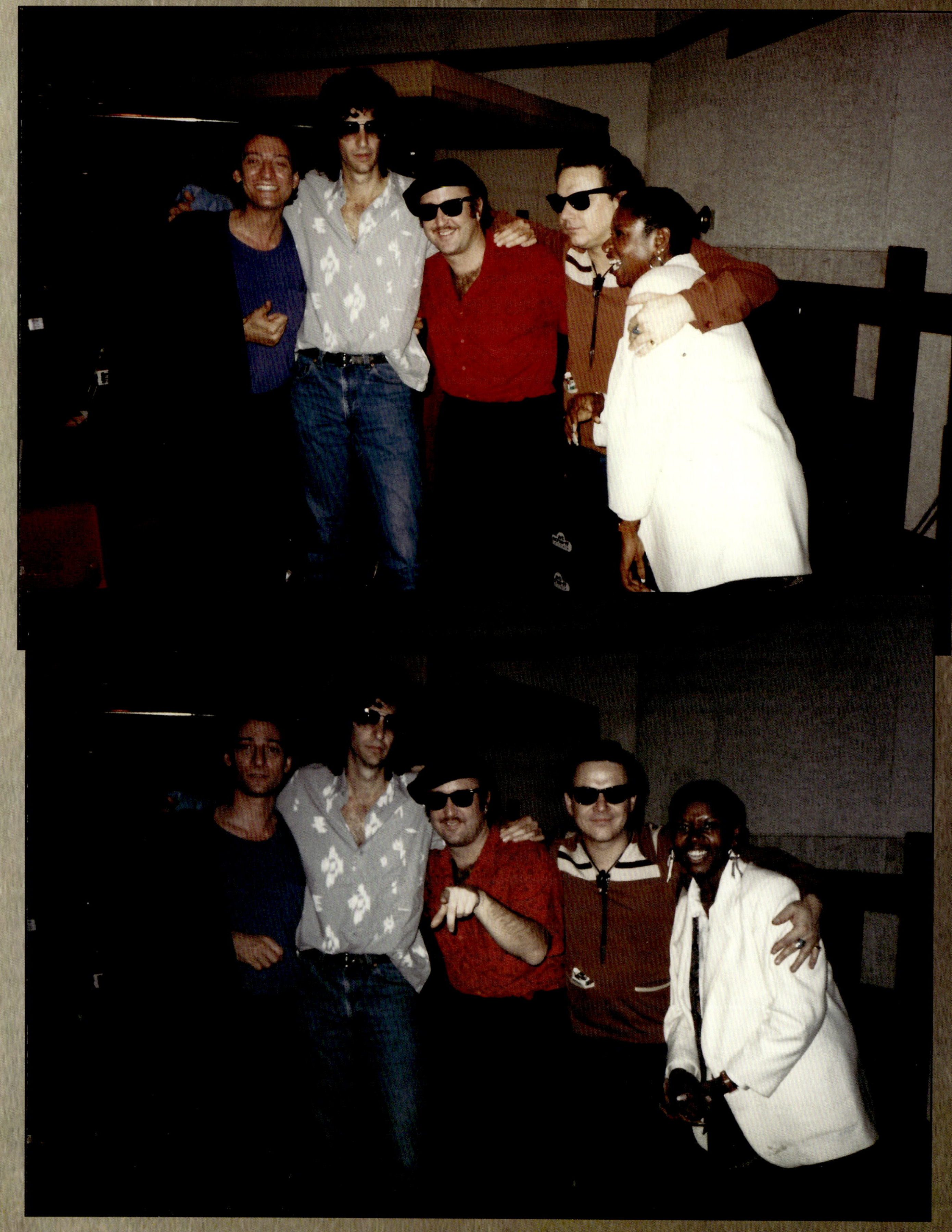

HOWARD STERN & ROBIN QUIVERS
NY, NY 1986

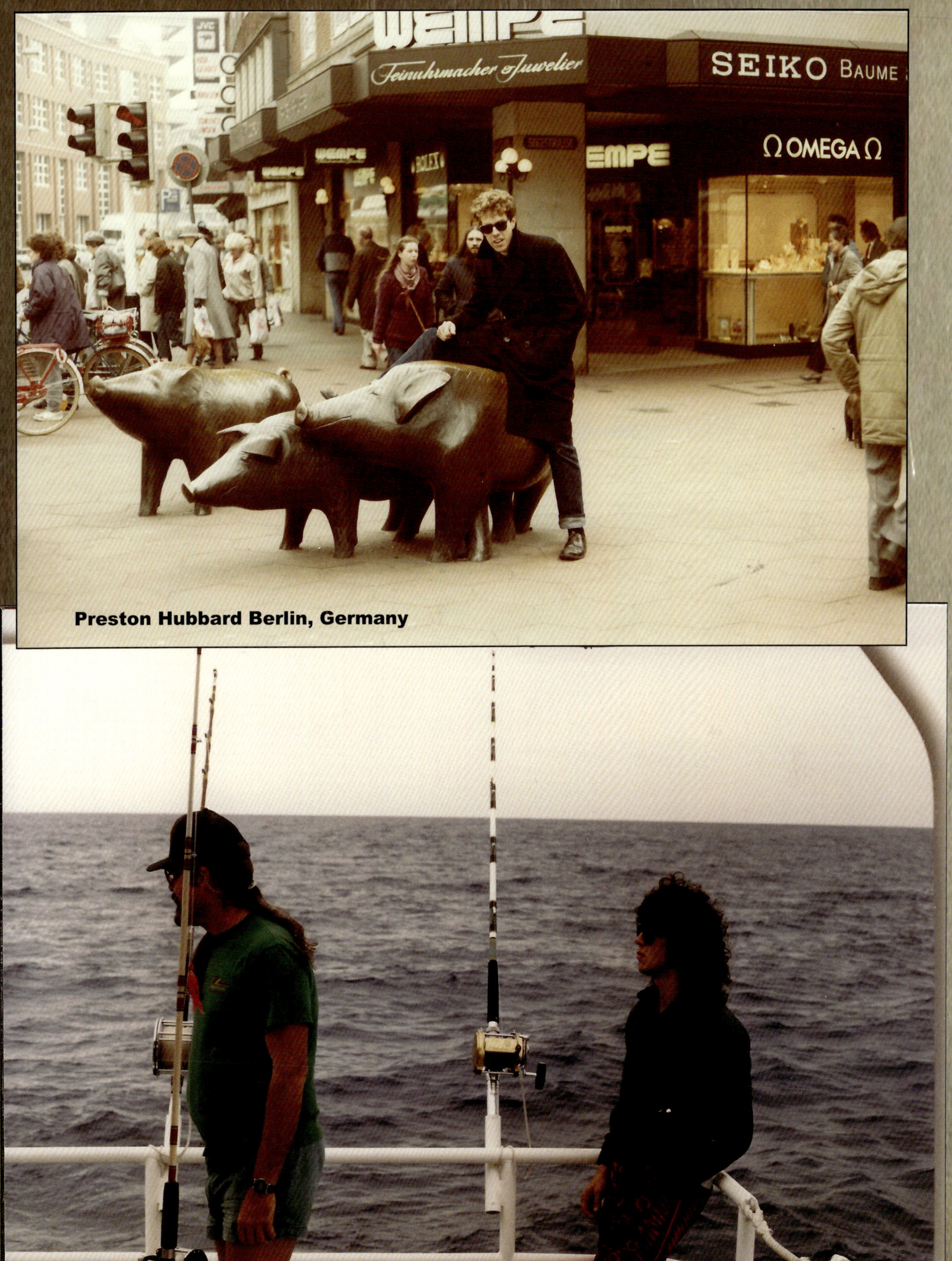

Preston Hubbard Berlin, Germany

T-Bird sound engineer Doug Chappell & Doyle Bramhall II fishing out on the open ocean while in Hawaii

SRV & JLV 1987

At a Fabulous Thunderbirds show Chris Kelly of Robin Guitars presented Jimmie Vaughan with a beautiful sunburst double neck guitar. This unusual guitar found a place in our large rolling coffin case which held about 8 guitars but rarely found its way out of the case and onto the stage. About this time the T-Birds and SRV were touring together on a regular basis and now the two brothers were finally sharing the same stage. At one show's encore that double neck guitar was pulled from its case and handed to Stevie Ray who walked to center stage and started to riff away. At the same time JV seemed to sneak up behind Stevie grabbing the second neck and played along with his brother. The crowd roared with their approval and this same scene played out in many encores to come.

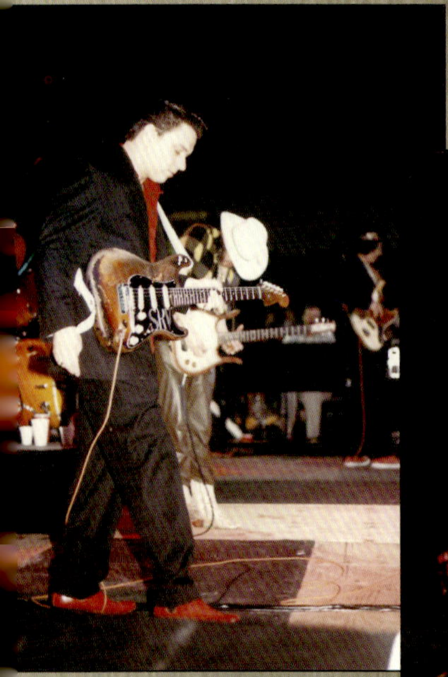

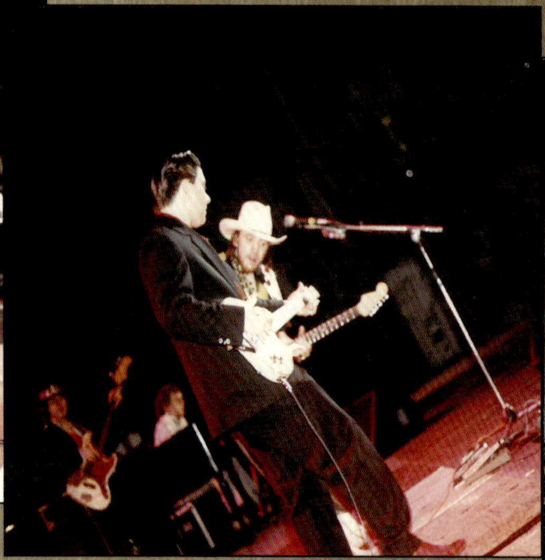

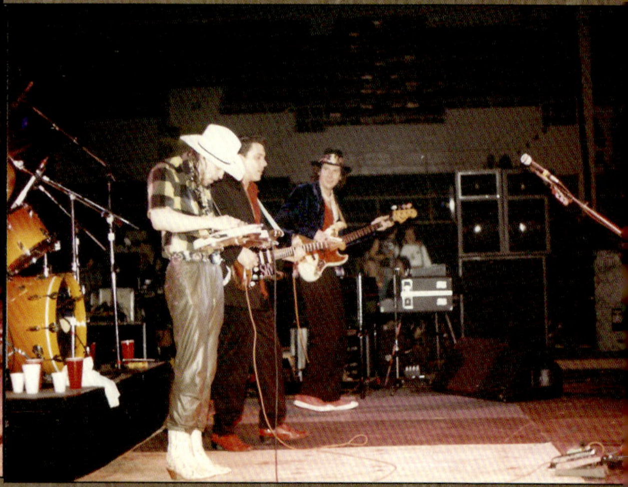

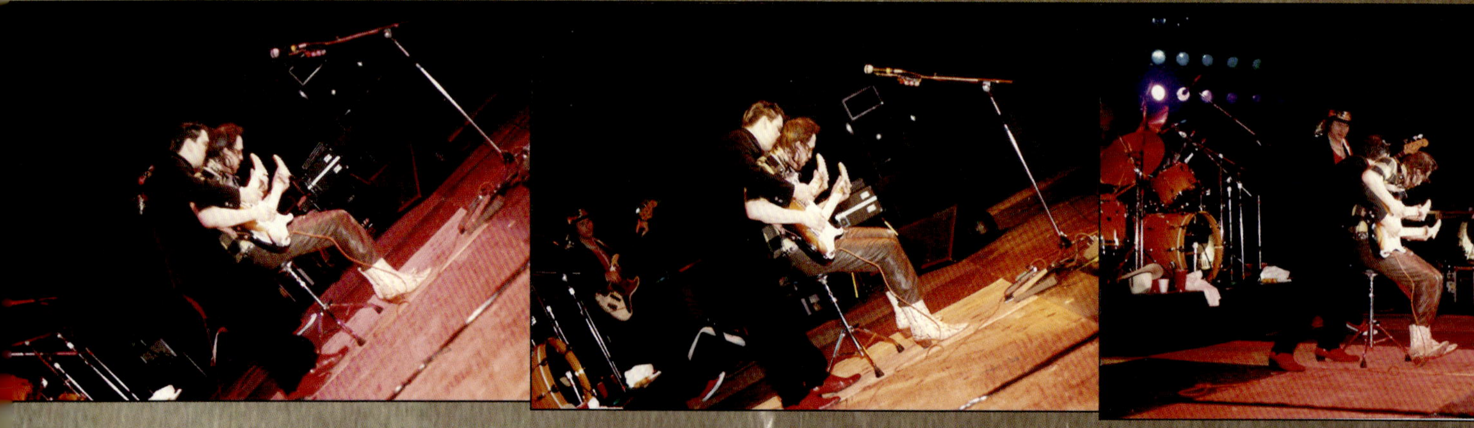

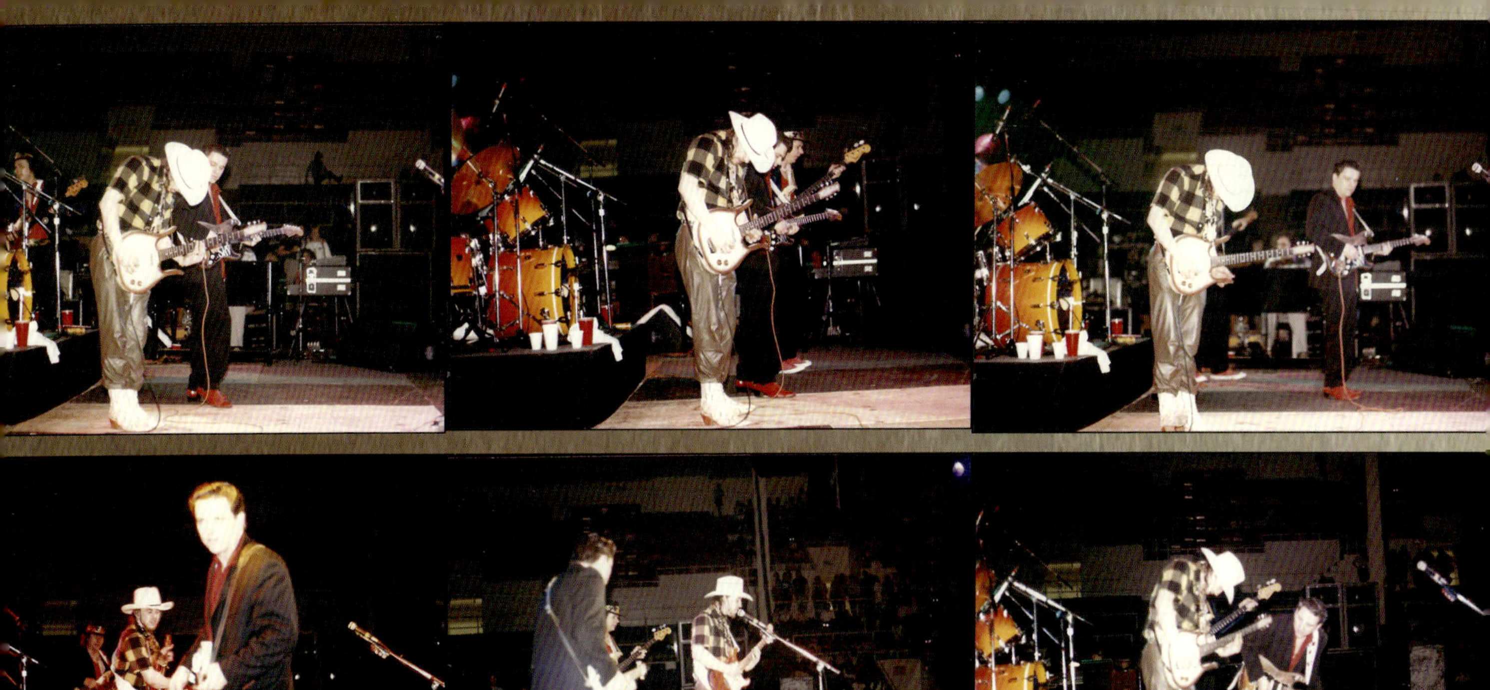

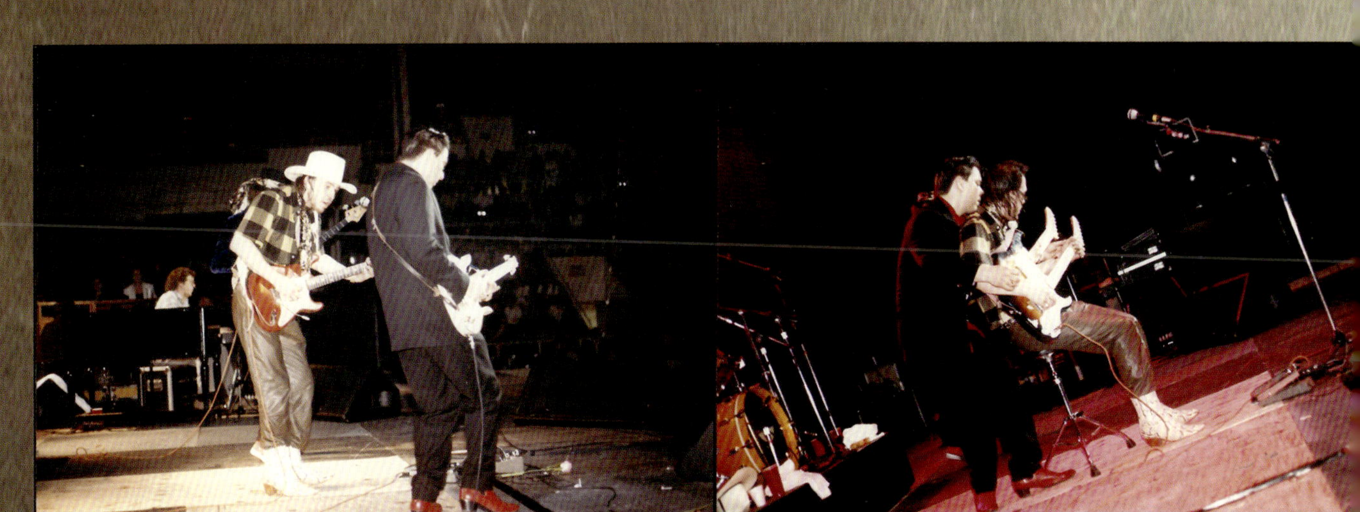

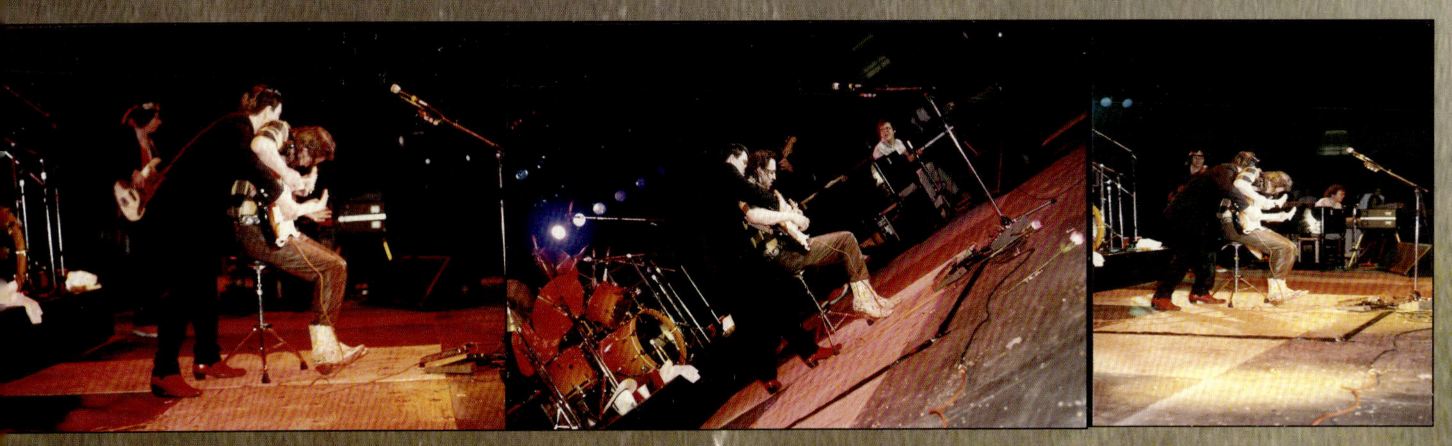

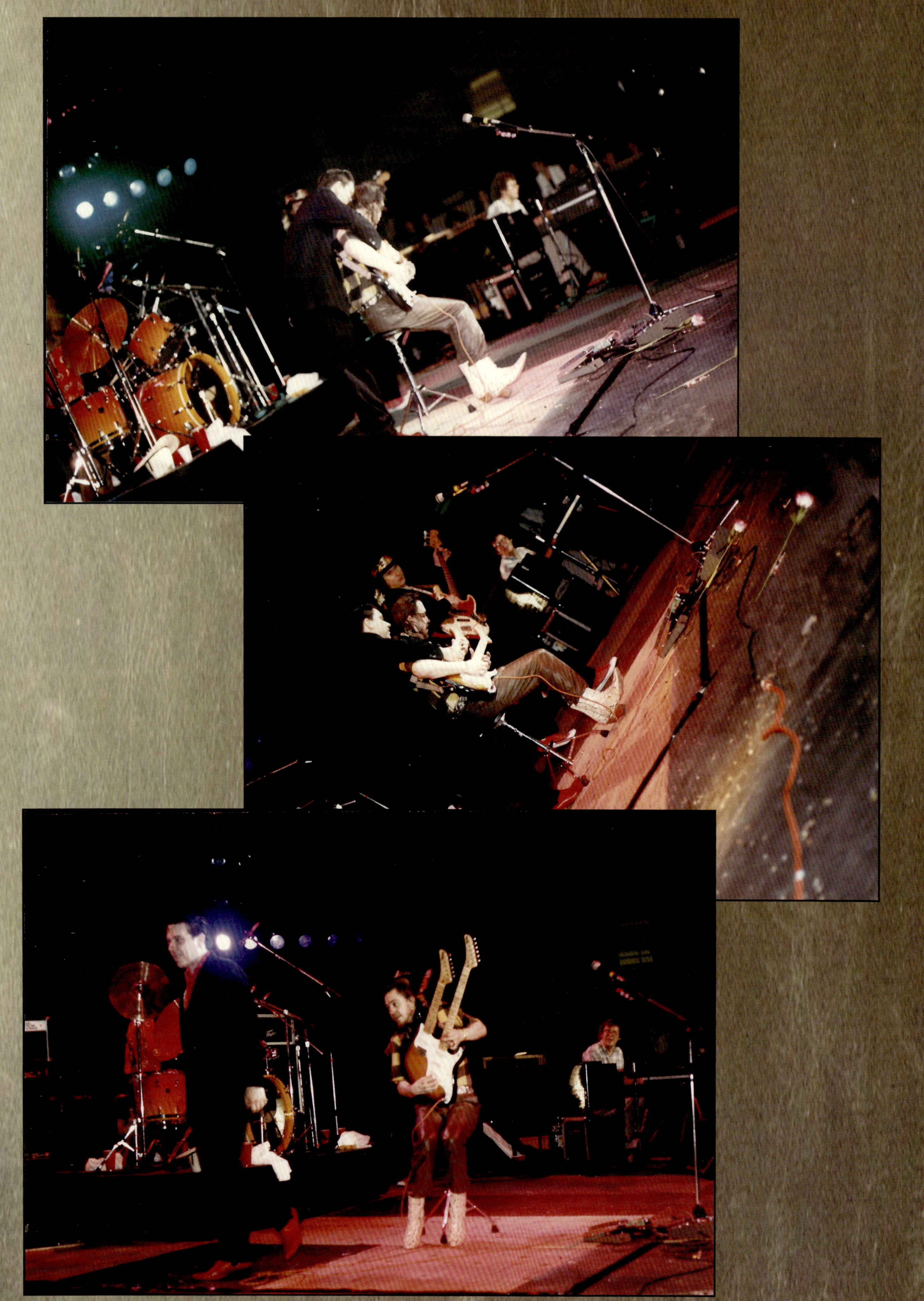

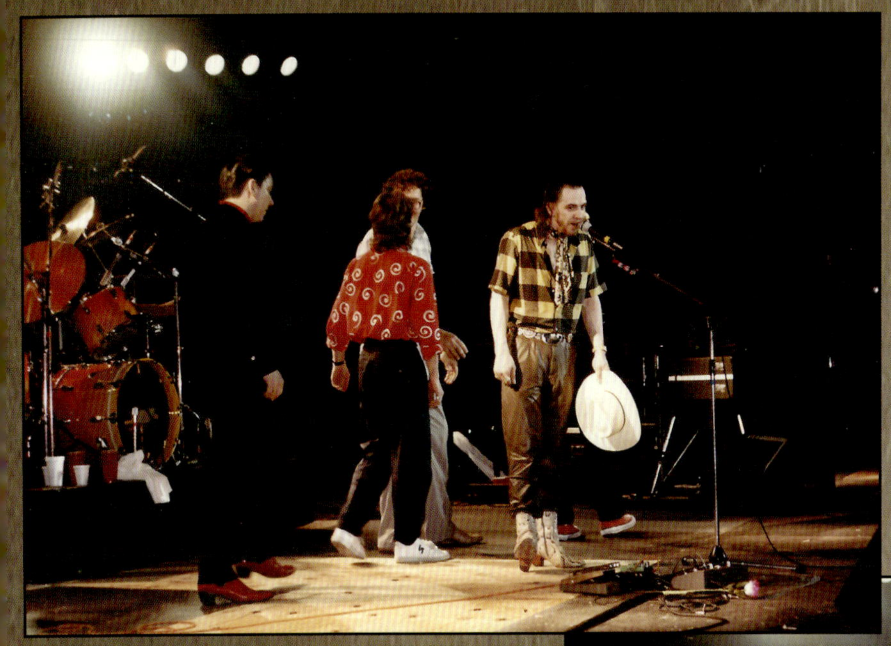

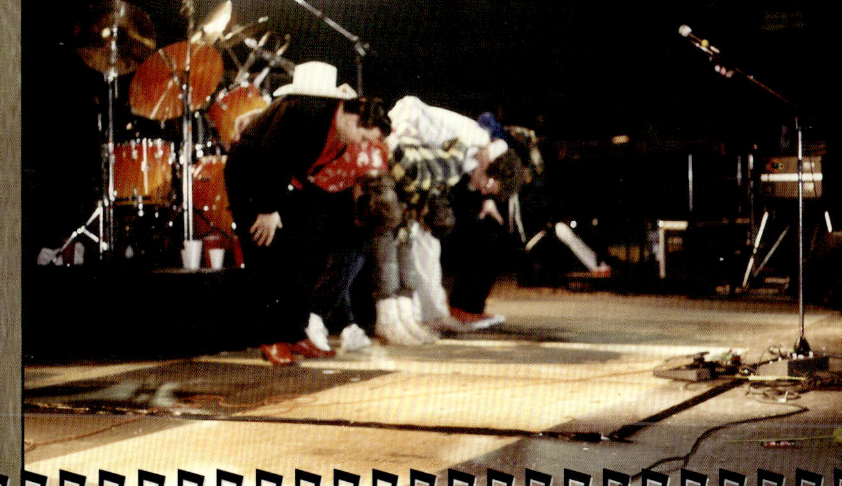

Chapter 12: Wrap It Up

In 1988 it was time for the T-Birds to start recording the follow up album to Tuff Enuff. Dave Edmunds would once again produce the album but this time it would be recorded at Ardent Studios in Memphis, TN. This was the start of a long relationship with Memphis and Austin as the bands I was working with were attracted to both the studios and the musical heritage of Memphis.

Ardent Studios was the place to record at that time, as you could always find a who's who of musicians recording at any given time. From ZZ Top to Joe Walsh to REM or Al Green. There were three working studios but all the musicians would take their breaks in the same lounge.

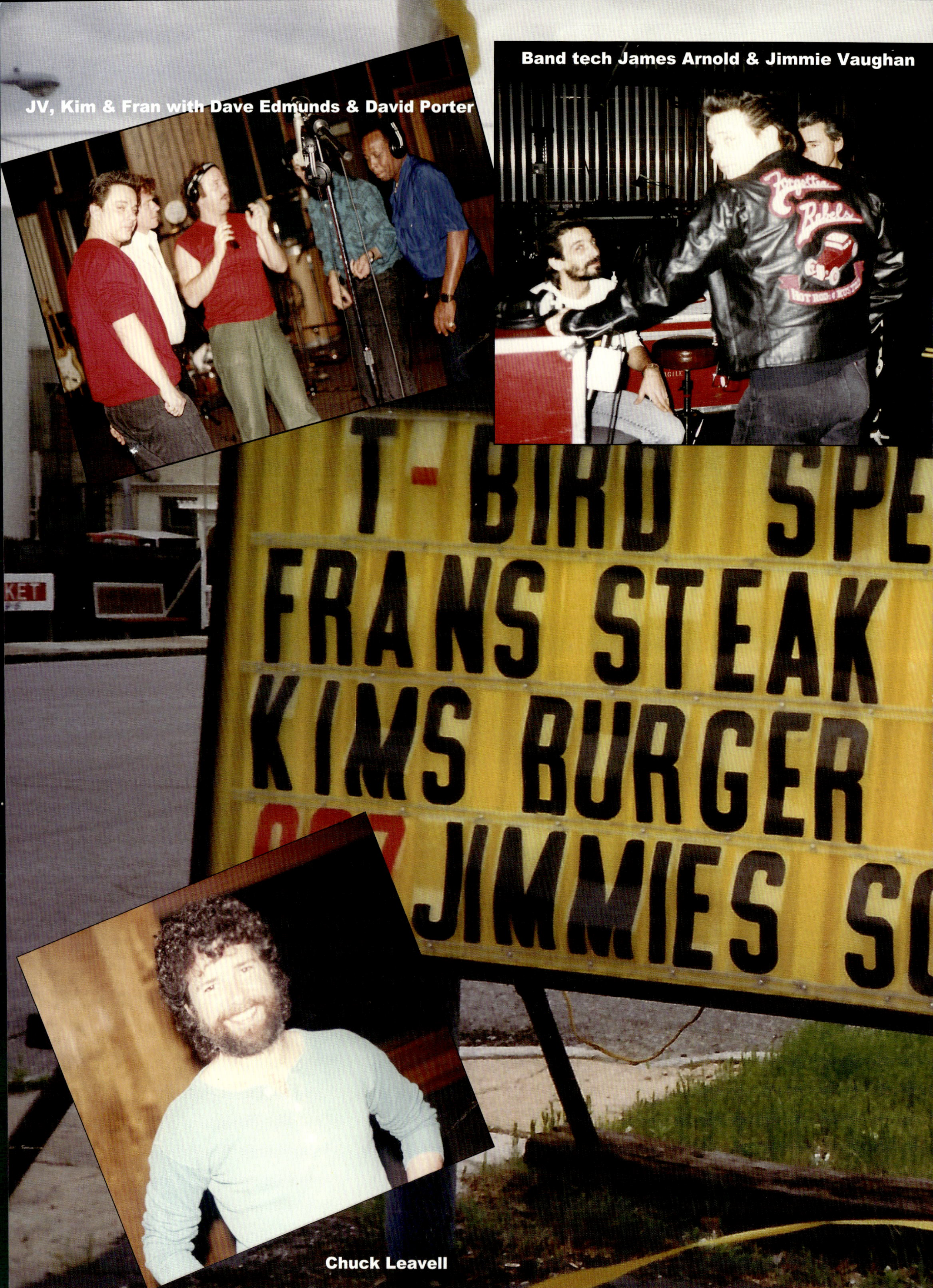

JV, Kim & Fran with Dave Edmunds & David Porter

Band tech James Arnold & Jimmie Vaughan

Chuck Leavell

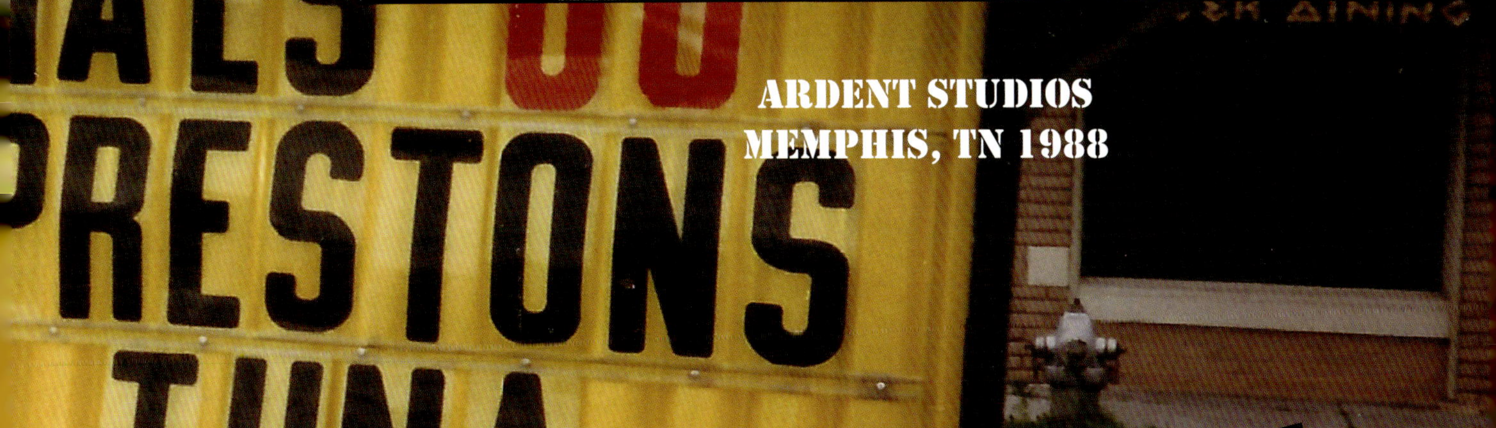

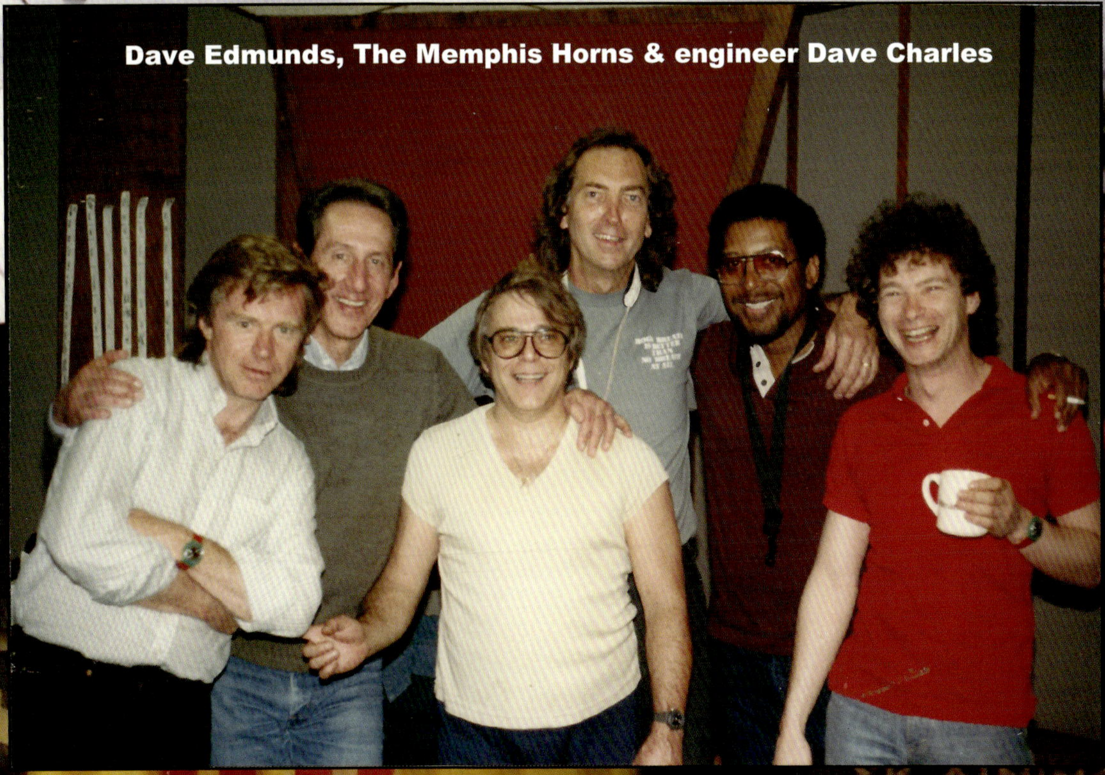

Dave Edmunds, The Memphis Horns & engineer Dave Charles

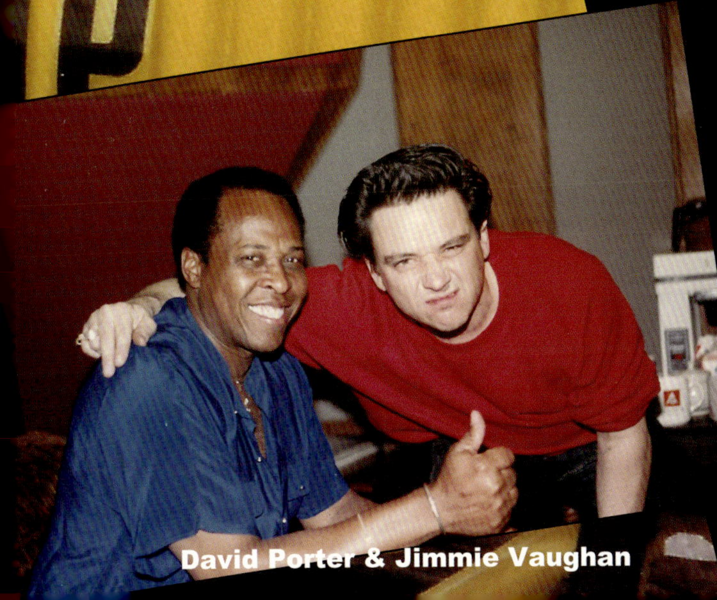

ARDENT STUDIOS
MEMPHIS, TN 1988

David Porter & Jimmie Vaughan

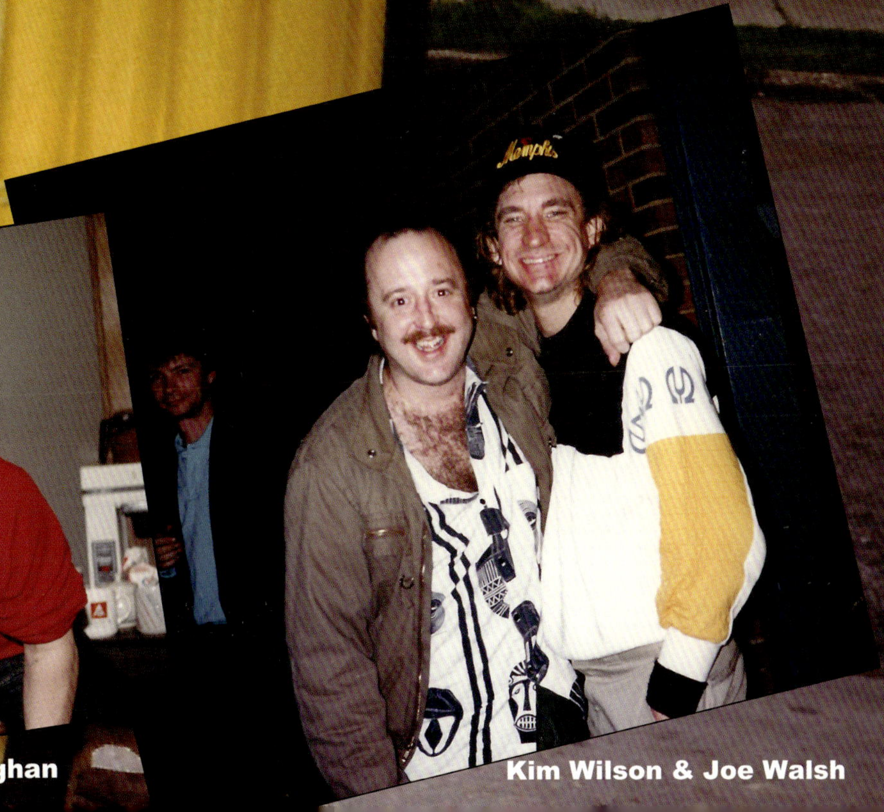

Kim Wilson & Joe Walsh

Chapter 13: The Red White and Blue Ball – Lee Atwater's Blues

In 1989 GOP Chairman Lee Atwater organized one of the George W. Bush Inaugural balls, The Red, White & Blues Ball. As a big fan of the blues he organized a star studded event which included Stevie and Jimmie Vaughan, BB King, Albert King, Joe Cocker, Delbert McClinton, Ron Wood and a host of others. The great thing about music is that no matter what party you're a part of every party gets the blues and Lee Atwater loved the blues like no other political operative.

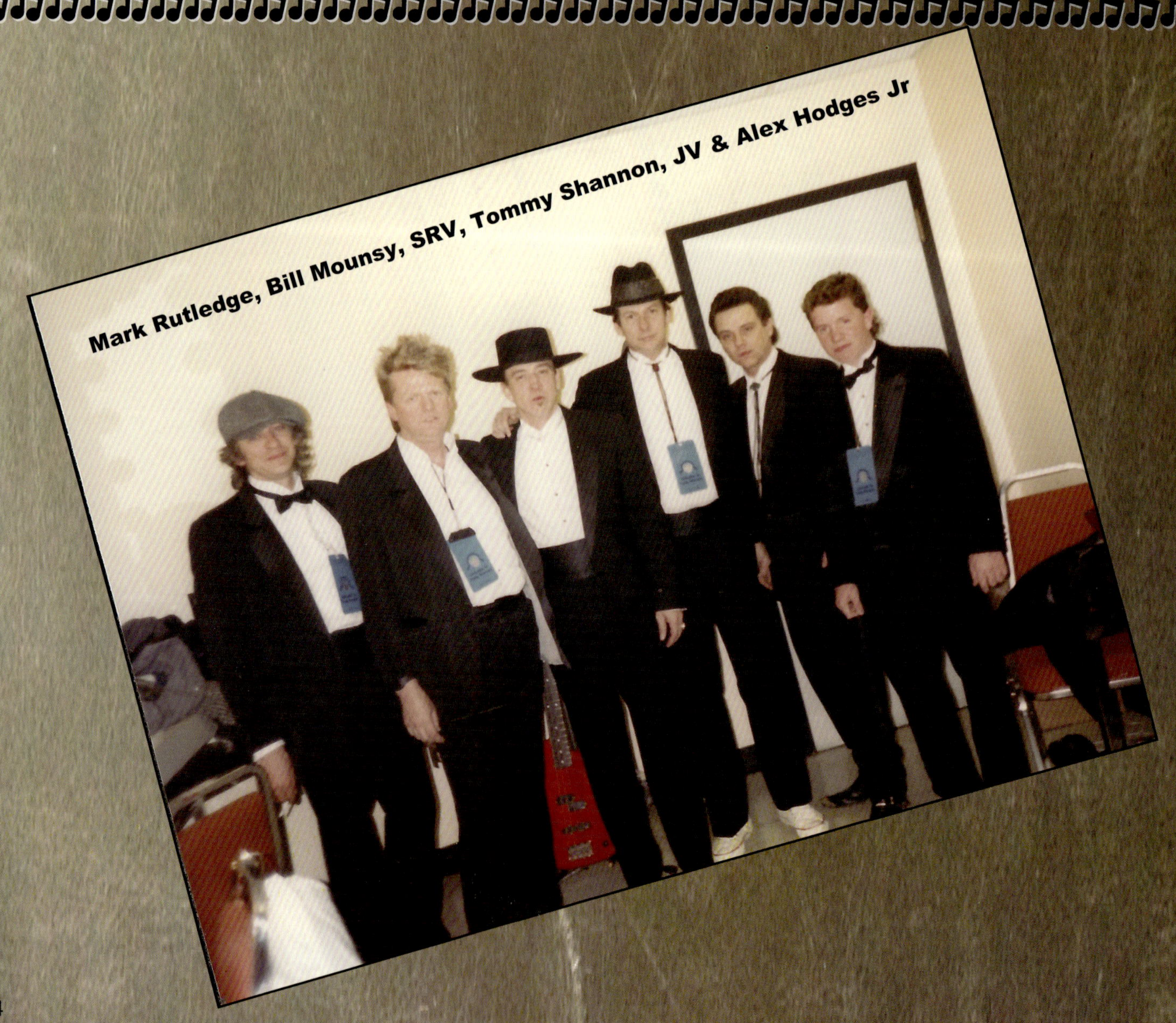
Mark Rutledge, Bill Mounsy, SRV, Tommy Shannon, JV & Alex Hodges Jr

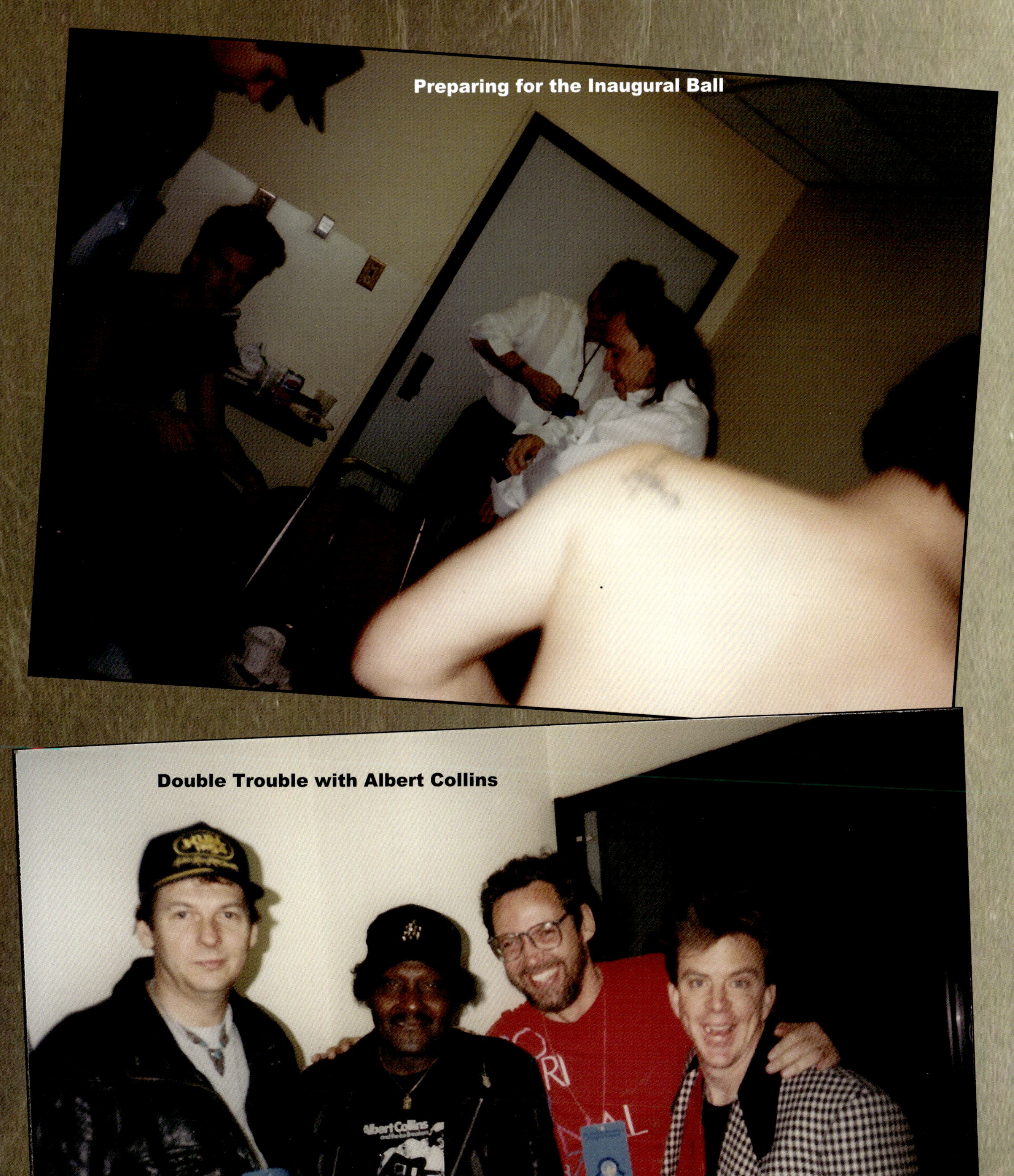

Preparing for the Inaugural Ball

Double Trouble with Albert Collins

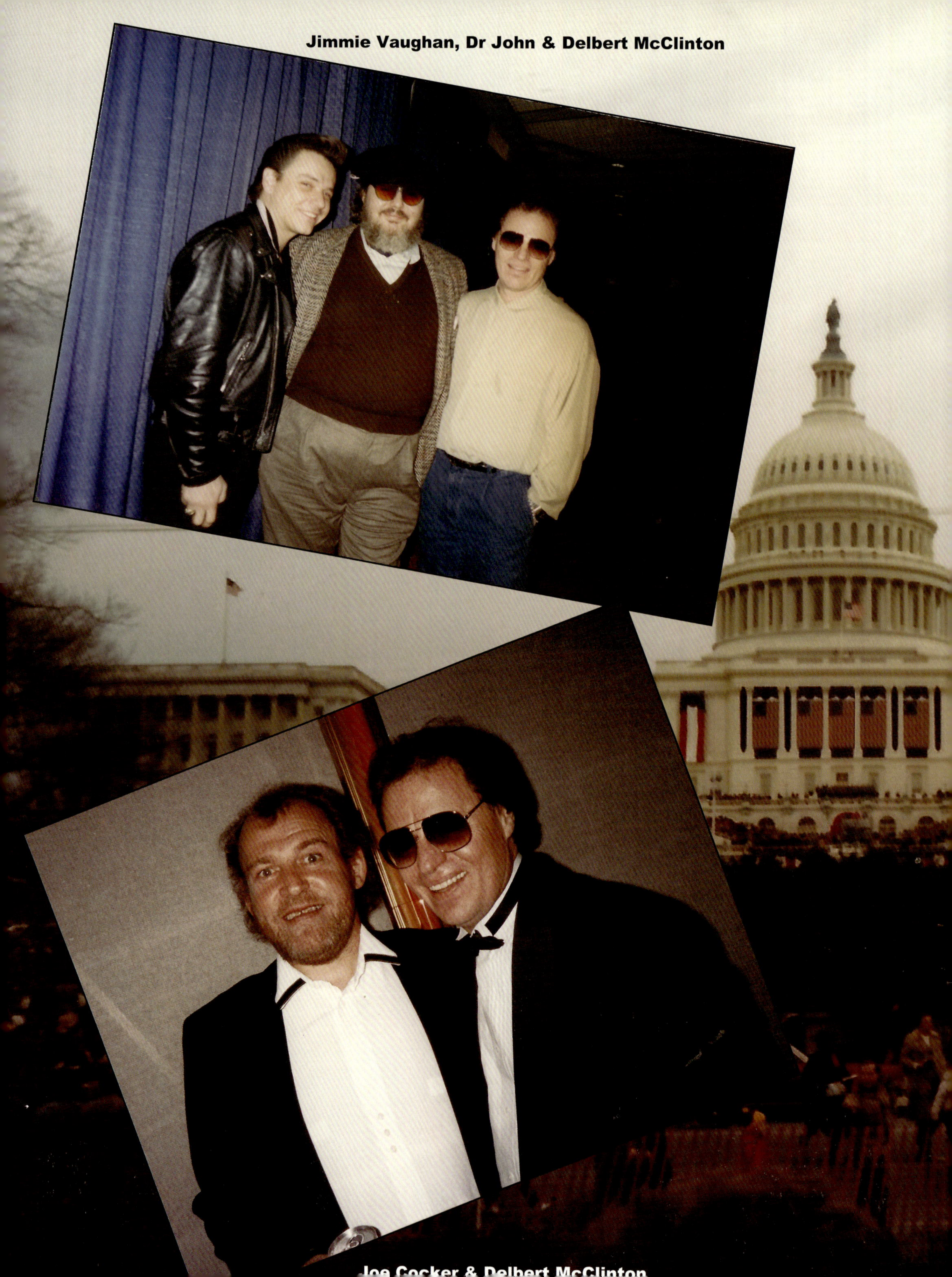

Jimmie Vaughan, Dr John & Delbert McClinton

Joe Cocker & Delbert McClinton

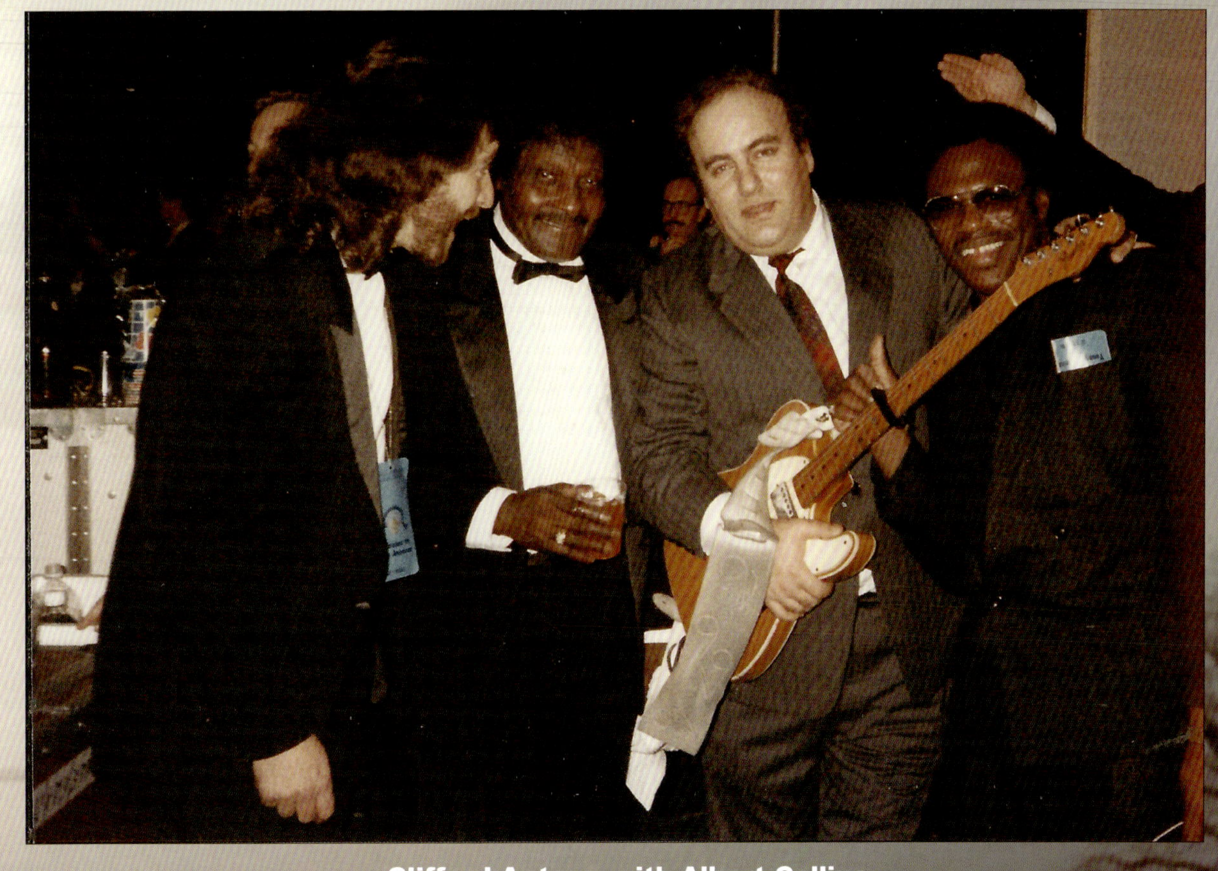

Clifford Antone with Albert Collins

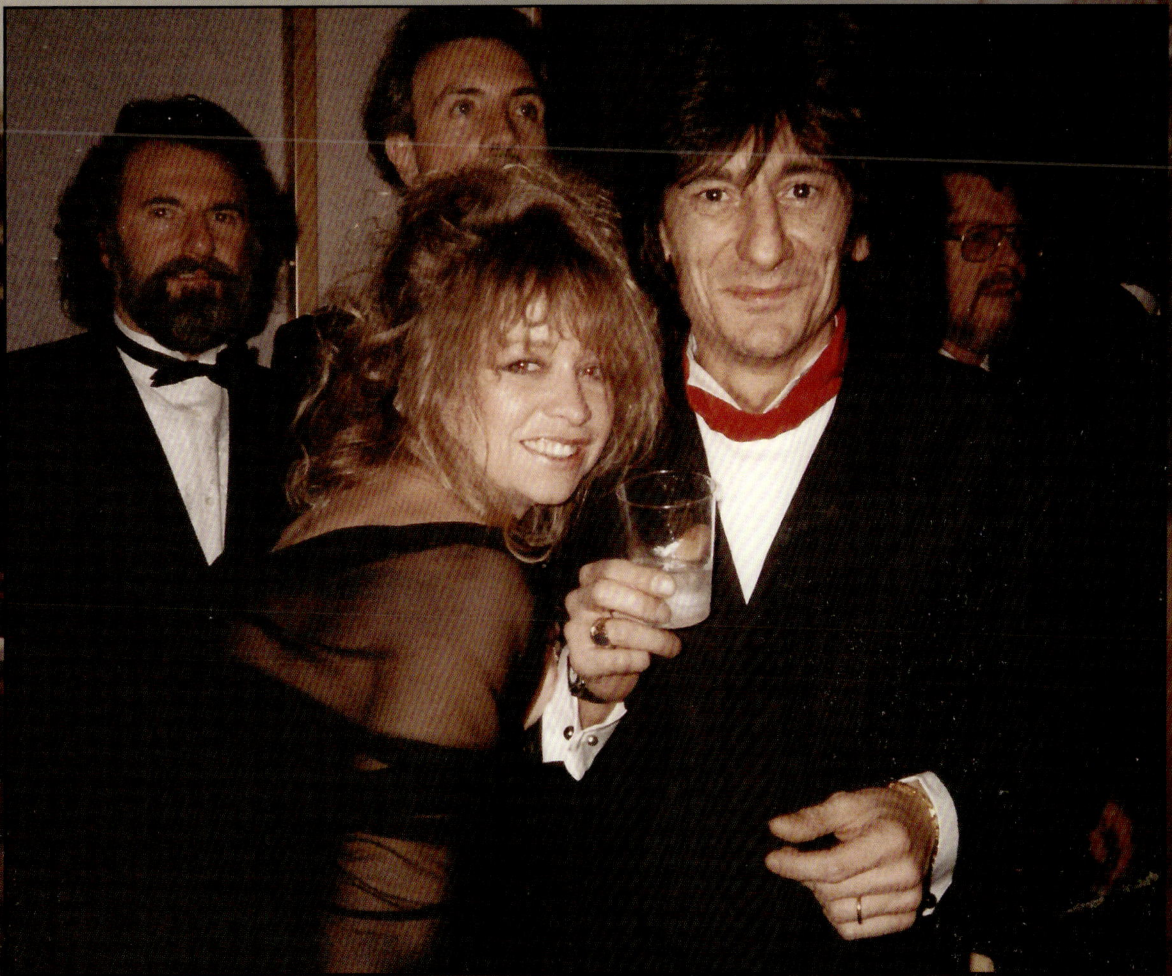

Jo Wood and Ronnie Wood

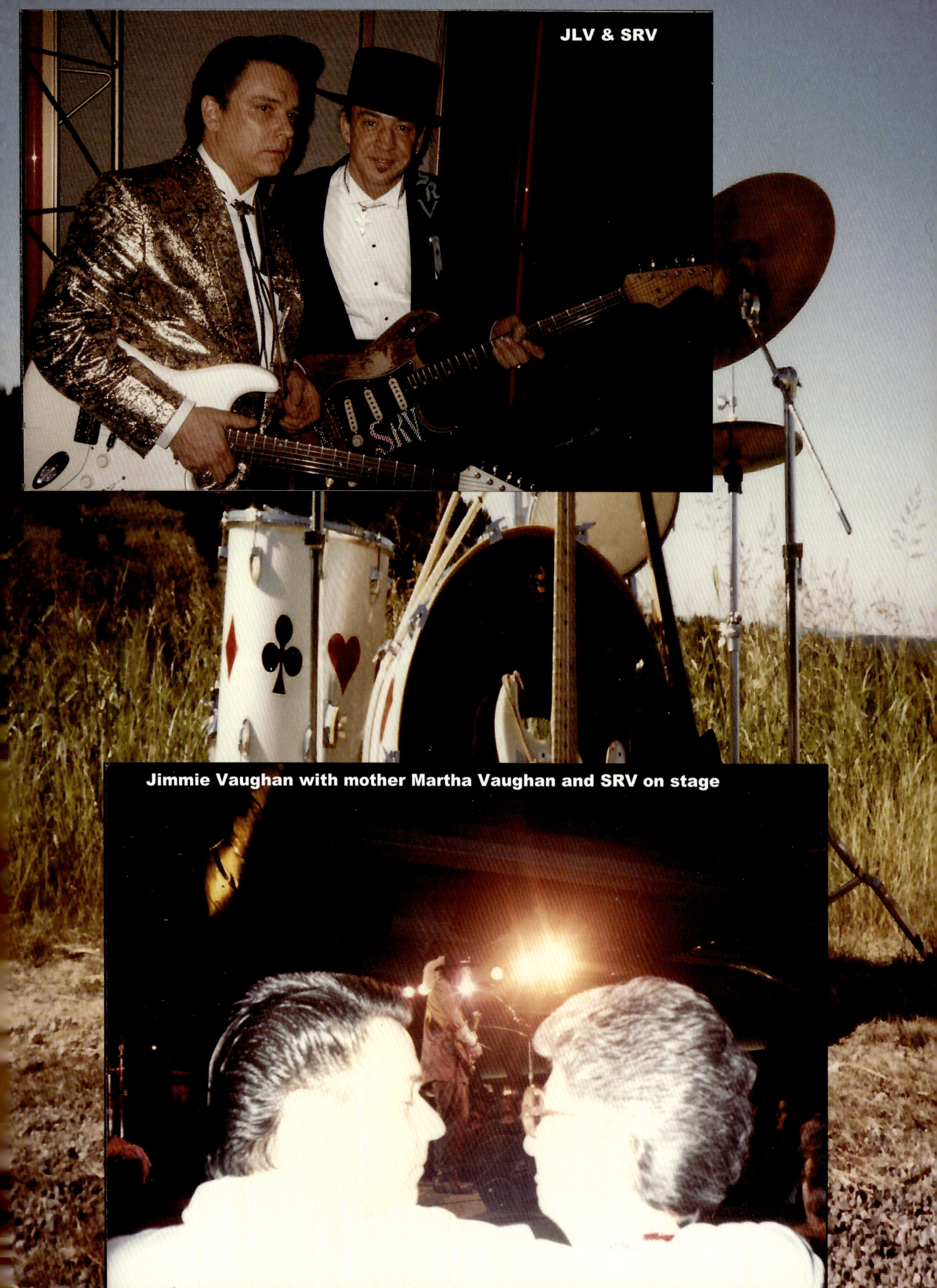
JLV & SRV

Jimmie Vaughan with mother Martha Vaughan and SRV on stage

Chapter 14: Long Way from Home with Jimmie & Stevie Ray Vaughan

In 1989 my world was met with some big changes as Jimmie Vaughan announced his departure from the Fabulous Thunderbirds. For months Sony Music (Formerly CBS Records) had hounded me about a Vaughan Brothers album. Finally Jimmie and Stevie were sitting down and planning a record together. With producer Nile Rodgers we returned to Memphis to start the recording of Family Style. The recording was started at Ardent Studios then completed back in Texas at The Dallas Sound Lab. The album everyone had been hoping for was now finished and set to be released in late September of 1990.

Six Strings Down SRV

In July of 1990 all of the Sony Music senior executives flew to Dallas for a listening party to celebrate the completion of Family Style. Up to this point the label had not heard a single song from the studio sessions but in Dallas they had lots to celebrate as the album well exceeded their expectations. Everybody had a smile on their faces especially Jimmie and Stevie who couldn't have been happier. While I worked with Sony setting up the new album for its September release Stevie went back on the road to fulfill his summer touring obligations.

One weekend looked particularly interesting as SRV & DT were set to perform with Eric Clapton and Robert Cray at the Alpine Valley Amphitheatre in WI. Jimmie and I thought it would be fun to attend these shows so we planned to be there on August 29 and 30. Of course this was a bittersweet weekend with incredible performances by both Clapton and Stevie with Jimmie joining both onstage for the evening's encore. The evening ended in tragedy as the helicopter carrying Stevie Ray and Clapton's crew members crashed on take off killing all on board. A weekend that would change many lives including mine forever. My thoughts and emotions could fill a book but my experiences of spending the prior seven months with two brothers was so very special and will never be forgotten.

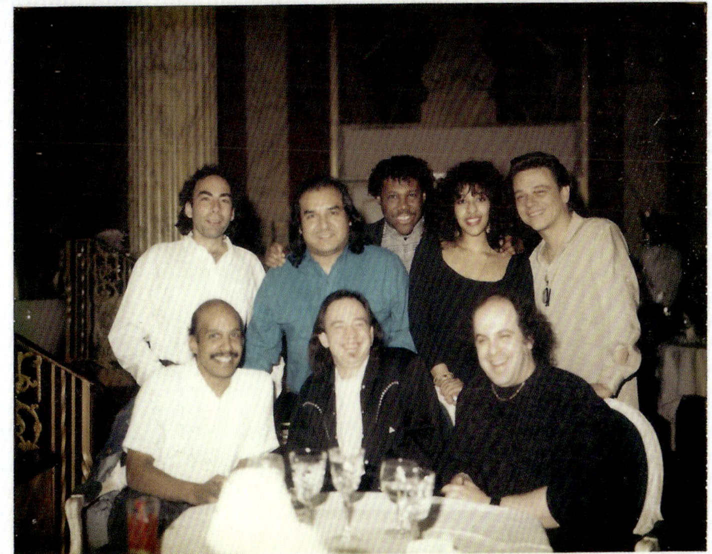

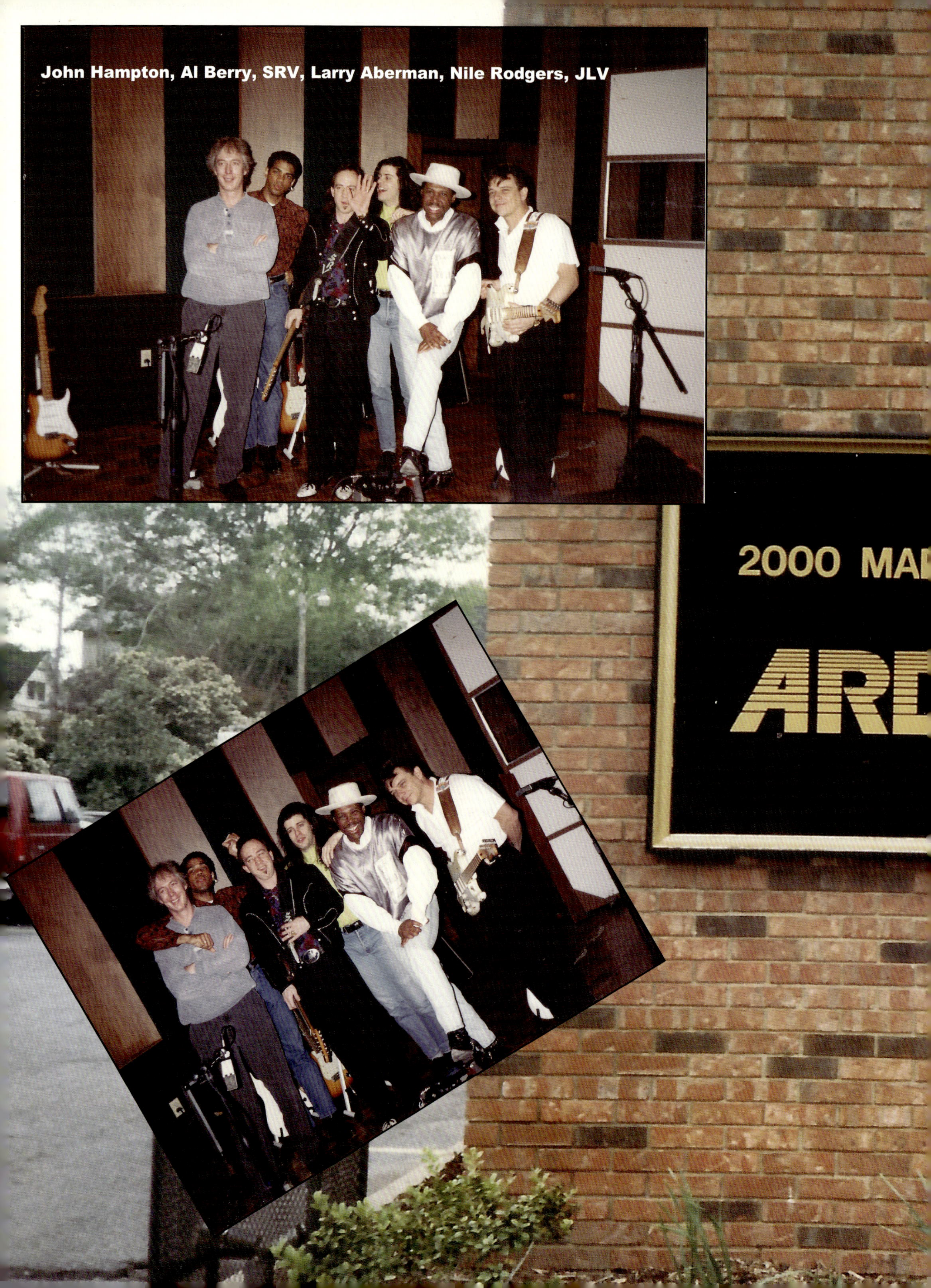

John Hampton, Al Berry, SRV, Larry Aberman, Nile Rodgers, JLV

Richard Hilton, JLV, Al Berry, Larry Aberman, SRV, Nile Rodgers

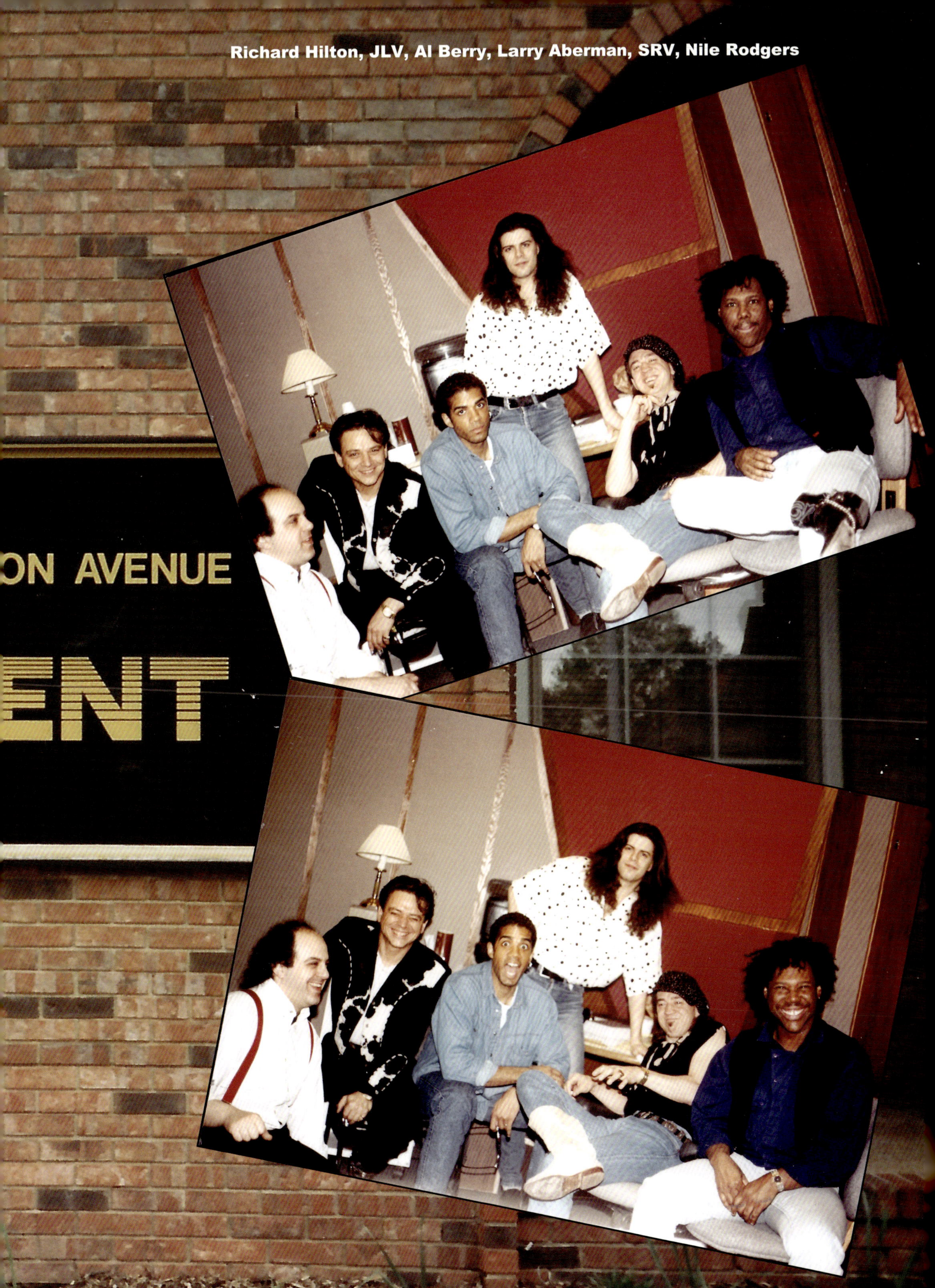

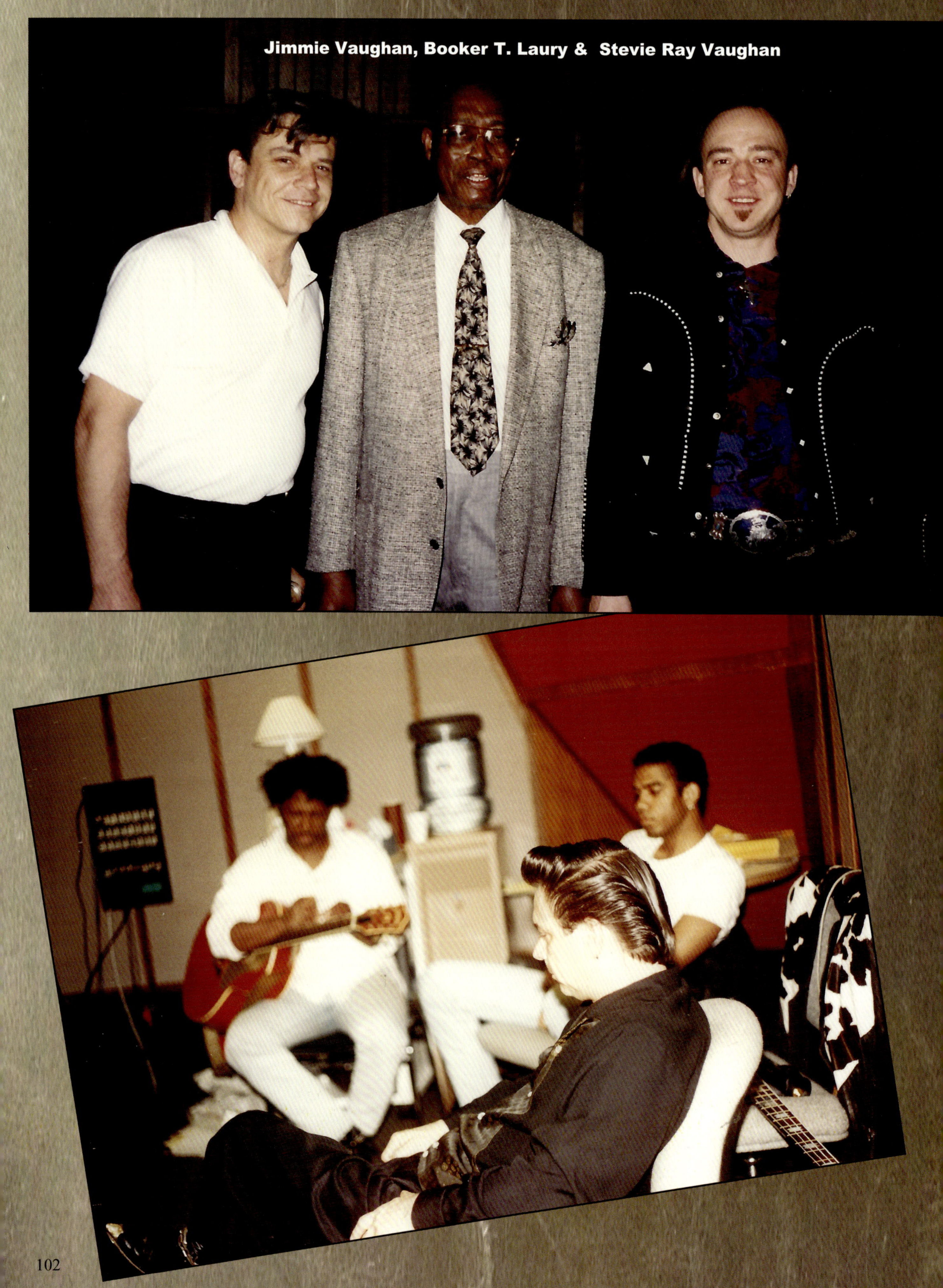
Jimmie Vaughan, Booker T. Laury & Stevie Ray Vaughan

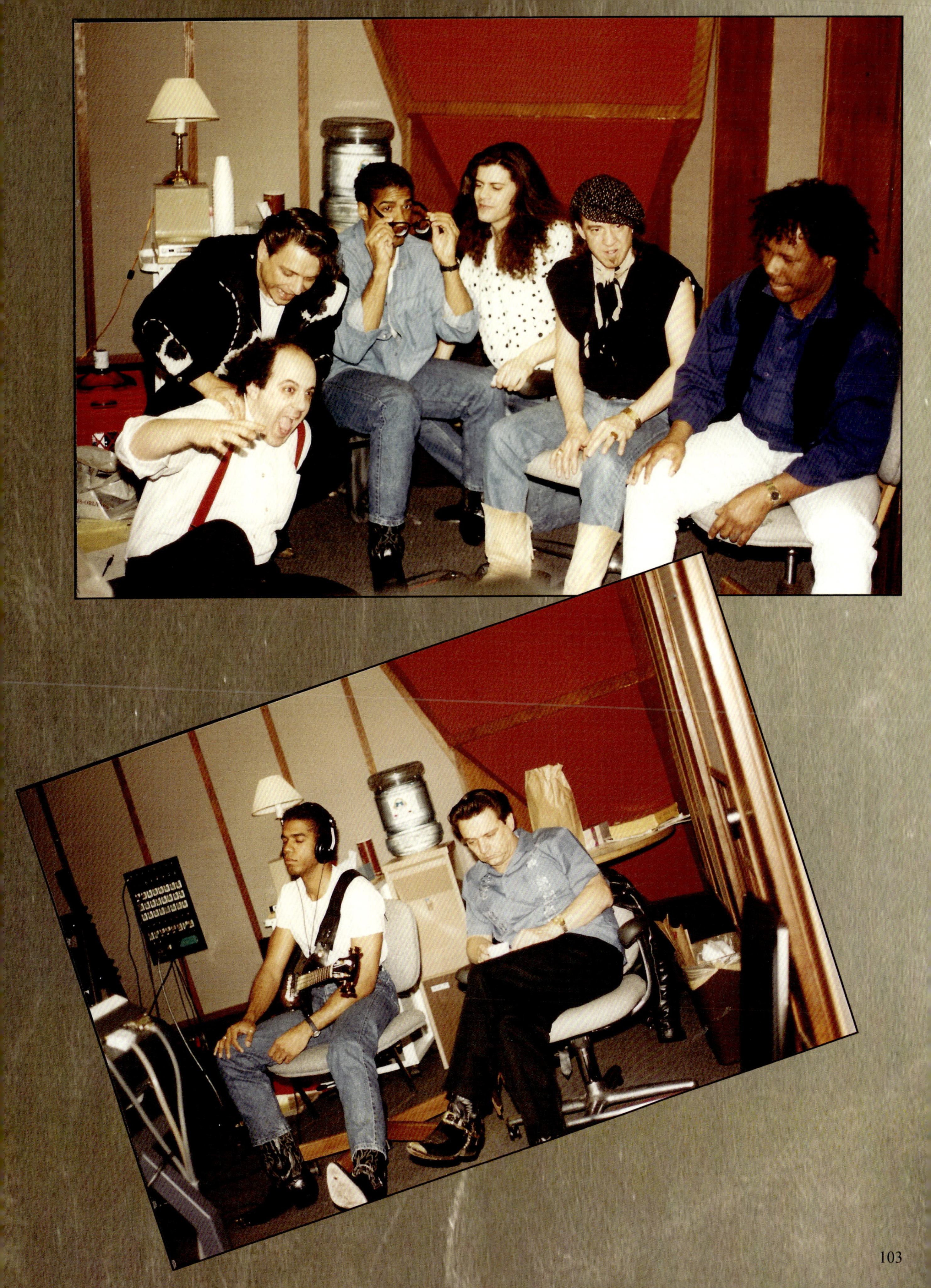

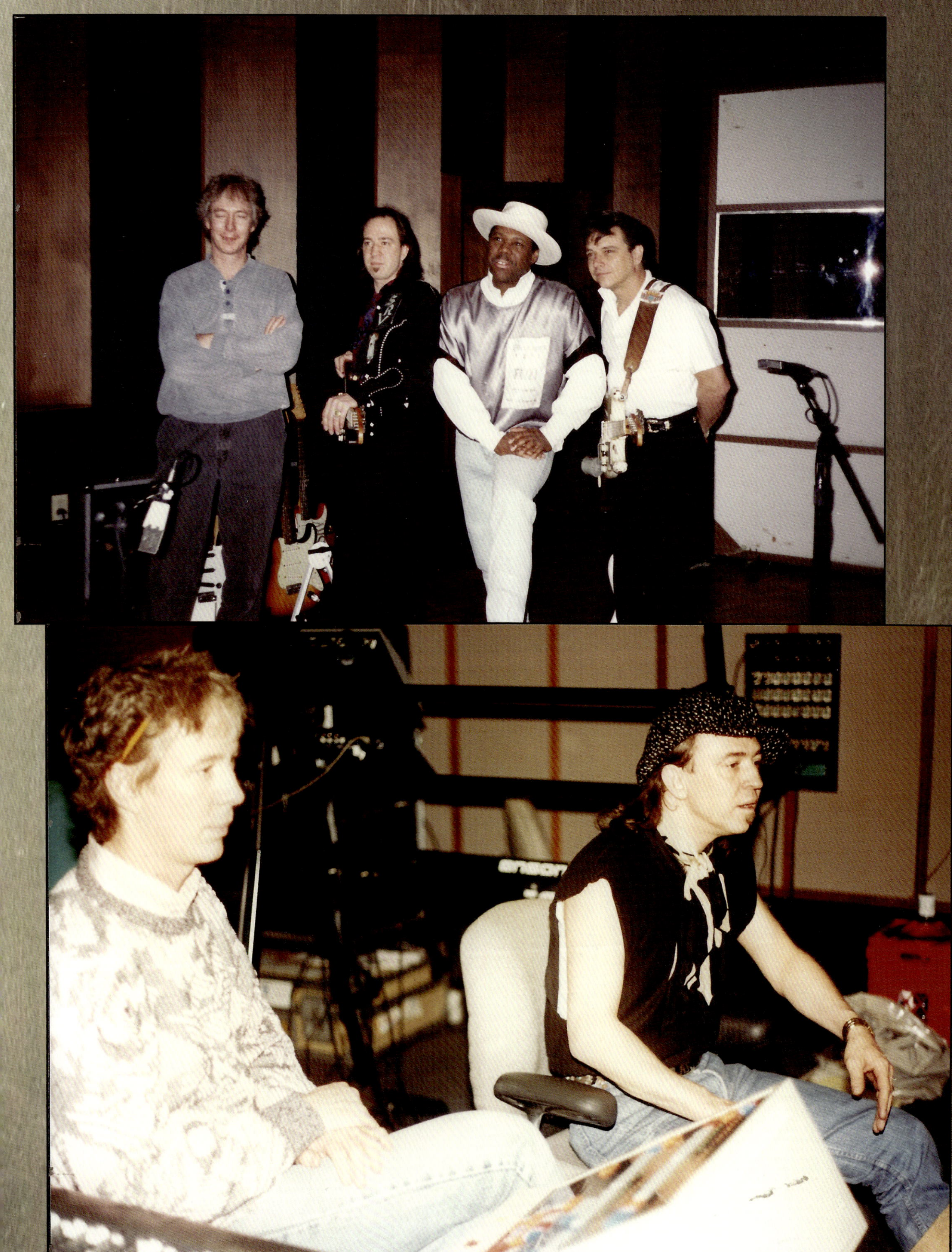

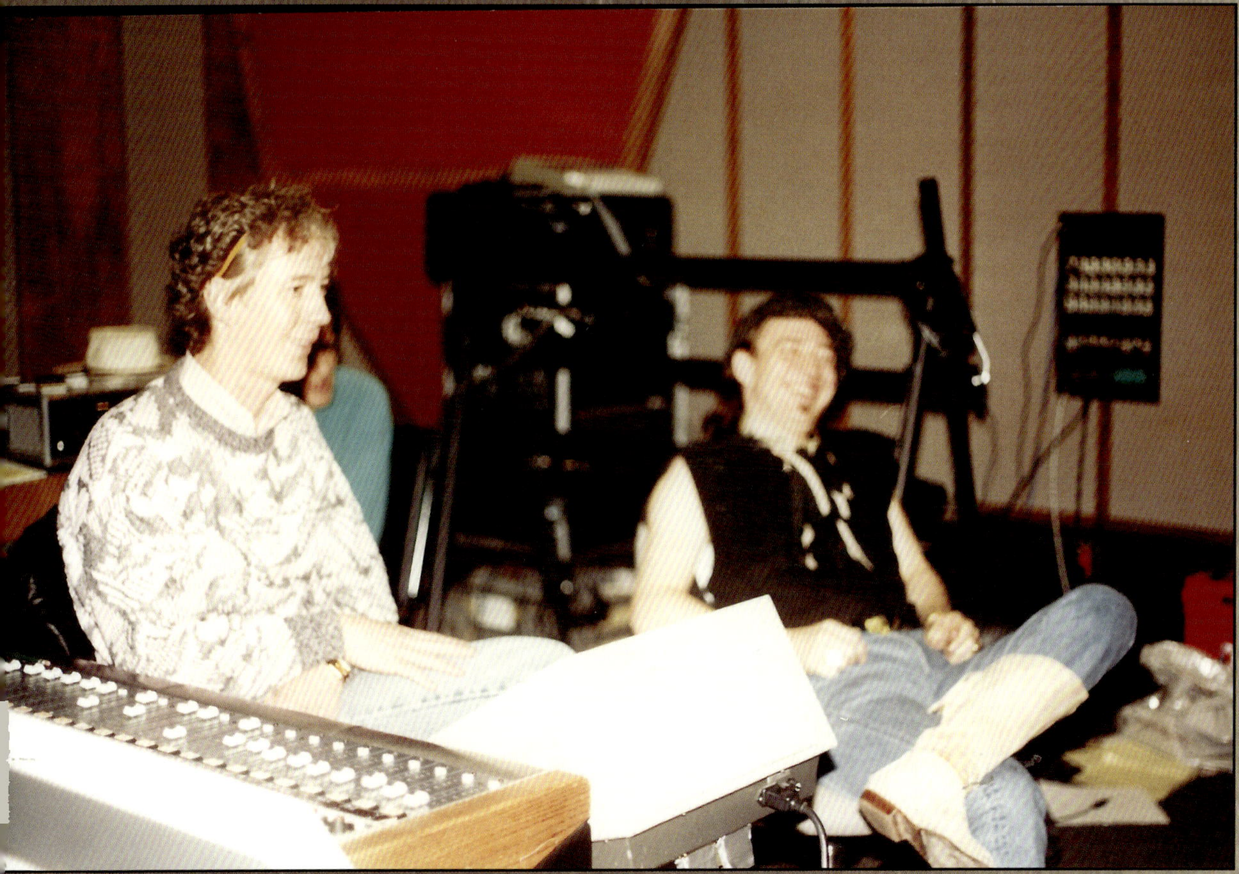

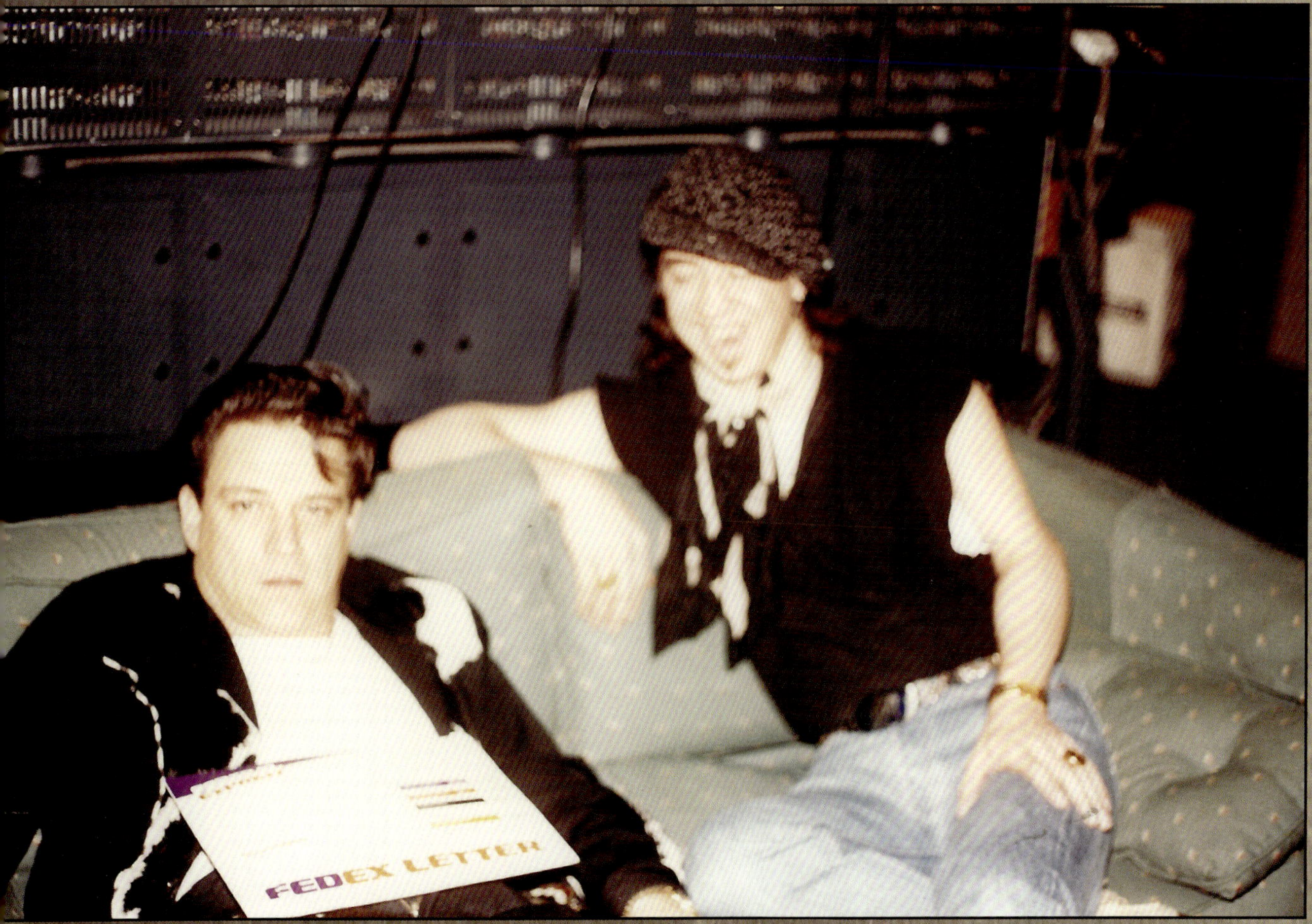

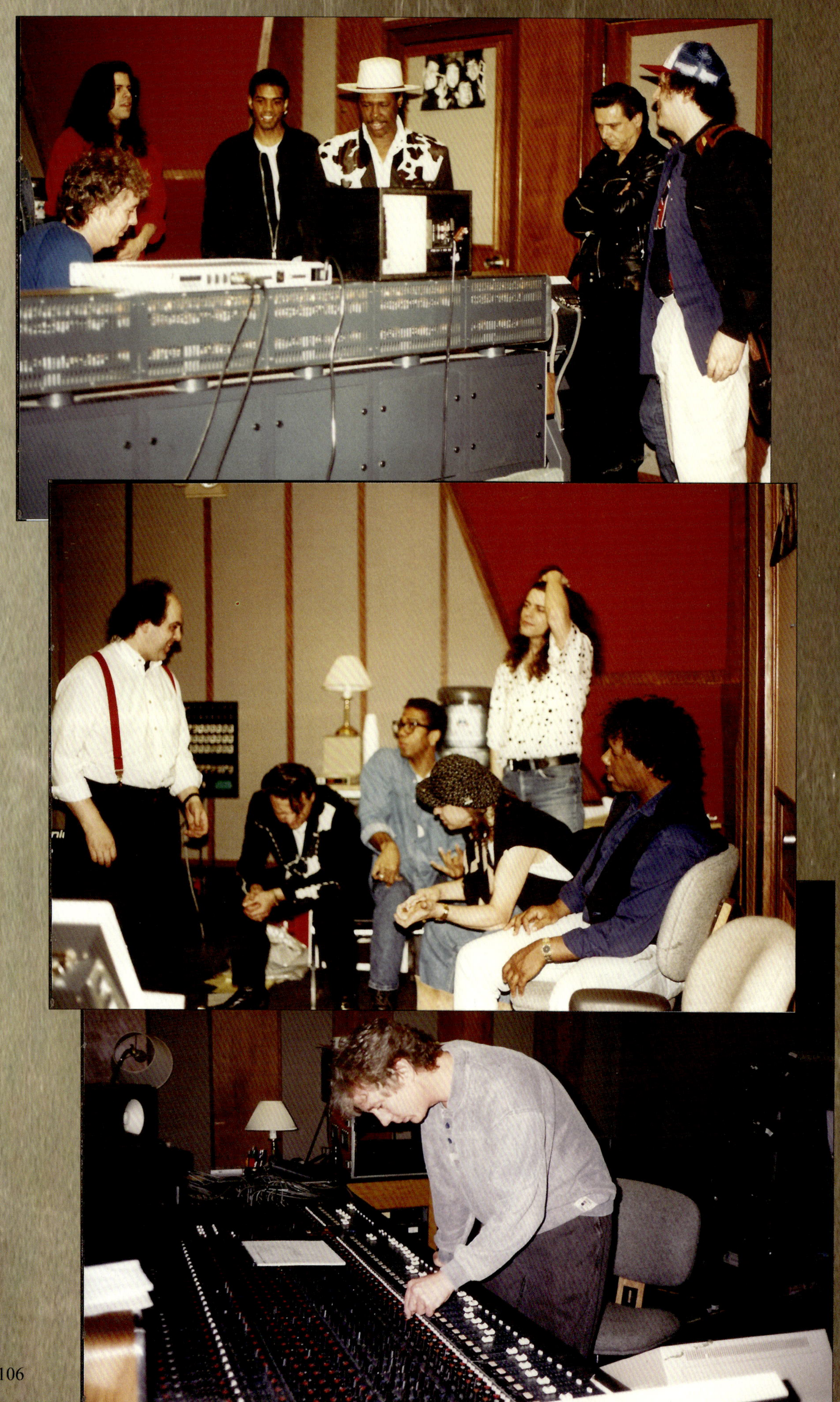

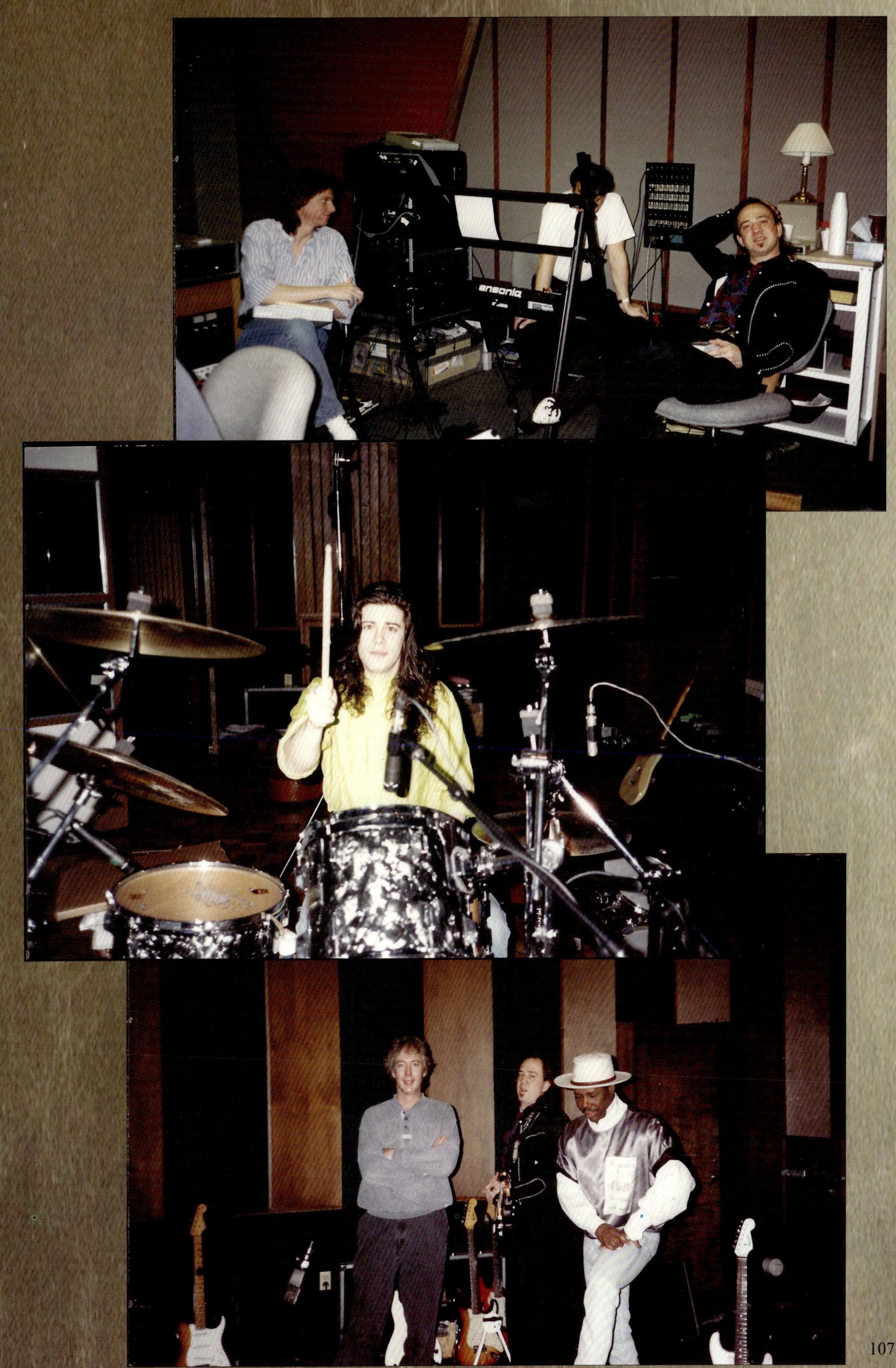
ensoniq

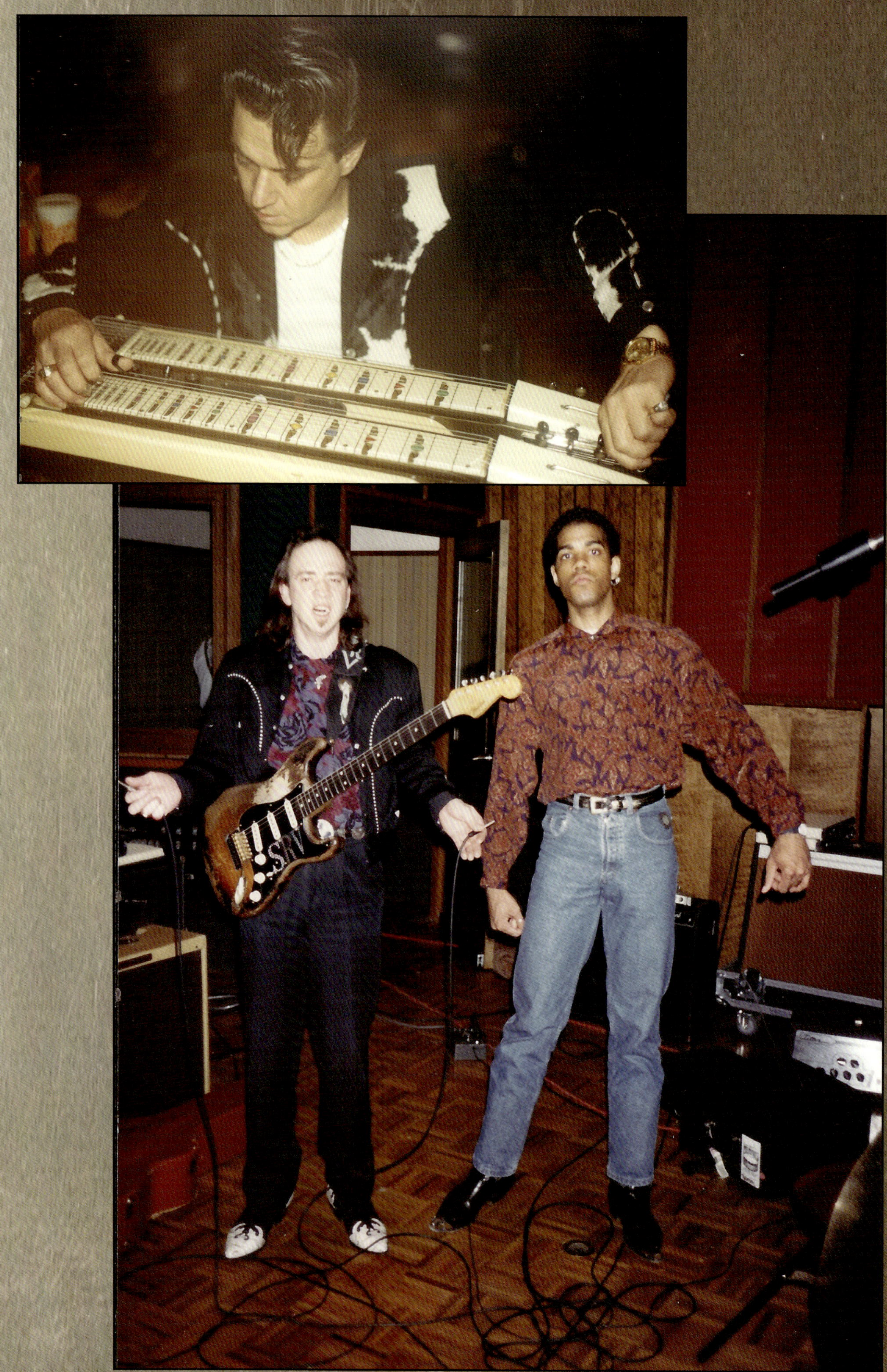
SRV

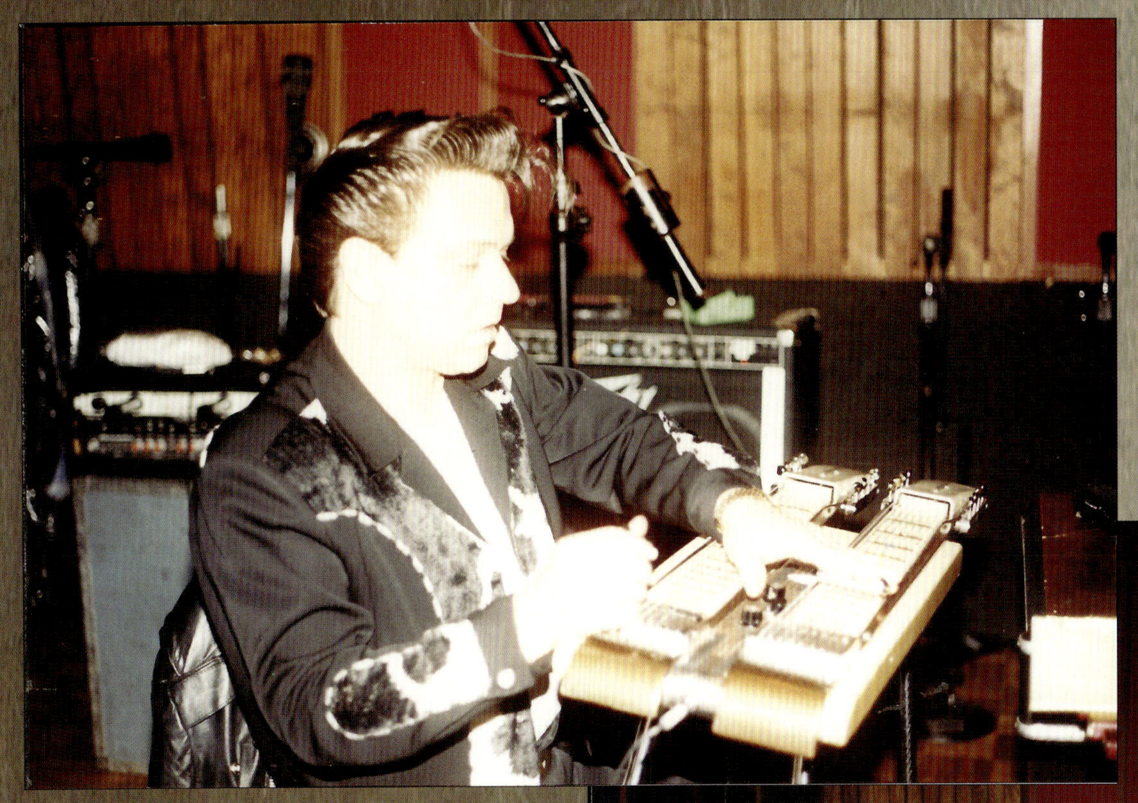

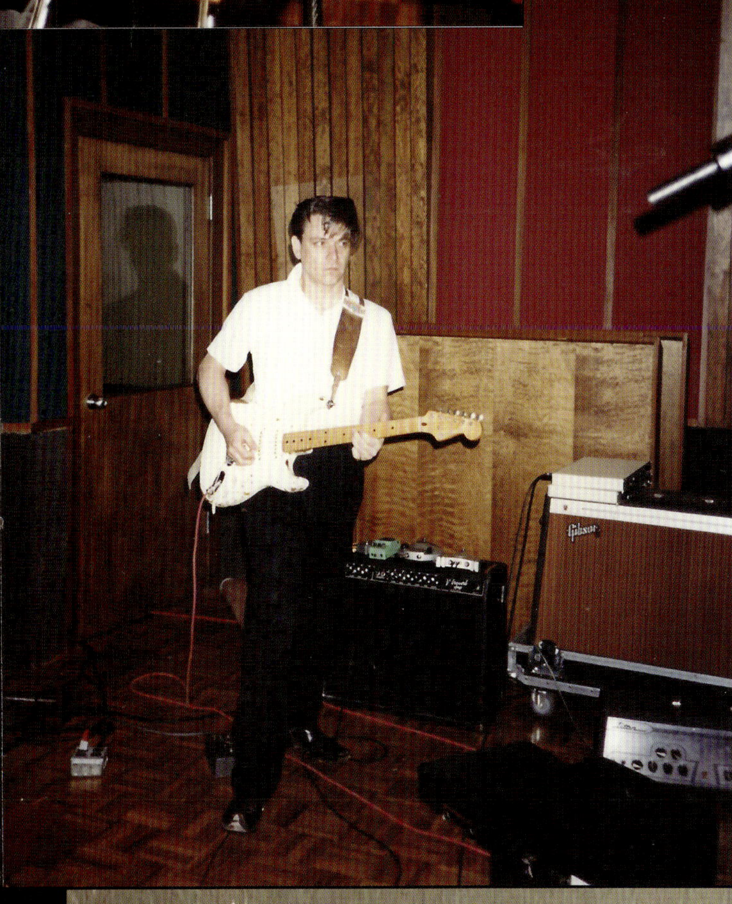
Gibson

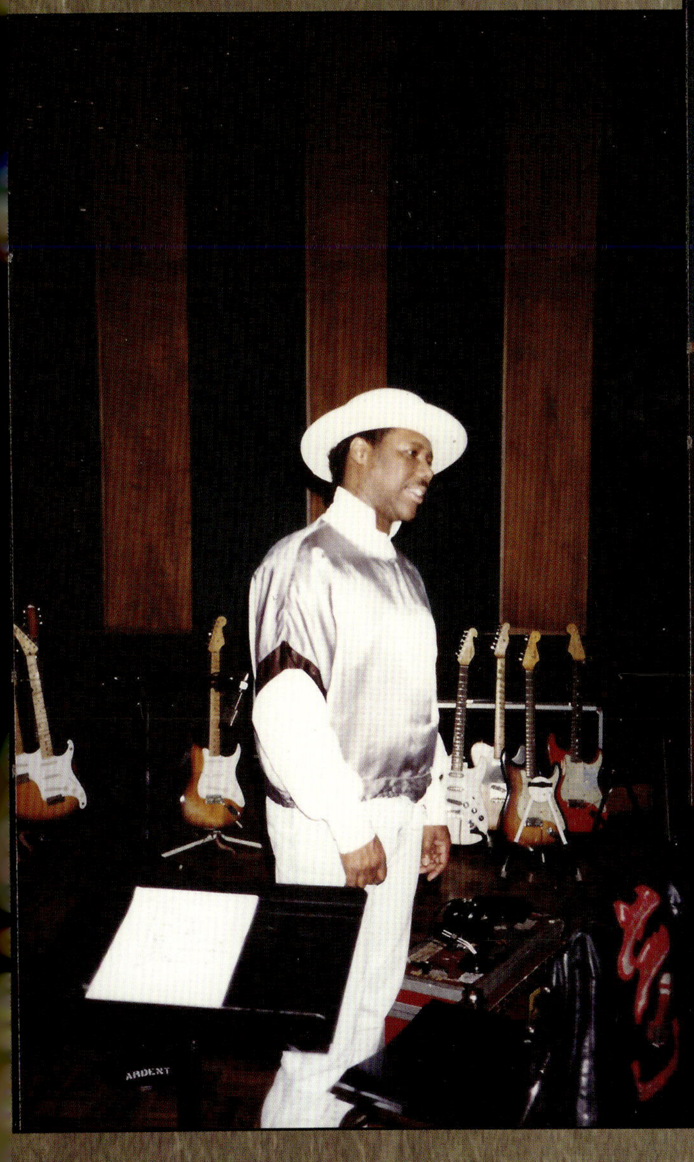
ARDENT

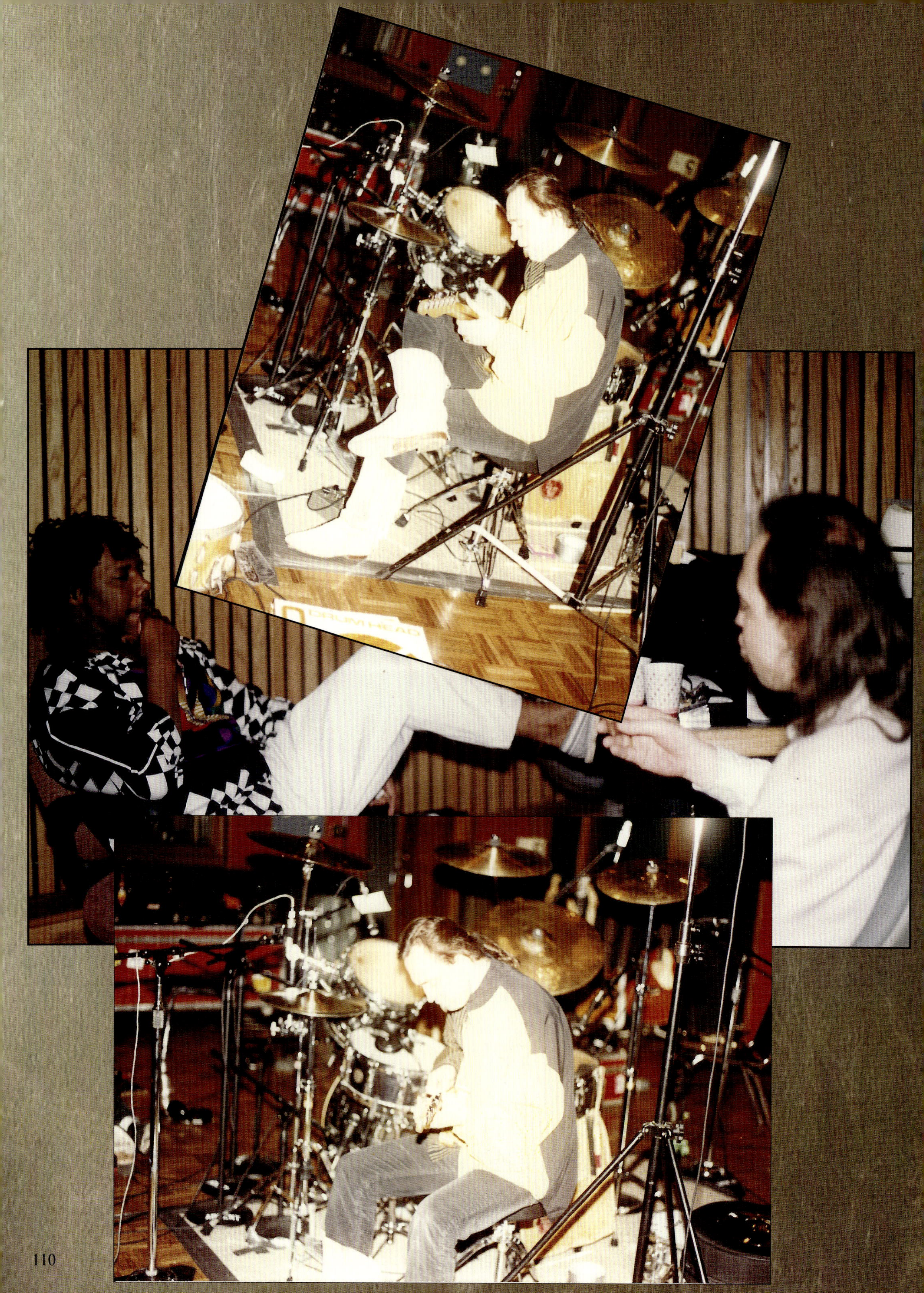

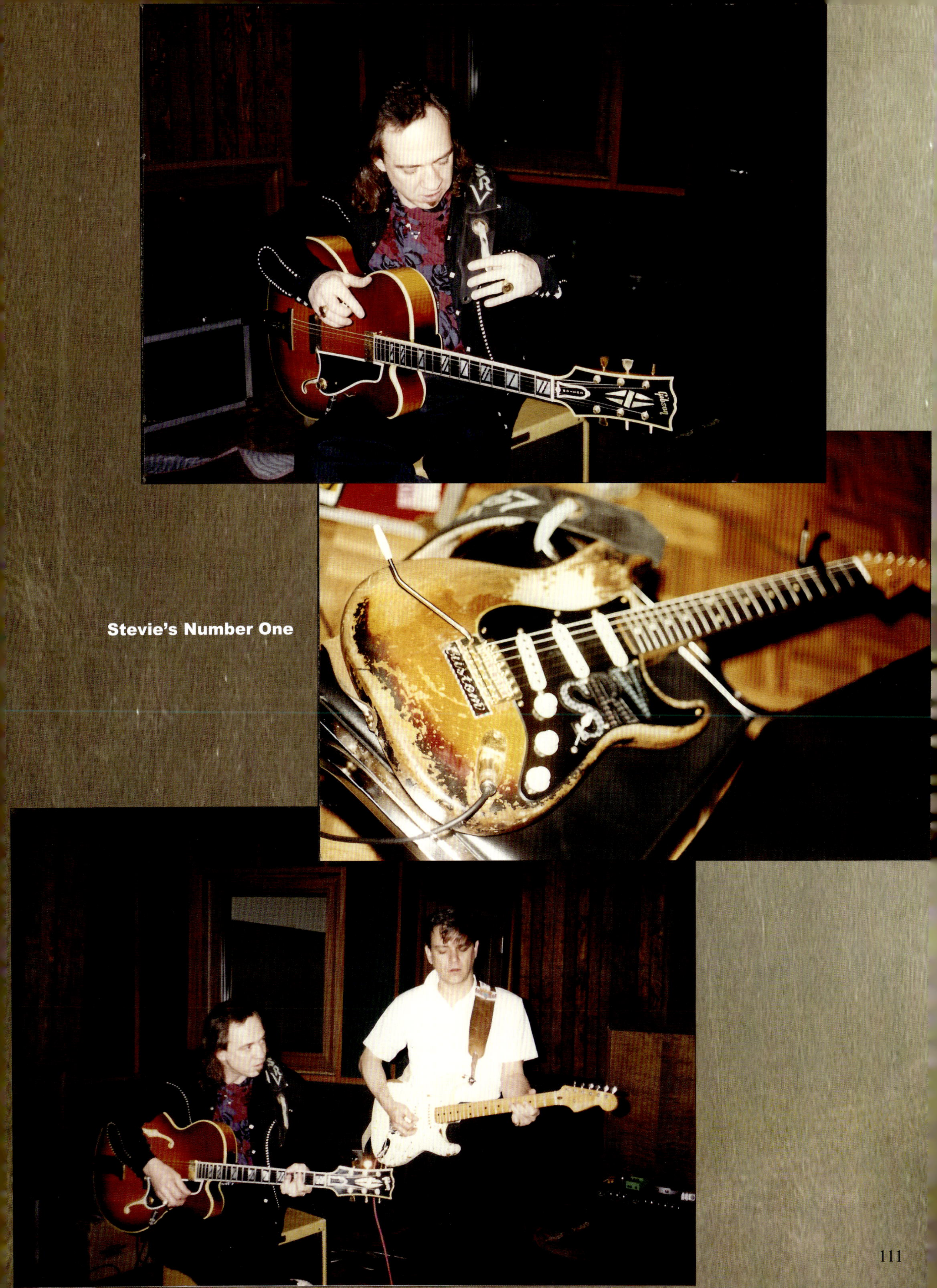

Stevie's Number One

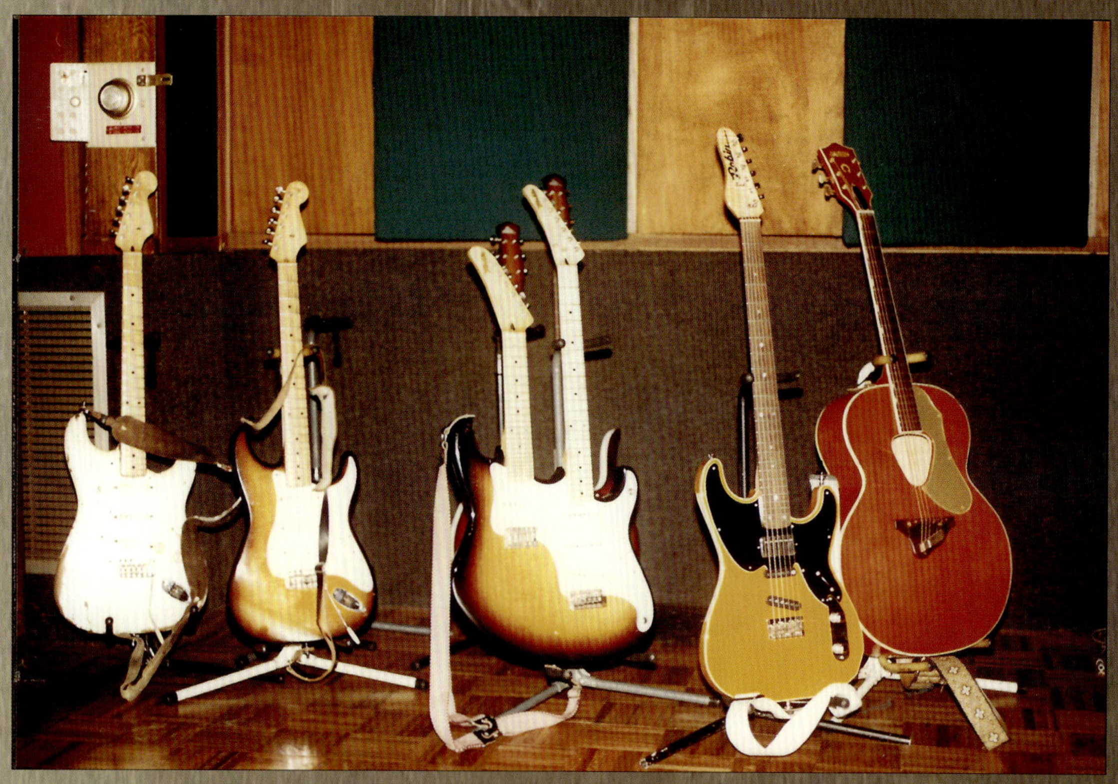

SRV & JLV guitars

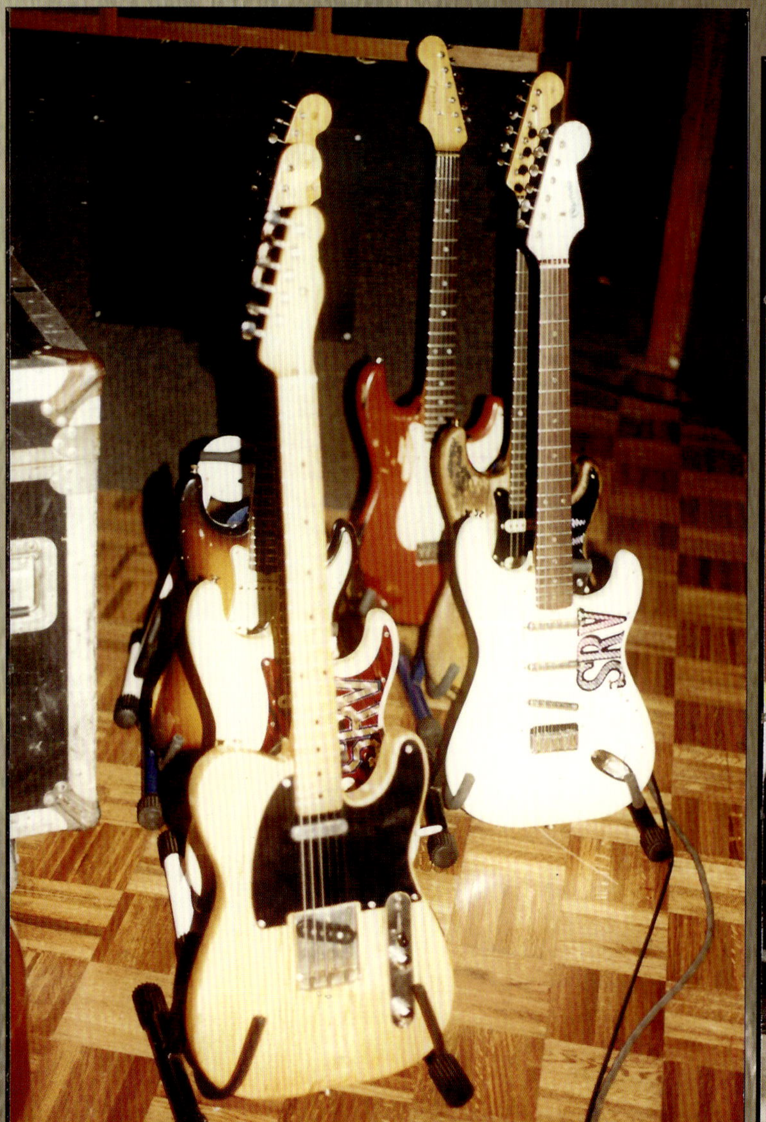

Jimmie Vaughan

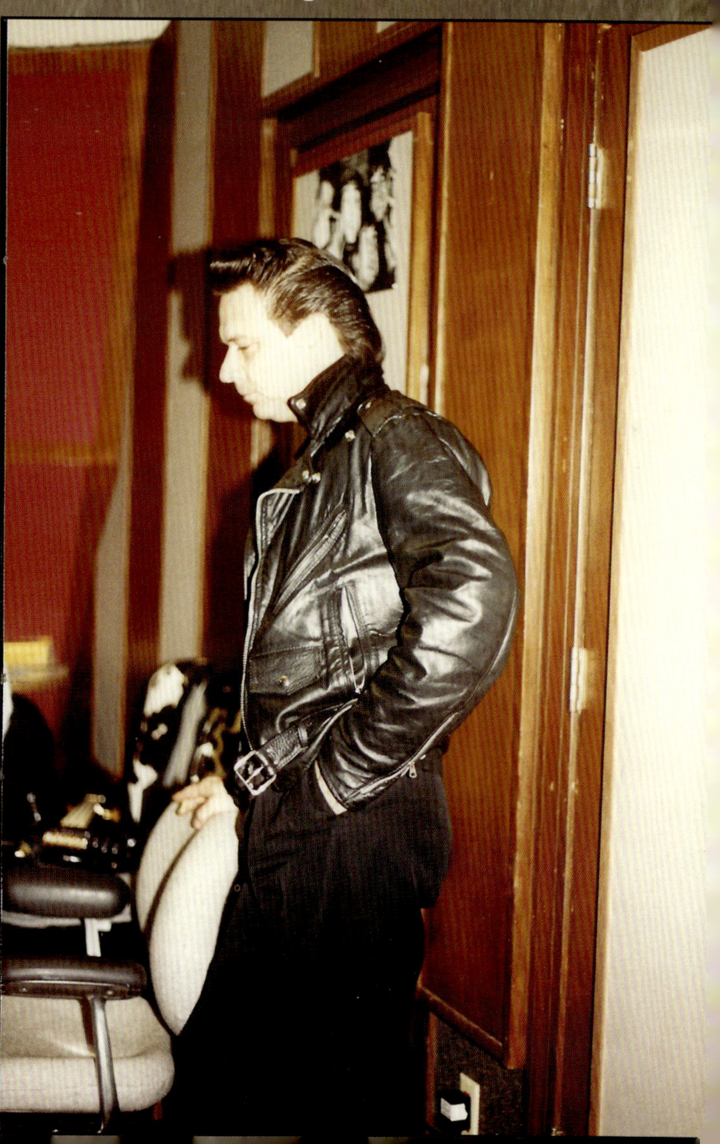

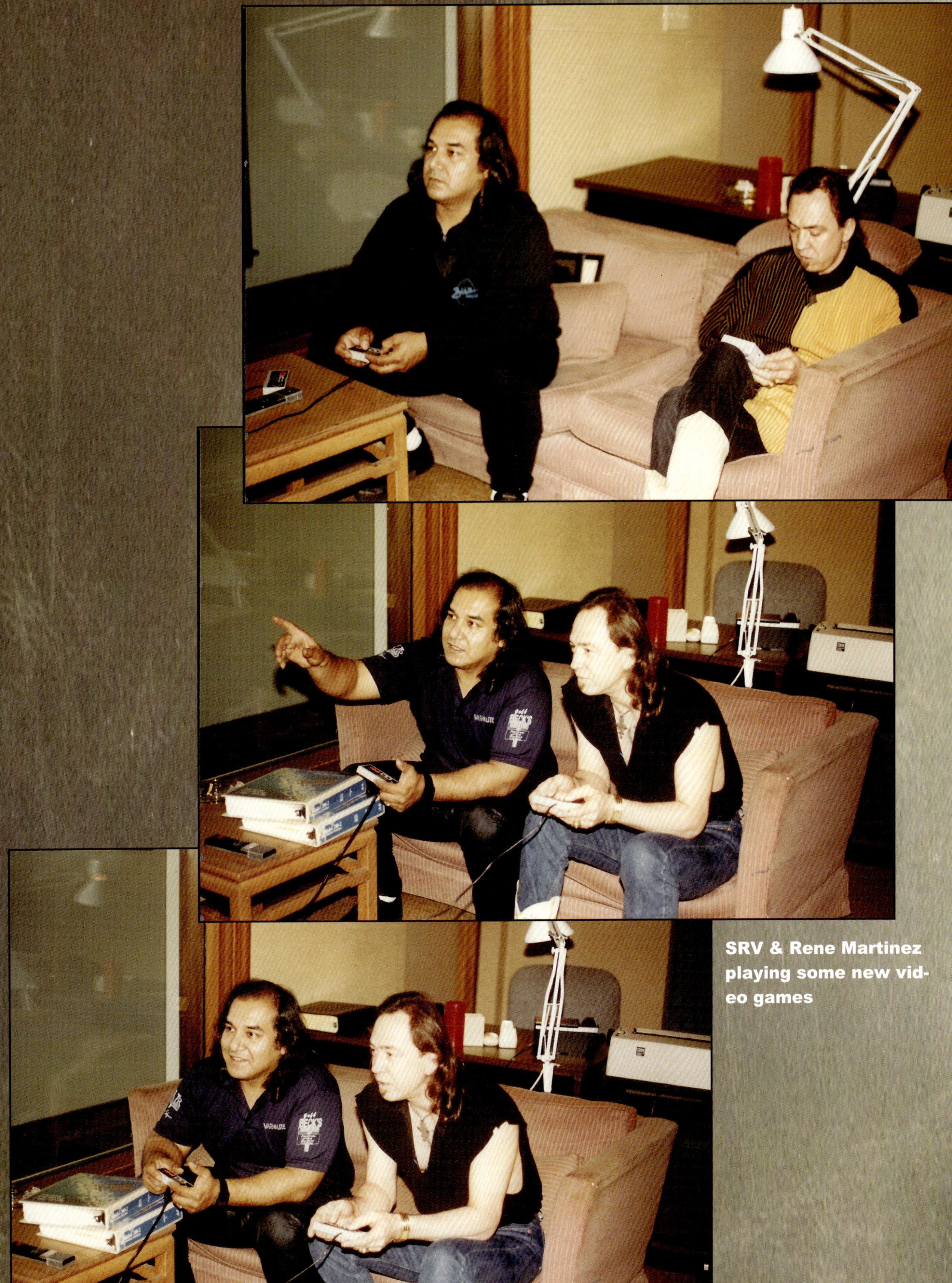

SRV & Rene Martinez playing some new video games

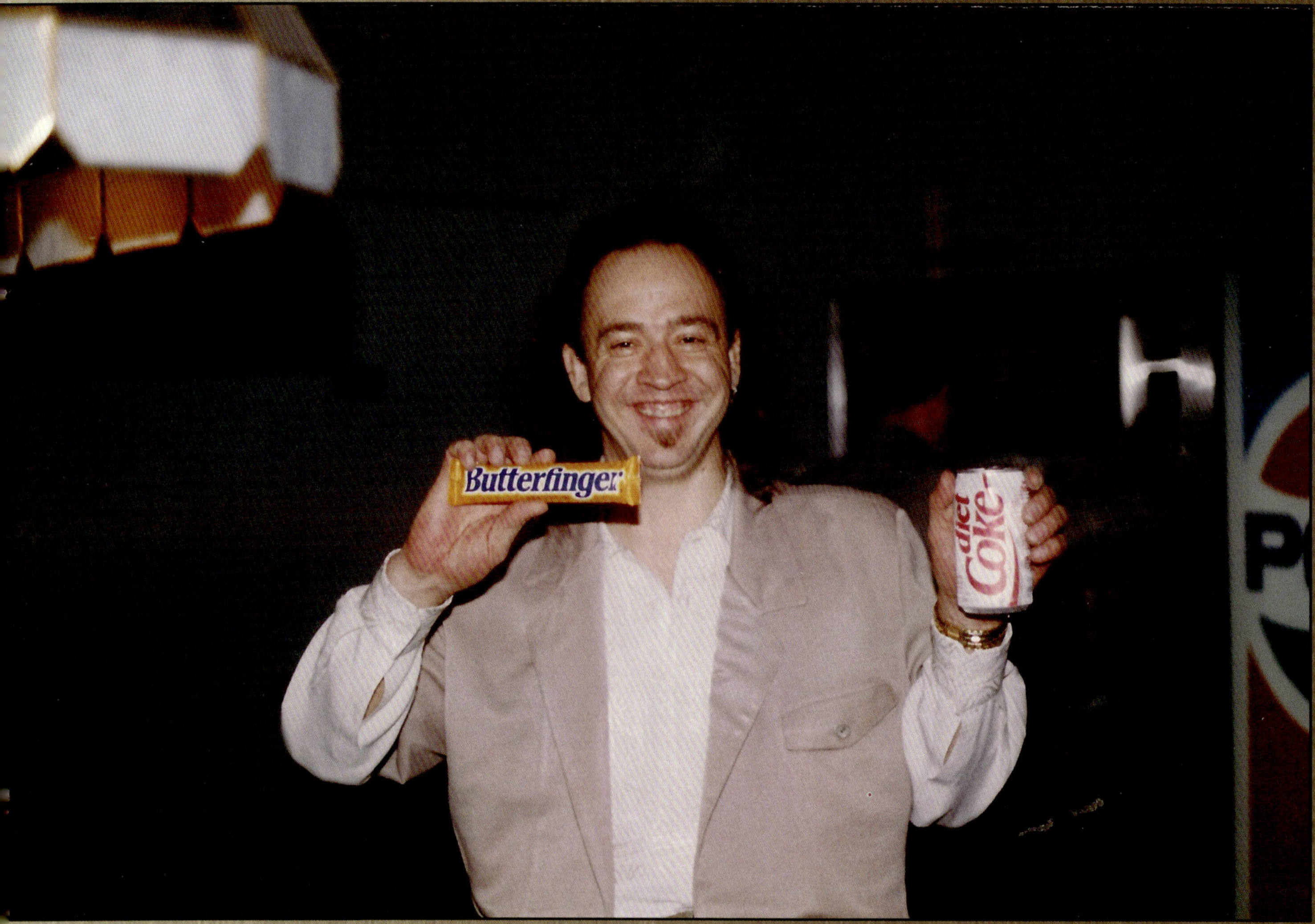
Butterfinger
diet Coke

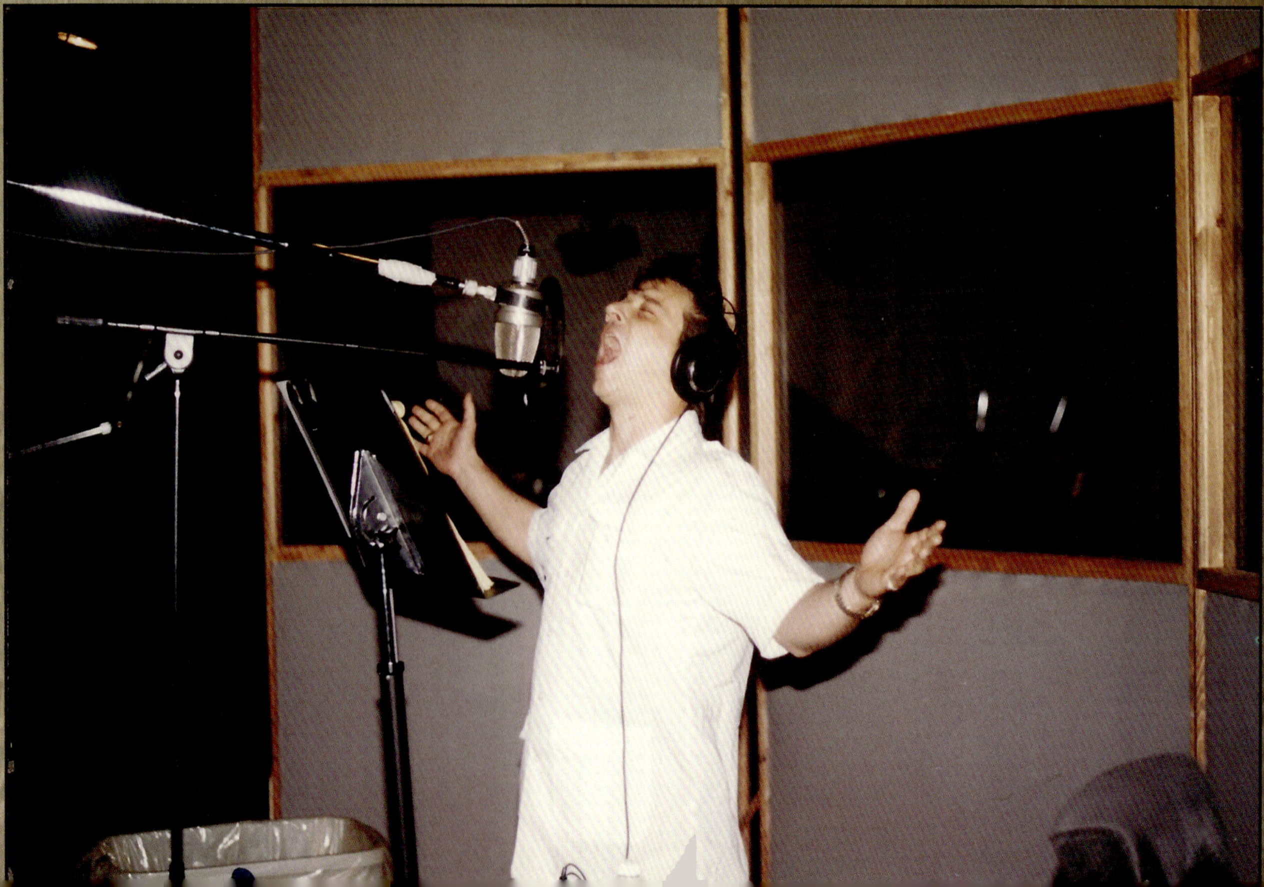

DALLAS SOUND LAB
LAS COLINAS 1990

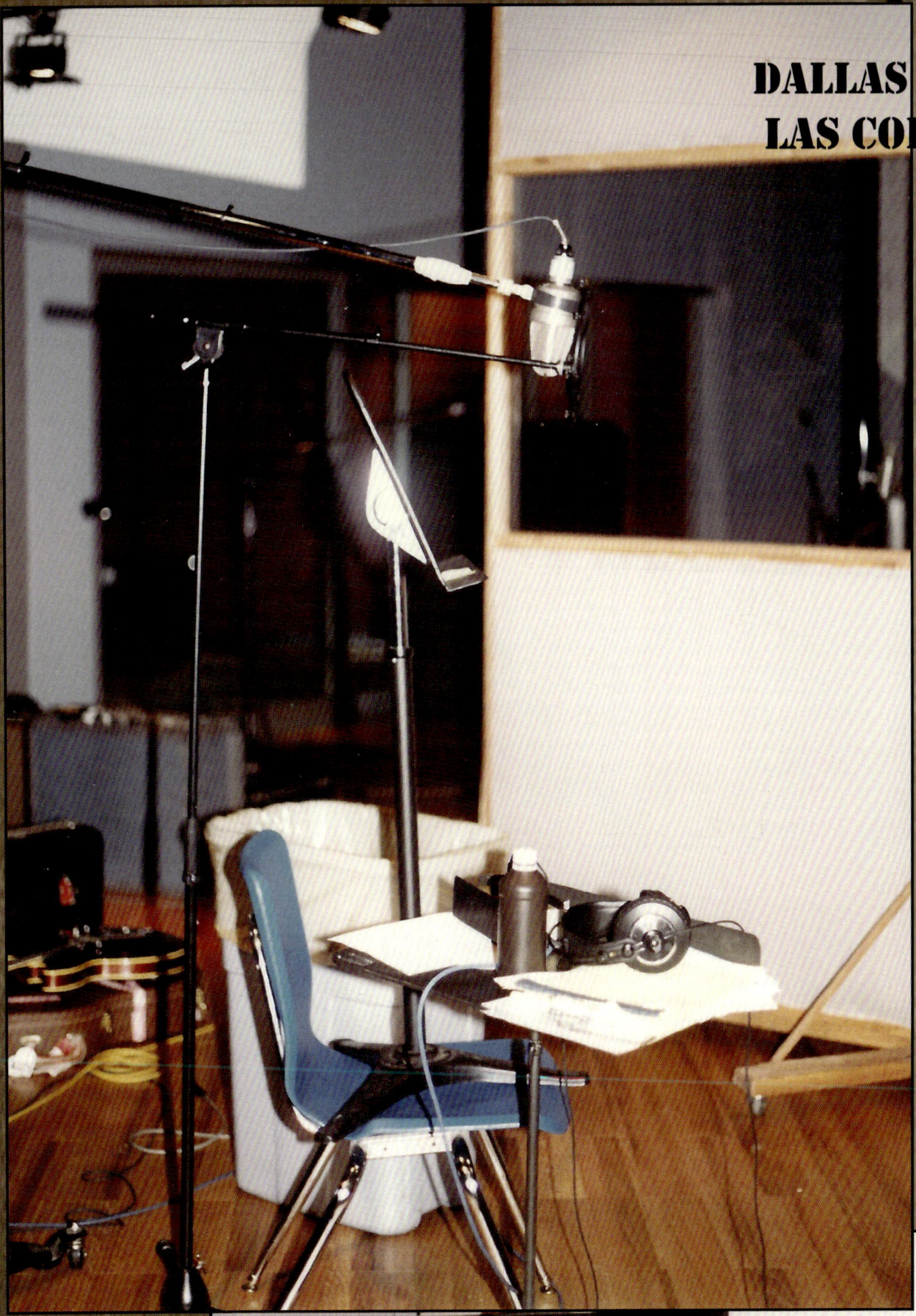

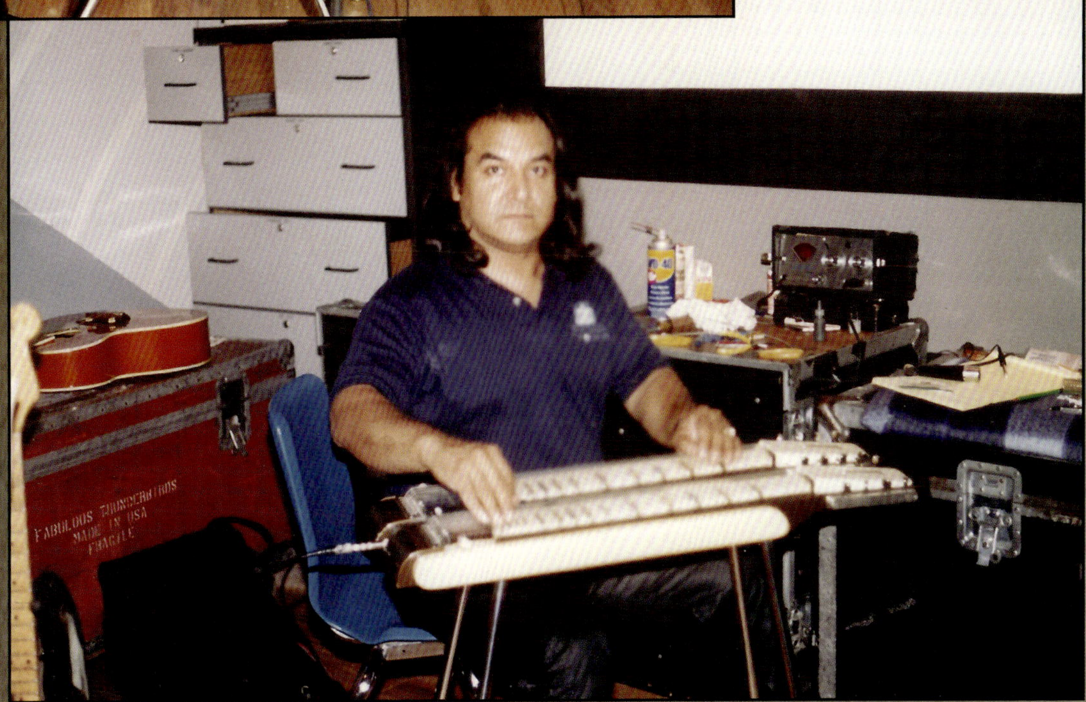

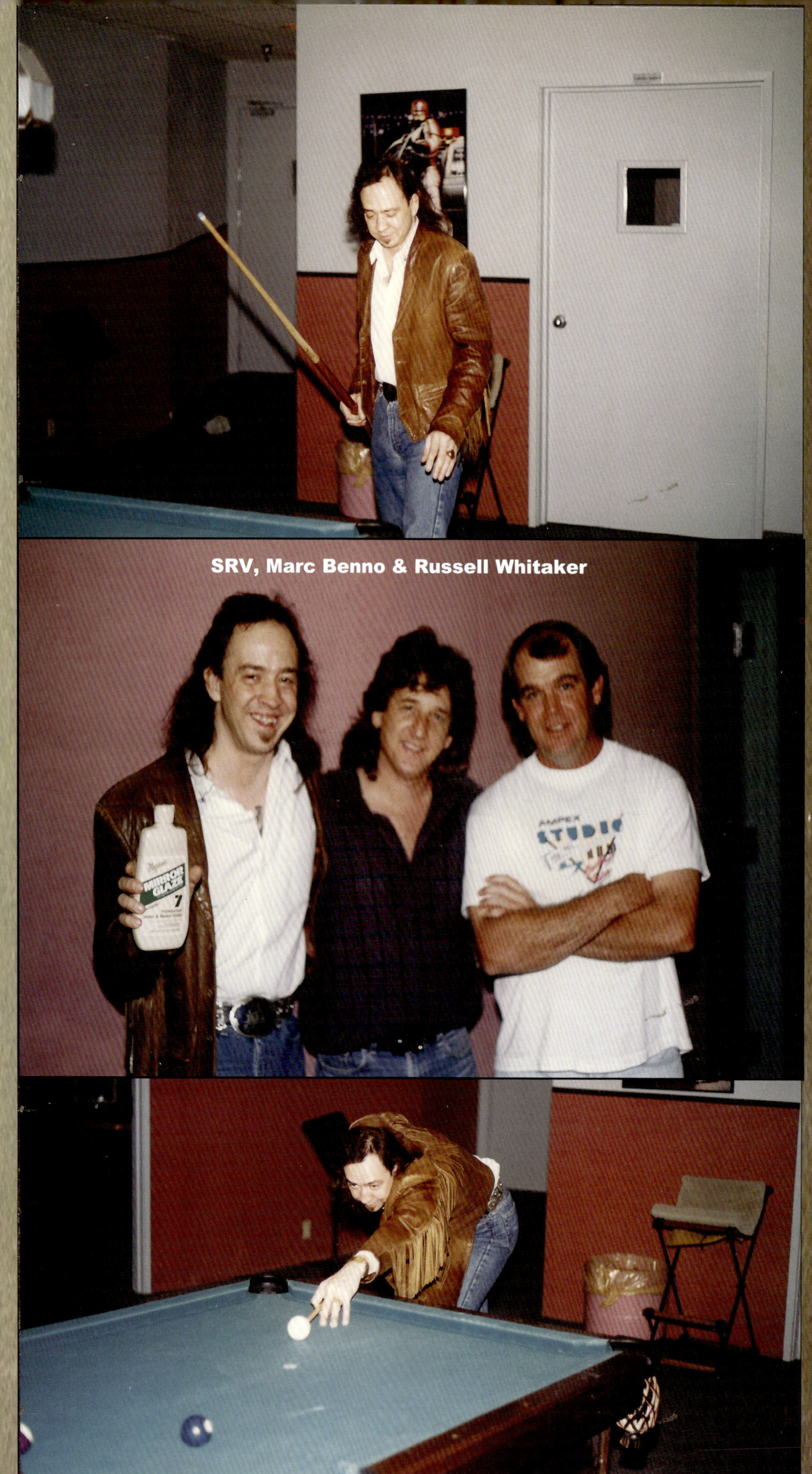

SRV, Marc Benno & Russell Whitaker

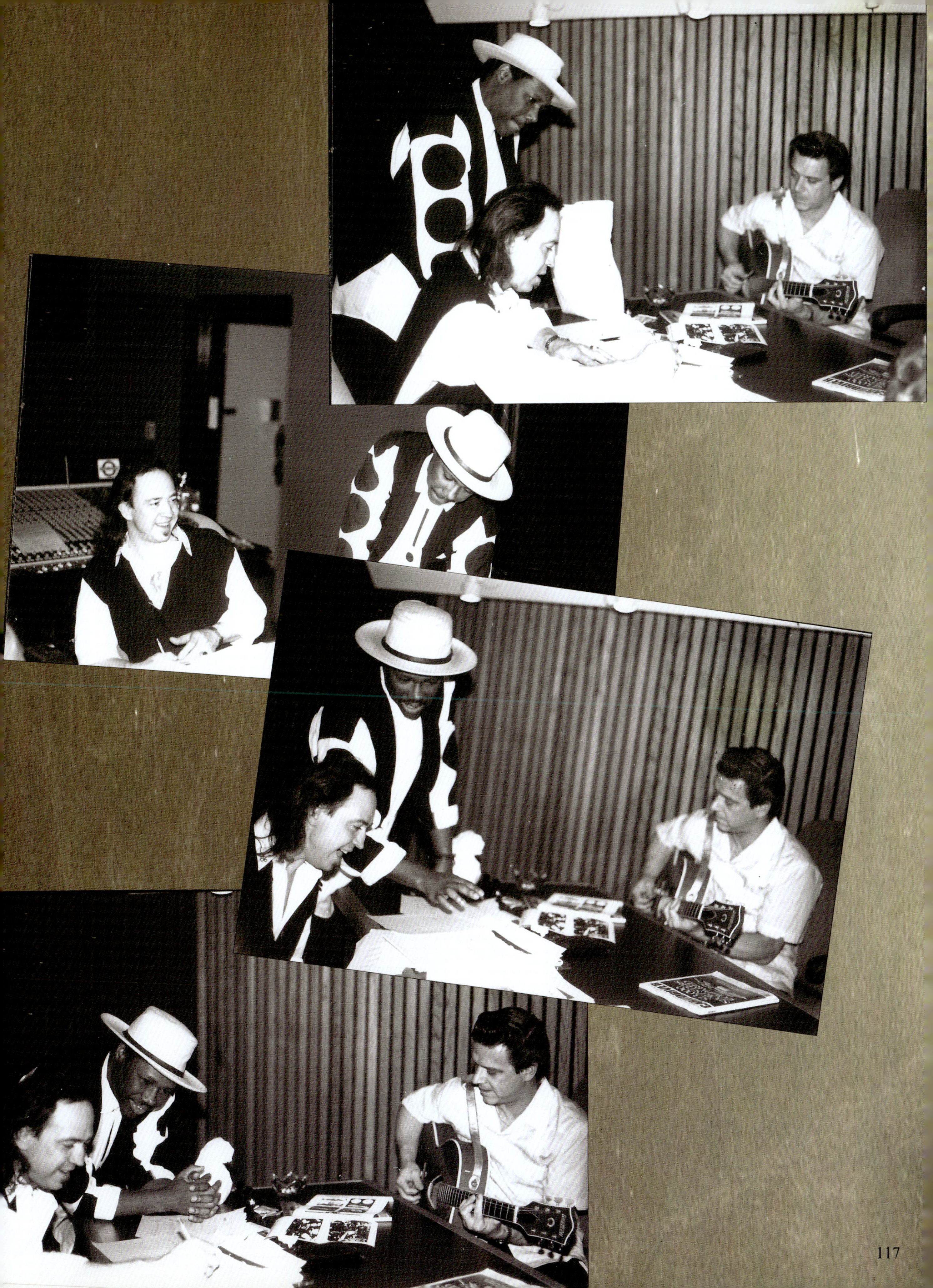

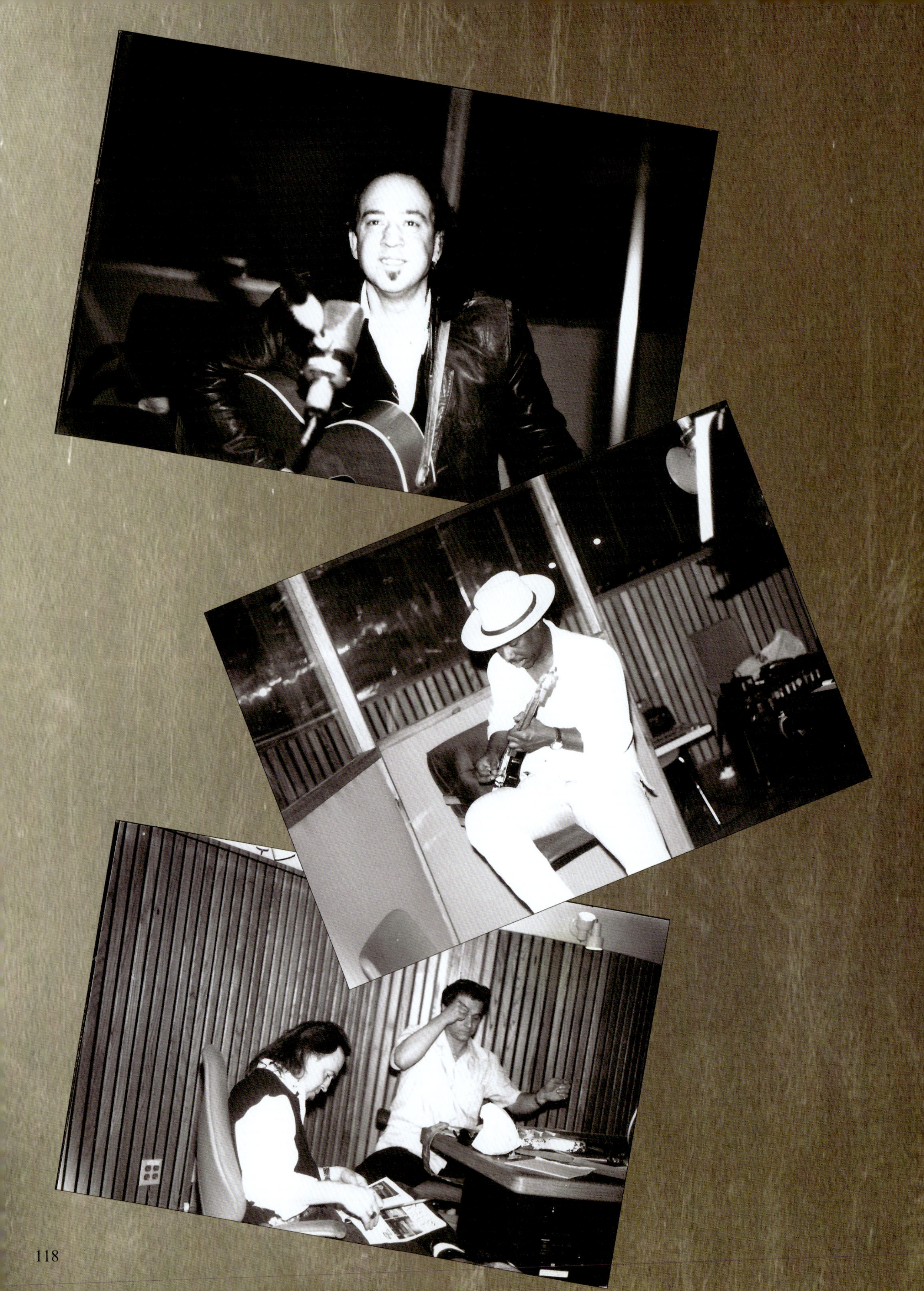

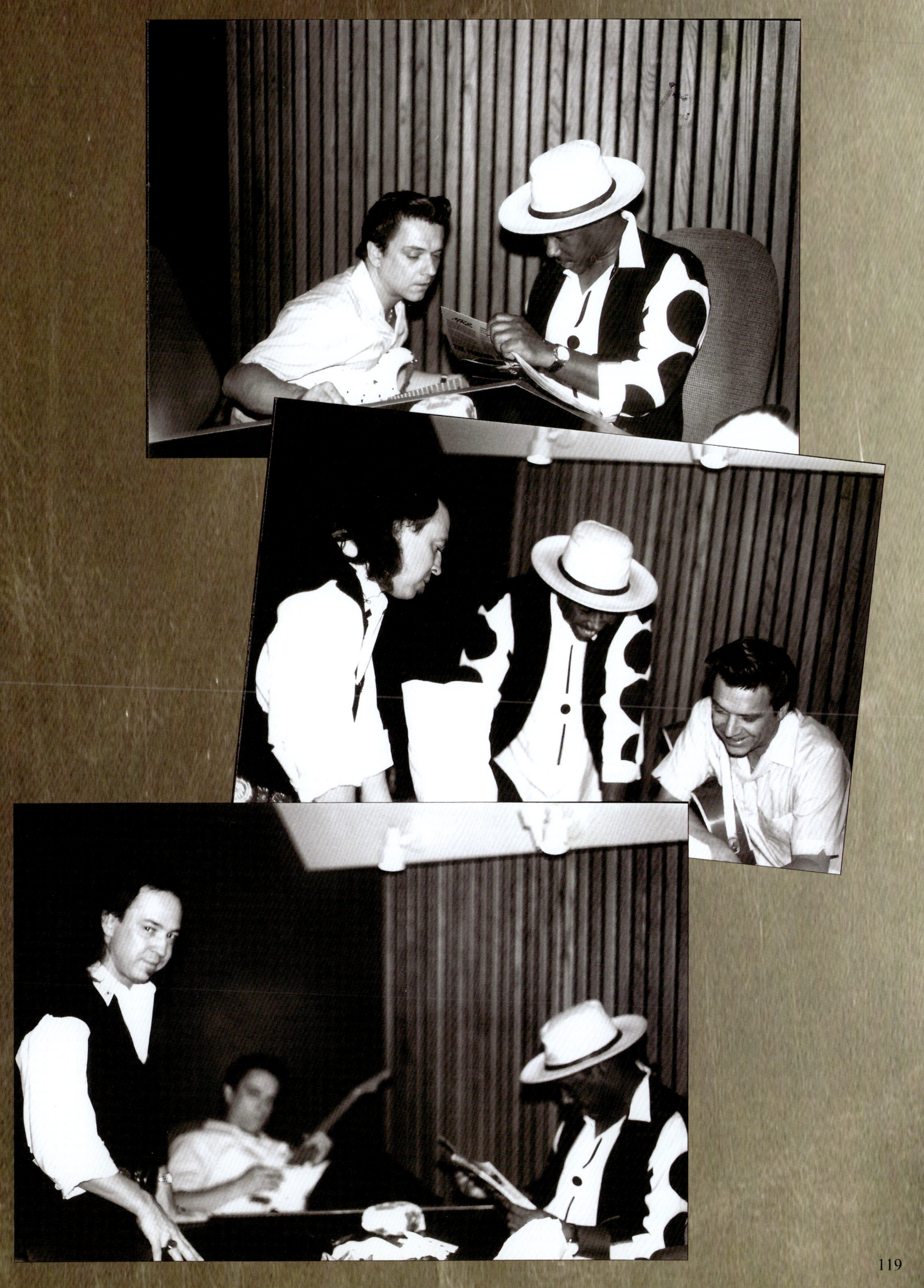

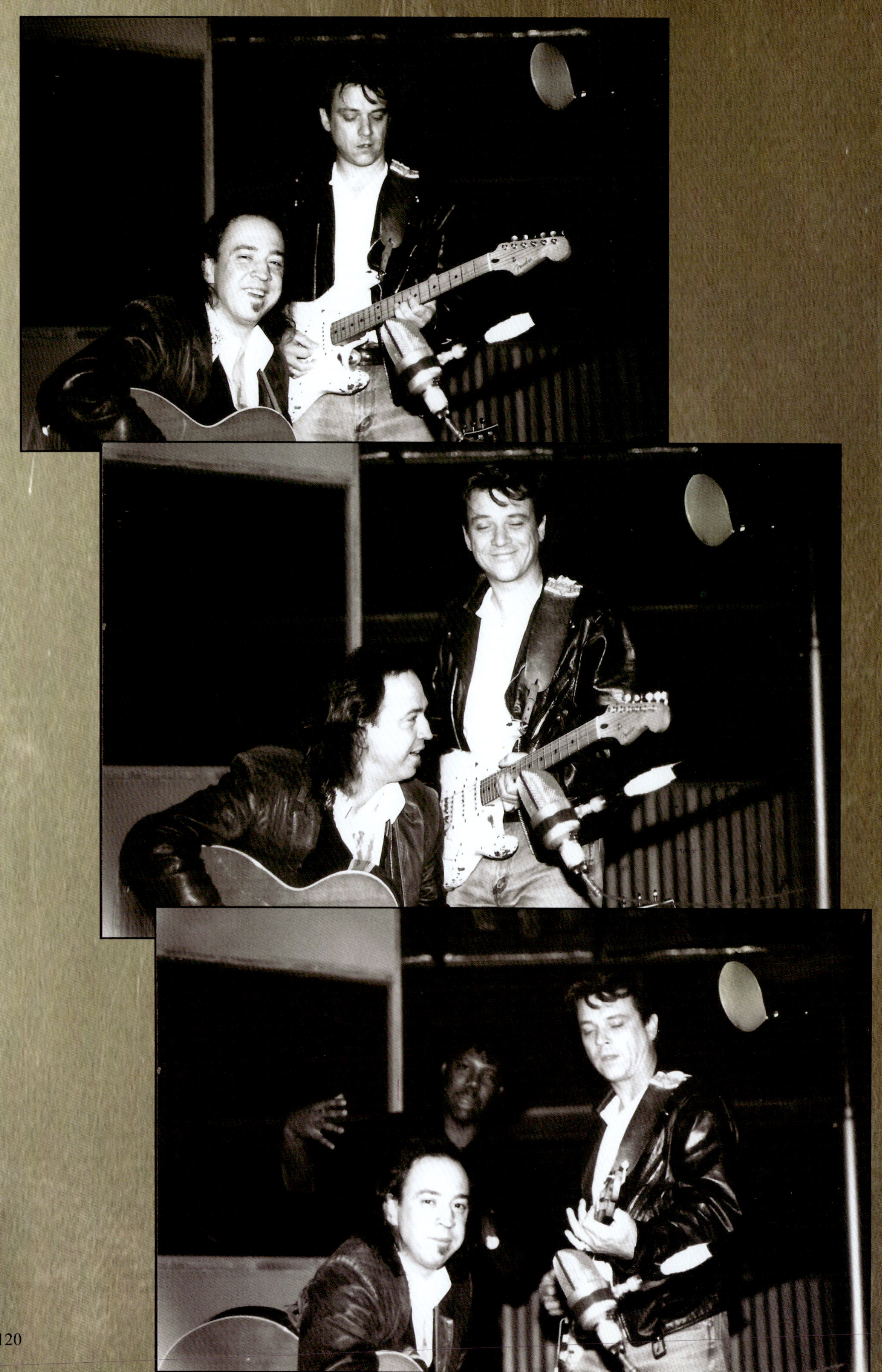

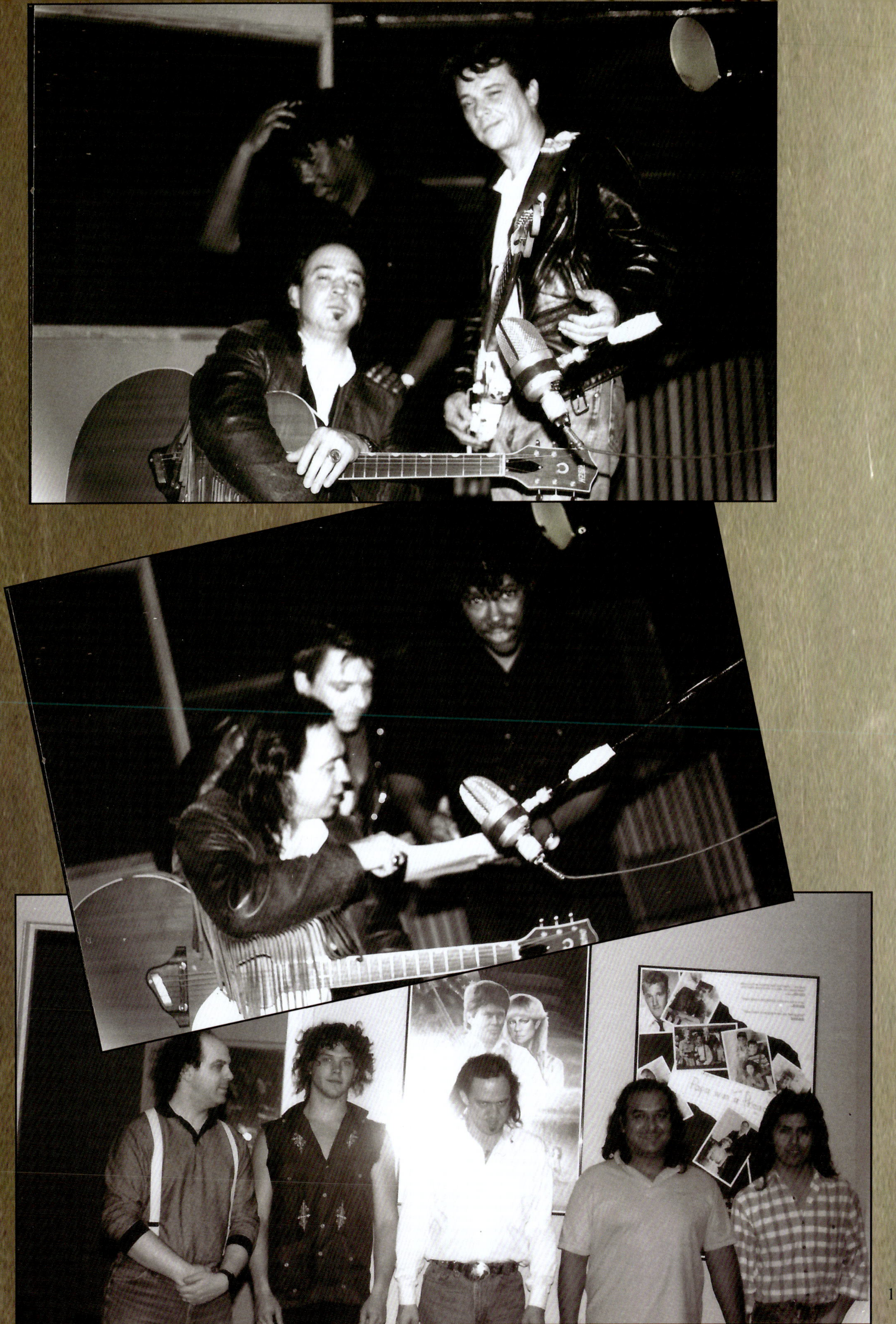

Doyle Bramhall & SRV

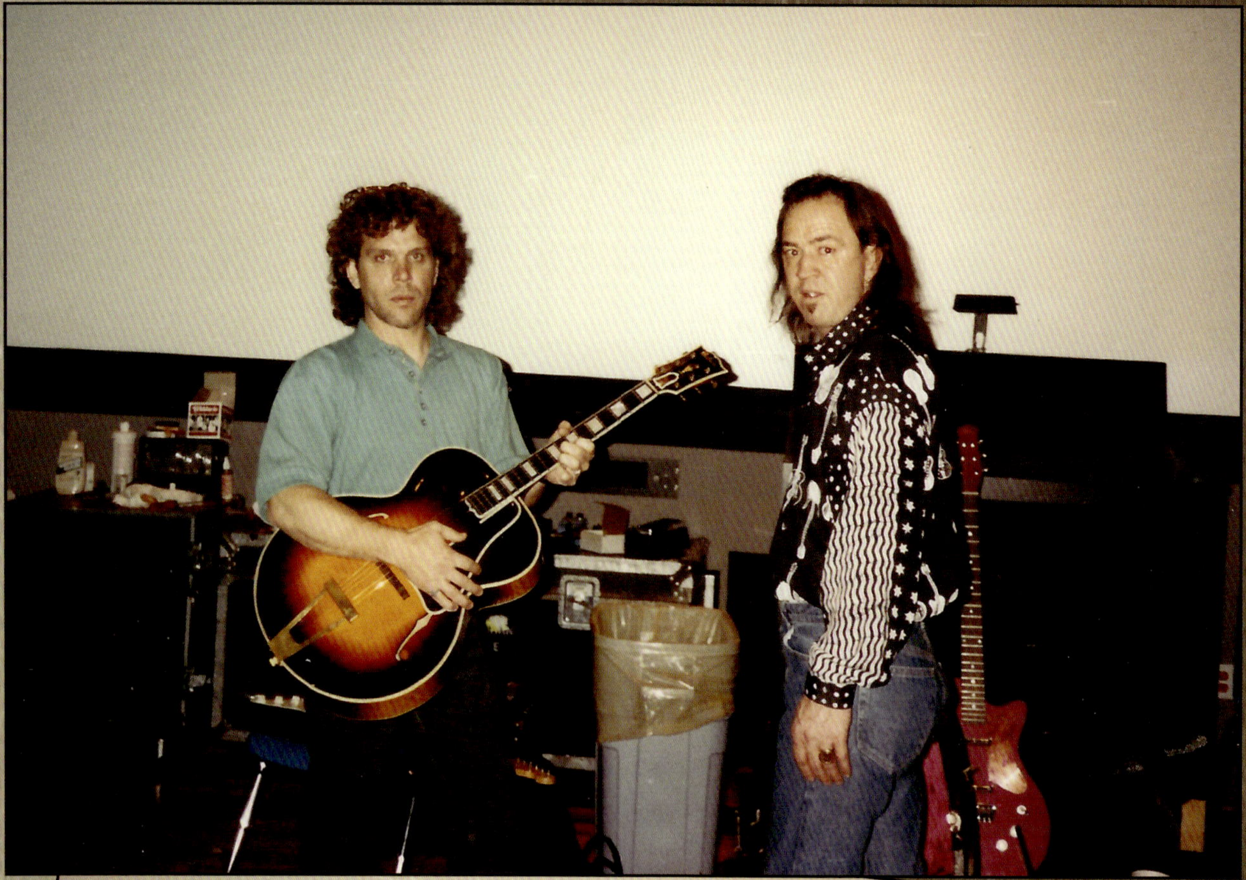

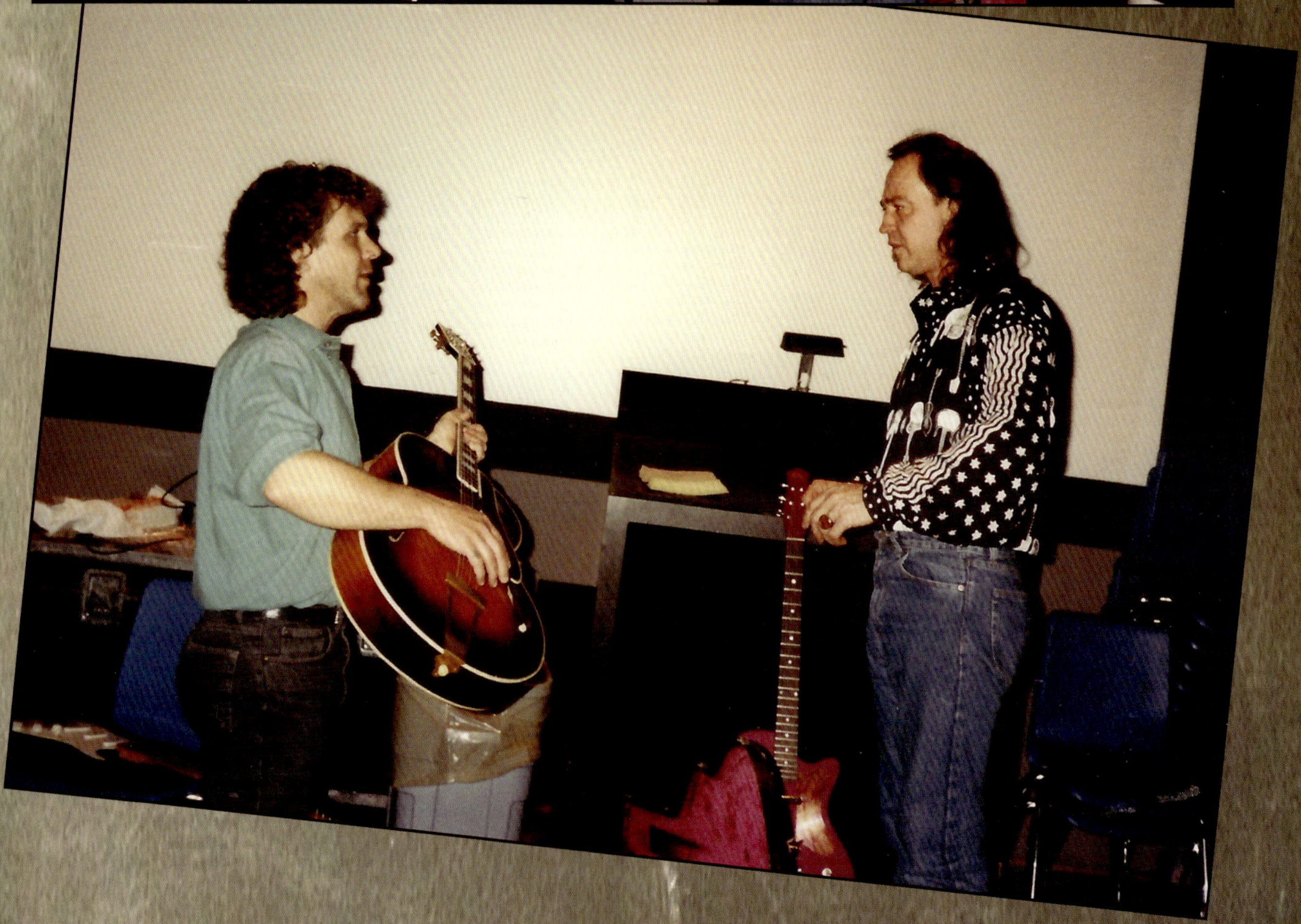

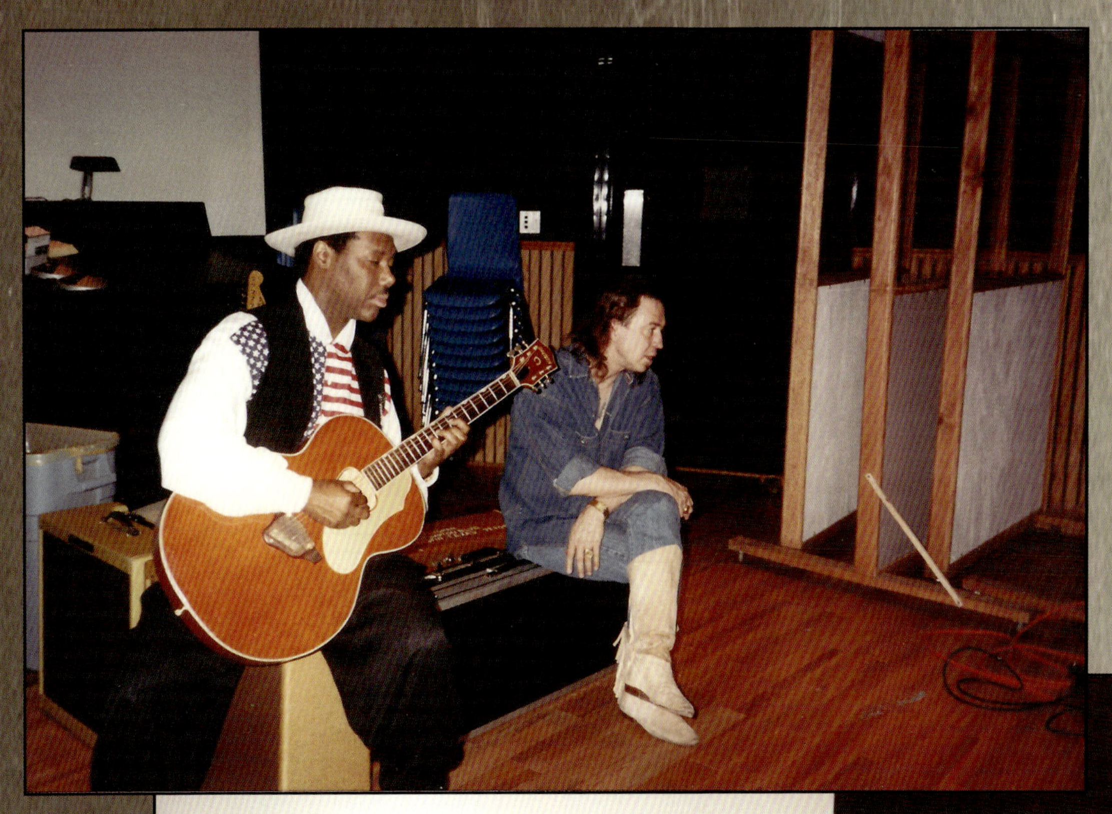

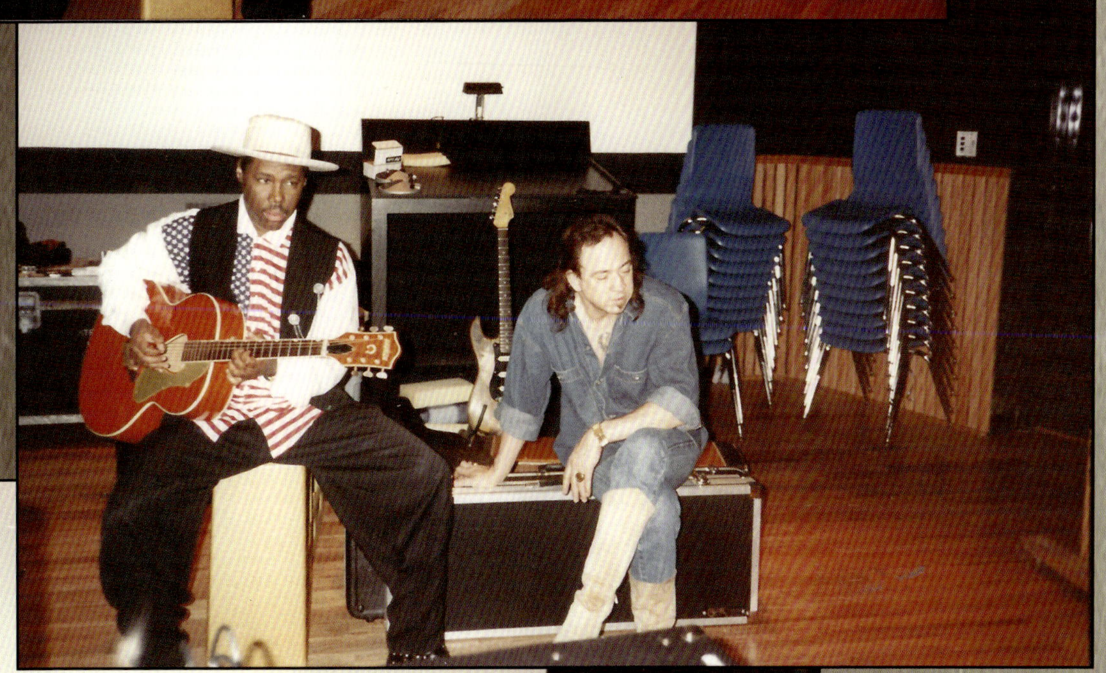

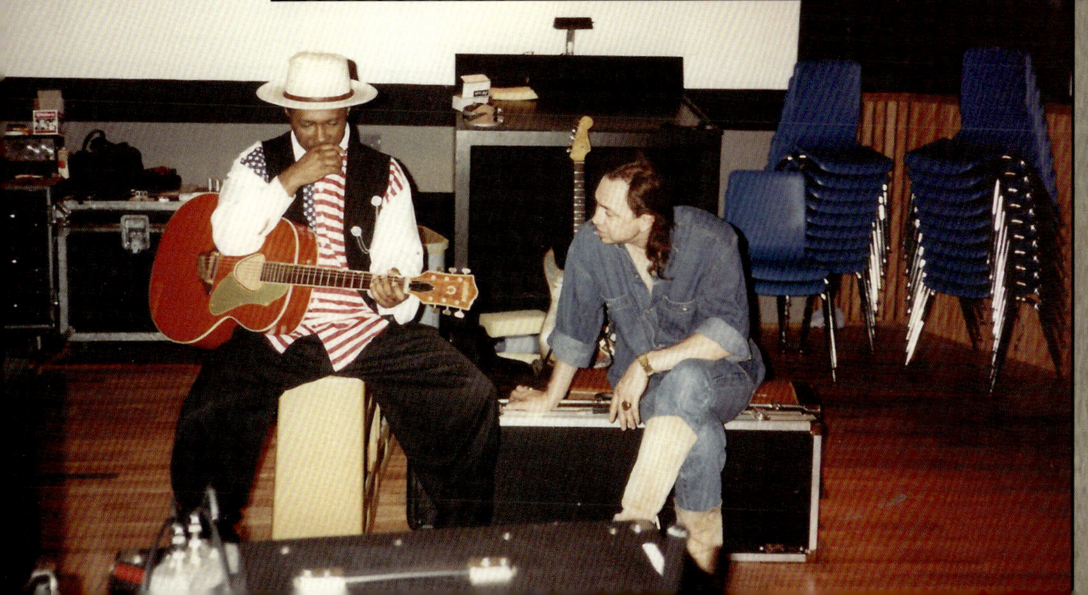

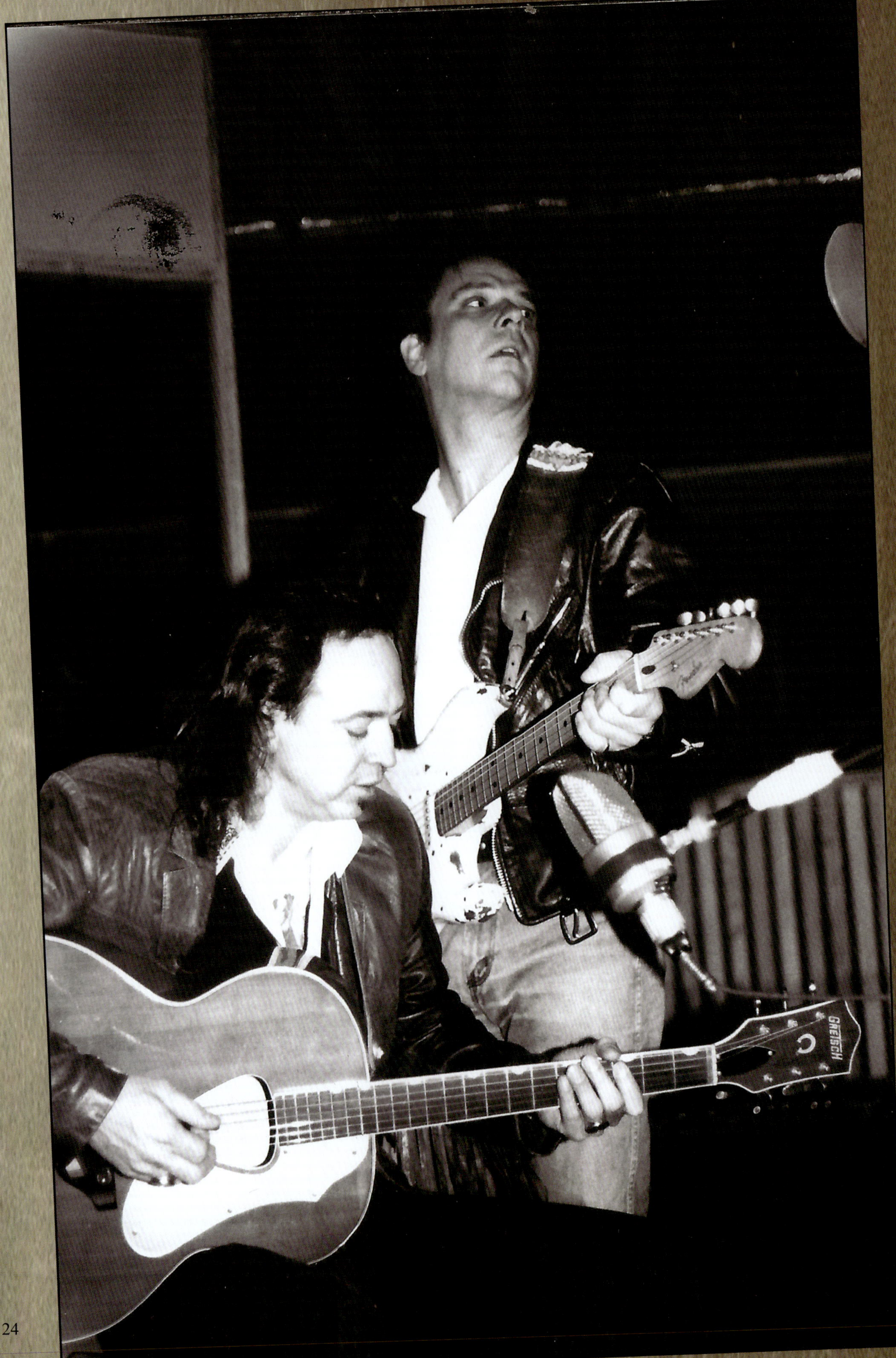
GRETSCH

Chapter 15: Royal Albert Hall – Jimmie Vaughan

A year had passed since Stevie Ray's death and Jimmie Vaughan stayed off the stage and out of the spotlight until 1991 when I received a call from Eric Clapton's office inviting Jimmie to perform with EC at the Royal Albert Hall as part of Eric's blues band along with Buddy Guy, Albert Collins and Robert Cray. Jimmie accepted the invitation and once again we set off for London.

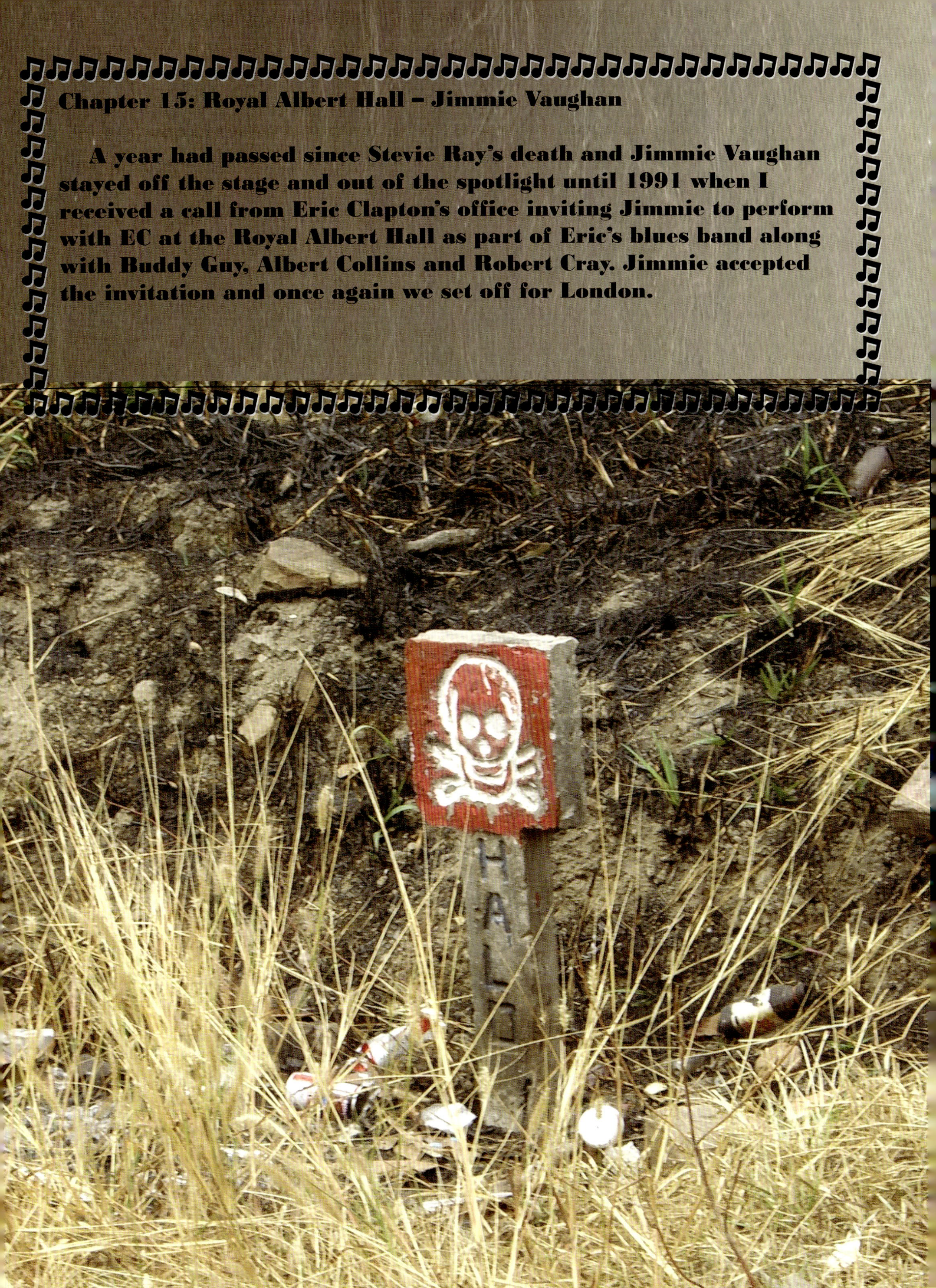

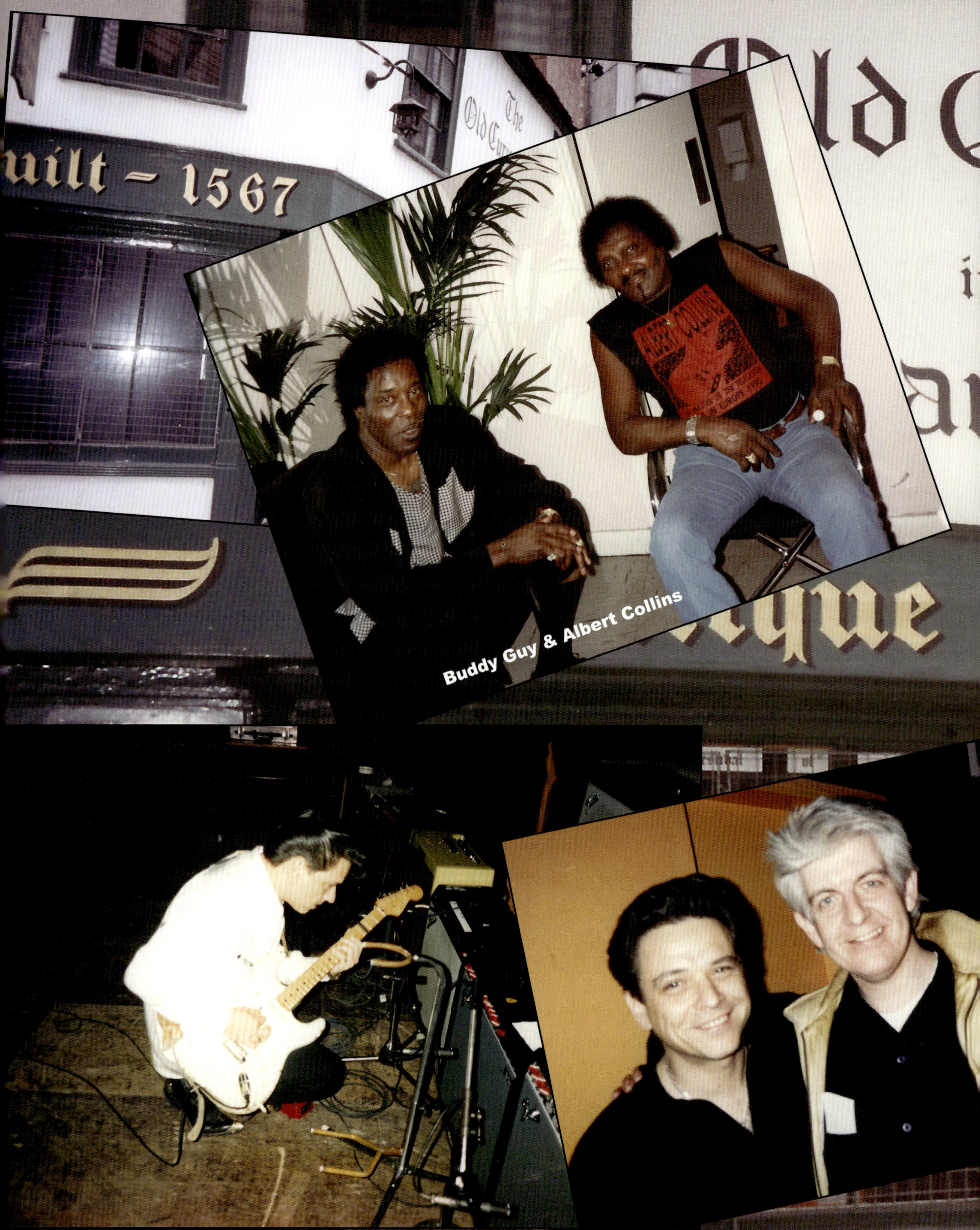

Buddy Guy & Albert Collins

Jimmie Vaughan at The Royal Albert Hall

Jimmie Vaughan & Nick Lowe

Jimmie Vaughan & Albert Collins

Johnnie Johnson & Chuck Leavell

Chapter 16: Living in a Dream with the Arc Angels

October of 1990 and we all still felt lost and looking for some direction. At the time I was managing Doyle Bramhall II who had just signed a deal with Geffen Records. He was writing and rehearsing at the Austin Rehearsal Complex along with Tommy Shannon and Chris Layton (Double Trouble) who at the time were just trying to keep themselves busy. Also Charlie Sexton who had just returned to Austin after living in Los Angeles had a small rehearsal room where he was spending more and more time. It didn't take long before these four musicians were in one room and playing together.

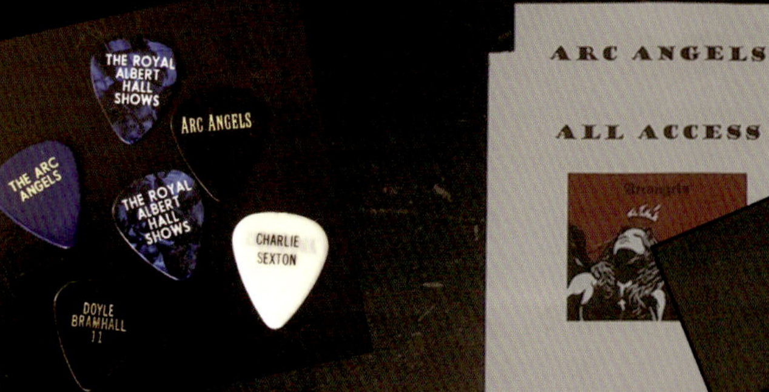

At about the same time I ran into Tim O'Conner owner of the Austin Opera House and he told me about an upcoming Robert Cray show. I asked him if he needed an opening act and told him I had the perfect band. I went back to Doyle, Charlie, Chris and Tommy and asked if they could put together a 45 minute set to open the Robert Cray show. They agreed to play but still didn't have a name for the group. That was solved when standing outside of the rehearsal complex Chris Layton looked up at the Austin Rehearsal Complex sign and came back with "How about the ARC Angels".

The ARC Angels went on to record for Geffen Records, toured extensively but was short-lived and the band broke up in 1995.

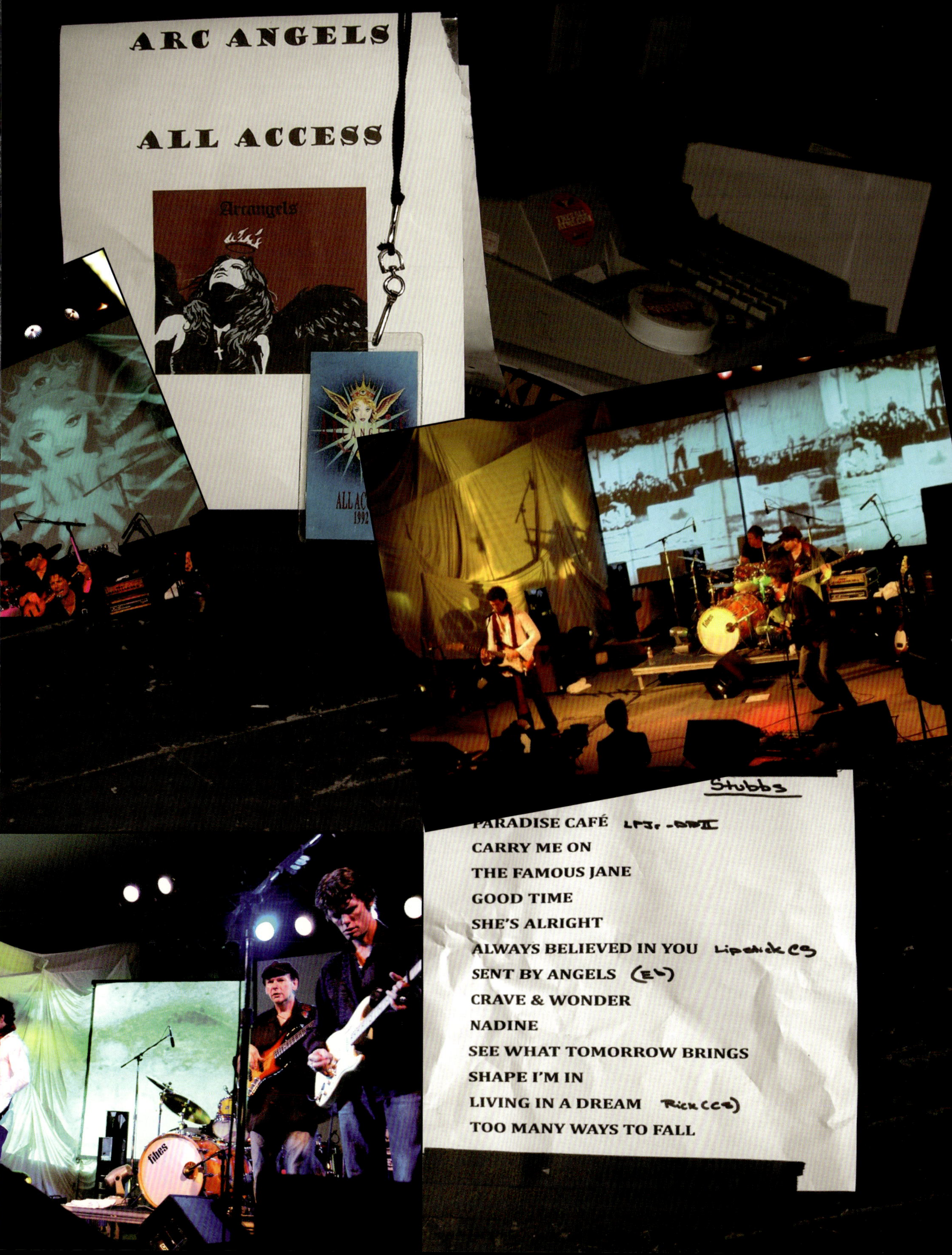
ARC ANGELS
ALL ACCESS
Arcangels
ALL AC
1992
Stubbs
PARADISE CAFÉ
CARRY ME ON
THE FAMOUS JANE
GOOD TIME
SHE'S ALRIGHT
ALWAYS BELIEVED IN YOU
SENT BY ANGELS
CRAVE & WONDER
NADINE
SEE WHAT TOMORROW BRINGS
SHAPE I'M IN
LIVING IN A DREAM
TOO MANY WAYS TO FALL

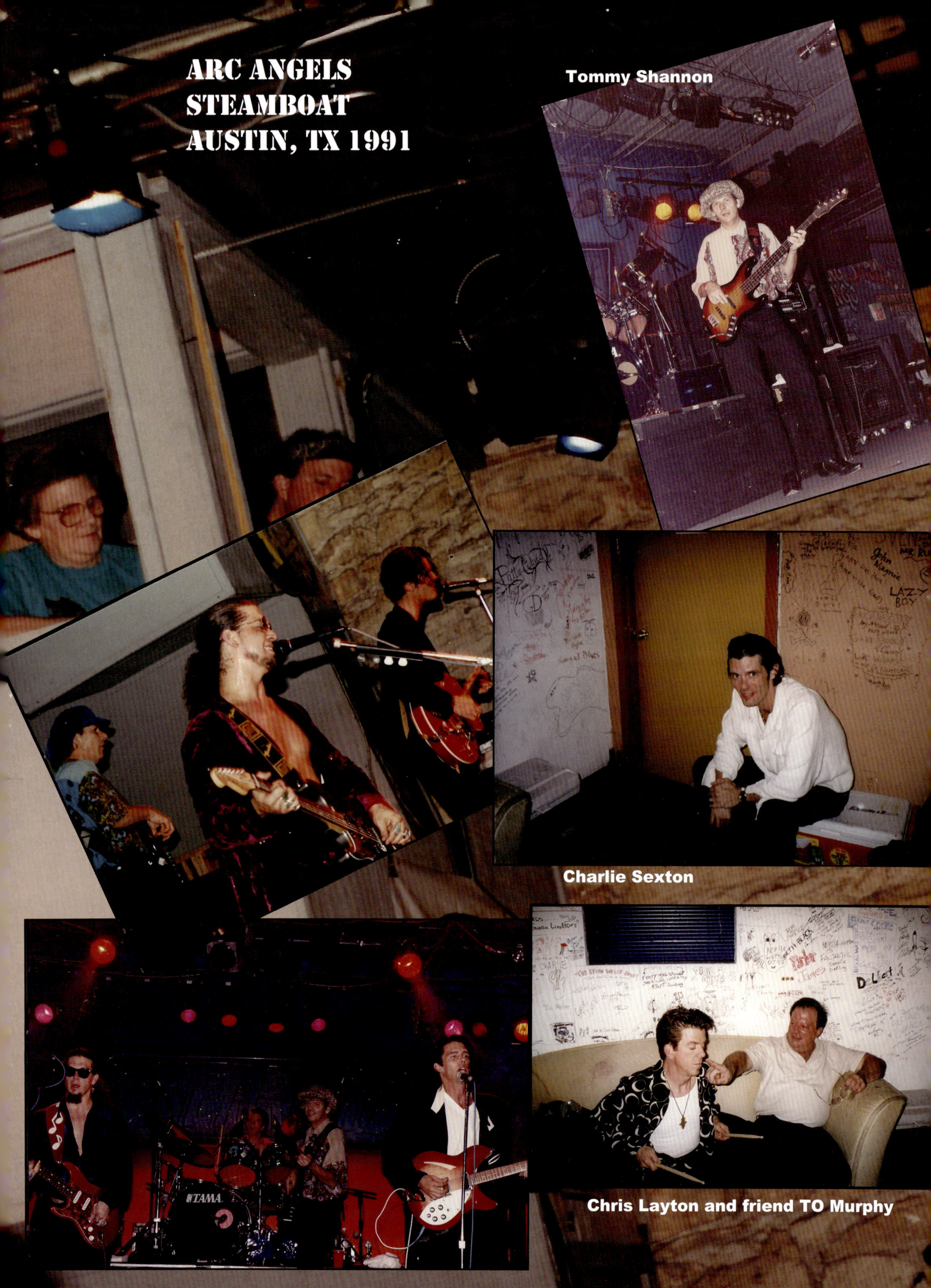

ARC ANGELS STEAMBOAT AUSTIN, TX 1991

Tommy Shannon

Charlie Sexton

Chris Layton and friend TO Murphy

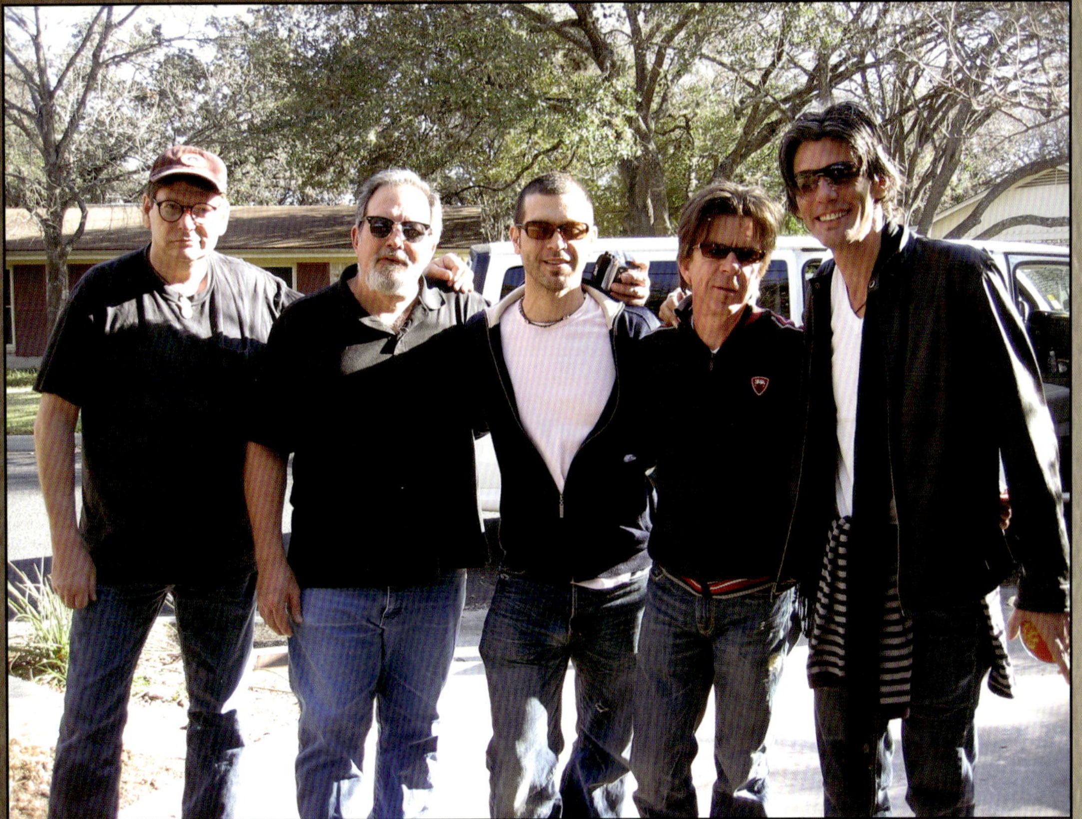

Tommy Shannon, TO Murphy, Doyle Bramhall II, Chris Layton, Charlie Sexton

ARC Angels with Billy Gibbons of ZZ Top at The Continental Club

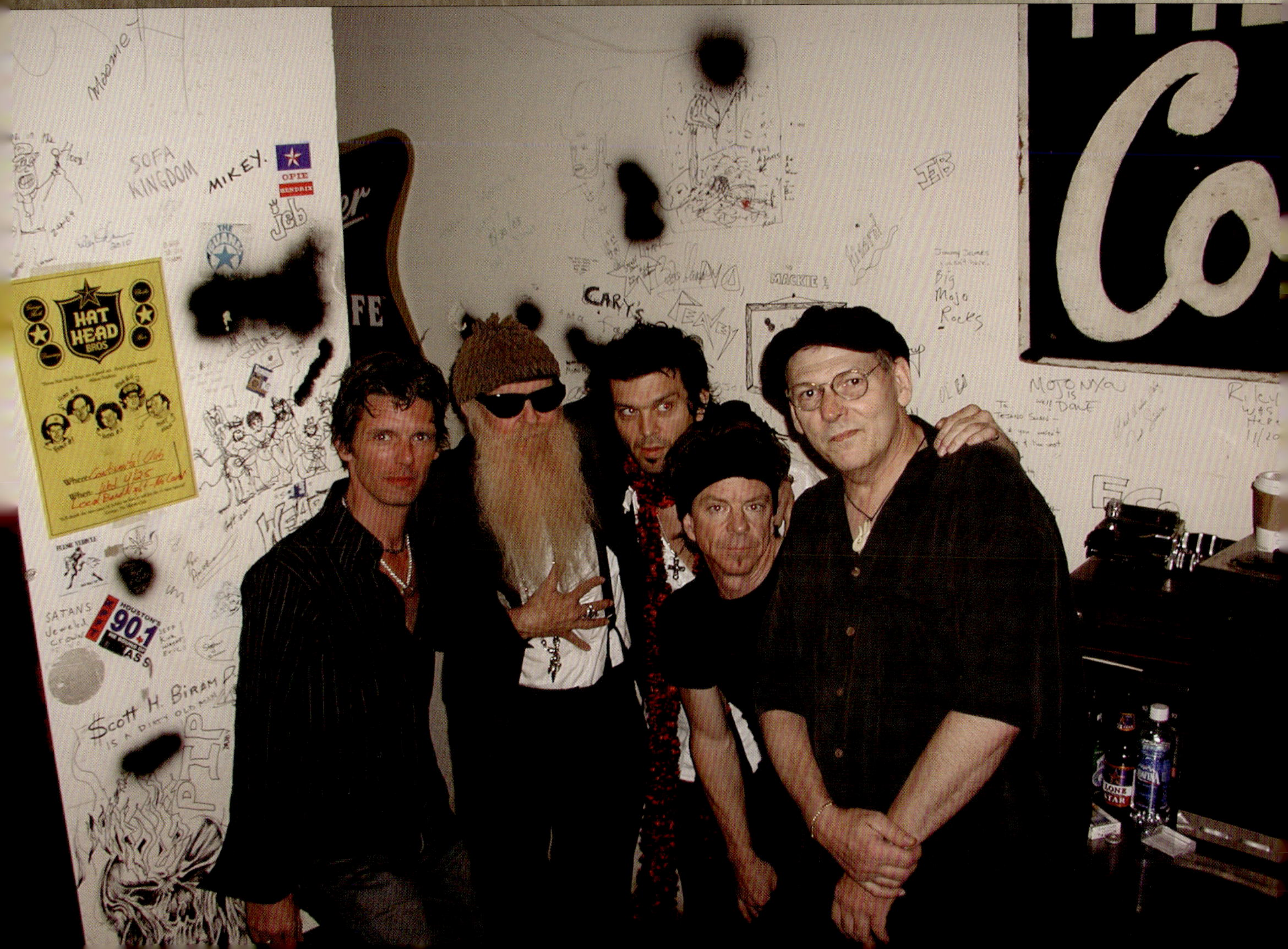

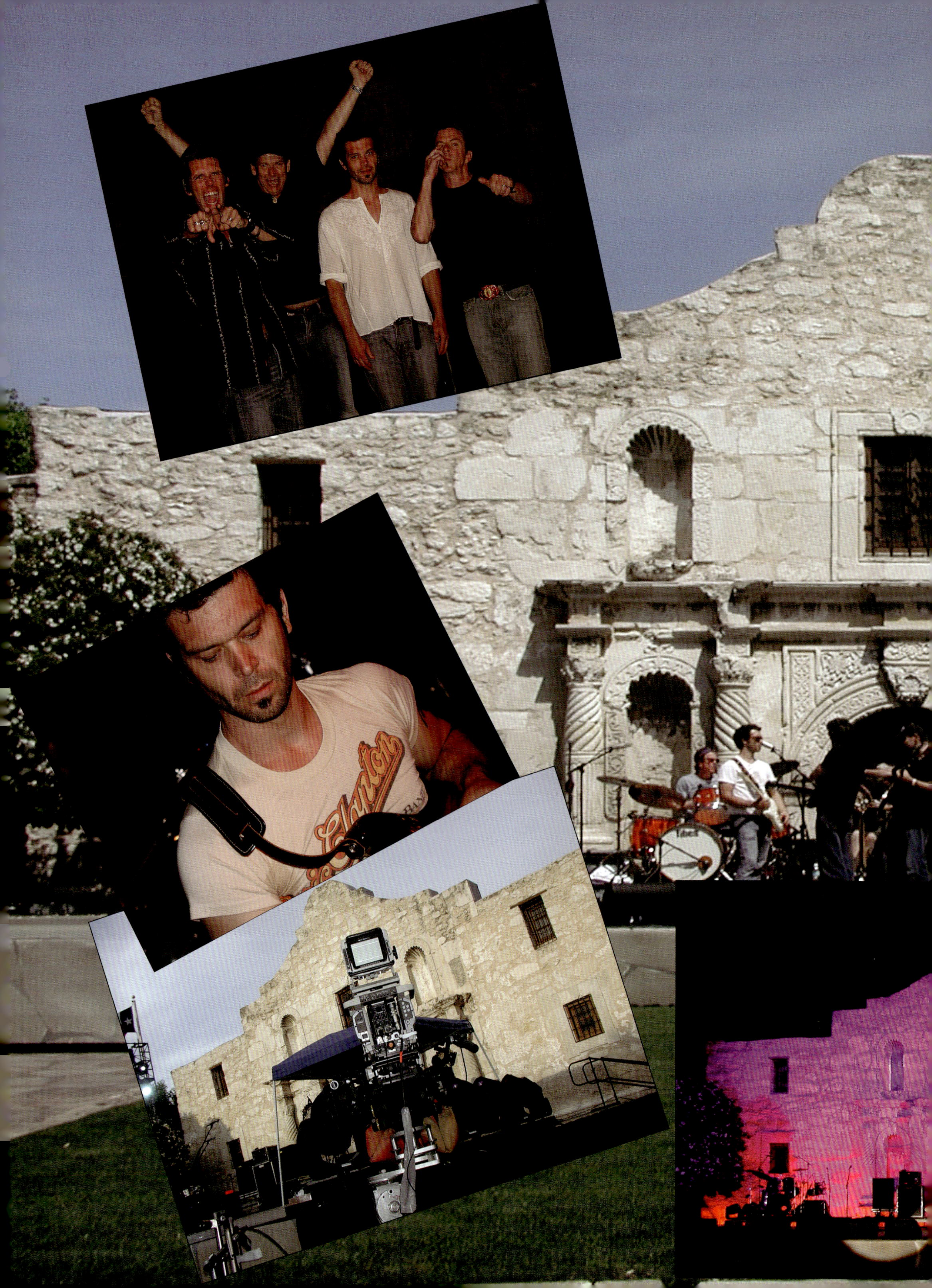
Clapton

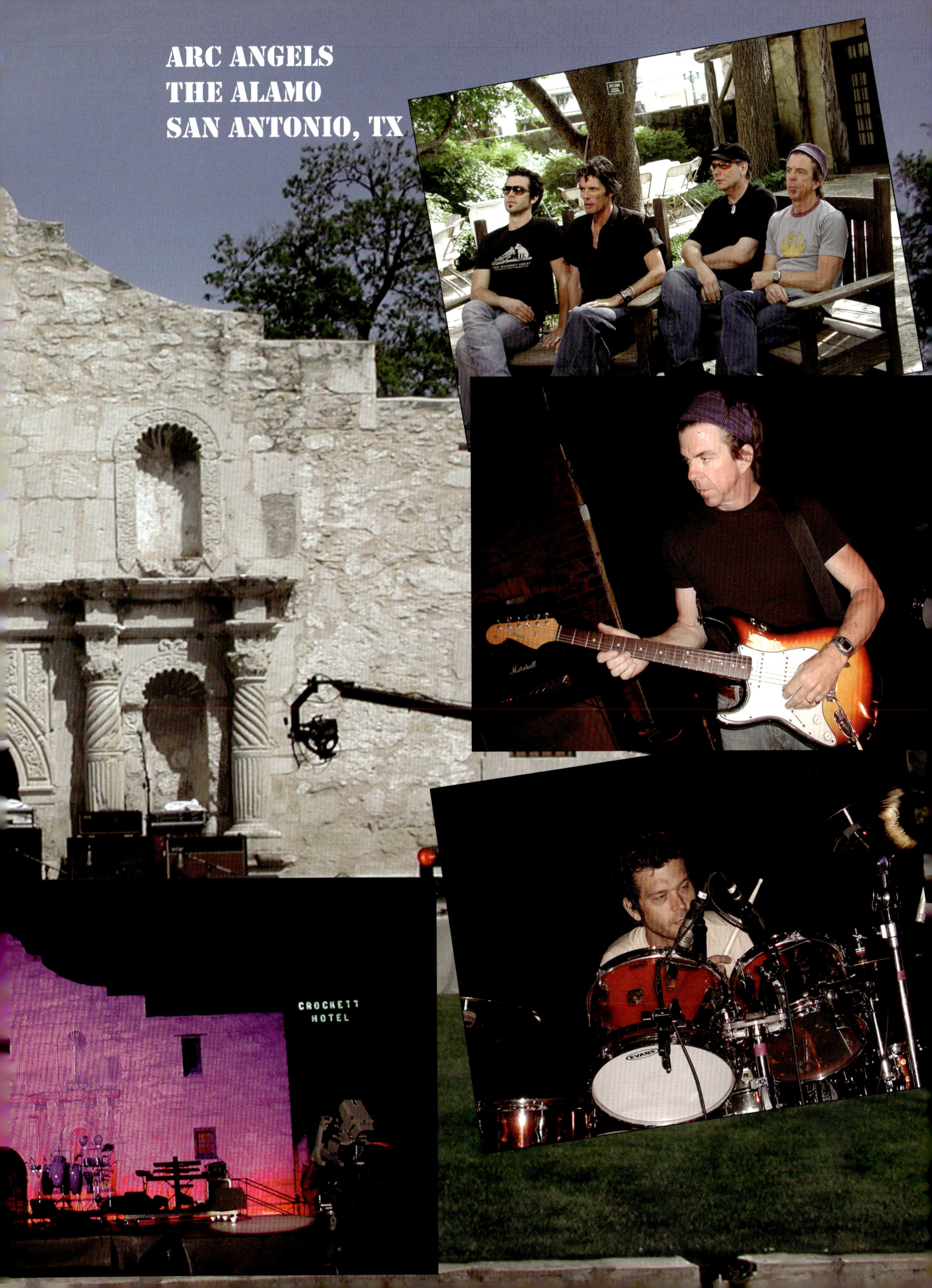
ARC ANGELS
THE ALAMO
SAN ANTONIO, TX
CROCKETT
HOTEL

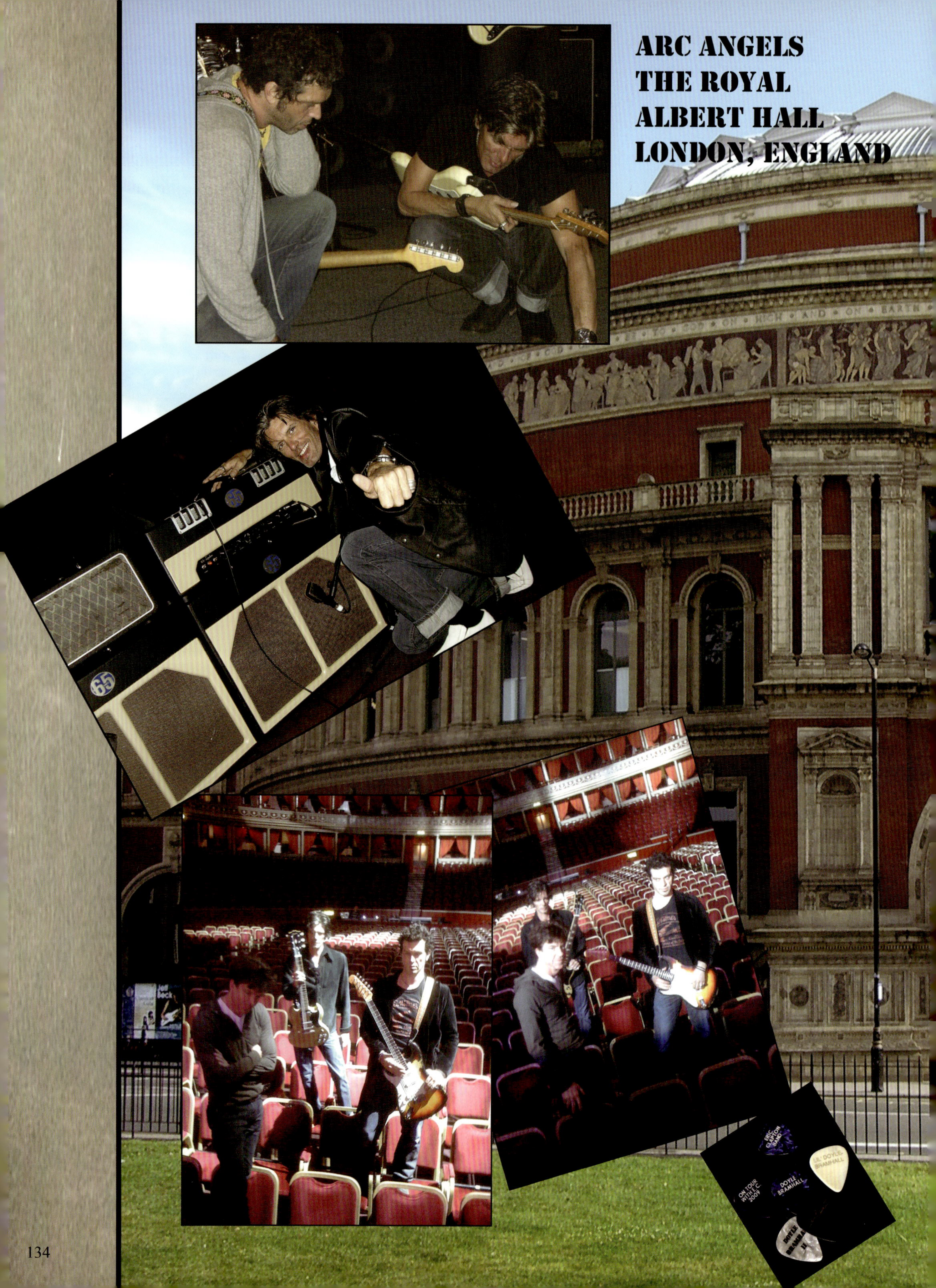
ARC ANGELS
THE ROYAL
ALBERT HALL
LONDON, ENGLAND
ERIC CLAPTON BAND
LIL' DOYLE BRAMHALL
ON TOUR WITH E.C. 2009
DOYLE BRAMHALL
DOYLE BRAMHALL II

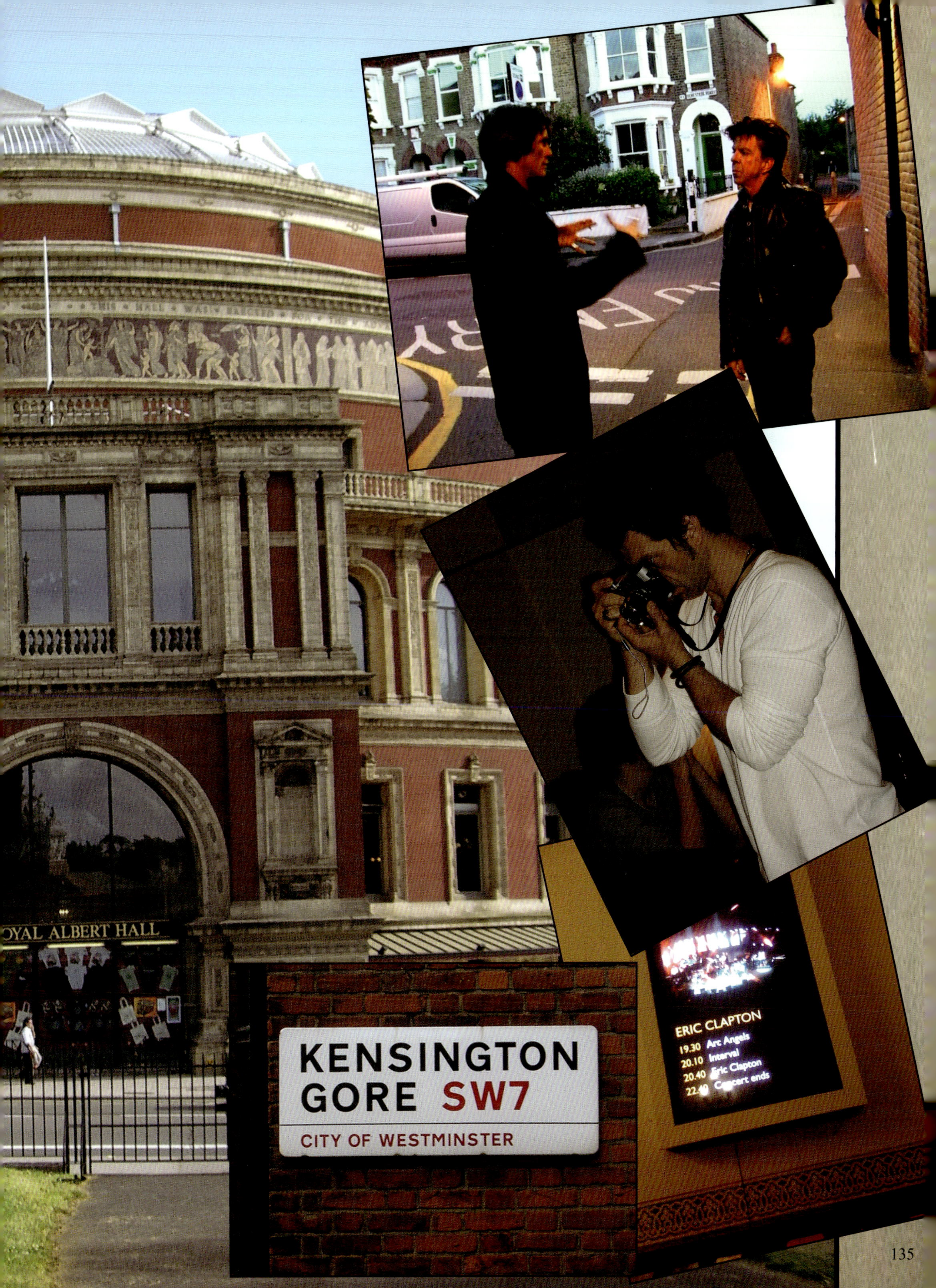
OYAL ALBERT HALL
KENSINGTON
GORE SW7
CITY OF WESTMINSTER
ERIC CLAPTON
19.30 Arc Angels
20.10 Interval
20.40 Eric Clapton
Concert ends

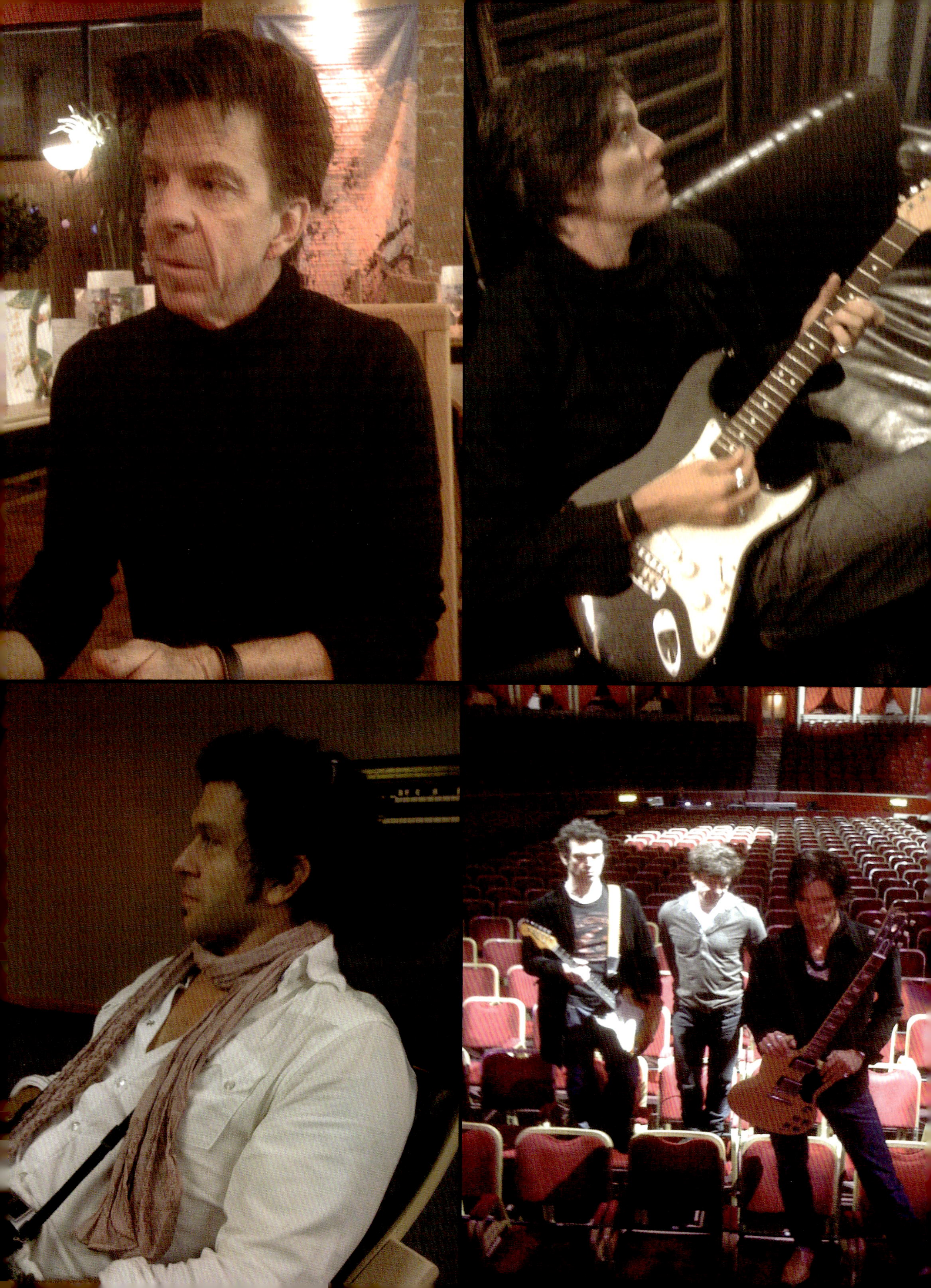

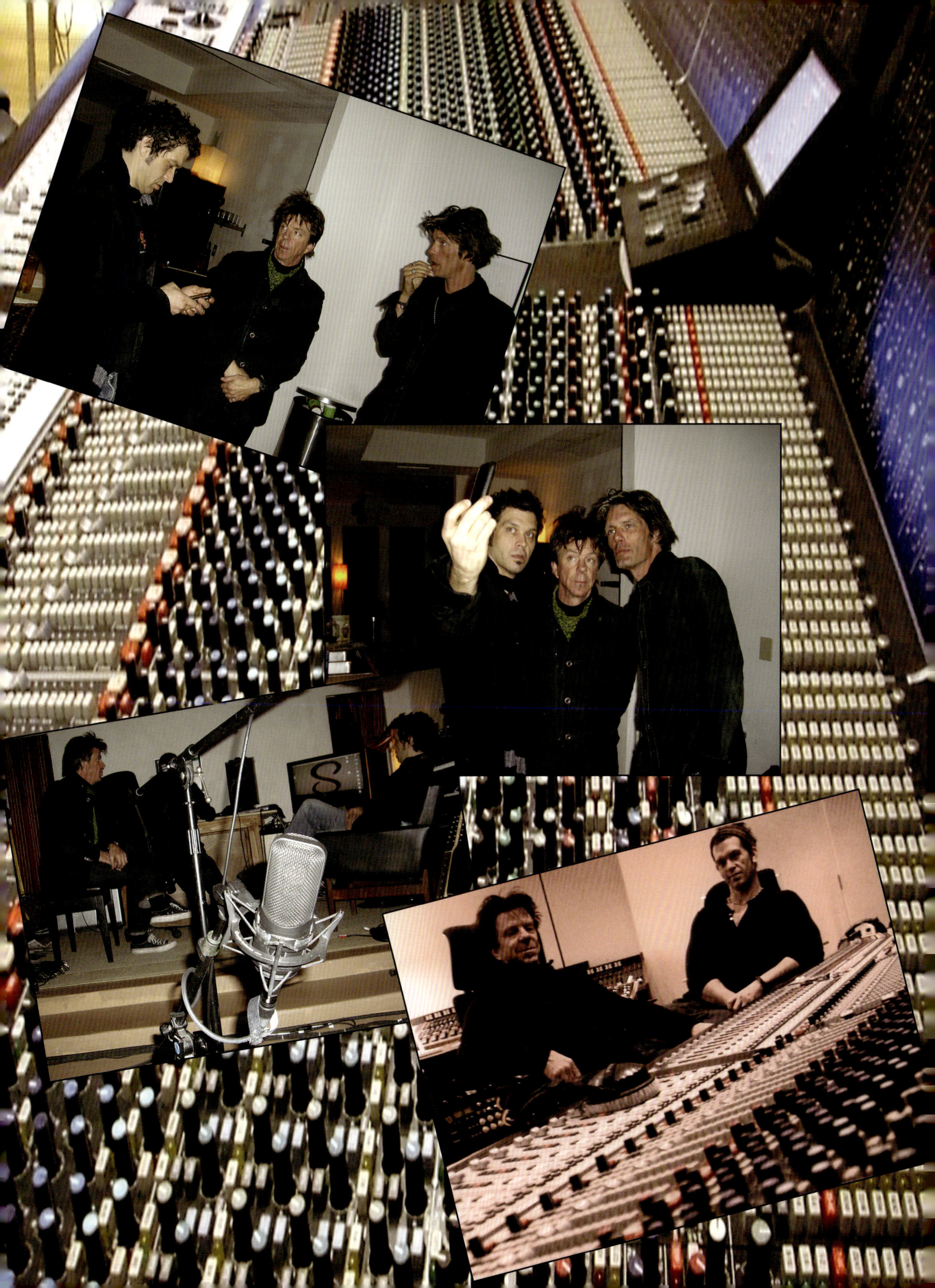

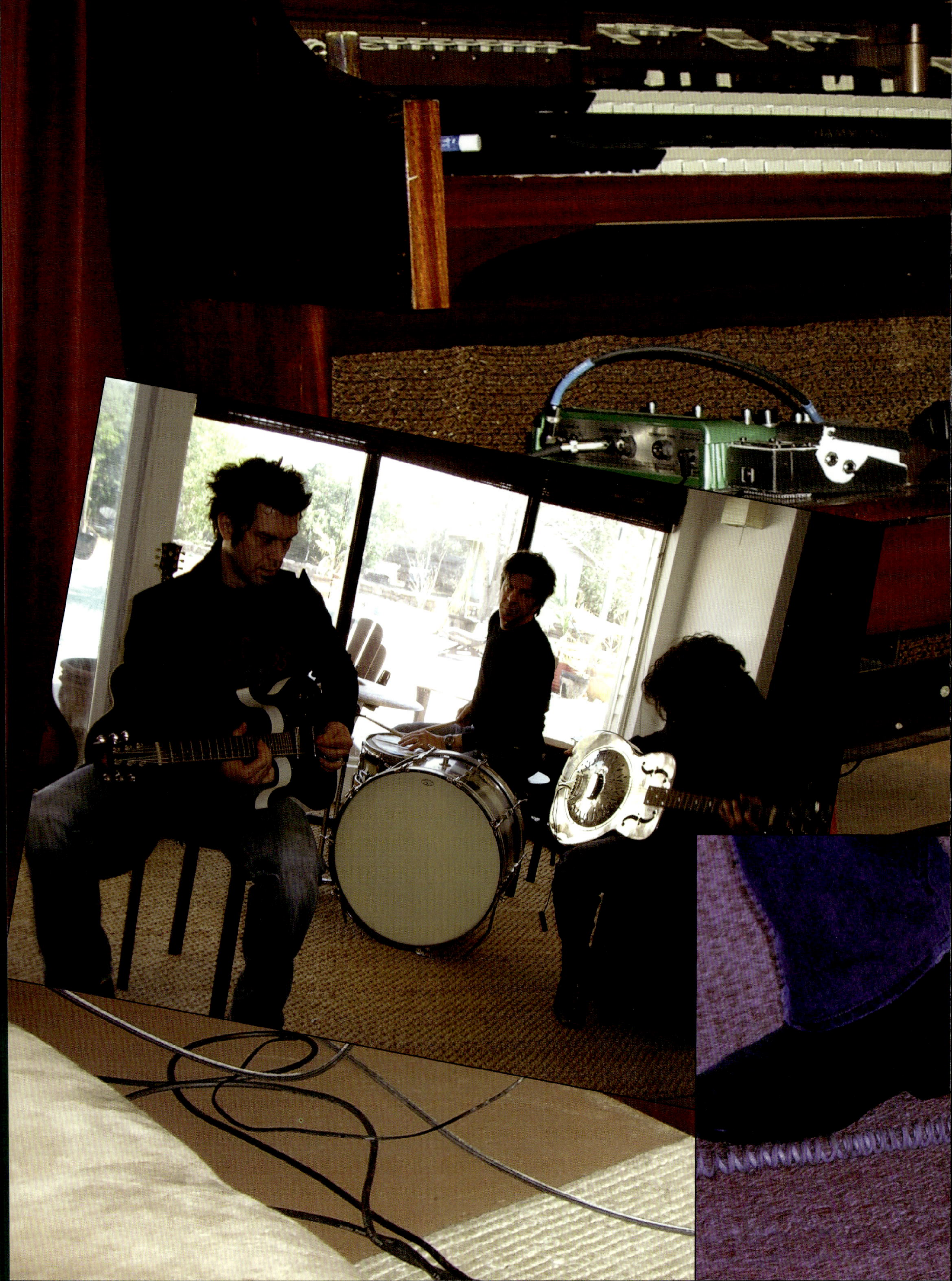

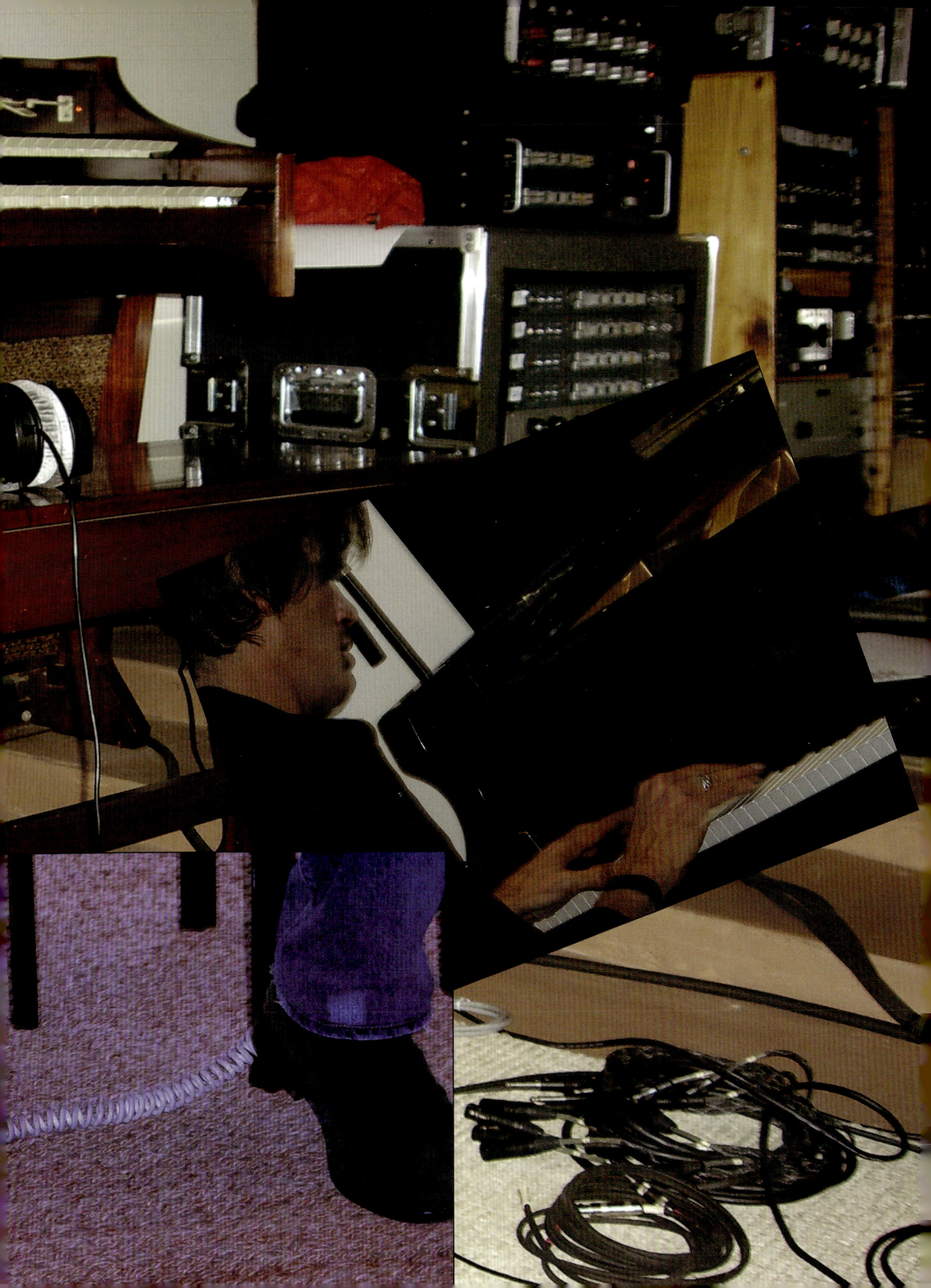

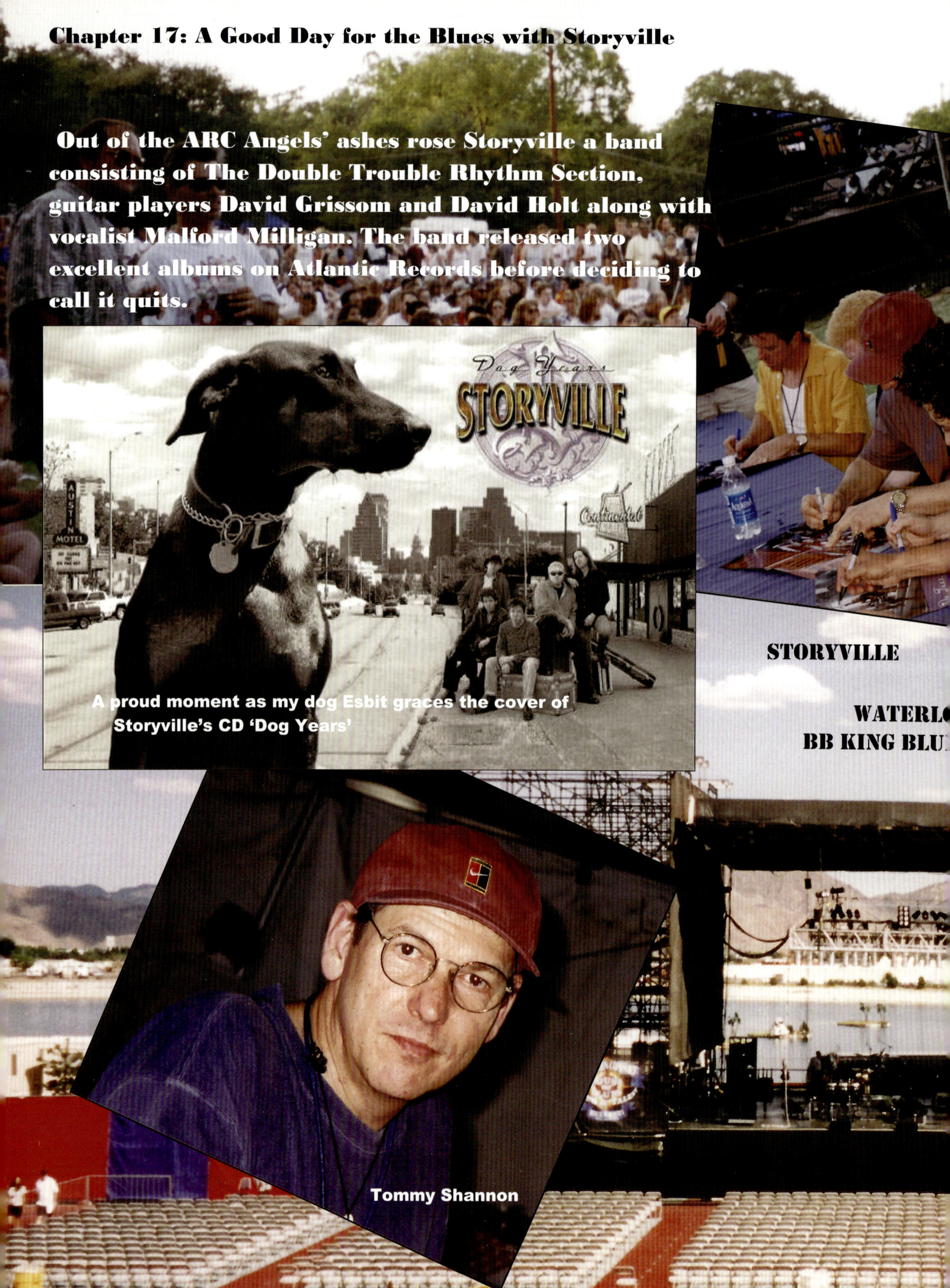

A proud moment as my dog Esbit graces the cover of Storyville's CD 'Dog Years'

Tommy Shannon

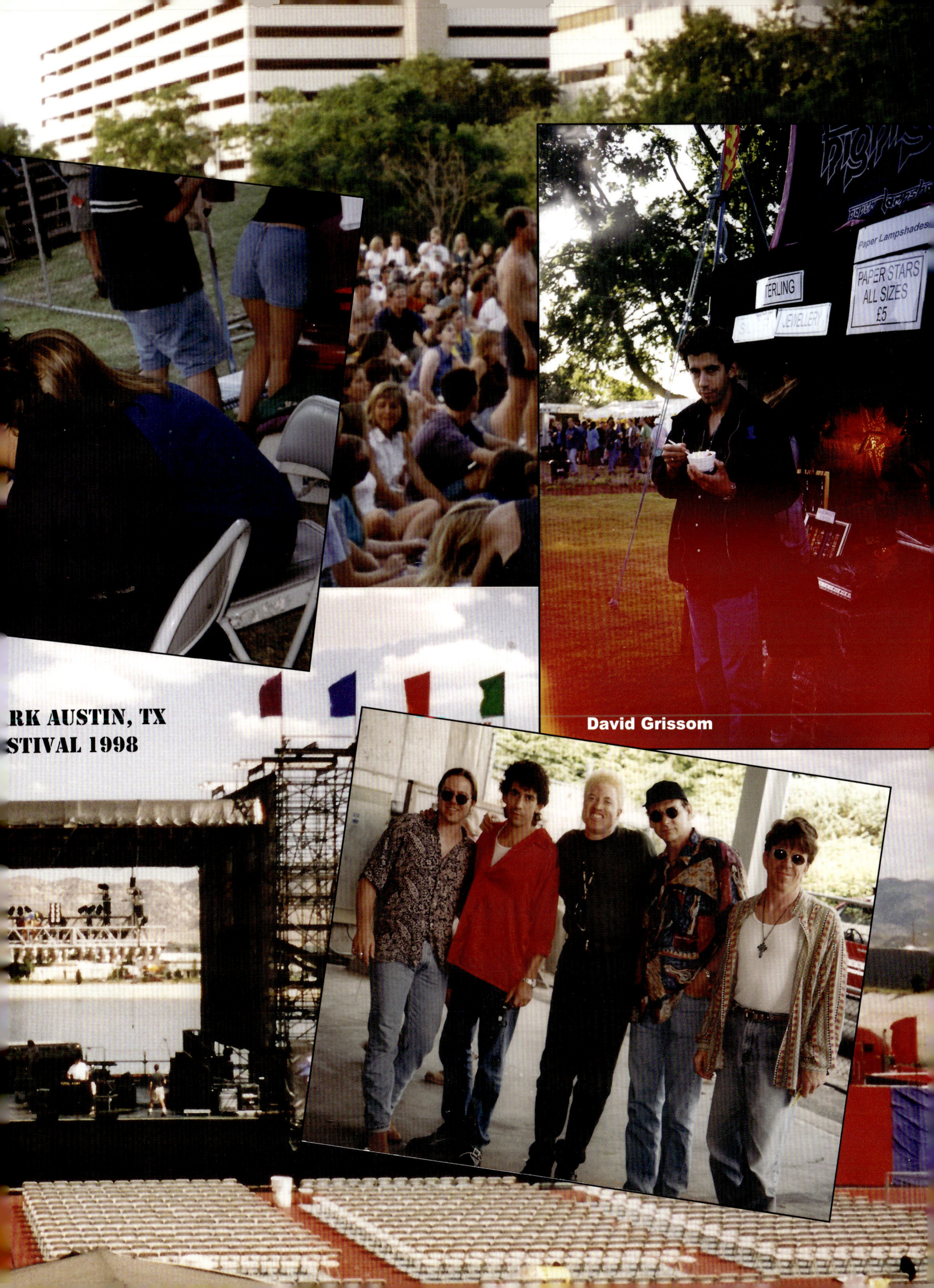

David Grissom

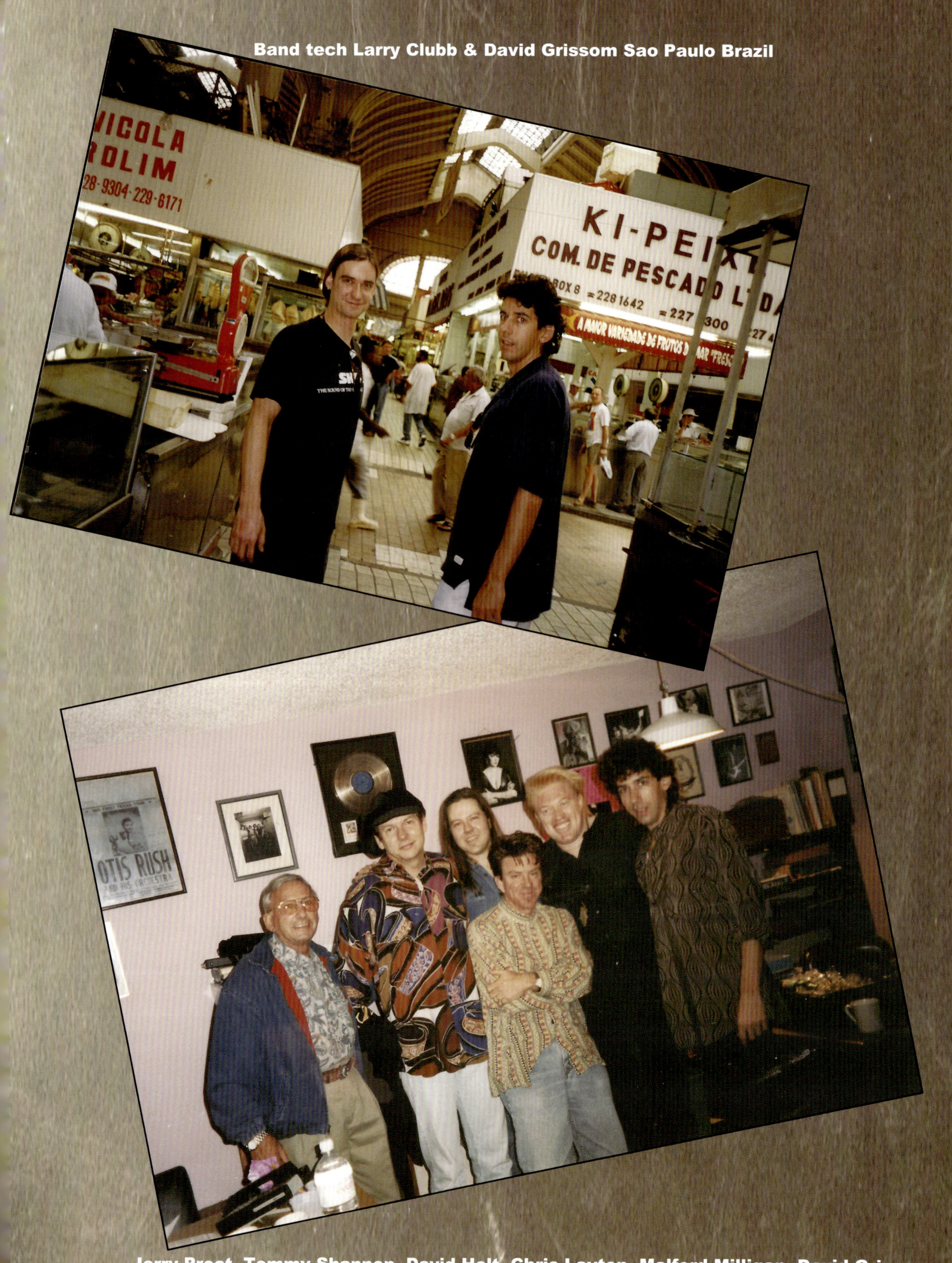

Band tech Larry Clubb & David Grissom Sao Paulo Brazil

Jerry Proct, Tommy Shannon, David Holt, Chris Layton, Malford Milligan, David Grissom

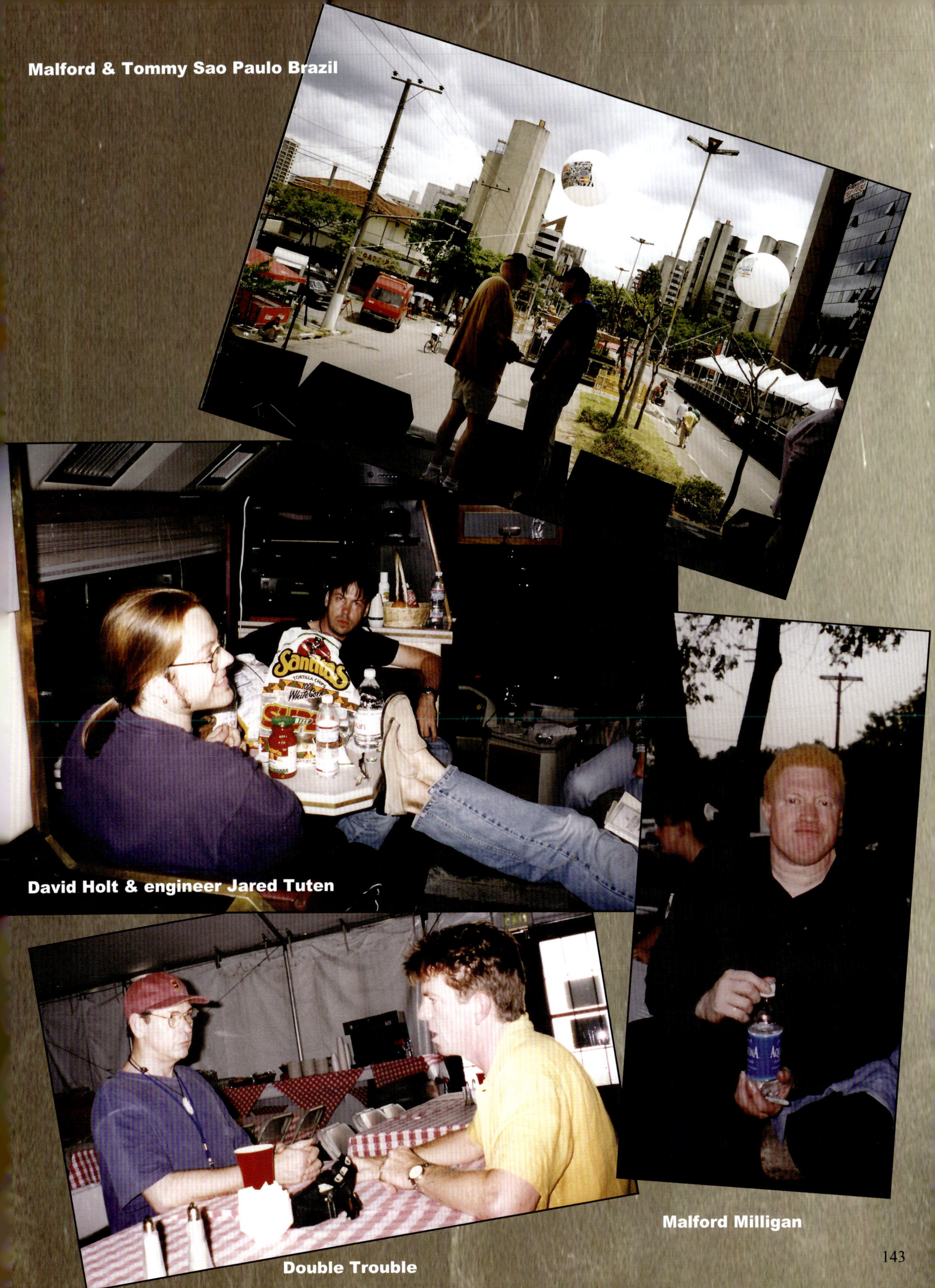

Malford & Tommy Sao Paulo Brazil

David Holt & engineer Jared Tuten

Malford Milligan

Double Trouble

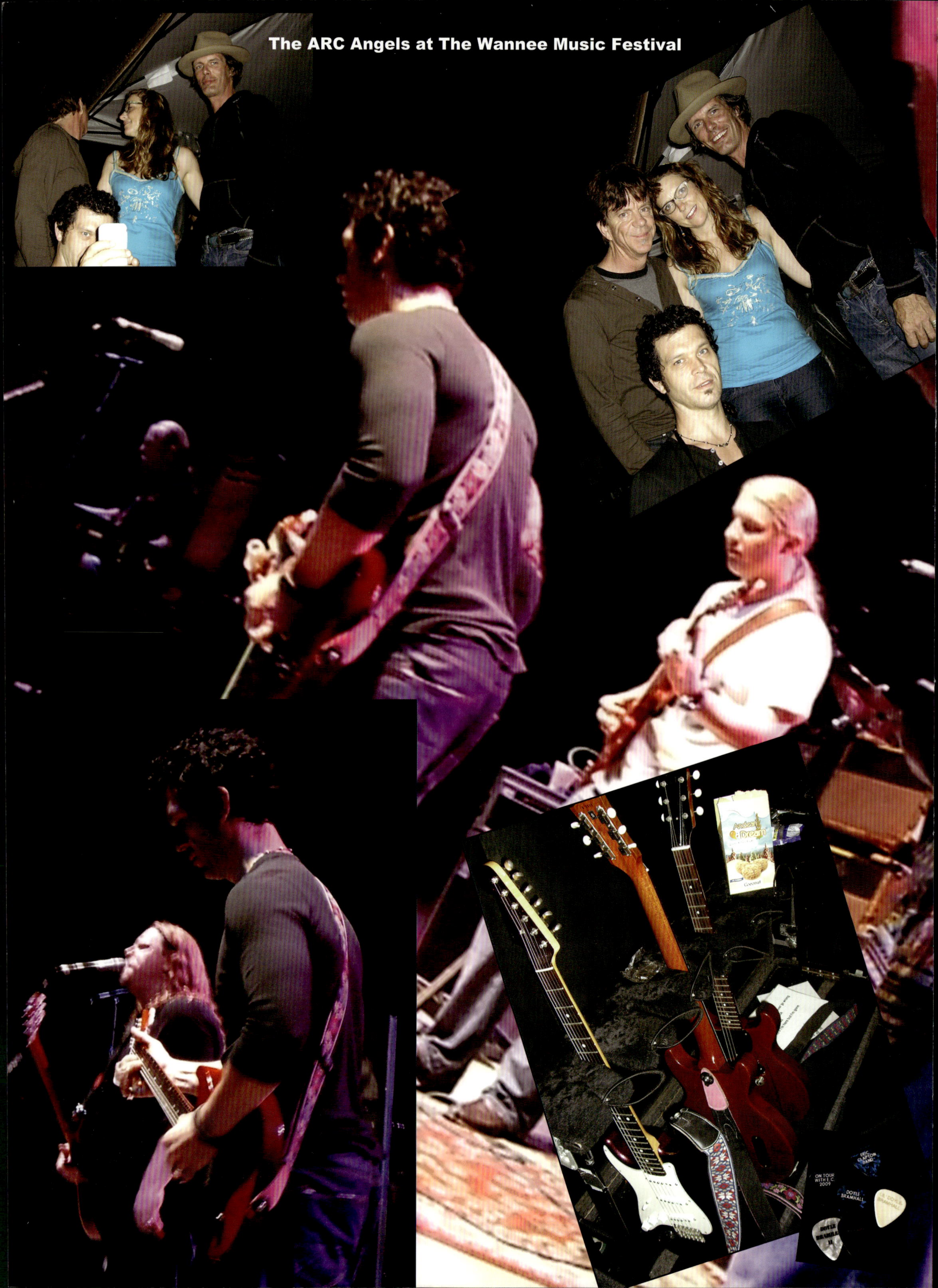
The ARC Angels at The Wannee Music Festival
ERIC CLAPTON BAND
ON TOUR WITH E.C. 2009
DOYLE BRAMHALL
DOYLE BRAMHALL

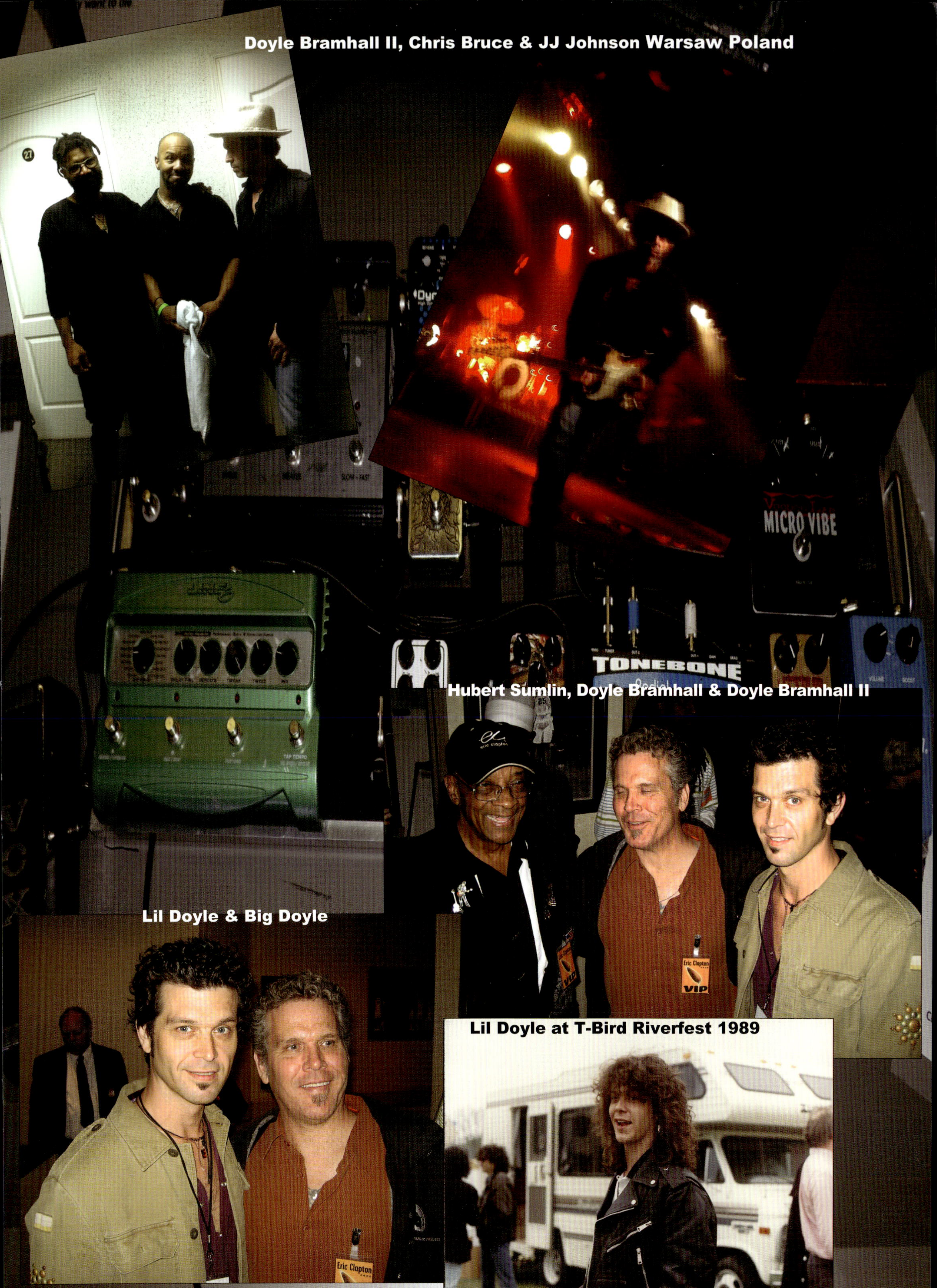

Doyle Bramhall II, Chris Bruce & JJ Johnson Warsaw Poland

Hubert Sumlin, Doyle Bramhall & Doyle Bramhall II

Lil Doyle & Big Doyle

Lil Doyle at T-Bird Riverfest 1989

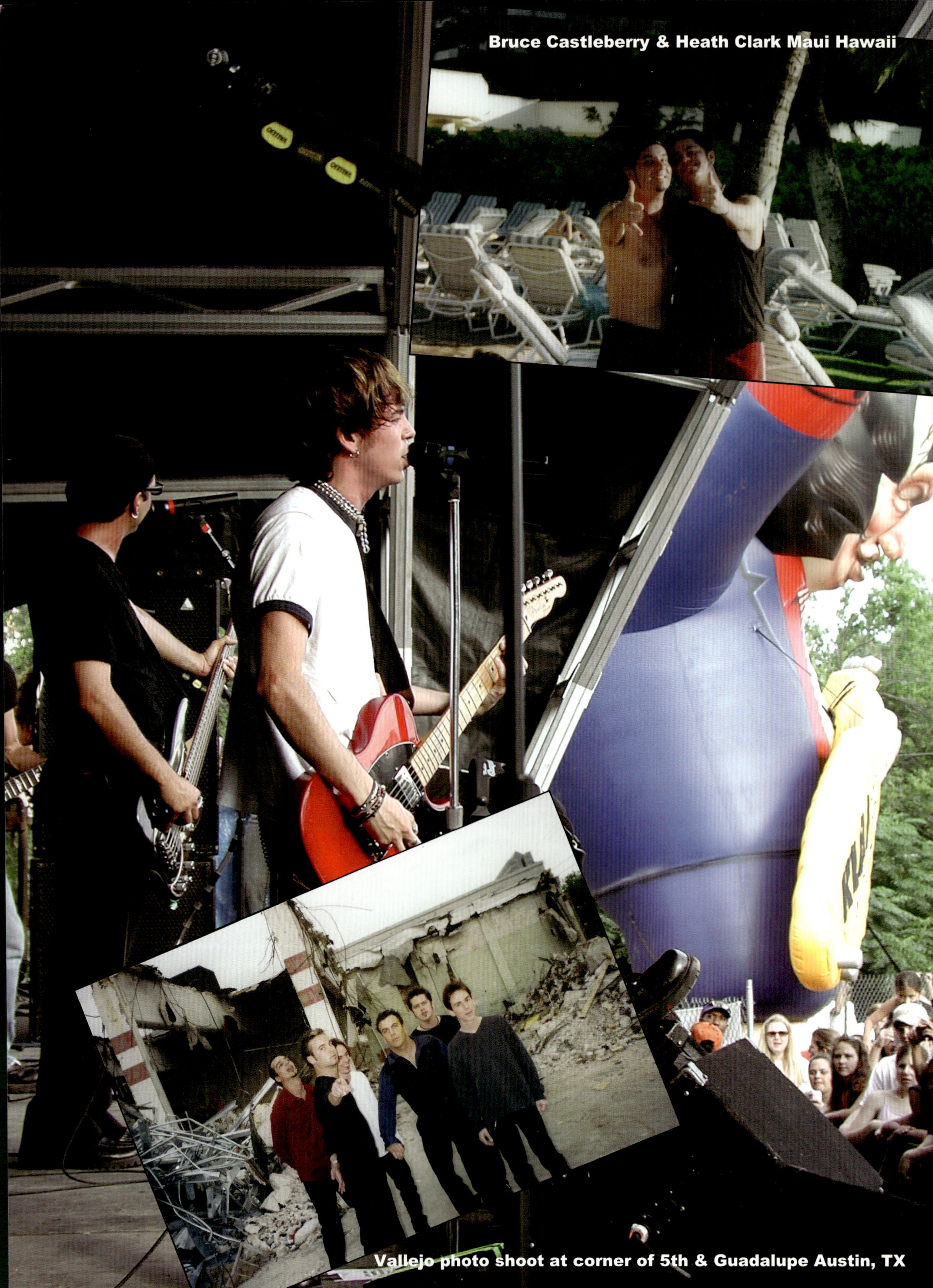

Bruce Castleberry & Heath Clark Maui Hawaii

Vallejo photo shoot at corner of 5th & Guadalupe Austin, TX

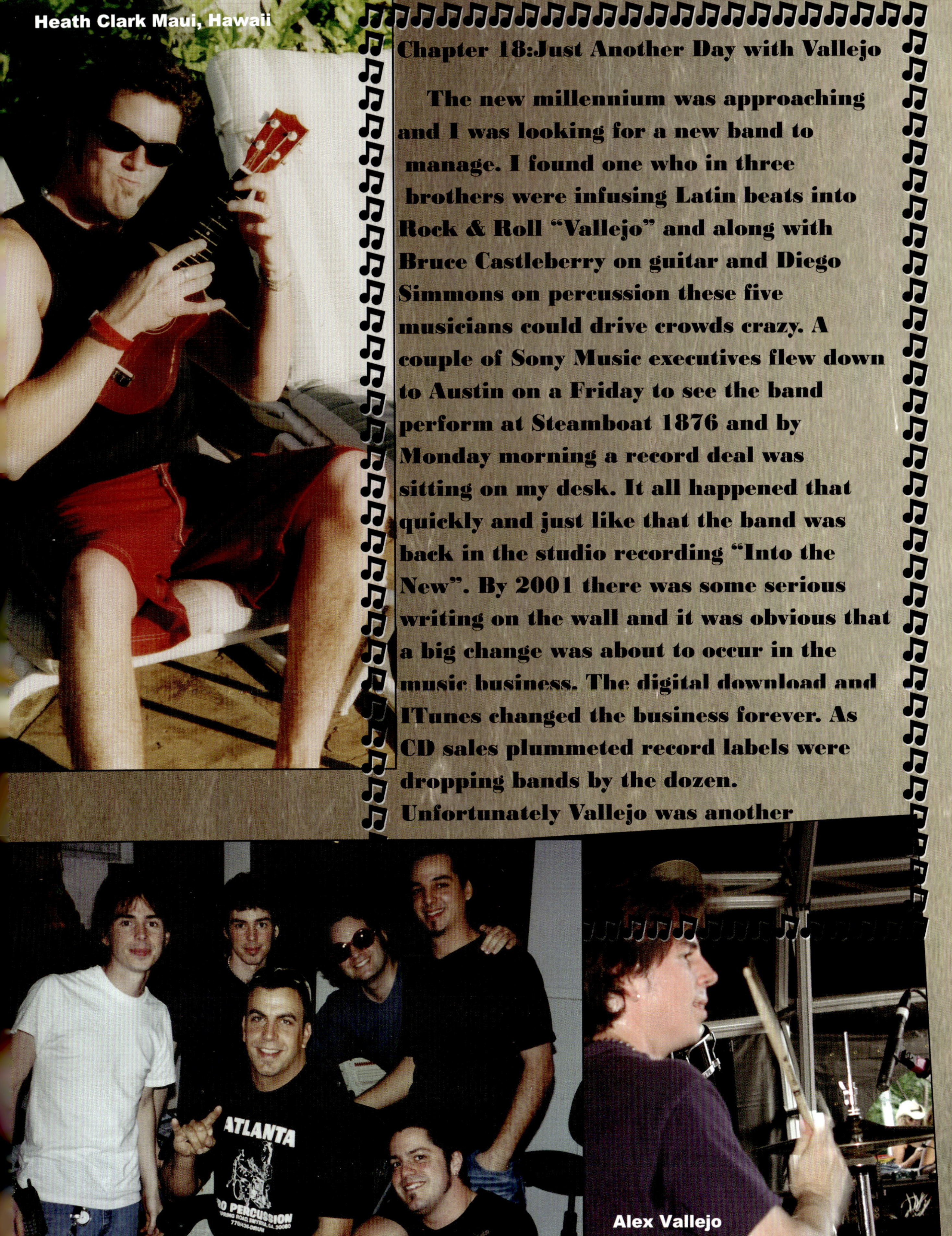

Heath Clark Maui, Hawaii

Chapter 18:Just Another Day with Vallejo

The new millennium was approaching and I was looking for a new band to manage. I found one who in three brothers were infusing Latin beats into Rock & Roll "Vallejo" and along with Bruce Castleberry on guitar and Diego Simmons on percussion these five musicians could drive crowds crazy. A couple of Sony Music executives flew down to Austin on a Friday to see the band perform at Steamboat 1876 and by Monday morning a record deal was sitting on my desk. It all happened that quickly and just like that the band was back in the studio recording "Into the New". By 2001 there was some serious writing on the wall and it was obvious that a big change was about to occur in the music business. The digital download and ITunes changed the business forever. As CD sales plummeted record labels were dropping bands by the dozen. Unfortunately Vallejo was another

Alex Vallejo

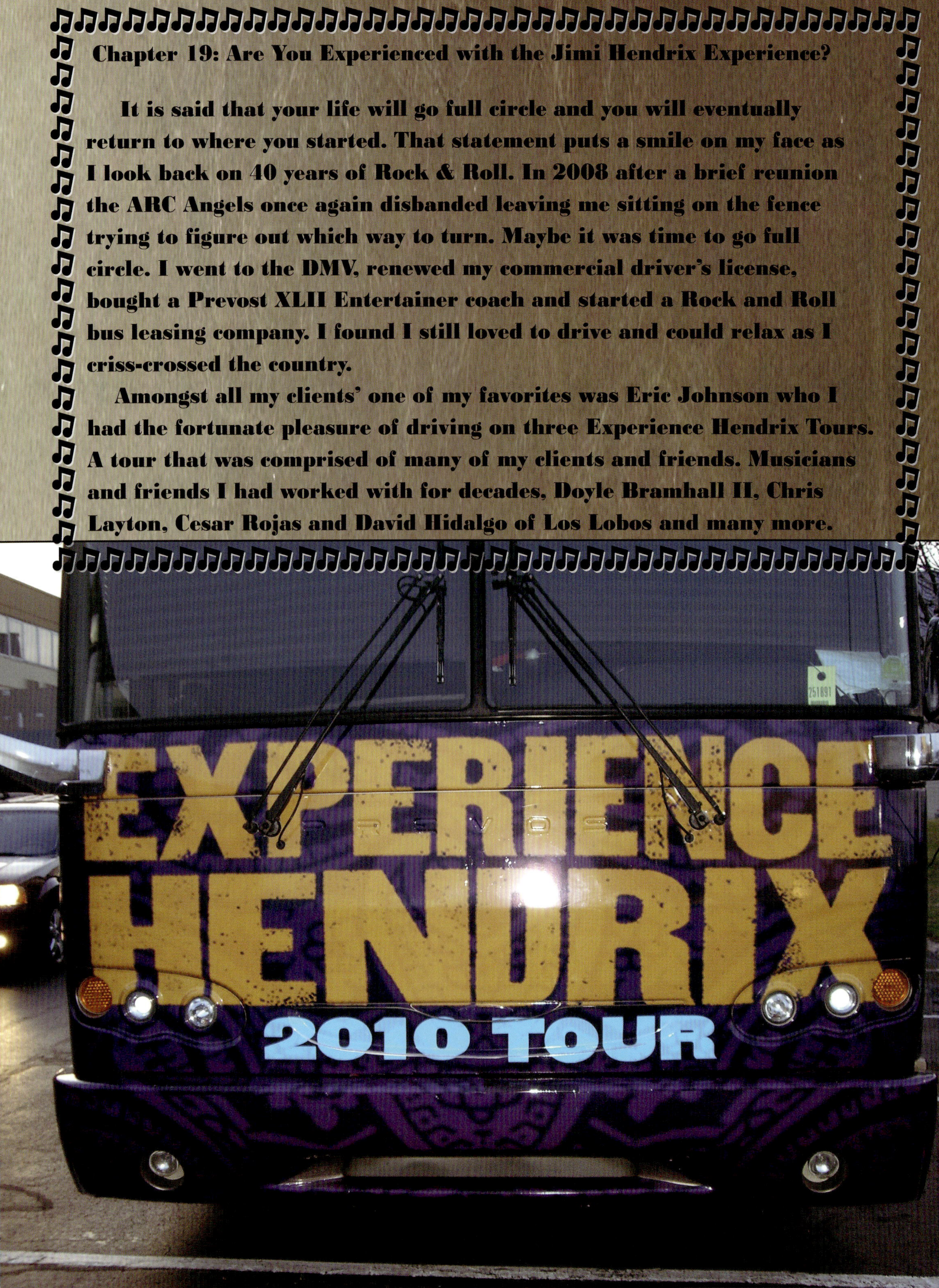

Chapter 19: Are You Experienced with the Jimi Hendrix Experience?

It is said that your life will go full circle and you will eventually return to where you started. That statement puts a smile on my face as I look back on 40 years of Rock & Roll. In 2008 after a brief reunion the ARC Angels once again disbanded leaving me sitting on the fence trying to figure out which way to turn. Maybe it was time to go full circle. I went to the DMV, renewed my commercial driver's license, bought a Prevost XLII Entertainer coach and started a Rock and Roll bus leasing company. I found I still loved to drive and could relax as I criss-crossed the country.

Amongst all my clients' one of my favorites was Eric Johnson who I had the fortunate pleasure of driving on three Experience Hendrix Tours. A tour that was comprised of many of my clients and friends. Musicians and friends I had worked with for decades, Doyle Bramhall II, Chris Layton, Cesar Rojas and David Hidalgo of Los Lobos and many more.

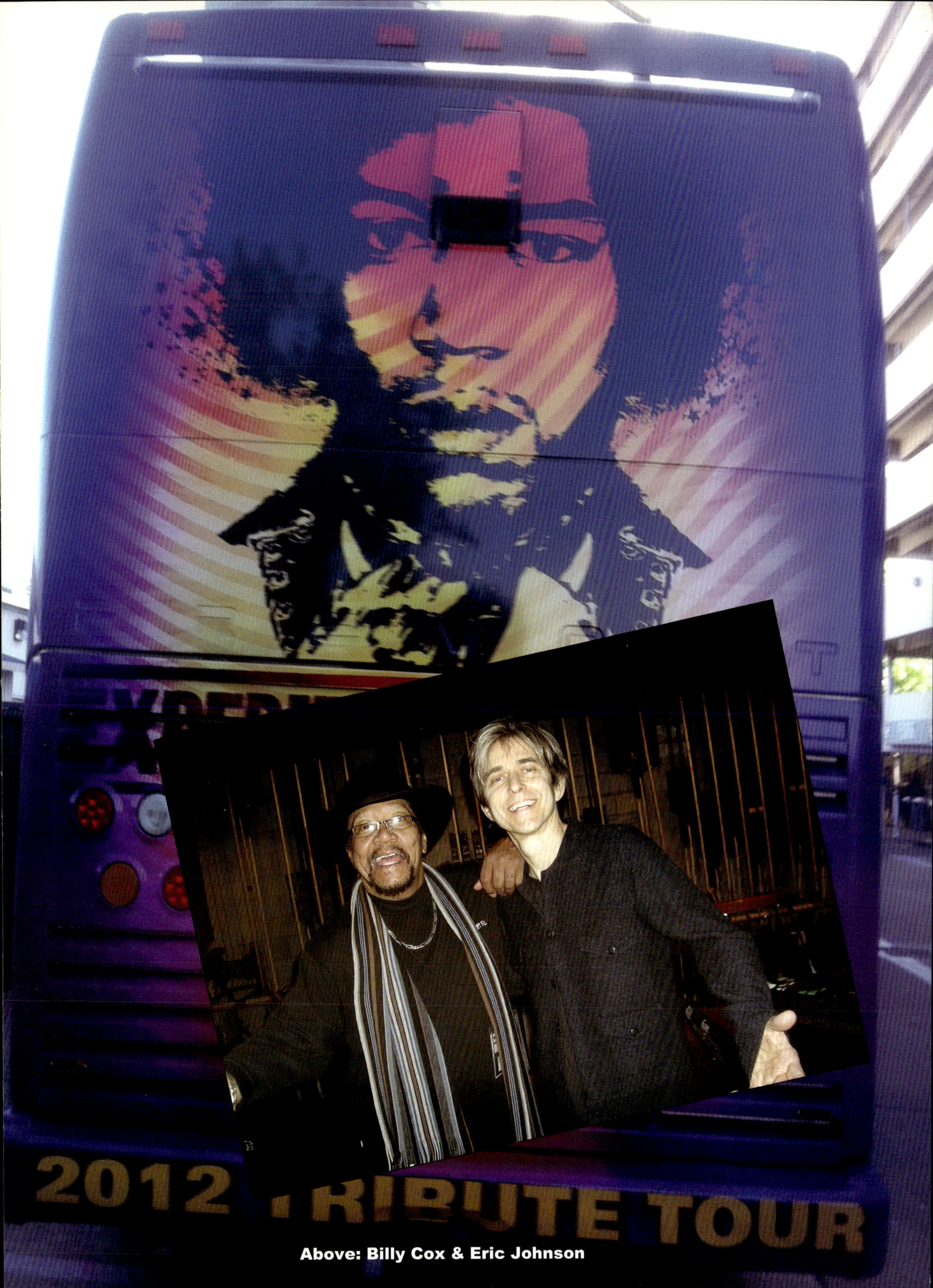

Above: Billy Cox & Eric Johnson

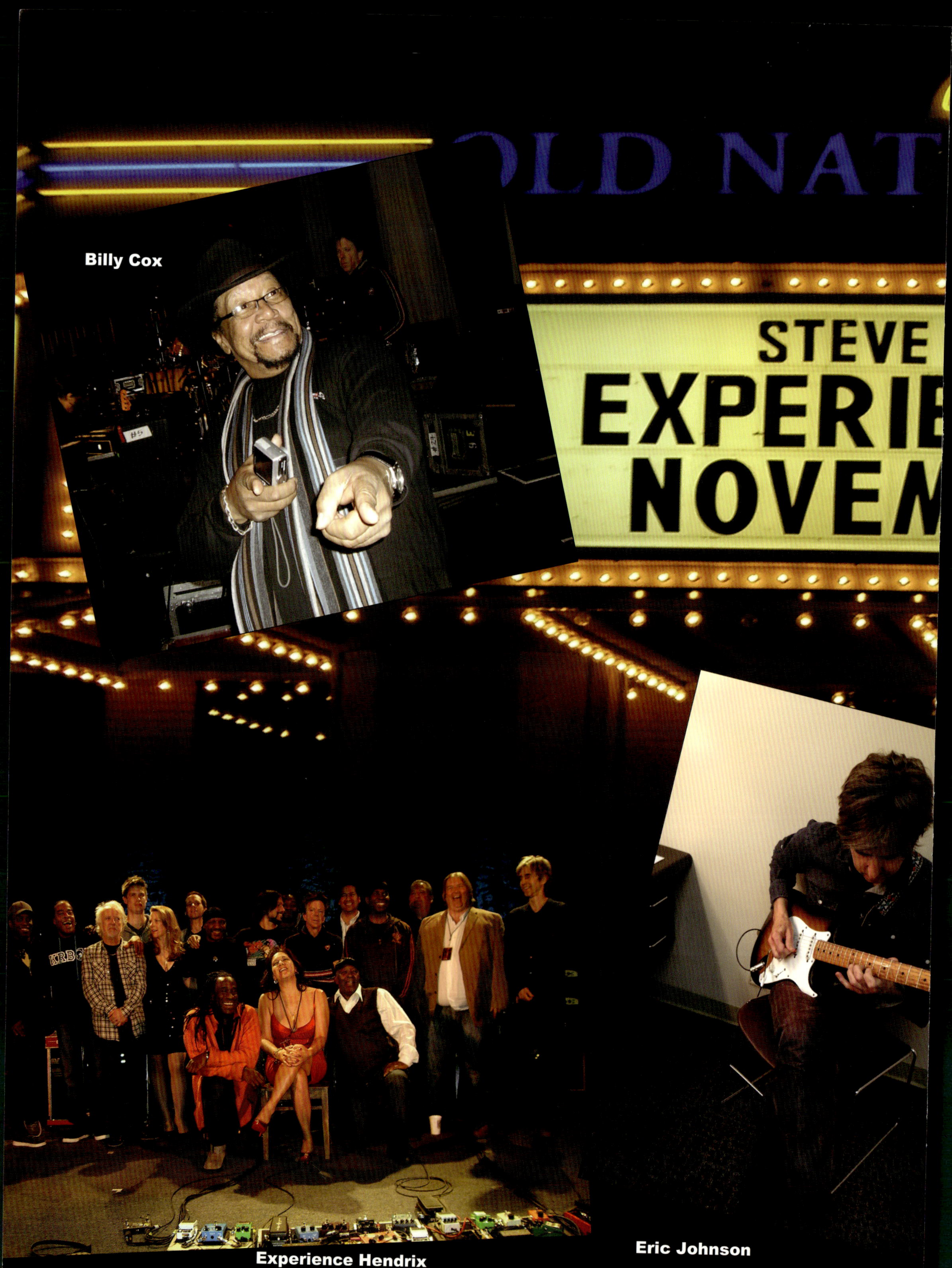

Billy Cox

Experience Hendrix

Eric Johnson

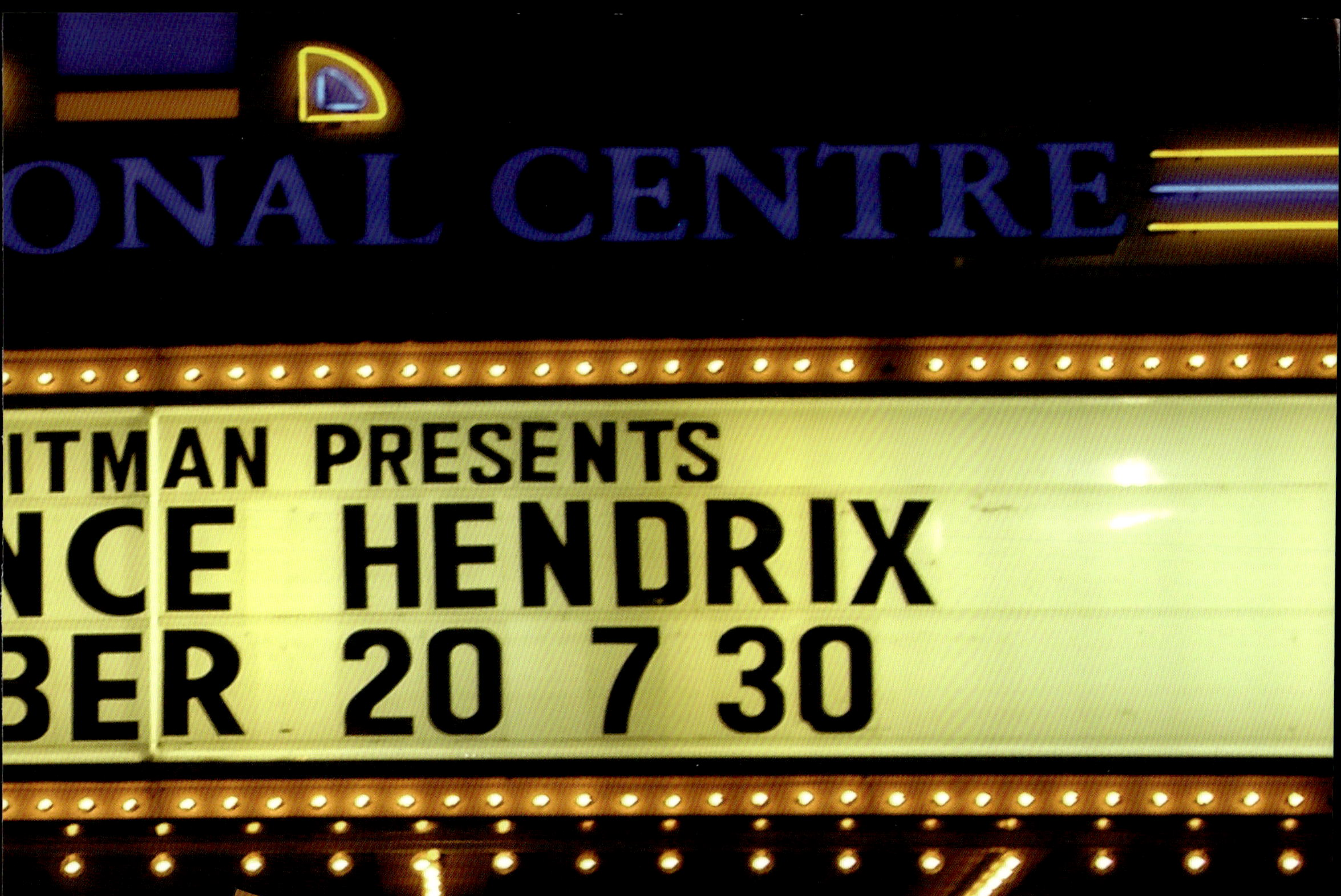

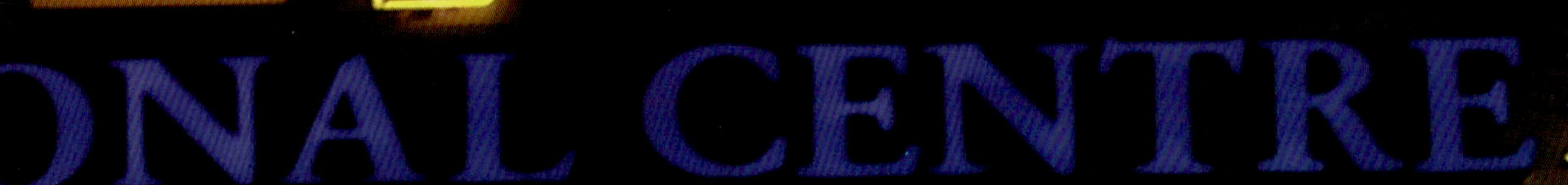

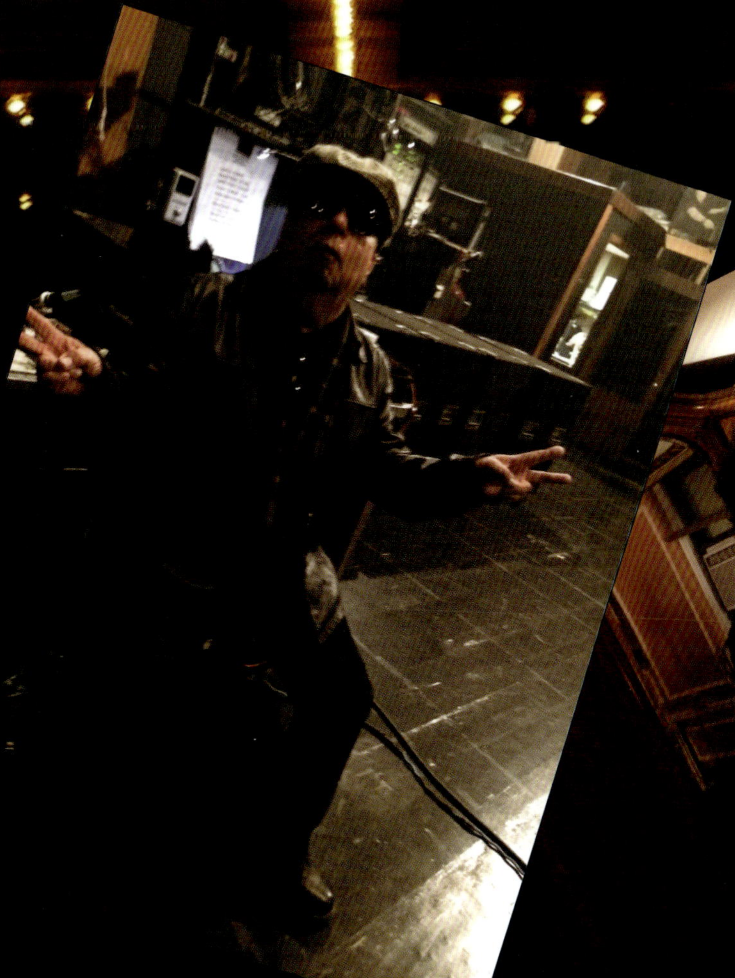

Cesar Rosas of Los Lobos

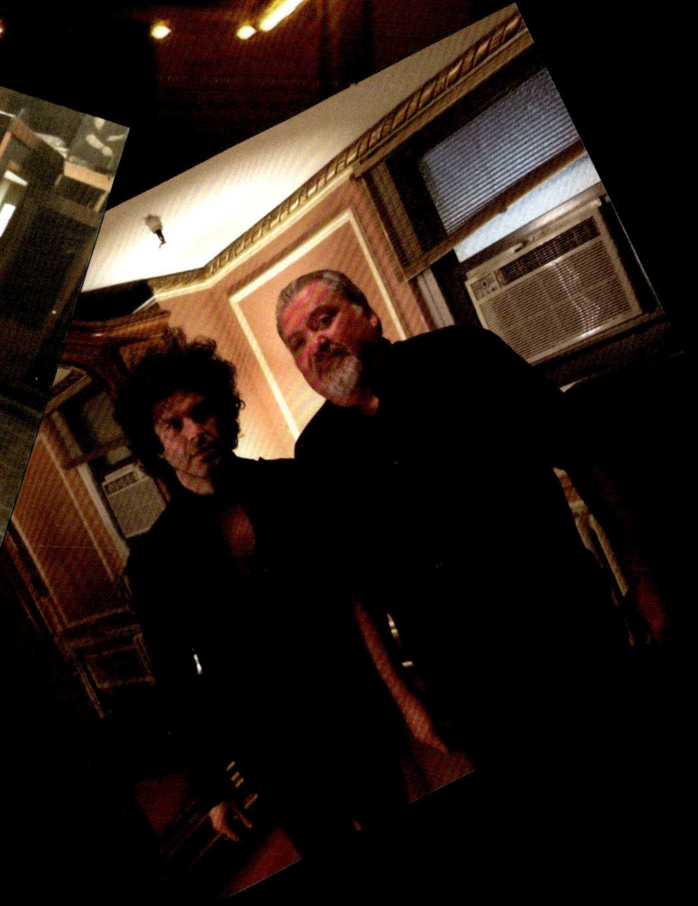

Doyle Bramhall II & David Hidalgo of Los Lobos

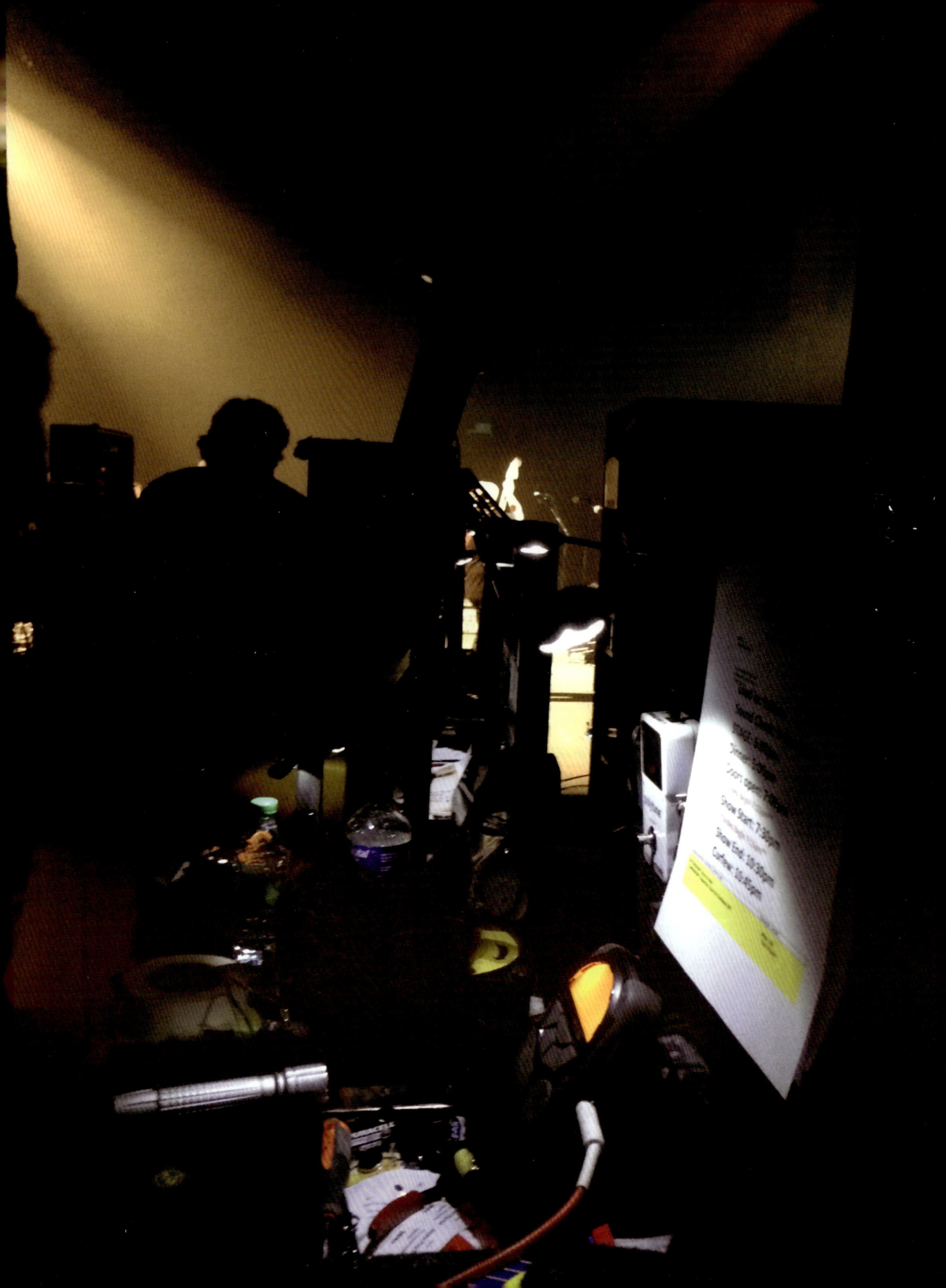
Show Start: 7:30pm
Show End: 10:30pm
Curfew: 10:45pm

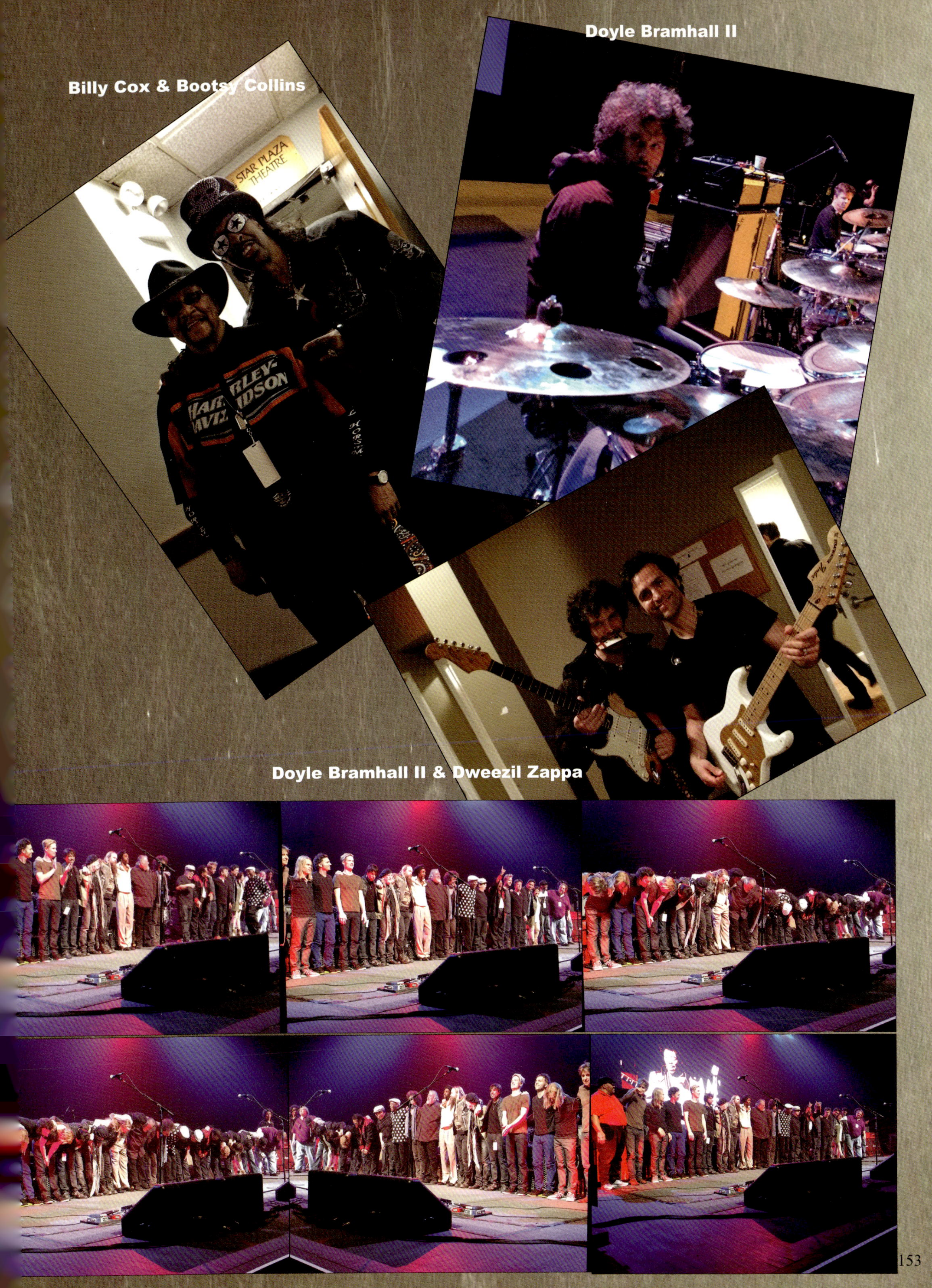

Billy Cox & Bootsy Collins

Doyle Bramhall II

Doyle Bramhall II & Dweezil Zappa

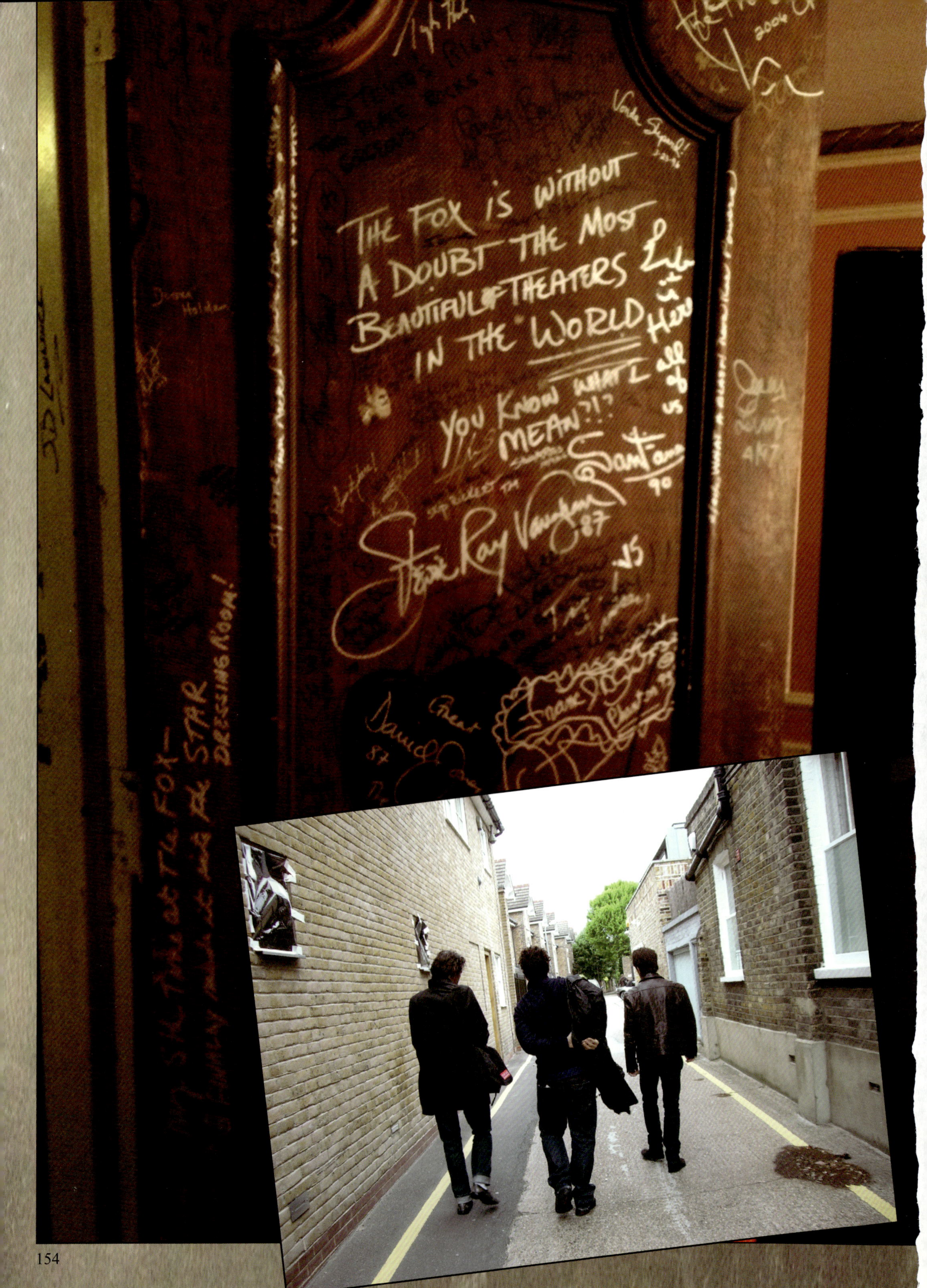
THE FOX IS WITHOUT
A DOUBT THE MOST
BEAUTIFUL OF THEATERS
IN THE WORLD
YOU KNOW WHAT I
MEAN?!?
Santana
90
Stevie Ray Vaughan
'87
STAR
DRESSING ROOM!

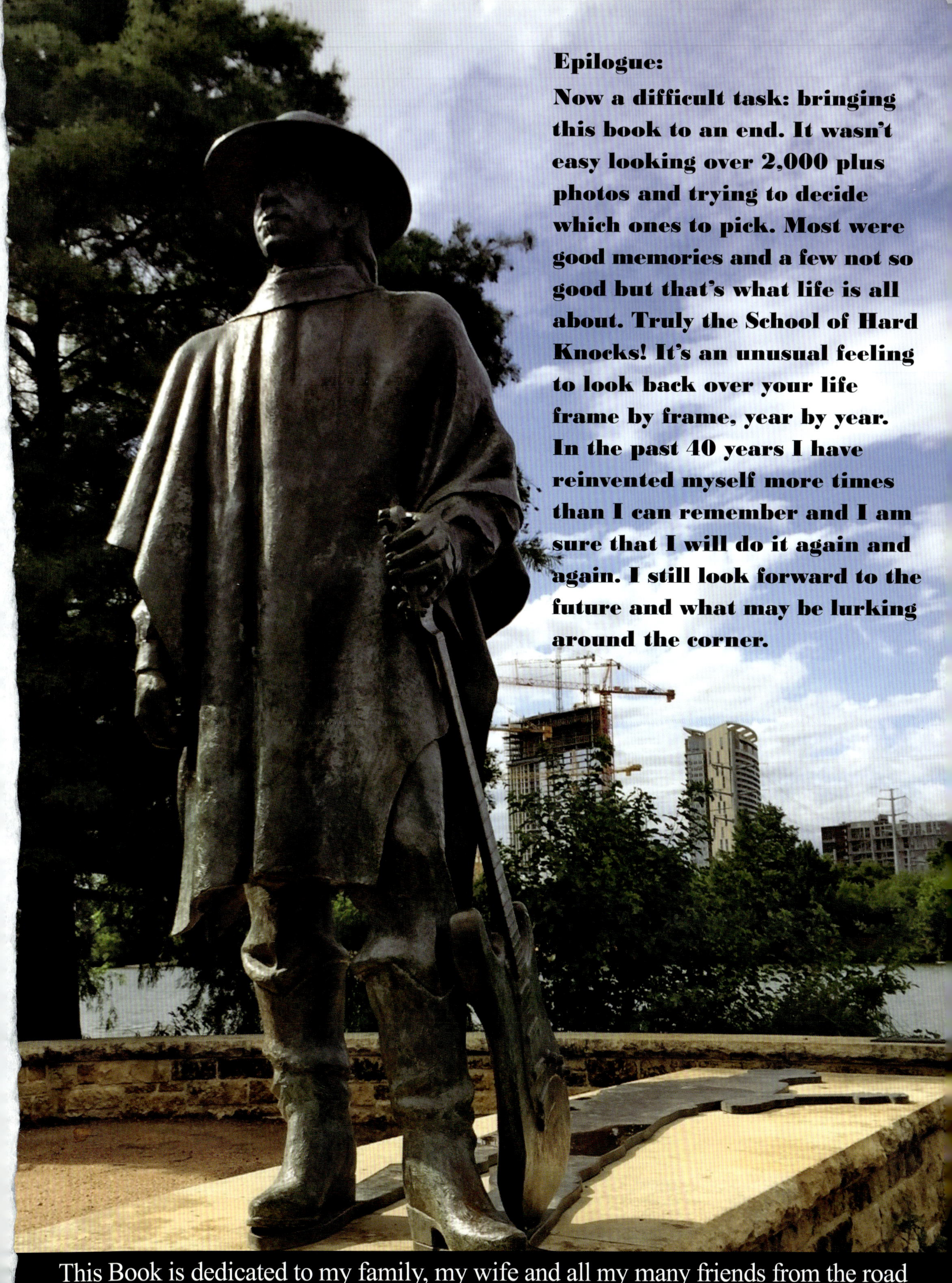

Epilogue:

Now a difficult task: bringing this book to an end. It wasn't easy looking over 2,000 plus photos and trying to decide which ones to pick. Most were good memories and a few not so good but that's what life is all about. Truly the School of Hard Knocks! It's an unusual feeling to look back over your life frame by frame, year by year. In the past 40 years I have reinvented myself more times than I can remember and I am sure that I will do it again and again. I still look forward to the future and what may be lurking around the corner.

This Book is dedicated to my family, my wife and all my many friends from the road